Committees and Commissions in India
1978

Concepts in Communication
Informatics & Librarianship-52

General Editor : **S.P. Agrawal**

Committees and Commissions in India 1978

Volume 16

PART B

A Concept's Project

Compiled by a team of professionals
guided by
VIRENDRA KUMAR

CONCEPT PUBLISHING COMPANY, NEW DELHI 110059

ISBN 81-7022-490-X (Vol. 16, Part B)

First Published 1994

Published and Printed by
Ashok Kumar Mittal
Concept Publishing Company
A/15-16, Commercial Block, Mohan Garden
NEW DELHI 110059 (India)

Lasertypeset by
Printing Express
H-13, Bali Nagar
NEW DELHI 110015

CONTENTS

PART B

19

NATIONAL COMMITTEE ON THE DEVELOPMENT OF BACKWARD AREAS, 1978 — REPORT ON DEVELOPMENT OF BACKWARD HILL AREAS[1]

Chairman	Shri B. Sivaraman, Member, Planning Commission
Members	Shri Som Dutt; Prof. Mrinal Datta Chaudhary (ceased to be member w.e.f. November 30, 1978); Shri S.S. Marathe (ceased to be member w.e.f. November 30, 1978); Shri Ranchor Prasad; Shri Ramakrishanayya; Shri K.P.A. Menon; Shri R.M. Honavar (ceased to be member w.e.f. January 31, 1981); Shri S.A. Dave, Dr. Y. Nayudamma; Shri Anand Sarup; Dr. B.D. Sharma; Shri Suresh Mathur; Dr. D.M. Nanjundappa; Shri S.M. Ghosh.
M. Secy.	Shri Nitin Desai.

Appointment

The Government have been pursuing certain policies and programmes in regard to the development of backward areas since the Fourth Five-Year Plan. It is now necessary to review the working of these various programmes and to set out a suitable strategy or strategies for the development of backward areas in the context of the priorities and objectives set out in the draft 1979-83 Plan. The Planning Commission have, therefore, decided to set up a Highlevel Committee to formulate appropriate strategy or strategies for effectively tackling the problem of Backward Areas vide its Resolution No. PC(P) 17/NCDBA/78-MLP dated November 30, 1978.

Terms of Reference

(i) To examine the validity of the various concepts of backward-

1. Planning Commission, Government of India, New Delhi, 1982, 76 p.

ness underlying the definitions in use for present policy purposes and recommend the criteria by which backward areas should be identified,

(ii) To review the working of: –

(a) the existing plans for dealing with the general developmental problems of backward areas like Tribal Sub-Plans, Plans for Hill Areas, etc., and

(b) the existing schemes for stimulating industrial development in backward areas such as the schemes for concessional finance, investment subsidy, transport subsidy, sales tax concessions, etc., similar schemes in the agricultural and allied fields like DPAP, and general measures for tackling the problems of poverty and unemployment with a view to find out their efficacy in the removal of backwardness; and

(iii) To recommend an appropriate strategy or strategies for effectively tackling the problem of backward areas, classified, if necessary, according to areas, causes of or prescribed remedies.

Contents

Summary of Recommendations; Introduction; Review of Past Efforts; Strategy for Development of Backward Areas; Watershed Management and Control of Shifting Cultivation; Forests; Water Utilization; Landuse and Cropping; Animal Husbandry and Dairy Development; Fisheries; Rural Electrification; Tourism; Industrial Development; Road and Communication; Organisation of Administrative and Financial Structure; Acknowledgement; Annexures from I to IV.

Recommendations

Introduction

1. In the Himalayas the Committee accepts the areas already demarcated as hill areas of U.P., West Bengal and Assam as backward hill areas for special consideration. The exclusively hill State of Jammu and Kashmir, Himachal Pradesh, Arunachal Pradesh, Manipur, Mizoram, Nagaland, Meghalaya, Sikkim and Tripura are already treated specially as backward States and the needs of the backward areas in these exclusively hill States should be looked after in the State

Plan on the basis of the guidelines given by the Committee for dealing backward areas. (Para 1.8)

2. Excluding the areas covered under tribal sub-plan for which separate provision exists, the rest of the hill areas above 600 metres contour in the Deccan belt should be considered backward hill areas for the purpose of special development. (Para 1.7)

3. The programme for hill areas should be an integrated development programme for building up of infrastructure and for supplying a package of inputs and other necessary services almost simultaneously. Each component of the programme has to be inter-related and coordinated with the other components, with the ultimate aim of maximising production and benefiting the hill people economically. (Para 1.16)

Strategy for Development of Backward Hill Areas

4. The strategy for development should be dictated by considerations of:–

(i) Benefiting the people as a whole rather than the status groups;
(ii) developing local resources and utilising local talents so that the need for out-migration of the adult males is no more necessary, or at least gets considerably reduced;
(iii) transforming a consumption-oriented economy into an investment-oriented one;
(iv) regulating inter-regional terms of trade in a manner that they cease to be exploitative for the backward regions;
(v) the States filling up the gaps in the marketing mechanism to give the backward areas fair return for labourers; and
(vi) maintaining the ecological balance. (Para 3.3)

5. In order to slow the progress of outmigration, generation of gainful employment locally has to receive a high priority. (Para 3.4)

6. Methods of reducing drudgery in the women's life have to be found so that the women can also become participants in the development process and yet remunerated for their labour in the time saved from drudgery. (Para 3.4)

7. Gearing up of the production system and creating a proper distributing machinery are from this point of view, the two primary requisites of ensuring flow of benefits of growth to the people. (Para 3.5)

8. In backward hill areas, self-sufficiency cannot be and should not be the goal of the development policy; but maximising the income from each unit of the development base, either land or water or domestic animal. Therefore, a policy of promoting spatial specialisation needs to be favoured. (Para 3.6)

9. The problem of food can be solved if in areas wherever the food crops are replaced by new cash crops if: (a) suitable marketing facilities are built into the system to buy the production at fair prices and take them off the hands of the farmers of the areas, (b) arrangements are made to supply the food grains commonly consumed in the area in fair price shops so that the farmer can buy his requirements at reasonable prices. An area approach of development will have to be taken up first in the zones which can be much more productive under the new strategies and on the communication routes. (Para 3.7)

10. It is suggested that:

(i) necessary knowhow and facilities be provided to ensure more efficient utilisation of available resources, particularly those of the forests, cattle, land and water;

(ii) the framework of focal points be used for a more realistic and a rational location of various services connected with education, health, etc; and

(iii) resources should not be frittered away by unconnected developmental schemes but used for an integrated rural development approach on an area basis, with emphasis on production and better investment by the State on the necessary and infrastructural base for the production strategy. (Para 3.8)

11. It is recommended that the watershed should be the primary planning unit, rather than a block or a district. The watershed approach provides a sound basis for programming of soil conservation, water harvesting and harnessing and landuse and planning social institutions. It is also possible to delineate watersheds into micro and mini-watersheds. A mini water-shed may be equated with our concept of a focal point and may cover an area of a cluster of villages with a population coverage of a 5000 or 6000 of a block population and micro watershed may cover an area of 1000 to 1500 hectares. (Para 3.9)

12. The strategy of entrepreneurial and skilled labour development that the Committee has recommended in its report on 'Industrial Dispersal' is all the more necessary in the backward hill areas. The

Committee would, therefore, recommend necessary action to superimpose the industrial development in these areas by following guidelines in that report. (Para 3.11)

13. Industrial development in the hill areas has to be based essentially on the promotion of such activities in which hills offer a distinct advantage like forest based industries, vegetable and fruit processing, etc. Another area in which hill areas offer an advantage in terms of climate and dust and pollution free environment is electronic and precision goods. The major advantage of such industries is that they do not involve heavy transportation of raw materials. These are mainly skill based industries where the value added is substantial. Necessary steps will have to be taken for training and skill development so as to prepare the environment for location of such industries. (Para 3.12)

14. Livestock has attained great importance in developing hill economy. Therefore, priority should be given for improving quality of livestock on commercial lines through cross breeding with exotic breeds. Pasture development programmes should taken up along with measures to improve cattle. (Para 3.13)

15. Social forestry on scientific lines is necessary to check soil erosion, maintain ecological balance and produce industrial new raw materials, conservation, extension and productive exploitation of forests has to go hand in hand to meet the industrial requirements and general needs of the people. (Para 3.14)

16. The administration is generally not committed to programmes of backward hill area development because most of the time, people do not choose to serve in these areas. Posting in the hills is generally seen as a form of punishment. Therefore, officers charged with development programmes should have feeling of commitment to these areas and be sensitive to the needs and aspirations of the people. (Para 3.16)

17. The sub-plan idea is conceptually a sound one and must be regarded as a breakthrough in our area development concept. The underlying idea is one of achieving internal consistency and integration among various on going programmes. It is an appropriate method of imparting some new orientation in area planning by taking note of the missing elements in the normal sectoral programmes of the State Governments. (Para 3.18)

18. While planning for big projects in under-developed hill areas, it would be necessary to build in adequate safeguards to project the environment on the one hand and the interest of the local population on the other by enabling them to avail of the job opportunities that arise.

(Para 4.2)

19. It would be necessary to work out suitable mechanism to replace the non-descript and unproductive livestock heads by introducing remunerative and fewer heads. It would be desirable to work out appropriate landuse patterns so as to ensure adequate feed and fodder for in approved livestock population. (Para 4.5)

20. Attempts should be to aim at appropriate landuse management in the hill areas, suiting to the specific site conditions, which would include wet cultivation and dry cultivation, horticultural and cash crop plantations and cultivation of utility trees/shrubs. (Para 4.6)

21. Watershed approach would mean planning and implementing soil conservation programmes for all types of lands and associated drainage system of selected watersheds within a reasonable time frame with the objective of providing maximum protection to existing land and water resources while optimising their use for increasing production and employment benefits. (Para 4.7)

22. In order to comprehend the total problem *vis-a-vis* the total potential and to draw up a programme which could be implemented within a reasonable period (say five years), the size of such watershed should be between 1,000 to 5,000 hectares. Once delineation and modification works are over, interse priorities and development of these watersheds are to be assigned taking into consideration the corrective factors for erosion and sedimentation ranging from physiography to climate and including proximity to the reservoirs. The Central and State Soil Conservation and Soil and Landuse Survey Organisations would have to take up this task to identify, at the earliest, watersheds on a priority basis for preparation of integrated management plans and implementation of the same. (Para 4.7)

23. Watershed management planning will need data pertaining to watershed characteristics such as topography, soils, geology, vegetation and climatic data, besides incidence of erosion flood and drought hazards. Therefore, there should be an adequate mechanism at the level for collection of such data through field State Headquarters and at field/units or from concerned agencies. The need for the basic data should be fully recognised and their collection, analysis and interpretation should be considered as a preinvestment towards proper planning and implementation of watershed management programmes. (Para 4.9)

24. The most logical step would appear to be to incorporate corrective measures in the existing landuse system to make the existing landuse practices less vulnerable to erosion and degradation hazards.

(Para 4.10)

25. Alternative management practices should be introduced slowly to encourage the beneficiaries to shift gradually to the improved landuse pattern. If the agro-silvicultural practices or agro-horticultural practices can be made profitable while practising mixed farming, it may be possible to achieve this gradual shift in landuse pattern and retiring the steeper slopes from cultivation of common agricultural crops, to productive and remunerative fodder or tree cover. (Para 4.10)

26. Once priority watersheds are identified and land classification completed it will be necessary to identify the areas needing treatment under agricultural, forest and other landuse practices. Depending upon a number of factors, such as slope, soils, rainfall, etc. Package of treatment measures will have to be chosen. These measures would include bench terracing, outlets with drop pits, riser protection, rehabilitate deteriorating terraces, hill side ditches on the agricultural lands. (Para 4.11)

27. For pasture lands combination of grasses, legumes and fodder frees and bushes will have to be chosen. Closures and erosion control measures like dykes may have to be adopted here as well. (Para 4.11)

28. Water harvesting structures such as low canal sills, diversion weirs and some ponds in suitable locations, could be considered for appropriate utilisation of available run off. Check dams, revetments and spurs will be necessary for controlling gullies and erosion along the stream banks and beds as well as land slips along the roads. (Para 4.11)

29. Some arrangements will need to be made in the planning Cell for collecting representative base level data for typical areas representing dominant combination of practices such as bench terracing, afforestation, water harvesting system, pasture, etc. (Para 4.13)

30. There are practical difficulties in mobilisation of self-labour in innumerable individual holdings in a single terrace for subsidised working through extension methods under the Soil Conservation Acts. Land records need updating. All this has resulted in the concept of integrated watershed management being rarely achieved, particularly when a large number of farmers are reluctant to joint in the working. At the same time, any soil conservation programme would be self-defeating if the people on whose lands these are carried out are not only involved in it effectively but have some stake in improving the land and maintaining it. Considering all this, the Committee would recommend:

(i) that the existing practice of subsidising private works on farmers' lands to the extent of 50 per cent should be continued;
(ii) if there are any works on the private lands like construction and renovation of risers, which would benefit not only the land on which they are located but also other lands belonging to other farmers, these should be treated as items of benefit to the community and financed to the extent of 100 per cent by the State; and
(iii) the existing practice of financing the soil conservation programme on community land on 100 per cent basis should continue. (Para 4.17)

31. It is necessary to develop production programmes which, whilst preserving the soil, will gradually improve the economic condition of the people of the area. The strategy outlined below has been developed after careful consideration of the pros and cons of the matter;

(i) reclaiming land, where necessary, and providing minor irrigation, where possible, so as to encourage settled cultivation in villages and on terraced slopes on the lines adopted by the Savaras of Orissa and the Angamis in Nagaland, assuring at the same time inputs, fair price shops, communication and marketing facilities;
(ii) identifying the areas suitable for plantation crops such as tea, coffee, rubber, which would give subsidiary occupation for a family on the basis of the one hectare of plantation each;
(ii) developing gross reserves to support a subsidiary programme of animal husbandry; and
(iv) developing suitable areas for agro-silvicultural operations and commercial forest plantations, which would give full occupation to large number of village population. (Para 4.21)

32. An important change which has to be brought about is the change over from the hoe cultivation to plough cultivation and settled agriculture. For the resettled cultivation, the farmer has to learn the use of the plough, breeding of cattle and care of crops. Therefore, wherever such resettlement is being done, there has to be close supervision and training of the farmer families so that they can learn the new technology. (Para 4.22)

33. People living in the catchment areas necessarily require pasture lands for grazing and also land to raise their food requirements. Unless, therefore, an integrated watershed area development programme becomes a part of the treatment of catchment of the river valley project, the problem is not going to be solved. The first priority has to be provided for the needs of the local people for grazing, fuel wood and other requirements. (Para 4.27)

34. It is recommended that the maintenance of the assets created in the catchment should become an integral part of the whole scheme. The Committee would also recommend that top most priority should be given to the critically eroded areas of the catchments, particularly those lying within the 'hill areas'. (Paras 4.28 and 4.29)

35. As scientific implementation of the soil conservation programme would require a multi-disciplinary programme and approach, the integrated watershed management approach cannot be planned or implemented unless a multi-disciplinary organisation is created. (Para 4.30)

36. It has also been found that the organisations handling soil conservation programmes are mono-disciplinary. Sufficient sub-divisions should be created which should of multi-disciplinary type. (Paras 4.31 and 4.32)

37. It would be necessary to provide refresher and reorientation courses to the officers of other departments involved in the problem of watershed management. (Para 4.32)

38. It is necessary to devise a cadre of soil conservationists with the basic background such as forest, soil science or science and agricultural engineering. It is equally necessary to acquaint the policy makers, administrators and financiers with the role of soil conservation in the areas of national and regional priorities effecting various development programmes of the country. (Para 4.33)

Forests

39. Hill areas which are thickly forested or are in close prominity of thickly forested areas are highly suitable to horticulture, plantation crops, orchards. inter-culture, floriculture and pasture development. (Para 5.10)

40. Himalayan hills are suitable for raising mulbery trees and boost the silk production. Floriculture is turning out to be a flourishing business. The demand for cut flowers is increasing rapidly and hill

areas are most suited to growing flowers of different kinds. (Para 5.11)

41. Hill areas are equally suitable for pasture development which will not only make a firm base for a Dairy development but would also check the growing menace of soil erosion. (Para 5.12)

42. Hill areas offer ample scope for agro-forestry based industries and handicrafts. In those of the hill areas which are richly endowed with forest wealth, there is enormous scope for setting up a large number of small industries. Those may include pulp paper and hard board, rosin and turpentine, sports goods, pencil industry, wicker-work, match industry, drug and pharmaceuticals, aroma chemicals and a large variety of other industrial enterprises. (Para 5.13)

43. The Committee recommend the following Action-oriented Programmes: –

(i) Survey of landuse and delineation of micro-watersheds requiring various degrees and types of treatment required and preparation of action plans;

(ii) Taking up required soil and water conservation measures including engineering as well as vegetative methods such as land shaping, gull plugging, construction of check dams, soil binding plant species, etc. These have been covered in Chapter 4 dealing with integrated watershed management;

(ii) Improvement of pastures and afforestation of degraded lands or waste lands belonging to Government or community, should be taken up under social forestry and other programmes;

(iv) Introduction of species suitable for use as fodder, fuel and small timber of a very short duration. There should be adequate research support and the species should be chosen with care so that the local population can feel the impact of the benefits at the shortest possible time;

(v) Association of voluntary bodies and panchayats in afforestation and pasture development must be secured. Raising of community forests even on Government lands where ownership to Government but the management given to the community where a strong panchayat or a voluntary body exists should be taken up;

(vi) Replacement of contractors by departmental felling or by forest labour cooperatives and destruction of felling in vulnerable areas should be forthwith done. The Government of U.P. has issued an order that no felling should be carried in slopes above

45°, felling between 30° and 45° should be on selection system and no felling above 3000 metre altitude should be done. Some such regulations are necessary in other States also;

(vii) Animal husbandry improvement scheme must be introduced simultaneously to reduce the number, while improving the quality of the stock. A very hard and unpopular decision at the political level is required to be taken about calling of any unremunerative cattle as recommended by the National Commission on Agriculture;

(viii) Creation of some biosphere reserves and more national parks so as to cover at least 10 per cent of the forest areas in the Himalayas with very careful management in the above surrounds of such reserves and parks;

(ix) Diversion of forest land for non-forestry uses in the Himalayas must be stopped immediately. All lands under agriculture should be properly shaped and terraced and water courses regulated to do the least damage;

(x) In the matter of road construction whether under Central or State agencies cost for taking up conservation measures to eliminate damage due to cutting up of the hill sides should be included in the project itself, and its execution should be integral part of the roads programme;

(xi) Improvement should be carried out in the alpine pastures and grazing conditions along migration routes and in the lower ranges use for grazing by migratory graziers in winter. For that purpose there must be socio-economic coupled with agrostrological studies, regarding migratory grazing, conditions of graziers, intensity of grazing, availability of alpine pastures, the ownership, pattern of the livestock which the migratory graziers take to alpine pastures etc;

(xii) Horticulture (Himachal Pradesh as an example) is becoming very popular in this region. Care will have to be taken that this important economy for the development of hill areas does not result in degradation of environment and deforestation due to increasing demand of boxes for packing cases. (Para 5.21)

44. Steps would also have to be taken to ensure that it is made obligatory on orchards to replant the forest areas from where trees have been *felled* to pack the fruits. (Para 5.21)

45. The more important steps to eliminate the deforestation to

meet the demand of packing would be the introduction of alternative packing material like hardboard. Alternative material packing would have to be persuaded vigorously if the expanding demand of boxes for packing is to be met, without large scale deforestation. (Para 5.21)

46. There is some hostility between the Forest Department staff and the local population, and this distress can be removed only through proper extension efforts and much closer contact between the two, so that each other problems and limitations are better understood. (Para 5.22)

47. The continual over-exploitation of trees and shrubs for fuel will go on unless a successful policy of first halting the trend and then reversing the process can be thought of and implemented. This is the most important aspect of the forest in the hill areas. Over exploitation of grass lands by the growing cattle and sheep population, without any attempt to regenerate the cover and control the grazing, has now led to a position where very little grass is available annually for the cattle and sheep wealth. The policy will have to aim at gradually halting this process of deterioration and building up the pastures of the hill areas so that a balance may be struck between the cattle and sheep wealth and available fodder in the first instance. (Para 5.35)

48. As a general policy, the nation has laid down that the purchase of minor forest produce in the forest areas must be departmentally managed so that the collectors of minor forest produce are given a fair price for their labourers. This policy has yet to be developed on large scale and it is also noticed that some States have a habit of going back on the national policy deliberately. A consistent policy will have to be developed to ensure that the tree wealth which gives the minor forest produce is not only maintained but developed so that steady source of income will be available to the local population. Thereby encouraging them to see to the preservation of these trees. Secondly, a fair price should be given to the produce not necessarily based on the labour charges alone but by complete departmentalisation of minor forest produce collection so that the urge to over-exploits is also curbed. (Para 5.35)

49. If the backward area is to be developed the local population should get every opportunity to benefit by the various developmental and employment opportunities that can arise in the area. Forests being an important part of the economy in the hill areas, every opportunity available in the forest for benefiting the local population and for giving them employment opportunities should obviously be availed of.

(Para 5.37)

50. It will be useful to compile a list of purely protective forests for each of the States or Union Territories. It is obvious that very stringent tests will have to be applied to take out an area entirely from the orbit of productive forests and to earmark if for protection of terrain only (Para 5.38)

51. The Committee advise that an immediate examination should be made of all such areas in the backward hill areas which should legitimately be brought within the classification of protected forests and steps taken to declare them as protected forests. Then a systematic programme should be taken up to see that the forest cover is brought back in all these protection forests within a reasonable time frame utilising the finances for 'social forestry'. This, in the view of the Committee, is of priority in the Himalayan hill ranges. (Para 5.38)

52. Although the position may not have such serious consequence in the forest areas of the backward hill areas of the Deccan, still it is serious enough to warrant a similar action to identify the areas which should be put under protection forests. A period bound programme should then be taken up to ensure that such areas are afforested quickly and maintained as protection forests. (Para 5.39)

53. There are large forest areas which need replantation with economic species and commercial species. In the backward hill areas, economic forestry should include the types of timber trees and fodder trees which can solve the problem of raw material for village industries and fodder for the animal wealth. (Para 5.42)

54. Serious attempt should be made by forest administrations in the backward hilly areas to involve the local population in the operations connected with the forest managements which are remunerative so that the local population can see the benefit of the forests from their economic angle. Similarly, the involvement of the local population in collection of minor forest produce and paying them a fair remuneration for the collected produce is another aspect which needs wide acceptance by the forest departments and the Governments of the States. (Para 5.44)

55. In backward hill areas, therefore, where forests are important, the forest administration must learn in involve the local people so that they benefit from the forests and see the benefit in real terms. (Para 5.44)

56. Cold arid areas occur in the Ladakh region of Jammu and Kashmir (Ladakh and Kargil Districts) and Lahaul and Spiti region and

Hongrang Valley of Himachal Pradesh. Land availability will be no limiting factor. The concerned States have already taken up a programme of afforestation, soil conservation and fodder development. This may be continued. Range management and grass land development should be an important part of the programme. The local people are not migratory and hence provision of improved fodder should have the utmost priority for the local livestock. Natural grass land are not abundantly available in the region. The extremes of climate and high altitude also limit their choice. For any large scale programme, pastures will have to be raised artificially where irrigation is available. In summer, graziers from outside migrate to the area with their livestock and cause destruction of natural vegetation. It will be necessary to regulate the entry of such migratory graziers strictly in accordance with the carrying capacity of the grazing runs. (Paras 5.46 and 5.49)

57. The Committee would strongly endorse the recommendation of the National Commission on Agriculture to set up a centre for forest research on cold desert to undertake forest research on the following:

(i) Identification of areas for pasture development and growing of forest trees to provide fodder for the grazing animals, small timber and fuel for the local population, and stabilisation of areas threatened with erosion;
(ii) Selection of suitable indigenous and exotic species and testing their performance;
(iii) Ecological and physiological studies in relation to photosynthesis and respiration at high elevation;
(iv) Studies of socio-economic aspects in relation to rangelands, soil and fater conservation; and
(v) Study of the effect of shelter-belts and wind-break against high velocity wind. (Para 5.50)

Water Utilisation

58. The cost of construction of irrigation works in hill areas is higher in view of the topographical conditions. Following would appear to be the most appropriate methods for developing irrigational facilities in the hill areas:

(a) contour channels, with storages or diversion structures;
(b) lift irrigation from storages or running streams; and

(c) hydraulic rams. (Paras 6.5 and 6.6)

59. In order to minimise the damage to contour channels, it is desirable to explore the possibilities of utilising polythene and alkathene pipes. (Para 6.7)

60. It has also been brought to the notice of the Committee that in Himachal Pradesh the rights of the farmers are standing in the way of optimum utilisation of kulh irrigation. We recommend that the State Government should review the entire position and devise suitable measures to ensure that there is full utilisation of the water and all the farmers within the command of the kulh receive a share. (Para 6.8)

61. Lift irrigation from the running streams can go a long way in meeting the water needs for irrigation and drinking purposes. The Committee would recommend that valleys need to be identified where lift irrigation schemes are feasible and these should be suitably brought into a Master Plan of Construction quickly. (Para 6.9)

62. Fast rising prices of diesel oil and other fossil fuel have made it imperative to find out alternative sources of energy. This would point towards the need for further efforts in developing the technology for utilising the kinetic energy of water which mostly go waste at present and devices like Hydraulic Rams, Himalayan Mill and Floating Mill which do not involve very high cost or long gestation period will be very useful. (Para 6.10)

63. Minor and Medium Irrigation in the Deccan Plateau are much simpler schemes than in the Himalayan Ranges. A Master Plan for Minor Irrigation in the Backward Hill areas is very necessary and the Committee recommends an early examination of the potential and a time bound programme for execution. (Para 6.16)

Landuse and Cropping

64. Quick growing economic species preferably handy fruit bearing (like walnut, peanuts and fodder) trees may be planted in these areas, if considered possible, so as to keep the interests of the owners alive. (Para 7.6)

65. Cultivation on hill slopes should be discouraged as far as possible as this causes erosion. Even the high value crops like potatoes which cause erosion should not be encouraged on slopes. There should be long term policy for covering such areas under perennial crops. Degrees of slopes beyond which cultivation should not be allowed may be

specified for different regions. (Para 7.7)

66. As far as possible, horticulture should be encouraged in combination with sod cultivation. Sod should preferably be comprised of grass clover mixtures suitable to the locality. This will provide a very good combination for horticulture and animal husbandry both of which are complementary. (Para 7.8)

67. The Committee recommends strongly that the Agricultural Universities in the States which have the hill areas should now take up in right earnest firstly, applied research in the different zones of the various high yielding materials that have been developed in the country. At the same time, breeding of varieties suitable to the climatic conditions of the various zones of hill areas will have to be taken up strongly by these universities. The Committee recommends that the ICAR may not take active leadership in ensuring that this basic work for hill area development is now undertaken on a systematic manner. (Para 7.12)

68. The research has to be two-fold – firstly to identify the crops and zones where basic seed material of high quality can be supplied to the rest of the country and secondly pest and environmental problems leading to crop damage. Special attention will have to be paid in regional stations of the Agricultural Universities to these problems. (Para 7.13)

69. The landuse in the hill areas as in other parts of the country has been guided mostly by the pressure of the population on land and the tendency is to bring under cereal production even marginal lands unsuitable for cultivation. The problem specially is acute in the hill areas leading thereby to cultivation on slopes and on this soil profiles thereby leading to very rapid soil erosion and a permanent loss to the productive areas. It is, therefore, necessary to see that the landuse is adjusted to the potential of the land without leading to land deterioration. Pasture and horticultural development, the former on thin soil and the latter on sloping terrain which even now are largely practised in the hill areas, will have to replace the agricultural crops in marginal terrain. This can only be done by an active and intelligent extension approach. (Para 7.14)

70. Under the climatic conditions a horticultural or a vegetable crop can be much more profitable per unit of land than cereal production. The Agricultural Universities will have to take up detailed investigations of profitable landuse under the climatic conditions and the right type of crop to be grown in the various zones under various

environmental conditions. This will be an exercise extending the idea that has been postulated by the NCA about fitting the right type of food crop to the hill area. The Committee recommends that this research work should be done.

71. Today no householder in the backward areas with the paucity of an administrative support and communications will risk the possibility or not producing a certain minimum food crop for his own family and depend on other people for his food. The change over, therefore, cannot take place all over the hill areas and on mere statement of policy but some selective approach will be necessary. The problem can be solved if wherever the good crops are replaced by new cash crops whether cereal, agricultural raw materials, horticulture or animal husbandry products, suitable marketing facilities are built into the system to buy the production at their fair prices and take them off the hands of the farmers of the area. Parallel to this organisation there has to be an organisation to supply the food crop prevalent in the area in fair price shops so that the farmer can buy his necessities from the fair price shops. (Para 7.16)

72. An area approach of development taking the more productive zones which can be still more productive and on the communication routes will have to be taken up first. The administrative support and the technical support will have to be laid on as a necessary part of the programme. The Committee recommends that this vast approach of development and change over of the cropping pattern to the best landuse should be brought about in the hill area at least substantially by 2000 A.D. A vast programmc should be built into the Five-Year Plans. (Para 7.16)

73. It is necessary that the productivity and income per unit of land is increased so that the hill areas can sell in the plains and get their needs from the plains balancing or improving the balance towards their side by the greater income per unit of land. (Para 7.17)

74. An important problem in expanding horticulture in the hill areas is the difficulty of communications in the Himalayan areas making it difficult to transport perishable fruits quickly to the consuming markets. Firstly, it is necessary to ensure that wherever active propagation of horticulture is being done as a remunerative replacement for the subsistence cereal economy, care should be taken to see that a suitable marketing system can be run in these areas to remove the produce quickly to the marketing areas. Where communications are difficult or cannot be established before the trees come into fruition,

other methods of handling the fruits so as to give remunerative return to the farmer needs examination. (Para 7.23)

75. Achievement of high productivity is not sufficient by itself. The grower must get incentive return so as to enable him to maintain the orchard properly. This is only possible if the post-harvest handling and marketing systems are modernised and streamlined. (Para 7.26)

76. Presently, all packing of fruits in the hills is done in wooden cases. The availability of wood will outstrip the demand. Therefore, the forests will be devastated and then Horticulture Industry will reach a dead end by the end of the century. Introduction of alternative packing cases is, therefore, a must. (Para 7.28)

77. The Committee recommends that firstly research work in fruit processing and preservation should carried out as a priority subject in the Agricultural Universities in the States where hill areas are important. Secondly, imaginative schemes for fruit preservation should be launched in time to take off all the fresh fruit in difficult areas and the fresh fruit during flush seasons in the regions where horticulture is being deliberately expanded. (Para 7.30)

78. It is proposed that some minimum limit say 15 per cent for use of fruit juices in all sorts of drinks may be recommended. The incidence of duties and taxes should be reduced with the increase in percentage of juice in such drinks. (Para 7.31)

79. Horticulture, should be treated at par with the industries in the backward areas for the purposes of advance of capital and interest. (Para 7.33)

80. Horticultural planning should be integrated covering all important aspects such as Production (Production of planting material, orchard management, etc.) post-harvest handling, marketing and processing. All these should have a strong backing of Research. (Para 7.34)

81. Temperate vegetables can be grown best in the middle levels of the hill areas both in the Himalayan ranges and in the Western Ghats. Proper planning of the right type of vegetables for the various areas and the adjustment of the seasons to give them a scarcity value in the plains market in various seasons should now be taken up seriously by the Horticulture Administration of States. Along with the increase of irrigation, providing for a tree crop routine in parts of the hill areas, introduction of vegetable growing in the crop routines will give greater remuneration to the farmers than following purely cereal routine. (Para 7.35)

82. Plantations have not come up in a big way in the Himalayan hills in the Western and Middle parts. Some amount of research will have to be done about the possibility of plantation crops in these areas. The country has found new areas for planting tea, rubber, coffee and so on through the various Boards taking an active part on promotion and identifying suitable areas with suitable climatic conditions. This work should be done in a wider way in the Himalayan hills. (Para 7.36)

83. In all the hill areas, the relevant varieties of trees will have to be identified for tasar programme and for a fodder tree programme. As pasture and animal husbandry development is of special significance in both the Himalayan hills and the Western Ghats, a fodder tree plantation will be of special benefit to the rural population. (Para 7.37)

84. The hill areas provide good scope for floriculture. The need is to organise and expand production and marketing to make floriculture more lucrative. (Para 7.38)

85. Another direction in which the hill areas can specialise is aromatic and medicinal plants. Many of those are wild growth in the hill forests. (Para 7.39)

86. The Committee recommends that the Central Silk Board should explore the possibility of expanding sericulture extensively in the hill areas. Extension of tasar culture throughout the oak belt of the Himalayas should be vigorously pursued by the Central Silk Board. (Para 7.40)

87. The Central Silk Board should organise seed multiplication and distribution, if necessary, by importing exotic strains. The Department of Agriculture can deal with sericulture aspect up to the process ing stage of cocoons. Short terms in service training to junior staff and familiarisation training of farmers and rearers should be introduced. (Para 7.40)

88. Possibility also exists for taking up tasar culture, which is now largely confined to Assam, throughout the oak belt of the Himalayas. The development of tasar hybrid, which thrives well on oak, has production of high quality material. Similarly muga culture at present practised in Assam can be extended to other parts of the north eastern regions. (Para 7.41)

89. Apiculture, i.e., production collection and marketing of honey and honey products could be a useful subsidiary occupation giving supplemental income to the people in the hills. There is great scope for increasing honey yields through organised apiculture, horticulture and forests. Detailed survey of the vegetation of forests with regard to

floristic composition should be carried out. (Para 7.42)

Animal Husbandry and Dairy Development

90. No reliable data is yet available about the possible contribution which the rearing of animals, sheep, goat and pigs and poultry can make to the economics of farming in the hill areas. It is, therefore, necessary that detailed studies should be taken up in various agro-climatic hill conditions for determining:

(i) the minimum economic unit and type of the livestock for each unit of holding for a specific situation;
(ii) the increase in income in a mixed farm that is attributable to livestock and other components; and
(iii) the extent of utilisation of potential farm, family labour and farm livestock. (Para 8.10)

91. In the high altitude areas of the western Himalayan region, encouragement should be given for rearing small stationary sheep flocks in the apple orchards in Himachal Pradesh and Jammu and Kashmir. Limited experience gathered so far has shown that legume grass mixture could be grown in the orchards for the maintenance of sheep. (Para 8.11)

92. Before we can opt for an aggressive programme of cattle development, the initial move should be to develop fodder and develop the hill pastures. (Para 8.12)

93. The common pastures have to be rapidly brought back to massive production according to land potential. Jammu and Kashmir introduced several exotic clovers in their common pasture and especially in the Alpine pasture with significant advantage. This method should now be spread to the Hill areas of Uttar Pradesh, Darjeeling, Sikkim and Assam. For good effect, pasture should be closed for grazing in a rotation and given a year at least to recoup. After that rotation grazing should be enforced. As additional boost to growth, an initial fertiliser application for the legume grass mixture is necessary. The experiment of J & K in fertilising their pastures can be carried out on a war footing in much larger areas. Whilst the initial expenditure may look prohibitive from the ordinary standards, as this will lead to the cattle revolution and sheep revolution ultimately in these areas and boost the annual income of the families, the initial investment is worthwhile and is strongly recommended by the Committee. (Para 8.13)

94. Nomadic husbandry is a very essential part of the hill economy. Improvement of cattle and sheep has to be done in the nomadic population also if there is to be general uplift. For this, two essential initial steps have to be taken. Firstly, the summer pastures in the Alpine hills will have to be fertilised and sown with legume grass, and high quality rotation grazing principle instituted. Secondly, on the seasonal migration routes, at least a couple of kilometres from the main route on other side will have to be intensively developed for fodder, so that the nomadic movement does not impinge on the traditional village pastures. Both these are priority issues and the Committee recommends that improvement of nomadic pastures and the traditional paths should be taken up on a priority basis. (Para 8.14)

95. Our objective in plantation being to give a cover to the land against soil and wind erosion till the new plantations provide complete canopy over the lands, the land continues to be liable to erosion till the canopy develops completely. During this period as a necessary part of the social forestry and for soil conservation, the land has to be covered by a pasture of Legume and grass which are quick growing. (Para 8.15)

96. As the Social Forestry programme includes growing of fodder trees on degraded forests, systematic building up of degraded forests near cattle and sheep concentration with trees fit for leaf fodder will go a long way towards improving fodder availability. (Para 8.15)

97. An aggressive cross-breeding programme can succeed only when artificial insemination can be done promptly on the heat of the he village cow and there is a nearby market for the fluid milk that the cow gives in daily lactation. (Para 8.16)

98. There is considerable scope for developing milksheds in the hills of Kerala and Maharashtra (Ratnagiri, Satara, Poona, and Kolhapur districts) and we recommend that this potential should be suitably exploited. (Para 8.18)

99. The farmer should be encouraged to rear cross breed heifer upto the age of bearing so that these could be sold to milk sheds areas in the plains, giving an annual income to the breeder. (Para 8.18)

100. The State Animal Husbandry/Sheep Departments should set-up service centres on the migration routes and take up a systematic and integrated programme of shearing, grading and marketing of wool to alleviate the difficulties of the nomads. (Para 8.19)

101. The practice of letting goats loose in the forest areas should be discouraged as this species, due to its browsing and acrobatic habits, causes immense damage to growing plants. We are not in favour of

increasing the number of goats but their quality must be improved to get more milk and meat. (Para 8.22)

102. There is good potential for development of poultry in the hill regions since the demand for eggs specially that for meat is substantial. The type of poultry keeping, however, has to be tailored according to level of management practices available. (Para 8.24)

103. There is a good scope of growing tapioca in hill areas and this can comprise a major component of poultry feed and help rearing poultry at a comparatively cheaper rate if casava can be grown and utilised in large quantity. (Para 8.24)

104. In the areas where the poultry rearing is purely backward operation, it is necessary to improve the quality of local birds by crossing them with exotic/crossbreed male birds. (Para 8.24)

105. There is also very good scope for introducing improved duck rearing in some of the North-Eastern States. The cross-breeding programme has been successfully taken up on pilot basis in Tripura and Assam. This programme needs to be intensified. (Para 8.24)

106. The National Commission on Agriculture in its interim report on poultry, sheep and livestock have identified the districts and also the measures necessary for development of poultry in north eastern States and other hill districts. The Committee recommends that these measures should be taken up earnestly and vigorously. (Para 8.24)

107. An integrated programme of piggery development which envisages setting up of farms with cross-breed pigs and improved pig management practices could be taken up in rural areas. (Para 8.25)

108. Regular supply of cross-breed pigs for field programme depends mainly on Government pig breeding farms. (Para 8.25)

109. The problem of higher cost compounded pig feed could be solved to some extent by use of agricultural waste and agricultural bio-products. Necessary advice to this end could come from Agricultural Universities. Meanwhile compounded pig feed could be subsidised. This subsidy may be related to the performance of individual farms. (Para 8.25)

110. The other difficulties of marketing pigs at remunerative price could be overcome by organising cooperative societies of primary pig producers and by forceful efforts for making pork popular. (Para 8.25)

111. In view of the difficult terrains, mobile veterinary units should be established in order to cover remote areas. It is necessary to strengthen disease investigation facilities in these regions. The hilly terrains are largely free from rinderpest. Hence entry of unvaccinated

animals should be prohibited. For this purpose rinderpest check posts should be set up on important cattle movement routes entering such terrains. (Para 8.26)

112. It would be necessary to protect valuable exotic and cross-breed cattle against Food and Mouth Diseases (FMD). (Para 8.26)

113. Since the FMD vaccine is costly it would be necessary to subsidise it suitably for the benefit of the weaker sections in these areas. (Para 8.26)

114. The FMD virus typing/epidemiological centres of the ICAR's coordinated project on 'Epidemiology of Foot and Mouth Disease' should prepare maps showing prevalence of various types of FMD virus in the hilly regions, with a view to explore the possibility of evolving a monovalent vaccination programme there. (Para 8.26)

115. Among pigs, swine fever is most important in the North-Eastern Region. Therefore, it would be necessary to protect the pig population of this region against this disease. (Para 8.26)

Fisheries

116. In the high altitudes, there is potential for development of cold water fisheries. Considering the demand for fish from the local population and also as an added attraction for tourists, hill areas offer good scope for the development of fisheries both for commercial and sport purposes. (Para 9.1)

117. The water resources on the high altitude would continue to be mainly the cold streams and lakes. However, in low regions, many ponds, tanks and beels will have to be suitably reclaimed for developing culture fisheries of major carps. Reservoirs too can be profitably exploited. But emphasis has to be on intensive pisci-culture practices. (Para 9.4)

118. In the lower regions, culture of Indian major carps, Chinese carps and European common carps would be considered. The technology is fairly well-known and there should be no difficulty in implementing this scheme. (Para 9.5)

119. There seems to be distinct scope for introducing grass carps in some of the weed infested lakes in high altitudes. Such a measures besides resulting in increased fish production could also keep the excessive vegetation under check. (Para 9.6)

120. It is essential that the States take energetic steps to introduce innovations in hatchery practice and developing artificial feeds which

would assure higher survival of the young trout. (Para 9.9)

121. The ecology and fishery biology of the species comprising the main fishery of the snow trout should be studied with a view to improving the indigenous fishery. (Para 9.11)

122. The cold water fisheries Research Unit of the CIFRI has identified the localities for the collection of seedfish of snow trout. It is, therefore, suggested that cultural possibilities of snow trout should be explored by the concerned State in the water of the Western, Central and Eastern Himalayas. (Para 9.11)

123. The Committee strongly stresses the importance of availability of scientific data in respect of ecological and biological conditions, the absence of which greatly hamper the development of fisheries in hill areas. There is also need for hydrographic surveys of water areas suitable for pisci-culture. Training of officers of fisheries in the techniques of cold water fishery is equally important. (Para 9.12)

Rural Electrification

124. Considering the present-critical situation of the availability of kerosene oil and diesel oil and also the need to preserve our precious forests in the hill areas, it is essential to spread electrification in the hill areas to the maximum extent possible not only to reduce the dependence of the hill people on kerosene for lighting purposes, but also to persuade them to give up to the extent possible, the use of fuelwood and diesel oil as energy base. (Para 10.1)

125. While planning big power projects in the hill areas adequate safeguards would need to be taken to protect the environment on the one hand and the interest of the local population on the other by providing greater opportunities for job employment in order to improve the economic conditions of the rural people. (Para 10.3)

126. The approach in regard to the electrification of the hill areas has necessarily to be based on the principle of 'growth point' development. (Para 10.4)

127. Rural electrification programmes should not only cater to domestic/light requirements, but should also cover pumping projects service connections, for commercial purpose, agro-based industries, village, tiny and cottage industries. This approach would not only improve the viability of the rural electrification schemes but would also contribute in improving the economic lot of backward hill area people. (Para 10.4)

128. The Committee would strongly urge that the norms for rural electrification in the hill areas should be realised to the maximum extent possible considering the pattern and the situation prevailing in the hill areas, normal norms cannot be applied if rural electrification has to make a real headway in the hill areas. (Para 10.5)

129. Use of wooden poles which are largely available with proper creasoting agent should be encouraged more vigorously in place of conventional steel tubular or rail type poles. (Para 10.6)

130. Realistic Integrated Area Development Programme be chalked out in certain pockets, which should take care of development of small/medium industries. The power development programme should be so framed so as to meet the time bound requirement of electricity demand in these pockets. (Para 10.7)

131. The backwardness of the region calls for building up of infrastructure for future development of the areas and a special tariff for electric supply in these areas should be framed, keeping in view of the social objectives of developing the area and reducing the cost to the extent possible by using cheap material and methods. (Para 10.8)

132. The emphasis should be on taking up small micro-hydel projects for which there is considerable scope in these areas. It would be in the national interest to subsidise the power tariff as the increasing use of electricity by the villagers would prevent deforestation also. (Para 10.8)

133. There is also considerable scope for undertaking extensive programmes for rural forestry and of bio-gas plants, depending upon the availability of cattle. In this context, there is also need for research on the economic possibilities of solar energy in the hill areas. (Para 10.9)

Tourism

134. The decision for formulating appropriate policies should be taken keeping in view the need for developing the backward hill areas and providing opportunities for the middle level tourists and keeping the common man in view so that all the developments and economic activities arising out of promotion of tourism are focussed on his overall benefit. Obviously this objective can best be fulfilled by promoting domestic tourism at modest cost and attending to that minority of foreign tourism who travel on a shoe-string budget and would settle for any place which is cheap and comfortable. (Paras 11.3 and 11.4)

135. Most of the hill areas are a trekkers paradise. Trekking and mountaineering are two of the most important activities which can not only develop the economic conditions of the poor hill people in the backward areas but also provide a spirit of adventure in our youngsters. (Para 11.4)

136. The most important type of traffic from our point of view is the pilgrim traffic: Lakhs of people visit Badrinath, Kedarnath, Gangotary, Yamnotri, Amarnath, Vaishnodevi and such centres and quite a large number cannot make it to these places because of lack of facilities and inadequacy of transport services. It past trend is any indication, the number of pilgrims, given improved facilities, is likely to increase by leaps and bounds. (Para 11.4)

137. An integrated approach, encompassing an integrated development of various activities with reference to each other, would not only lead to dispersal of tourist activities and its attendant economic benefit but also would be a step towards the improvement of the economic conditions of the common man residing in the backward hill areas. (Para 11.5)

138. The State Tourist Development Corporations should play an active role in the development of the superstructure of tourism as well as the basic infrastructure such as adequate and regular supply of water and electricity, surface transportation to reach the various centres, public health and medical facilities, etc. (Para 11.6)

139. As a first step towards the promotion of this tourist traffic, each State must identify the *yatra* and trekking routes. It is equally essential to bear in mind the travel circuit concept. It is desirable that travel circuits radiating from specified centres are identified for developing tourist intrastructure in an integrated manner in the area. This exercise will help in developing tourist facilities in a planned and regulated manner. (Para 11.7)

140. Pilgrim centres are at present awfully lacking in adequate accommodation and other facilities. The example of Tirupati and Guruvayoor where income from the temples is utilised for providing adequate facilities and development of these centres is worth emulating in the northern hill area shrines. Necessary legal and other measures be taken if necessary on the lines of what has been done at Tirupati and other such centres in South India. (Para 11.10)

141. Initiative for providing cheap and suitable accommodation on identified *yatra* and trekking routes should be taken up in a coordinated manner by the State Tourism Development Corporations. (Para 11.11)

142. A more liberalised policy will have to be followed in the matter of offering accommodation in the P.W.D. and forest rest houses to the tourist and in many cases, it may also be desirable to set up annexes to rest houses, and camping sites within the compound of the main rest houses so that tourists can use the common facilities provided there. (Para 11.12)

143. Where an experiment has been tried to clear the ground and provide tents, people prefer to stay in camps provided the rent is not too high and other common facilities are available. Development of such sites with proper facilities of power, water and basic hygiene may be considered. (Para 11.13)

144. There is considerable scope for encouraging private individuals particularly the ex-servicemen and such of the educated youngmen who have migrated out side the hill areas, to take loans and construct suitable accommodation for this purpose. Norms could be laid down for these private persons and preconditions of licensing could also be imposed on the loans before institutional loans are made available. This will of course involve a basic change in the present tending policies of banks and financial institutions. More and more youth hostels should be provided. (Para 11.14)

145. The State Tourist Development Corporation should be specifically entrusted with this responsibility and it should be its duty to ensure that whatever facilities are created in the identified centres and routes, they are properly maintained and run. If necessary, the Corporations should be given adequate powers to enforce this discipline. (Para 11.15)

146. Improved transport arrangements will have to be made for the places identified for development. More buses, taxis, etc., will have to be provided to meet the transport requirements for development of the places likely to be developed. Improved bus-stands, better reservation facilities and more coordination between the railways and the road operators also have to be organised. (Para 11.16)

147. In almost all the places with the potential for development of tourism, there is an acute shortage of water supply as a result of which even the present tourist traffic is put to a lot of inconvenience. Water supply schemes will have to be worked out in detail and L.S.G.D. Departments will have to be asked to give priority to these schemes for places which are selected for development. (Para 11.17)

148. Adequate medical facilities are not generally available in backward hill areas. These facilities will have to be provided so that, in

case of emergency, tourists are not stranded without medical aid. In these places, where the permanent population does not warrant the establishment of regular hospital or a dispensary, temporary shifting of a dispensary or posting of a doctor during the season could be resorted to. (Para 11.18)

149. Hardly any way side amenities worth the name are available in this region. Punjab and Haryana offer good examples where standard but cheap way side amenities have been provided and this should be encouraged. (Para 11.19)

150. Publicity will have to be regarded as a specialised job for which either proper machinery will have to be created within the Tourist Department or private agencies which may be capable of handling this job, will have to be pressed into service. (Para 11.20)

151. The State Tourist Development Corporation should take up in right earnest the publicity campaign and other connected matters in collaboration with hotel organisation, etc. (Para 11.20)

152. Forests can play an important role in the hill areas to provide recreational facilities. (Para 11.21)

153. It is recommended that each State Government should take up the preparation of Master Plans which should:–

(a) take account of the basic natural factors contributing to the attractiveness of a place of tourist interest and identify pilgrim and trekking routes;

(b) study with reference to the existing and the expected volume of tourist traffic, the availability of the civic medical and public health, water supply and accommodation facilities, to determine the steps required for their augmentation and improvement;

(c) appraise the variety and quality of boarding, catering and other facilities and work out the measures needed for their improvement;

(d) the approach should not be to confine planning with reference to the development of tourism but to look upon the various places of tourist interest situated within a reasonable distance of each other as a complex of inter-related facilities and to draw up plans for integrated development, including vegetable growing, poultry, souvenir production, etc.;

(e) In any Master Plan, the importance of preserving the environment in the hill areas must be kept in view. The need to maintain the ecological balance while taking up tourism development in the hill areas, the need to assess the absorption capacity of each centre before taking up development so that ecological balance is maintained, the need to evolve the requisite architectural and building guidelines for the development proposed in the hill areas, etc., are important in connection with the preparation of Master Plan. (Para 11.23)

Industrial Development

154. There is great potential in the hill areas particularly in regard to cottage and village industries based on forest material and wood, horticultural and vegetable, mineral products, apart from such units which can be economically established in the hill areas because of the area having salubrious climate, thereby saving lot of expenditures on air conditioning, etc., like precision instruments, electronics, watches, etc. (Para 12.2)

155. The major effort in the industrialisation programme to the backward hill areas has necessarily to be based on the exploitation of the raw materials available in plenty and the traditional skills particularly for the development of handloom, village and cottage industries, carpets, etc. Further, there is scope for wool industry using sheep and goat wherever possible. The recent revolution in manifold increase in the production horticultural crops, particularly fruits, have opened up vast possibilities of establishing industries based on these raw materials. (Para 12.4)

156. Industries utilising local raw materials cannot provide a sufficient basis for industrial development of hill areas. In many cases raw material based activities will be transport intensive and face handicaps in marketing because of the heavy incidence of transport costs. Hence a special effort has to be made to direct to these areas certain types of footloose industries which produce high value low weight products like pharmaceuticals, watches, electronic devices, etc. (Para 12.6)

157. If the occupational structures in hill areas is to be diversified those footloose type of industries have to be pushed to hill areas because the extent of transport cost disadvantages will not be significant and because other, more transport intensive, footloose units cannot be promoted effectively in these areas. Thus the approach to industrial development of hill areas must be based not merely on the exploitation of local raw materials but also on a deliberate effort to ensure that these areas get a fair share in the overall natural development in foot-

loose industries. (Para 12.6)

158. There is ample scope for establishment of some Industrial Estate in these areas on the lines advocated in its Report on 'Industrial Dispersal'. These estates should be designed so as to attract specific categories of industries. Where possible functional estates with common service facilities should be promoted to attract the type of footloose industries mentioned earlier. Wherever, public sector projects are set up, industrial estates should be set up to support ancillarisation in local area. (Para 12.7)

159. It is time that, as a first step towards effective development of agro-processing units in the backward areas, action is initiated toward the development of regulated markets covering horticultural based crops, with professional supervision. As pointed out in the Report on Industrial Dispersal, this appears to be the more hopeful for an organisation which will handled the needs of the farmer and at the same time command a professional management for efficient running of the industry. (Para 12.8)

160. The Committee would like to emphasise the need for the concerned States to identify the skills that are necessary to develop the type of industries, discussed in this chapter and suited to the hill areas, the extent they are not available locally and the manner in which local population should be trained to fill these gaps. The potential source of entrepreneurship would have to be tapped. (Para 12.10)

161. A large number of educated people from the hill areas have migrated outside their own homes. Attempts should be made to attract them back by providing them necessary facilities and training. In particular, the training of entrepreneurs should include provision of initial help to the trainees, suitable accommodation and stipends, supply of blueprint of the industries which the selected applicants wants to start, good consultancy aids, continuous technical guidance and assistance during the period of operation, etc. (Para 12.10)

162. The margin money for the entrepreneurs in the hill areas should be kept to the minimum and should not in any case exceed 20 per cent of which 15 per cent should be available from the subsidy and the balance 5 per cent alone should be found by the entrepreneurs. Similarly, margin money for working capital will have to be allowed and should not exceed 50 per cent of the normal requirements as specified by the monitoring authorities in non-backward areas. In addition, both term loans and production loans should be available as a package from a credit institution so that internal wrangling on security

can be overcome. (Para 12.10)

163. Howsoever, one may wish, industrial development cannot be brought about solely with the help of subsidies, provision of infrastructure and State help. While these are no doubt essential, more important is the economics of agglomeration and to lay emphasis only on such industries which provide a specific advantage, *vis-a-vis* the non-hill areas and concentrate its efforts only on the development of such industries. (Para 12.11)

Road and Communication

164. The Committee would urge that apart from following the traditional methods of constructing roads, carefully study should be made about the design and specifications of roads in the hill areas, depending upon the intensity of the traffic and availability of local raw materials and efforts should be made to utilise them to the extent possible. Another easy mode of transport in the hill areas is the extensive use of ropeways. The latter should be explored and encouraged to the maximum extent possible as it is much cheaper than the traditional cost of construction of roads. (Para 13.6)

165. The P&T Department has also decided to provide a LDPCO in each village having a population of 2500 or more in hilly and backward areas without any conditions of minimum revenue. In tribal areas, the population limit of 2500 for a single village has been relaxed to cover a group of villages within a radius of 10 kms. of a bigger central village provided no two public telephones will be opened on this basis within a radial distance of 10 kms. of each other. The Committee would recommend that a similar criteria should be thought of in hilly areas and wherever there is a police station under the charge of Sub-Inspector of Police or above, a LDPCO has to be provided even when the revenue does not cover the annual recurring expenditure in the maintenance of the LDPCO. (Para 13.10)

Organisation of Administrative and Financial Structures

166. For the purpose of the administrative and financial organisation, the structure has to be adjusted to these three classes:

(i) Backward hill areas in the Deccan plateau and part of the States having hill areas like Uttar Pradesh, West Bengal and Assam;

(ii) Backward hill areas to the hill States of the Himalayas comprising Jammu & Kashmir, Himachal Pradesh, Arunachal Pradesh, Manipur, Meghalaya, Nagaland, Mizoram, Tripura and Sikkim; and

(iii) Forward hill areas in the hill States mentioned in item (ii) above. (Para 14.2)

167. The National Committee's report on "Organisation of Administrative and Financial Structure for Backward Areas Development" has recommended integrated development project approach for a project area comprising 2 or 3 blocks in backward areas. The Committee would recommended that this project approach with the necessary implications about administrative autonomy and financial autonomy should be implemented in the area comprising items (i) and (ii) in paragraph 14.2 above. (Para 14.3)

168. A multi-disciplinary approach is essential for following watershed management strategy. (Para 14.5)

169. It will be necessary to ensure that the Hill Area Development Commissioners wherever they exist and wherever the creation of such posts is considered necessary, depending upon hill area to be developed, are given adequate staff support and administrative and financial powers. The National Committee would recommend that the Hill Area Development Commissioners should enjoy the same powers and status as have been recommended in respect of the development of backward areas for officers to be designated as Backward Areas Development Commissioners. (Para 14.6)

170. The National Committee would like to recommend that the Steps suggested by it in Chapter 7 "Personnel Policies" of the Report on Organisation of Administrative and Financial Structures for Backward Areas Development must be properly enforced particularly in the hill areas to ensure that adequate staff support is available. (Para 14.7)

171. The Committee would like to emphasised people's participation and thereby providing built in seeds of success in the integrated watershed management programme. The Committee's observations in Chapter 9 dealing with people's participation in its report on Organisation of Administrative and Financial Structure would have to be consistently kept in mind while drawing up plans and programmes for implementation in the hill areas. (Para 14.8)

172. Detailed strategies have been suggested for formulation of sub-plans, budgetary control and delegation of adequate financial

powers. In such States as are not wholly hill States, there is already a sub-plan for development of hill areas. So far as these States are concerned, these are covered by what has been recommended in the main report on Organisation of Administrative and Financial Structure. (Para 14.9)

173. The Committee suggests that the needs of backward hill areas would be taken into consideration whilst allotting special funds for States in the Plan. (Para 14.10)

20

NATIONAL COMMITTEE ON THE DEVELOPMENT OF BACKWARD AREAS, 1978 — REPORT ON DEVELOPMENT OF CHRONICALLY FLOOD AFFECTED AREAS[1]

Chairman Shri B. Sivaraman, Member, Planning Commission

Members Shri Som Dutt; Prof. Mrinal Datta Chaudhary (ceased to be member w.e.f. November 30, 1978), Shri S.S. Marathe (ceased to be member w.e.f. November 30, 1978); Shri Ranchor Prasad; Shri Ramakrishanayya; Shri K.P.A. Menon; Shri R.M. Honavar (ceased to be member w.e.f. January 31, 1981); Shri S.A. Dave; Dr. Y. Nayudamma; Shri Anand Swarup; Dr. B.D. Sharma; Shri Suresh Mathur; Dr. D.M. Nanjundappa; Shri S.M. Ghosh.

M. Secy. Shri Nitin Desai

Appointment

The Government have been pursuing certain policies and programmes in regard to the development of backward areas since the Fourth Five Year Plan. It is now necessary to review the working of these various programmes and to set out a suitable strategy or strategies for the development of Backward Areas in the context of the priorities and objectives set out in the draft 1979-83 plan. The Planning Commission have, therefore, decided to set up a High Level Committee to formulate appropriate strategy or strategies for effectively tackling the problems of Backward Areas vide its Resolution No. PC(P)17/NCDBA/78-MLP dated November 30, 1978.

1. Planning Commission, Government of India, New Delhi, 1982, V, 40 p.

Terms of Reference

(i) To examine validity of the various concepts of backwardness underlying the definitions in use for present policy purposes and recommend the criteria by which backward areas should be identified,

(ii) To review the working of: —

(a) the existing plans for dealing with the general developmental problems of backward areas such as Tribal Sub-Plans, Plans for Hill Areas, etc., and

(b) the existing schemes for stimulating industrial development in backward areas such as the schemes for concessional finance, investment subsidy, transport subsidy, sales tax concessions, etc., similar schemes in the agricultural and allied fields like DPAP, and general measures for tackling the problems of poverty and unemployment with a view to find out their efficacy in the removal of backwardness; and

(iii) To recommend an appropriate strategy or strategies for effectively tackling the problem of backward areas, classified, if necessary, according to areas, causes of or prescribed remedies.

Contents

Summary of Conclusions and Recommendations; Introduction; Identification of Chronically Flood Affected Areas and Strategy towards Development; Cropping Strategy; Irrigation Strategy; Measures to Mitigate Flood Damages; Annexures; Chapter 2; Annexures 2.1 to 2.4, Chapter 5; Annexure 5.1.

Recommendations

Introduction

1. Chronically flood affected areas should be treated as backward areas, and special measures instituted for dealing with their problems, and promoting their economic development. (Para 1.1)

2. It is necessary to identify the ameliorating steps necessary for the development of the affected areas where damage is caused by natural havoc and is in the flood plains where neither any embankment

exists nor are provided in the Master Plan. This is where nature's direct havoc on the economy is felt and this havoc, if chronic, creates the problems of backwardness. (Para 1.11)

Identification of Chronically Flood Affected Areas and Strategy Towards Development

3. The following criteria should be used for identification of the chronically flood prone areas:

(i) flood frequency of at least once in three years;
(ii) flood duration of at least 7 days period at a stretch;
(iii) flood depth of more than the standing paddy at that time; and
(iv) flash floods with strong current liable to uproot plants even if the duration is less than 7 days. (Para 2.4)

4. In all flood plains, one single Department must be designated as the Department to maintain sufficient hydraulic data. It is only this data which would enable a demarcation of the chronically flood affected areas and the nature and the change in such areas over time. (Para 2.5).

5. In all the blocks affected by floods, the exercise to refine the identification of chronically flood affected areas requiring amelioration may be done within the next two years so that a realistic and satisfactory ameliorative programme can be introduced. (Para 2.8)

6. Unlike the demarcation area of a block which the committee has deemed useful for planning in its reports already submitted, the area considered appropriate for the present report, for obvious reasons, is a water basin or sub-basin. (Para 2.9)

7. Measures to mitigate flood losses need to be part of a comprehensive scheme where in modification of floods, reduced damage susceptibilities of infrastructure and property are looked at an integrated fashion. (Para 2.15)

8. For developmental purposes it should not be difficult for project approach to be implemented covering part areas of the blocks so long as they fall in a basin or sub-basin. (Para 2.16)

9. Crop damage is one of the worst damages caused in floods. An appropriate cropping strategy and other steps have therefore to be adopted in these areas. The obvious pathways would be to popularise suitable flood escaping or flood tolerant cropping system or intensive crop production with irrigation in the flood free months there. The

Committee considers that maximum utilisation of the water resources available in these areas and introduction of suitable cropping strategies would be the most important steps for the development of these areas. (Para 2.17)

10. Regarding the damage caused to houses, property and infrastructure, strengthening of house structure, raising the level of whole villages or providing ring bunds around villages have been considered as possible alternatives. Each of these alternatives has positive and negative aspects; yet the fact remains that something has got to be done to provide protection to the human settlement. (Para 2.18)

11. The Committee would also like to emphasise the importance of pre-disaster preparedness measures since they can change a major disaster into a minor one and mitigate the suffering of those likely to be affected. (Para 2.19)

12. The Meteorological Department is reported to have drawn up a comprehensive scheme for improving meteorological telecommunication network for collection of data and its prompt dissemination to the appropriate quarters. The Committee would suggest early decision on these proposals. (Para 2.24)

13. The Central Flood Forecasting Organisation is maintaining a network of observation stations where gauges have been installed to record river flows, sediment discharge, etc. The Rashtriya Barh Ayog have pointed out that there is need for complete review and preparation of a comprehensive plan with a view to bring the network to standards laid down by W.M.O. The network should come into operation within 5 years. Similar action is necessary in respect of gauges maintained by the Irrigation Department of the States. (Paras 2.26 and 2.27)

14. There are wide gaps in the hydrological data. No regular information has been maintained about the behaviours of the rivers. The river beds of some of the rivers reported to have gone up due to reduced velocity of the flood and consequent accumulation of sand. This needs to be verified in the field. (Para 2.28)

15. The Rashtriya Barh Ayog has referred to the new technologies developed for collection, transmission, storage and retrieval of basic data. While we may not be able to modernise completely collection, transmission, processing and storage of data, a minimum programme should be taken up for meeting the essential requirement of flood forecasting. (Para 2.29)

16. The present restriction on use of margin money on disaster preparedness measures should be reviewed. Funds need to be provided.

(Para 2.34)

17. The Committee has already recommended a sub-plan approach for allocation of plan funds in respect of the backward areas. It has also dealt with extensively about the allocation of financial resources, etc. The Sub-Plan approach would equally be applicable to the chronically flood affected areas identified by the States in accordance with the criteria recommended by the Committee. The Committee has recommended a special grant of Rs. 5 lakhs per block, on a phased basis, to take care of certain special items like surveys, investigation, etc. As in the case of chronically flood affected areas, a block would not be the unit for identification, but a basin or a sub-basin, the allocation may be on an area basis. A suitable formula would have to be devised so that this additional allocation is also available in respect of the chronically flood affected areas. (Para 2.36)

Cropping Strategy

18. Adequate research support needs to be provided to solve 'Diara' land problems. Suitable research projects should be taken up on crop and varietal improvement, efficient methods of village for timely operations, efficient use of irrigation water, pests and disease management, etc. Organised marketing system to pick up the farm produce from the producers and fetch remunerative prices will go a long way to promote this cropping strategy. (Para 3.4)

19. Given such facilities, and subject to local requirements, the general cropping pattern for the chronically flood prone areas of U.P. should be (a) intensive 'Rabi' cropping after recession of flood water with irrigation and raising crops with improved varieties of wheat, potato, peas and mustard; (b) after 'Rabi' irrigated summer cropping (Zaid) be practised, using suitable short duration varieties of summer maize, mung or paddy so as to harvest the crops before rains; and (c) 'Kharif' cropping when taken up, mostly flood tolerant paddy varieties like Madhukar, Chakia–59, etc., may be adopted. (Para 3.5)

20. The 'Diara' land in Bihar constitutes the most flood affected areas of the State. Diara lands of Bihar are similar in character to those for eastern Uttar Pradesh. The various practices in the 'Diara' land can be applied to other chronically flood affected areas wherever suitable. (Para 3.6 and 3.7)

21. Access to irrigation water is essential for promoting intensive crop production programmes during flood free months in chronically

flood prone areas of Bihar. Adequate research support as advocated for 'Diara' lands in Uttar Pradesh holds good for Bihar. (Para 3.7)

22. Flood incidence has been observed to be worst near the confluence of rivers in Assam. These areas which are chronically flood prone may continue to lack adequate flood protection for long years to come. Hence there is an urgent need for restructuring the cropping programme to minimise crop damage and loss of production. (Para 3.8)

23. In Assam Valley worst floods are experienced in the months of July and August, although in some years floods have been reported in early June or in end of September. In general, however, the cropping has to be restricted to avoid the months of July and August. (Para 3.9)

24. Recognising the flooding, pattern occurring in the riverine areas, the appropriate cropping strategy would be to raise early *Ahu* paddy from February to June, followed by late transplanted *Sali* paddy from September to December. However, farmers' acceptance of this strategy hinges on the availability of irrigation water for early planting of *Ahu* and for saving the *Sali* paddy from moisture stress in the valley for year round surface flow irrigation due to topography, the ground water resources appear to be abundant. It is indeed, reported, that in most parts of the valley, groundwater is available within a few metres of the surface and offers great scope for exploitation at fairly low cost. The Committee advocates that steps should be taken to popularise an irrigated cropping programme of early *Ahu* paddy or jute, in the pre-flood season, followed by late *Sali* paddy or *Rabi* wheat, mustard or pulses in the post-flood season. The State's efforts in the direction needs to be intensified using available high yielding varieties and technology. (Para 3.11)

25. In the low lying deep water areas, farmers raise crop mixtures of *Ahu* and *Bao* paddy. For *Bao* paddy varieties like *Kekola Bao*, *Negheri Bao*, etc., are recommended. Nevertheless, the modern technology of paddy cultivation has not yet benefited the deep water paddy culture and there is no break-through yet in deep water paddy cultivation. More intensive research has to be undertaken on deep water paddy. (Paddy 3.12)

26. An alternate pathway to improve production from such land would warrant systematic development of deeper areas as organised water bodies for aquaculture and use the same as a supplementary irrigation source for intensifying crop production in the remaining peripheral areas when properly drained. Recognising its merit, the committee considers it would be worth-while to test the economic

viability of this concept by undertaking a few operational pilot projects in the State before its large scale adoption. (Para 3.13)

27. The Committee endorses the contingent crop plans and alternate cropping pattern envisaged by the Government of West Bengal. (Para 3.15)

28. In general, agriculture on Orissa, means raising of paddy. The October-January sown crop of paddy, though covers only upto 5 per cent of the State's paddy area, is practically free from flood and performs best. The season is comparatively cloudless and favours increased photo-synthetic efficiency from November onwards. All efforts should be made to expand paddy area in the October-January season. The Committee advocates this strategy in the flood prone coastal area of Orissa. (Para 3.18)

29. The success of such a strategy depends on the availability of irrigation water. The Committee, therefore, reiterates its recommendations that immediate steps should be taken to increase irrigation facilities in the flood prone areas. (Para 3.19)

30. Intensive research, carried out in the country by the scientists of the Central Rice Research Institute, Cuttack, Agricultural Universities, etc., and elsewhere on paddy, now offers newer varieties and technology suitable for flood prone areas. Photosensitive high yielding varieties like CR—1009, CR—1011, CR—1018, Pankaj and Jagnath can successfully be grown in rainfed, shallow and intermediate waterlogged areas (15 to 50 cm water depth). For recurrent flood areas, flood resistant varieties like FRG-7, FRG-8, BR-13, BR-14, FR-13A and FR-43B are recommended. Where semi-deep (50 to 100 cm) flood water conditions are experienced, rice varieties like CR-1030, CR-260-30, CR-260-31, etc., would be the suitable varieties. Floating rice varieties like Jaisuria, CNDW 332, 327, 326 and 325 have shown great ecological adaptability and are recommended for deep water areas. (Para 3.20)

31. The Committee advocates the restructuring of the cropping, which can escape or tolerate flood damage in the flood prone areas. For popularising such a cropping strategy, it is reiterated that steps should be taken to make available irrigation facilities in such areas. (Para 3.21)

32. Due to management difficulties, deep water paddy produces low grain yields, ranging from 0.5 to 1 tonne per hectare. Suitable varieties are to be evolved to tolerate long periods of complete submergence. Nevertheless, there appears no breakthrough in deep water

paddy cultivation. In view of the importance of deep water paddy, in the flood prone areas and the formidable problems faced for attaining any break-through in its production. The Committee strongly advocates intensification of scientific research on deep water paddy on priority basis. (Para 3.22)

Irrigation Strategy

33. A strategy to retain some water in the natural depressions for providing lift irrigation during the later part of the rabi season and during hot weather season should be considered. (Para 4.6)

34. It should be possible to carry canal water for irrigating lands rendered flood-free during Rabi and summer seasons if there is any major, medium or minor surface irrigation scheme operating in the relatively higher areas in the neighbourhood. The distribution arrangements can be made from the nearest canal water course either through portable pipes or through underground pipe system which may remain undisturbed during the floods. Such irrigation will provide gravity flow to the areas rendered free from floods for Rabi and hot weather crops in and around natural depressions. Drip irrigation and sprinkler irrigation may be tried to secure economy in water use. (Para 4.6)

35. Wells could be sunk in the areas. They would be normally covered during the period of submergence and can be used for irrigation purposes with manual or animal operated devices as well as with portable pump sets to lift water from the wells in the flood free season after the monsoon. (Para 4.7)

36. In West Bengal many channels keep on flowing after the monsoon season even after the lands are rendered flood free. To raise boro paddy or wheat the farmers are used to put up kucha bunds across the flowing channels to impound water and lift the same for irrigating the areas. The system is very crude and adversely affects the regimes of the natural streams or the drainage channels. Instead of putting up temporary earthen bunds, if a systematic programme of construction of sluices with gates are drawn up and construction undertaken, perhaps the purpose will be better achieved and during the monsoon season the gates can be kept opened to allow flood water to pass freely. (Para 4.8)

37. A system of lifting water during the Rabi and summer season is already in vogue in some parts of the Assam State. This programme should be accelerated. (Para 4.9)

38. So far as areas subjected to flash floods are concerned, the same

strategy of tube wells, wells and river lifts can be considered with similar portable arrangements for pumps, motors and distribution system for providing irrigation during Rabi and hot-weather seasons. In such areas it is most advisable not to try any crops during flood periods. (Para 4.12)

Measures to Mitigate Flood Damages

39. It is fully realised that absolute immunity from flood damage is not physically possible even in the distant future because of unpredictability of several natural forces which might cause in unprecedented situation. (Para 5.1)

40. The full potential of the Landsat Imagery be utilised to know precise details about the behaviour of various upper reaches in the country. (Para 5.8)

41. The moderation of run-off would directly help the chronically flood affected areas. For reduction of run-off, the committee would recommend (i) prohibition of production in the hilly catchments; (ii) construction of flood detention reservoirs; (iii) contour bunding in hilly catchments; (iv) small check dams on the tributaries to delay run-off to point of concentration; and (v) elaborate arrangement for flood fighting arrangements at vulnerable points with adequate support of flood forecasting and warning thereof. (Para 5.11)

42. A number of smaller flood retention reservoirs of suitable capacity should be constructed on or near each river, by excavation if necessary. This will serve to regulate the ferocity of flash floods down-stream of these reservoirs. The retained flood waters in various reservoirs can provide ample water supply during the dry season. (Para 5.13)

43. The upper reaches management can be most effective on a watershed management basis. However, at times a judicious choice between conflicting alternatives has to be made. (Para 5.14)

44. Any individualistic attempts at soil conservation measures may not yield the effective results. The whole watershed needs tackling in totality by the Governments and the individual farmers should be made to work within the prescribed norms. In consonance with the overall objectives, any financial needs of the individual farmers should be satisfactorily backed by governmental agencies. (Para 5.15)

45. Embankment construction has been one of the age old method of reducing flooding. The Committee agree that the object of remedial

measures of the protection of a chronically flood affected area should be to train the rivers on their way to the sea by constructing protective embankments, judicious dredging, flood escapes, etc. One of the main reasons attributed to such frequent breaches has been found to be inadequate maintenance. The Committee endorses the Seventh Finance Commission recommendations on the subject. (Para 5.17)

46. The importance of preparing a comprehensive plan of action assumes greater strength in the context of drainage management. The Committee would like to emphasise involvement of all the concerned authorities/agencies which would be responsible for sanctioned construction works in the flood plain areas. (Para 5.18)

47. The maintenance of drainage by dredging and utilisation of the material thus dredged for filling up the hollow areas on the other side of the embankments is a possibility. The maintenance of major/medium drainages wherever maintained by Revenue Department, must be taken over by the Irrigation Department. (Para 5.19)

48. The Committee, while endorsing the comprehensive treatment of the subject of drainages by the Rashtriya Barh Ayog would like to re-emphasise and recommend the following measures:—

(i) There is need for closer coordination amongst concerned agencies like the Railways, National Highways, State Irrigation/Flood Control Departments so as to ensure that structures such as bridges, road, railways, etc., do not aggravate flood problems;

(ii) Prior consultation by National Highway authorities, State P.W.Ds and Railways with the State Irrigation/Flood, Control Departments should be made obligatory. To facilitate an expeditious check, the Government of India should evolve guidelines/checklist for the purpose of vetting of waterways by the State Irrigation/Flood Control Departments;

(iii) It should be mandatory that assessment of adequacy of existing waterways should be made by the State Committee of Engineers or some other Technical Board and the waterways for bridges to be constructed in the future should be vetted by the State Irrigation/Flood Control Department;

(iv) The Standing Committee for settling disputes on waterways and sharing of costs, headed by the Chairman, Central Water Commission, should be vested with statutory powers for implementation of its decisions;

(v) The State should undertake legislation to prevent unauthorised river bed cultivation and encroachments into drains etc. and where such laws already exist, the enforcement agencies should be strengthened. Cultivation of crops like watermelons, vegetables, etc., in river beds and berms, may however, be allowed with caution. The practice of cultivation in the abandoned beds of Dhars and which discharge into main rivers should be stopped; and

(vi) Where suitable legislation with a penal clause for unauthorised crossings over drains has not been enacted, the same should be done and enforced. (Para 5.20)

49. Flood relief channels should be constructed at suitable points to drain excess of flood water to remote artificial lakes; these should also be provided towards the downstreams and of enlarged channels to carry away surplus water to other artificial lakes. The flood relief channels can be used as feeders for minor irrigation canals. (Para 5.20)

50. A complete review of the operation of the systems of sluices for drawing up a necessary operational manual for the same is necessary. (Para 5.23)

51. The paucity of data on river bed behaviours inhibits in making any objective idea about the problem of sand casting. Studies should be undertaken whereby assessment of the problem in the right perspective can be had. (Para 5.25)

52. The problem of sand casting, beyond a limit, is quite harmful for the crop growth. The Committee would recommend the initiation of scientific studies on the subject so that suitable crop planning can be devised. (Para 5.26)

53. Rural houses, facing flood fury, are generally made of materials which cannot withstand a high degree of stresses and strains. In the event of raising *pucca* structures the damage susceptibility can be considerably reduced. Such a scheme should be supported in areas where alternatives are not found to be feasible. In case of its adoption strict enforcement would be desirable as otherwise additional numbers in the hope of receiving doles for construction may get settled in affected areas. (Para 5.29)

54. Raising of villages as a whole offers another alternative to mitigate the hardships of human settlements. Without liberal support from public funds the proposition can rarely succeed. In case of raising of villages, roads should not be raised correspondingly so as to avoid

any interference with drainage aspects. The roads may be allowed to get submerged during floods. Availability of country boats in sufficient numbers would be able to solve the problems of the chronically flood affected areas during that spell. (Para 5.31)

55. Construction of ring bunds around the villages or human settlements in another way which has been experimented at certain places. Such a scheme may be supported in the event of cost-benefit favouring the same in comparison to other alternatives. (Para 5.32)

56. Structural changes and land elevation wherever undertaken by individuals or groups, should be encouraged and suitable monetary and other assistance be provided keeping in view the overall policy objectives. (Para 5.33)

57. Strict regulation of landuse in the chronically flood affected areas is necessary. (Para 5.34)

58. The Planning Commission already provided for soil conservation and afforestation measures in the upper catchment of flood prone rivers. This programme will require to be implemented on sub-watershed basins after identifying the critically affected ones. Effective implementation of this programme will require building of inter-disciplinary teams for each of the basins. The pace of the programme will have to be accelerated along with effective measures to prevent deterioration of new areas. The Committee would recommend special efforts in this direction. (Para 5.34)

59. Disaster relief, while warding off, the immediate distress, encourages certain attitudes which need to be deplored. There is a tendency to consider relief measures as a right. This in turn tends to remove the incentive to avoid future flood losses and encourages persistent human occupancy of the flood plain. (Para 5.35)

60. Effective steps should be taken to train and organise local volunteers in fighting flood hazards due to threatened breaches in embankments and also to utilise effective steps to plug the breaches as and when the same occur. (Para 5.36)

61. The Committee feels that there should be a law to ensure that any building that is constructed in such areas should provide for a plinth above the normal flood level. (Para 5.37)

21

NATIONAL COMMITTEE ON THE DEVELOPMENT OF BACKWARD AREAS, 1978 — REPORT ON DEVELOPMENT OF DROUGHT PRONE AREAS AND DESERT AREAS

November 30, 1978 — September, 1981[1]

Chairman Shri B. Sivaraman, Member, Planning Commission

Member Shri Som Dutt; Prof. Mrinal Datta Chaudhary (ceased to be member w.e.f. November 30, 1979); Shri S.S. Marathe (ceased to be member w.e.f. November 30, 1978); Shri Ranchor Prasad; Shri Ramakrishanayya; Shri K.P.A. Menon; Shri R.M. Honavar (ceased to be member w.e.f. January 31, 1981); Shri S.A. Dave; Dr. Y. Nayudamma; Shri Anand Sarup; Dr. B.D. Sharma; Shri Suresh Mathur; Dr. D.M. Nanjundappa

M Secy. Shri Nitin Desai

Appointment

The Government have been pursuing certain policies and programmes in regard to the development of backward areas since the Fourth Five Years Plan. It is now necessary to review the working of these various programmes and to set out a suitable strategy or strategies for the development of Backward Areas in the context of the priorities and objectives set out in the draft 1979-83 plan. The Planning Commission have, therefore, decided to set up a High Level Committee to formulate appropriate strategy or strategies for effectively tackling the problems of Backward Areas vide its Resolution No. PC(P)17/NCDBA/78-MLP dated November 30, 1978.

1. Planning Commission, Government of India, New Delhi, 1981, xxvi + 143 p.

Terms of Reference

(i) To examine the validity of the various concepts of backwardness underlying the definitions in use for present policy purposes and recommend the criteria by which backward areas should be identified.

(ii) To review the working of:-

(a) Existing plans for dealing with the general development problems of backward areas like Tribal Sub-Plans, Plans for Hill Areas, etc.; and

(b) Existing schemes for stimulating industrial development in backward areas such as the schemes for concessional finance, investment subsidy, transport subsidy, sales tax concessions, etc., similar schemes in the agricultural and allied fields like DPAP and general measures for tackling the problems of poverty and unemployment with a view to find out their efficacy in the removal of backwardness.

(iii) To recommend an appropriate strategy or strategies of effectively tackling the problem of backward areas, classified, if necessary, according to areas, causes or prescribed remedies.

Contents

Summary of Conclusion and Recommendations; Introduction; Criteria for Delineation of Drought Prone Areas; Review of Past and Current Programmes; Strategy of Development; Watershed Approach; Role of Agrometeorology in Agricultural Planning; Soil and Water Conservation; Development and Management of Irrigation; Crop Planning and Productivity; Livestock Development; Pasture Development and Range Management; Horticulture Development; Afforestation; Sand Dunes Stabilisation in Arid Area Solar Energy and Wind Power Utilisation; Strategy for Transport of Technology; Nomad and Nomadism in Desert Area; Organisational and Financial Arrangements; Acknowledgements; *Annexures:* Chapter 1–I to II; Chapter 2–I to V; Chapter 3–I to IV; Chapter 10–I to VII; Chapter 11–I to VIII; Chapter 15–I; *Appendices*, Chapter 10–I to III; Chapter 19–I to II.

Recommendations

Introduction

1. Apart from the size and the geographical spread of the drought prone areas, another important considerations why it is necessary to formulate and implement an appropriate development strategy for these areas is that they represent a major factor contributing to regional imbalances in development of the country. (Para 1.5)

2. As compared to other areas, the drought prone tracts are more vulnerable to ecological degradation, leading to an increasing economic dependency and social deprivation. (Para 1.7)

Criteria for Delineation of Drought Prone Areas

3. The water balance technique seems to be the logical approach for the objective of drought prone area delineation. This approach takes into account precipitation, evapo-transpiration and soil moisture storage and attempts to arrive at a balance between water income and water loss. The Committee is of the view that while this may be an ideal approach, it does not appear to be practical at this stage for delineation purposes owing to paucity of experimental data on evapo-transpiration, soil moisture over the semi-arid and tropical regions and evolution of appropriate area specific agro-climatic models. As the objective of this Committee is drought prone area amelioration for planning and implementation of programmes for this purpose this approach will be ideal, provided the basic data on the essentials can be developed. This will, however, take time. Our objective being to find means of increasing and stabilising productivity in the concerned area, it seems reasonable to follow, for our purposes a synoptic definition that a Block can be defined as drought affected if the pattern and quantum of rain-precipitation, during the main crop season of the area, makes the traditional cultivation of the main crop of the area hazardous in three years or more out of every 10 years. (Paras 2.14 and 2.15)

4. Till the necessary data is collected, and a scientific assessment of drought prone Blocks is done, the present area brought under a drought prone area programme may continue to be handled under the special area programmes. It has been pointed out to the Committee

during its discussion with the States that even following the criterion now prevalent on the basis of which present identification has been done, there are marginal areas of Blocks which need to be brought within the drought prone area programme. The Committee would recommend that any such cases should be examined on merit on the existing definition and brought within the programme if they quality. At the same time keeping in view the recommendations of the National Commission on Agriculture that a periodic review of these areas is necessary because of the developments that are continuously taking place, it would only be reasonable to expect that those Blocks which have already come to a level of development which will put them outside the drougnt prone area category, should be removed from the programme. (Para 2.16)

5. Whilst some new areas may quality, some existing areas have to be deleted as non-qualifying. The Committee would, however, emphasise that a scientific delineation of areas is required it a scientific answer is to be found for the amelioration of the defect. (Para 2.17)

6. The list of the Districts and the Blocks in the State concerned which have been identified on the basis of the recommendations made by the National Commission on Agriculture and which have been taken up under the desert development programme, these may be looked into in case there has been any reorganisation of Districts or blocks. (Para 2.21)

Review of the Past and Current Programmes

7. The present approach is mainly confined to development of agriculture and allied sectors with its major focus on restoration of the ecological balance. But for an integrated development of any area, agricultural sector alone cannot help to achieve the desired objectives. One of the major reasons for deterioration in ecological balance in these areas is the excessive pressure of population on land. Without providing alternative sources of income, any attempt to promote optimum use of land and water cannot succeed inspite of the improved any land agricultural practices. (Para 3.54)

8. Comprehensive planning aiming at alround development of the area has yet to be taken up. Even the basic survey of existing resources has not been completed and there has been lack of coordination between various agencies and programmes in the district

for development. (Para 3.54)

9. The present concept is supposed to be based on the watershed approach. It was, however, only during last two or three years of the programme that attempts are being made to try out this concept and that too in a few district of Gujarat and Rajasthan. But in most other districts, sectoral officers considered DPAP and DDP only as a source of additional funds and intensified their activities without any attempt for integrated watershed development. The fundamental objectives of restoring ecological balance had not thus been able to get the desired attention. (Paras 3.55 and 3.56)

10. Though in some districts there was a mention of division of the district into major and sub-watersheds in the master plan, the actual planning and implementation were not done on the basis of watershed approach. In most districts, the land soil capability surveys, the resources inventory, etc., have not been fully completed. (Para 3.57)

11. In an integrated area development programme for the effective implementation of the approach, funding and expenditure should be controlled by the same agency. Unfortunately, however, this is not so. The programme for infrastructure development is substantially dependent on outlays in the State Sector. The priorities of the State organisations controlling such outlays meant for the entire State is, however, seldom in compatibility with the priorities of the drought prone area development administration. (Para 3.61)

12. Conceptually, an area development programme cannot and should not be designed on the basis of a certain fixed sum of money being repeated every year. Moreover, infrastructure such as dairying roads, electric transmission lines, have their impact over areas much larger than the blocks and even sometimes a district. The present system of funding leaves, therefore, much to be desired. (Para 3.63)

13. There is now sufficient technology available or increasing productivity in the drought prone areas of the country except in extremely difficult land and water situations. What is lacking, however, is an aggressive adaptive research and technological transfer programme through a proper extension machinery. (Para 3.73)

Strategy of Development

14. A block should be the local area for assessing drought proneness. On the principles evolved by the Department of Meteorology for assessing recurrence of the period of high deficiency

rainfall, an exercise should be done immediately to assess the position in the various blocks falling broadly in the region of the present drought prone areas demarcated in country. This exercise will be more relevant to the objective, the Committee is seeking than a broad classification by regions. (Para 4.4)

15. Experience over the years has shown that every year some part of this vast country or the other is susceptible to drought. Where the drought is severe, relief measures are the obvious answer. The entire country cannot be drought proofed. In the chronically drought affected areas, the economy of the population can be improved optimally with potential available in the environment to tide over the bad years. (Para 4.51)

16. Till the delineation under the new criterion is done with the necessary field data, the present area delineated as chronically drought prone may continue to be dealt with under the special area programme. (Para 4.6)

17. The problems of the desert areas are different in many ways from those in the semi-arid and dry sub-humid regions. An analysis of the situation shows a very complicated trend. Total cultivated area is much less than total areas available for cultivation. Animal wealth is under-exploited inspite of the fact that the tract can boast of the best Indian dual purpose breeds of cattle and recognizable breed of sheep. The livestock economy is migratory in character, mainly due to lack of all the year around grazing and water facilities. (Para 4.7)

18. In attempting the development of areas, the restoration of the ecological balance between the water, the soils, the plants, the human and animal population should be a basic consideration and should underline the development strategy. It indicates the need for bringing about an appropriate landuse pattern which will be conducive to attaining the necessary ecological balance. (Para 4.8)

19. There is sufficient technology available for increasing productivity in drought prone areas of the country except in extremely difficult land and water situations. An aggressive adaptive research and technological transfer through a proper extension machinery should be able to increase productivity substantially. (Para 4.11)

20. The aim and concept as outlined by the Committee in para 2.12 of Chapter 2 of its report on "Organisation of Administrative and Financial Structure for Backward Area Development", should be to improve the quality of life of the people in the backward areas. Policies and programmes should be conceptualised and designed, keeping this

overall concept in view, and administrative, social and economic institutions adapted and adjusted towards this end. (Para 4.14)

21. While a comprehensive frame will be the ultimate objective, the spread and the expectation will have to be adjusted to the present level of absorbable capacity of the population of new techniques and skills and the capacity of the administration and institutions to cover the field in the comprehensive manner required in a backward area. Under this approach, it should be borne in mind that the programmes, would have to be both area and beneficiary oriented. For beneficiary oriented programmes, "family" should be regarded as basic human unit for planning and development and for the area planning and development "Block" should be taken as the unit. (Para 4.14)

22. The whole country has been covered by aerial photography in black and white and this is to be repeated at an interval of 5 to 10 years. The Survey of India gets the areas photographed and the photo interpretation techniques have been very well developed, where one can see many things. We can interpret the photographs in terms of geology, geomorphology, geohydrology, landuse, soils and forestry and they give us very specific information and detailed maps can be prepared covering all these aspects. Combining all the data and maps available with suitable ground level, we can prepare optimal landuse and land capability maps, which would provide the basic guidelines for planning for agricultural and other development. This technique can be used on a large scale, district-wise, region-wise and basin-wise, to study in a scientific manner, our renewable resources for a proper land soil water management. (Para 4.16)

23. The effect of drought is a lack of water balance which involves the soil structure, evapotranspiration conditions of the various crops of the area and the rainfall pattern during the main rainfall season. This requires a much more detailed analysis of the environmental conditions for proper guidance on the types of crops and their varieties to be grown, proper land use in utilising pasture development, horticulture, plantations and forestry to make maximum use of the environmental conditions and land quality available. Utilising the macro guidance given by studies on the lines done by the CAZRI for districts in Rajasthan, the position will have to be refined for each block by suitably constituted inter-departmental groups, which will, after local check of. the various parameters and the scientific knowledge then available, guide the extension workers in the types of landuse that can be introduced, with profit. (Para 4.17)

24. The CAZRI may train state level teams to carry out macro surveys in the drought prone areas as has been done by them in Rajasthan. These state-level teams must have the necessary technical expertise to further refine the macro studies and to give recommendations at the blocks level for extension purposes. The Ministry of Agriculture may form a Working Group to develop this concept of a technical study team at the State level to perform this necessary function for drought prone area development. This working group may also go into the adaptive research work that will be necessary in each stage to refine the macro research conclusions on a location specific basis for the drought prone areas and identify the farms and the groups that will do the necessary adaptive research. (Para 4.18)

25. The States had been advised to form Land Use Boards which would undertake this work in the States. The Ministry of Agriculture is at present performing the functions of coordinating this work at the Central level. It was envisaged that a proper Land Use Board will be constituted at the Centre. The Committee places great reliance on a proper landuse capability survey, particularly, in the drought prone areas for maximising productivity of land under the hostile environment. (Para 4.19)

26. The basic sphere dominating the farm population is the possibility of drought and the famine, forcing it to produce as much as possible in a normal area not only for the home consumption but also as carry over for the next year when the food crops may fail. This fear complex leads to bad landuse and anyhow does not satisfy the requirements for foodgrains. If the farm population is to be brought out of this fear complex, and persuaded to grow more valuable cash crops on that land, which is now possible by the technology available, or change over to pasture development and animal husbandry, there must be some guarantee that they will get their food requirements throughout the year at a reasonable price from nearby fair price shops. The country with its vast food distribution organisation is now in a position to give this guarantee provided the requirements are estimated in detail at the block level, adjusting requirements to the changes in cropping that have taken place and providing the necessary foodgrains through the season at nearby fair price shops. The Committee would specially draw attention to this support for a proper land use strategy. (Para 4.21)

27. There are lot of research findings available in the All India

Coordinated Research Project for Dryland Agriculture. A continuous up dating of the technology has to be done in order to refine the field levels advice to the extension organisation. (Para 4.22)

28. Uni-disciplinary research now generally prevalent in the Agricultural Universities and Parallel Research being carried on in various institutions — Central and State — in various aspects of the sciences have to be brought together in a multi-disciplinary applied research programme in order to solve the specific problems of drought prone areas. (Para 4.22)

29. A joint team of the ICAR and the World Bank had recommended the constitution of regional research centres on a multi-disciplinary basis by Agricultural Universities in the country to deal specifically with a multi-disciplinary approach to regional agricultural programmes including crop husbandry, animal husbandry, forestry, horticulture and fisheries. The Committee will strongly recommend that this concept already enshrined in the reports of the Joint Committee be translated into effect by ICAR whether the World Bank is financing the same or not. Such multi-disciplinary regional research centres in each of many different regions of drought are vital to support the drought prone areas amelioration programme. (Para 4.22)

30. Whereas a lot can still be done by tapping available surface and ground water resources in the drought prone districts, it has long ago been realised that amelioration of drought prone districts can only be carried out effectively by transfer or water from more richly endowed basins to the drought prone areas. In future planning, the strategy will have to be to ensure that inter basin transfers are systematically developed and relief given to drought prone areas, particularly those which do not have much of natural precipitation. (Para 4.25)

31. Crops give maximum return when the evapo-transpirations balance is maintained during the crucial periods of crop growth. In other periods, slight stress can be stood by the crops without serious damage. A little under-watering in the other period is not a serious constraint. On the other hand, the mentality of sufficiency of water leads to save productivity. Here there is a need for the laboratory to get close to the land in translating the principle of proper and economic water use. (Para 4.26)

32. For making better use of available water in drought for crops to give maximum coverage in irrigation both by selection of crops

needing lower water duty and by rigid control of water use in the irrigation systems by bringing into effect all aids for such controls like linking of canals and canal controls—if this method is followed, may be much more than 30 per cent of gross cropped area will receive attention. This should be the objective. (Para 4.27)

33. Our first objective should be to ensure that each family in the area gets a reasonable firm base for his economy so that in serious droughts only marginal help will be needed for the family. Thereby also large scale migration of man and cattle can be prevented. There is, therefore, justification for bringing in the principle of social justice and equity in distribution of water to the families. The Committee would recommend seriously such an approach to be followed, it necessary, with a legislative support. (Para 4.29)

34. In middle India, it is generally noticed that in major irrigation schemes main canals pass through deep cuttings in several reaches and higher lands on both sides may be drought affected. It is desirable that where such situations exist, relief is given to the drought affected area by suitable lift irrigation projects. (Para 4.30)

35. The Committee notices that generally minor irrigation schemes of surface reservoirs are not designed and constructed for commands less than in some States 200 acres and in some States 100 acres. This is due to the responsibility cast on various organisations for minor irrigation and their present capacity to survey and design the projects. In drought prone areas the precipitation has to be conserved on a watershed basis starting from higher available point for storage and gradually going down and trying to hold back as much as of the precipitation as possible within the watershed. This will require a system of designing small ponds and minor irrigation reservoirs for very small areas of command. The construction will be simple. An organisation will have to be given the responsibility for planning such water holdings structures on a watershed basis in drought prone areas. The obvious organisation would be the soil conservation organisation suitably strengthened with the necessary expertise. (Para 4.31)

36. Ground water exploitation and conjunctive use of ground and surface water will be an essential ingredient, in agricultural development of drought prone areas. In some of the arid and semi-arid areas the ground water is saline. In such specially difficult areas, a proper planning of conjunctive use of saline and fresh water and suitable agronomic practices and selection of cultivars tolerating levels of salinity, will all have to be filled in to the programme. The objective

is maximum use of whatever water is available. In this context, the large scale experimentation by Haryana of utilising saline ground water in the canal system is worth looking into. (Para 4.32)

37. The Committee recommends that immediately the present stage of use of the reservoirs in the various drought prone areas, the system of reclamation and the cropping pattern may be investigated quickly and at least within the next year a proper plan of maximising the use of such water drawn up. (Para 4.34)

38. As a majority of the population in the drought prone areas depend on land based activities like crop-farming and animal husbandry, the core task for development will to be promote rational utilisation of land and available water. The research institutions working in agriculture and allied sectors have evolved considerable amount of technology for improving and stabilising the economy of watersheds in the drought prone areas. The major task now is its transfer, in a package, to the people residing in these watersheds. (Para 4.35)

39. The Task Force on Rural Development as well as the National Commission on Agriculture has therefore rightly stressed that the strategy for development of drought prone areas has necessarily to be built mainly around animal husbandry. Animal husbandry in conjunction with dairing is considered to offer a more stable based than crop farming for sustained income for the rural households in these areas. (Para 4.38)

40. Notwithstanding the land resource constraint, these areas do offer considerable scope for pasture and fodder development on the available areas if the latest technology for fodder crop and pasture development evolved at the Central Arid Zone Research Institute, Jodhpur, the Indian Fodder and Grasslands Research Institute, Jhansi, and other places is adopted appropriately. (Para 4.41)

41. The problem of employment has to be tackled by providing opportunities in the secondary and tertiary sectors. Unless the industries and service sectors absorb the unemployed and under employed, it will not be possible to reduce the pressure on land in the watershed area. These areas, however, have good potential to provide employment in the non-agricultural sector. Some of the drought prone districts have very good industrial resources like limestone, bauxite and manganese. (Para 4.42)

42. For the development of industrial sector in the drought prone areas, the growth centre approach will have to be synchronised with

the watershed approach so that a clear appreciation might emerge on the extent to which the plans for secondary and tertiary sectors are complementary and supplementary to the land based activities. (Para 3.43)

43. In the context of development of drought prone areas, where new activities or functions are proposed, their location becomes extremely important because such location at appropriate places will start a chain reaction of development with far reaching effects. Therefore, an understanding of functional inter-relationships in space goes a long way towards the development of a drought prone area. Further, decentralisation and the actual location of functions need to be done with in the framework of a region encompassing both urban and rural sectors. (Para 4.43)

44. In relation to the drought prone areas, separation of urban and rural areas spells harm from the point of view of the overall development of the region and its impact on the people. In the drought prone areas, a gradual urban rural continuum should develop with the intensity of watershed approach combined with growth centre concept. The Committee has already dealt with this aspect in its report on Industrial Dispersal and on the development of village and cottage Industries. (Para 4.43)

45. From many drought prone areas in the country there is seasonal out-migration of various types of labour to take advantage of the semi-skilled labour opportunities available in the large scale industrial and construction development taking place in the country. There has also been seasonal migration during the agricultural season like the sowing season and the harvesting season to the more agriculturally endowed areas to supplement the local labour in the crucial operations. In planning the development of a drought prone area, these outmigration opportunities should not be lost sight of. (Para 4.44)

46. It has been noticed that intensive agricultural activities in many parts of the endowed areas has resulted in high wage employment to a large number of outmigrants from the poor agricultural areas. It may be necessary to assess these opportunities and utilise them instead of trying to keep back people in the drought prone areas under low wage employment schemes like the Employment Guarantee Scheme in Maharashtra. (Para 4.44)

47. Many large project like irrigation projects in the country are today suffering from lack of the right type of semi-skilled labour for

completing their work on schedule. There is scope here for increasing the number of semi-skilled labour who can get into these opportunities. The obvious places to look for such labour for upgrading their skills are the drought prone area of the country. The Committee would emphasise that in planning labour for the peoplé in the drought prone areas, the question of skill and wages should be kept clearly in mind. Whether within the areas or by out-migration if the family can earn more and cross the poverty line, every step should be taken to see that the people are advised in the correct direction. Particularly, when moving large masses of labour to new opportunity centres, a good deal of State support in organisation and movement will be necessary. (Para 4.44)

48. As development takes place alongwith the desired lines, many agricultural commodities for local processing and semi-processing will be available. Extraction of sunflower oil, milk processing, wool grading and preliminary processing are instances. The scope for such economic activity needs to be assessed in each area and processing units located, where feasible. (Para 4.45)

49. The provision of drinking water supply is an important element in any programme of development in drought prone areas. These areas experience acute scarcity of drinking water, both for human population as well as livestock, because of low rainfall. In fact, no development of livestock is possible in potential areas without the facility of drinking water. Priority attention, therefore, needs to be given to locating sources of drinking water in those areas. (Para 4.46)

50. Since there is paucity of local water resources, water has to be inducted from outside the arid zone. The Rajasthan Canal Project is an instance of such an effort. This canal is designed to irrigate areas along the western boundary of Rajasthan but the interior desert areas do not derive any benefit from it. The project should be recast to exclude unsuitable areas, where the cost of land levelling and development will be high and to construct life canals to take some waterdeeper into the desert with a view to bringing more areas under irrigation and extending the benefit to a larger section of the community. A beginning has already been made in this direction. (Para 4.47)

51. For maximising the utilisation of the scanty rainwater, suitable water conservation techniques like Khadnis, bandhis and alhandhis will have to be adopted on a larger scale. (Para 4.48)

52. In the early stages of development of the canal command areas, there will be water to spare in the canals. This opportunity needs

to be utilised. As water becomes available in an area, a large scale programme of tree plantation, raising of shelter belts and wind breaks and rejuvenation of vegetable cover will have to be undertaken. This programme will arrest wind erosion, sand blowing and sand casting on arable fields and also reduce the desiccating effect of hot winds on crops. (Para 4.49)

53. The economy of the desert area should continue to be mainly animal husbandry oriented. The desert area has a natural endowment of several good breeds of cattle and sheep. A major thrust of the development programme has to be on the prevention, in a large measure of the nomadism of the cattle breeders and sheep owners. An organised programme of livestock development will have stabilising influence. (Para 4.50)

54. In canal command areas dairy development and milk chilling centres and milk products factories should be undertaken. (Para 4.50)

55. In the arid areas the major emphasis has to be on sheep development. The good breeds of sheep available in this region can be further improved both for wool and mutton. (Para 4.51)

56. Apart from improving the quality of sheep, wool shearing and grading centres have to be established and arrangements made for wool and meat marketings. Another dimension to this development is the possibility of creating more employment in the cottage industry by processing the wool locally. For this, adequate extension support will be necessary. (Para 4.51)

57. Attention has therefore to be paid to large scale development of pastures, regulated grazing to prevent over use and creation of grass reserves and fodder banks for supply of hay in scarcity years. In canal command areas, the cropping pattern has to be adjusted to bring 30 per cent of the area under fodder crops in mixed farming. (Para 4.52)

58. The cold desert in the country occurs in Ladakh valley in Jammu and Kashmir. The Lahaul Spiti Valleys and the Kinnaur region in Himachal Pradesh are also considered as cold semi arid. The population in these areas is sparse. The extreme climatic conditions, lack of communication and the level of education make development of these areas a difficult task. All efforts made so far to develop these areas achieved little success. The Committee would, however, like to emphasise that the available information is not sufficient for formulating the strategy for development and indicating the feasibility of different programmes. In our view, many more investigations and more extensive research based on local environmental

conditions—physical and socio-economic are required before viable economic programme can be implemented effectively in these areas. This has to be given the top most priority. (Paras 4.53 and 4.56)

Watershed Approach

59. For a complete watershed approach one has to bring soil conservation measures, water conservation and storage measures, dryland farming, animal husbandry, afforestation and minor irrigation as the minimum number of discipline under a coordinated approach. At present, the watershed approach in the DPAP is one of the many programmes that the district carries out under DPAP. It is taken as a separate programme by itself with a coordinated approach limited to few watersheds taken up under the programme. The Committee would, therefore, suggest that if the sub-plan approach that the Committee has recommended for all backward area development programmes in its report on 'Organisation of Administrative and Financial Structure for Backward Area Development' is now brought into effect in the DPAP district, this scattered handling of programmes, which should be brought together for maximum benefit, will not continue to affect growth. (Para 5.3)

60. For planning a proper watershed approach for any watershed, the basic physical features like the physiography, land slope, nature and depth of the soil and the hydrological behaviour of the soils and the slopes in the watershed have first to be studied and analysed. Scientific allocation of the various parts of the land for the right type of vegetative cover, grass, trees or agricultural crops will depend on this initial analysis of the physical characters. The type of soil-conservation measures and moisture conservation measures can be planned on the basis of the physiographic data. The present landuse and the hazards in soil and water deterioration that this leads to, have then to be studied in detail so that initially a programme of stopping the deterioration, with a follow up programme of rehabilitation of the areas that have deteriorated can be suitably designed. (Para 5.5)

61. The watershed characteristic vary according to the permutations and combinations of the basic factors of land, slope, nature and depth of soil, precipitation and induction of water from outside. Thus, planning for two watersheds cannot be made on an identical pattern. A watershed management plan has to be highly location specific. It can, therefore, be carried out only by a technical group of experts who

understand the variations of these factors in planning a watershed management programme. The planning cannot be left to lower levels of field workers. This group expertise should be available bale at the project level, supported by higher expertise in the line departments. (Para 5.5)

62. Till a comprehensive attack on the problem can be made on a sub-plan basis in the DPAP district, it is essential anyhow to ensure that the departmental schemes are suitably examined by the project authorities to ensure than they do not create the hazards and where such hazards exist due corrections are made in the project on a continuing basis. (Para 5.6)

63. Normally a watershed management approach and plan would have been based on the rainfall precipitation within the watershed. All other aspects of planning like soil and water conservation, cropping, etc., would naturally follow this basic factor. On the other hand, as and when the master plans for minor irrigation, medium irrigation and major irrigation are carried out in the various districts it may so happen that the irrigation system will create complications in the plan already done and lead to substantial modifications in the watershed management programme. In order to avoid this, it is desirable to examine the watershed planning in a drought prone district against a master plan for irrigation and then work out a suitable plan of adjustment as the programmes of irrigation come into operation. This will have to be a continuous process of examination and adjustment. (Para 5.7)

64. A monitoring of the soil and water loss from the watershed will be a correct measure of the extent of success that has been achieved in the planning and execution of a watershed management. Monitoring of both soil and water loss is easy in a watershed approach if the monitoring unit is located at a point at the outlet of the drainage system of the watershed. A time series of soil and water loss at this point will enable the monitoring authorities to estimate the effectiveness of the action. Where the monitoring shows no significant improvement as expected, the monitoring authority can work back to the minor watersheds within the watershed and identify the particular mini watershed which has to be dealt with in detail for better soil and moisture conservation. This action will have to be a continuous process of monitoring and improvement. (Para 5.9)

65. If we have to carry out large scale development on a watershed basis quickly, it may be desirable to handle large watersheds

in the initial planning. On the other hand, a watershed management programme requires the cooperation of the villages. If too many villages are brought within the watershed, it may be difficult to get the human cooperation that is necessary for effectiveness of the operation. Basing on these considerations, the Committee would recommend that generally in drought prone areas a watershed of the order of 5000 hectares would be a workable proposition. Of course, in specially difficult areas the approach may have to be changed to different limits. (Para 5.11)

66. Watersheds of smaller size have distinct advantage of involving a small number of villages within a resource unit that share the common historical, social and economic patterns. Selection of large watershed entailing large financial outlay for its development should be avoided because the larger the area of the water, the greater will be the heterogeneity in other watershed characteristics like soil, vegetation, slope, landuse and socio-economic conditions. Hence, integrated planning will be complex for larger watersheds. (Para 5.12)

67. As the funds for area development would naturally be limited, some priority in action will have to be brought in the planning. Where general deterioration has to be stopped and areas rehabilitated, the programmes would generally be soil conservation and afforestation including pasture development. For this purpose, the watershed in the project area will have to be analysed for identifying mini watersheds falling under the following three classes:-

(i) substantial deterioration needing prompt action;
(ii) moderate deterioration where investments can be spread over a longer time; and
(iii) reasonably low deterioration areas which can be improved by mere human action in utilisation of the land and resources.

The large soil conservation programmes that the State undertake every year should be worked out on above listed priority schedule. (Para 5.14)

68. There should be an adequate mechanism at the State Headquarters and at field level for collection of data through field units or from concerned agencies. The need for the basic data should be fully recognised and their collection, analysis and interpretation should be considered as a pre-investment towards proper planning and implementation of watershed management programmes. (Para 5.15)

69. The most logical step would appear to be to incorporate corrective measures in the existing landuse system to make the present landuse practices less vulnerable to erosion and degradation hazards. Simultaneously, alternative management practices should be introduced with demonstration of best practice slowly to encourage the beneficiaries to shoft gradually to the improved landuse pattern. If the agro-silvicultural practices or agro-horticultural practices can be made profitable while practising mixed farming, it may be possible to achieve this gradual shift in landuse pattern, and retiring the marginal and sub-marginal land from cultivation of common agricultural crops to productive and remunerative alternative uses. (Para 5.16)

70. Some arrangements will need to be made in the planning cell for collecting representative base level data for typical areas representing dominant combination of practices such as bench terracing, afforestation, water harvesting system, pasture, etc. (Para 5.17)

71. After the creation of the Department of Rural Development which handles the DPAP in the Ministry of Agriculture and Irrigation, the technical expertise rests in the Department of Agriculture whereas the responsibility for carrying out these programmes rests in the Department of Rural Development (now Ministry of Rural Reconstruction). There is, therefore, a need for bringing together the line hierarchies responsible for technical development and technical planners comprehensively into the DPAP planning and implementation at all levels from the project upwards. (Para 5.18)

72. At the project level, the project authorities must have directly under their control technical officers of sufficient capacity in water and soil management and afforestation. (Para 5.19)

73. Super imposition of other capital facilities, which improve the logistic support and thereby economic conditions, should be taken care of at a much higher level, say the District Planning Cells and suitable coordination with corresponding organisations should be made at that level. At watershed level, too many line departments should not be brought together, as that would create confusion. (Para 5.20)

Role of Agro-Meteorology in Agricultural Planning

74. Reliability of occurrence of conditions suitable for sowing and identification of such specific periods are of considerable, importance to agriculture. In this context, the water balance technique seems to be

a dependable approach for the objective of drought prone area amelioration as it takes into account precipitation, evapo-transpiration and soil moisture storage and attempts to arrive at a balance between water income and water loss. However, owing to paucity of experimental data on evapo-transpiration and soil moisture over the semi-arid tropical regions of the country and evolution of appropriate area specific agroclimatic models, it is necessary to make a start with the preparation of a sowing rain commencement chart with available Climatic data, primarily to meet the needs of agricultural planning effectively and profitably. Such charts, in fact, have to be developed for different soil Zones of the country. Using long-term rainfall data and making certain assumptions, this method aims at mapping out the most probable time by which summer monsoon rains in a region would build up enough soil moisture to commence sowing. (Paras 6.4 and 6.5)

75. The new methodology for delineation of drought prone areas for a proper remedy to the situation would comprise:

(i) Assessment of the duration of the cropping seasons for various soil zones of the country. For this purpose, determination initially of the Commencement of Sowing Rains (CSR), utilising all available daily rainfall data and adopting a criterion (or criteria) that will contribute to the building of a moisture profile in thc soil;
(ii) determination of dispersion of CSR;
(iii) compilation of inter-spell duration and total rainfall realisation during the spells;
(iv) determination of frequency distribution of inter-spell duration in various ranges;
(v) superimposition of map showing medium dates of CSR and interspell duration on soil maps;
(vi) identification of drought prone areas of varying magnitudes depending on soil depths, texture infiltration rates and water holding capacity; and
(vii) re-assessment of most profitable cropping pattern. (Para 6.7)

76. The State Agricultural Universities, in collaboration with the Indian Meteorological Department and other concerned organisations, should take up analysis in hand immediately and prepare maps of drought pone areas, delineated on the basis of inter-disciplinary

exercises of superimposition of rainfall analysis of soil zones to provide the basis for drought proofing and modification of cropping patterns. The Committee would further recommend that such studies should be completed in respect of states having arid and semi-arid areas according to time bound programmes. Discussions with the concerned people indicate that it should be possible to complete such studies for different States substantially within a period of one year. (Para 6.12)

Soil and Water Conservation

77. The Committee is quite aware that the economic conditions of the farmers in these areas is poor and free self-labour availability of the farmers is low. There are practical difficulties in mobilising self-labour for subsidised working through extension methods under the Soil Conservation Acts. All these have resulted in the concept of integrated watershed management being rarely achieved, particularly when a large number of farmers are reluctant to join in the working. At the same time any soil conservation programme would be self-defeating unless the people, on whose lands these are carried out, are not only involved in it effectively but have some stake in improving the land and maintaining it. The Committee has suggested certain measures in this regard in Chapter 4 of its report on "Development of Backward Hill Areas and would like to reiterate the same here, namely:-

(i) that the existing practice of subsidising private works on farmers' lands should be continued;
(ii) if there are any works on the private lands like construction and renovation of risers, which would benefit not only the land on which they are located but also other lands belonging to other farmers, these should be treated as items of benefit to the community and financed to the extent of 100 per cent by the state; and
(iii) the existing practice of financing the soil conservation programme of community land on 100 per cent basis should continue. (Para 7.12)

78. The Committee understands that there is some amount of confusion in the financing of farm ponds. Farm ponds may be of two kinds—(1) farm pond to be utilised by the land-holding itself, and (2)

farm pond to be utilised on a joint basis by more than one holders. Where the farm pond is for the benefit of the holding itself, the expenditure has to be met by the farmer subject to such subsidies as are available in the State for the farm pond scheme for various levels of holding. For joint farm ponds, similarly the level of subsidies available in the State for such joint enterprise will have to be followed. The subsidies vary from State to State. (Para 7.13)

79. Soil and moisture conservation is a complex subject which calls for appreciation of role of other technical disciplines besides dominant involvement of a particular discipline. It is necessary to devise a cadre of soil conservation with the basic background such as forests, soil science, animal science or agriculture engineering. It is equally necessary to acquaint the policy-makers, administrators and financiers with the role of soil conservation in the area of national and regional priorities of affecting various development programme of the country. (Para 7.14)

Development and Management of Irrigation

80. Even with the improvement of existing works and the completion of projects under construction, the bulk of the drought prone areas will continue to be dependent on rainfall. The Irrigation Commission has, therefore, rightly emphasised the need for investigations into further possibilities of increasing irrigation by both surface and groundwater. We fully endorse this view. (Para 8.2)

81. The most striking feature of the drought prone areas is the absence of sizeable irrigation sources such as perennial rivers. Consequently, small works such as tanks, *bhandars* and dug-wells constitute the most important sources of irrigation, a large number of these works have at present structural and other deficiencies which need to be removed in order to improve their performance. (Para 8.7)

82. In certain areas, where ground water level is low and irrigation from wells is precarious, attention may have to be given towards construction of percolation tanks and check dams on a watershed basis. (Para 8.7)

83. It has long been realised that amelioration of drought prone district can only be carried out effectively by transfer of water from more richly endowed basins to the drought prone areas. In future planning, the strategy will have to be to ensure that such inter basin transfers are systematically developed and relief given to drought

prone areas, particularly those which do not have much of natural precipitation. (Para 8.8)

84. The Committee strongly urge that necessary studies and investigations for formulation of a National Plan to transfer water from one system to another in order to utilise the surplus water to meet the needs of drought prone and deficit areas in the country should be given a very high priority. It is only when these plans are executed that the picture in the drought prone area would undergo a substantial change. Till then, the Nation would have to be content with taking such other measures as are feasible for the development of drought prone areas keeping in mind the constraint that adequate water resources would not be available. (Para 8.13)

85. The schemes of inter-basin transfer or river water would take a very very long time to fructify, even if they are found technically feasible. In the meantime, it is local source of ground and surface water, to whatever extent, it is, available, which will have to be harnessed and reliance placed in the drought prone areas for bringing more area under irrigation. This underlines, among other things, the need for a quick and early completion of hydrological surveys in these areas. Recently, these has been a growing awareness on the part of the States to undertake these surveys. The Committee would strongly urge that this programme should be stepped up and both the Central Ground Water Board and the State Ground Water organisations should complete the hydrological surveys of all the arid and semi-arid areas as per a time bound programme. (Para 8.14)

86. Even with full exploitation of possible irrigation programmes in the drought prone district and with all transfers of water from other basins and may be possibly on a national basis, water will still remain a very valuable commodity for agriculture and human development. It is, therefore, necessary to ensure that available water is utilised of the maximum in improving the economics of the area. Here, there is a need for the laboratory to get close to the land in translating the principle of proper and economic water use. (Para 8.15)

87. The necessity is for making better use of available water in drought prone areas to give maximum coverage in irrigation by selection of crops needing lower water duty and by rigid control of water used in the irrigation systems by bringing into effect all aids for such controls like linking of canals, canals control, land shaping, field channels, etc. The Committee would strongly urge that the objective in all sources of irrigation in the drought prone areas should be to get

maximum return out of every unit of water. (Para 8.16)

88. Where there is a serious constraint of water in irrigation system, there is need for much more equitable distribution of available water keeping in view the principle of social justice. The Government of Maharashtra found that for such equitable distribution of water, proper legislation should be introduced so that such irrigation system in particularly bad drought areas may automatically control the distribution under a legal process. (Paras 8.17 and 8.18)

89. What is essential is that the limited water must be put to optimal use. This requires not only rationing of water but also banning the growing to such crops as require heavy irrigation like sugarcane, paddy, etc. The Committee would strongly urge that such an approach must be brought about if necessary with legislative support. (Para 8.20)

90. Another aspect is that there must be concerted effort towards avoidance of water losses. The Committee would, therefore, urge that it should be enjoined on all concerned that wherever an irrigation scheme of whichever type exists or is taken up utmost priority should be given to the introduction of optimum use of water practices. This also would go a long way in increasing the protection available to the farmers in these areas. (Paras 8.21)

91. The Committee notices that generally minor irrigation schemes of surface reservoirs are not designed and constructed for commands less than in some State 200 acres and in some States 100 acres. This is due largely because of the responsibility of such works being cast on Irrigation Departments, which are not attuned to design and undertake small projects. In drought prone areas the precipitation has to be conserved on a watershed basis starting from the highest available point for storage and gradually going down and trying to hold back as much of the precipitation as possible within the watershed. This will require to system of designing small ponds and minor irrigation reservoirs for very small areas of command. An organisation will have to be given the responsibility for planning such water holding structures on a watershed basis in drought prone areas. The obvious organisation would be the soil conservation organisation suitably strengthened with the necessary expertise. (Para 8.23)

92. In some of the arid and semi-arid areas the ground water is saline. In such specially difficult areas, a proper planning of conjunctive use of saline and fresh water and adoption of suitable agronomic practices and selection of cultivars tolerating some salinity, will have to be fitted into the programmes. The objective is maximum

use of whatever water is available. In the context, the large scale experimentation by Haryana of utilising saline ground water in the canal system would be worth looking into. (Para 8.24)

93. The present stage of use of the reservoirs in the various drought prone areas, the system of reclamation and the cropping pattern may be investigated quickly and, at least, within the next year a proper plan of maximising the use of such water drawn up. (Para 8.26)

Crop Planning and Productivity

94. Despite the technology being available and its economic feasibility established, still the farmers are not changing over to new pattern. The trouble is that every household is anxious to somehow produce sufficient foodgrains of the varieties most prevalent in the area. This basic fear dominating the farm population is the possibility of drought and famine, forcing it to produce as much as he can do not only to meet his current consumption, but also for a carry over for the next year when the food crops may fail. This fear complex leads to bad land use and anyhow it does not satisfy the requirement for foodgrain. If the farm population is to be brought out of this fear complex and persuaded to change the present pattern of land use, there must be some guarantee that they must get their food requirements throughout the year at a reasonable price and the type of food required by them from nearby fair price shop. The country with its vast distributing organisation should now be in a position to give this guarantee provided the requirements are estimated in detail at the block level, adjusting the requirements to the changes in cropping pattern that have taken place and providing the necessary foodgrains throughout the season at nearby fair price shops. This is the first essential and foremost support for a proper land use strategy. (Para 9.6)

95. The topmost priority in the drought prone areas must be given to prepare optimal land use and land capability maps, which will provide the basic guidelines for planning for agricultural and other development. Once such maps are available, it would be necessary for the concerned planning and development authority in the area to draw plans to take up relevant developmental strategy for such lands as are found unfit for crop cultivation, or are in a position to give better return if diverted to uses other than crop farming. The Committee considers this as a very essential step not only for proper land use, and improving the productivity and economic conditions of the people living in these

areas, but also in restoring the ecological balance which would go a long way in not only improving the conditions of the people in these areas but would also be in the larger national interests. (Para 9.8)

96. Successful dry land agriculture requires a two pronged strategy. When the monsoon is normal, is should be used most effectively. Making the best of it involves a good deal of attention and work—the best varieties, the best practices, inter-cropping and so on. The second part of the strategy comes into operation the moment the weather turns aberrant. This approach must outline for each agro-ecological region the list of anticipatory measures and alternative crop strategies that ought to be adopted when there is evidence of the incidence of drought. This kind of programme involves steps like:-

(a) Maximising production and altering crop patterns, when necessary, in irrigated areas;
(b) proper development and management of irrigation sources;
(c) mid season corrections in crop planning in un-irrigated areas;
(d) introduction of crop life saving practices; and
(e) building up of appropriate seed and fertiliser buffer to implement the drought cropping strategy. (Para 9.12)

97. There are crops that could give farmers something in return for his effort even in unfavourable years. These are fodder crops. Mixed cropping system comes into full play in this situation. If one crop fails, another comes to the rescue of the farmers. It is important to treat all practices as a package because it is the cumulative effect that enables a farmer to raise crops successfully in rainfed areas. It is needless to say that partial adoption of this package will not produce the desired result. This is the task which the State Agricultural Development Organisation in these areas must take up in right earnest and gear up the extension machinery as well as the input supply organisation towards this end. It requires a close and coordinated effort on the part of the various agencies involved in introducing this package approach and all have to work together as per a preconceived cropping programme, based on proper land use pattern. (Paras 9.13 and 9.14)

98. "Watershed based resource utilisation" involves the optimum use of the watershed precipitation for the improvement and stabilisation of agriculture on the watershed through improved water, soil and crop management. More effective utilisation of water for the production of crops can be facilitated by one or more of the following

means:

(i) Directly by improving infiltration of rainfall into the soil and thus making more soil water available for plant use;

(ii) through drainage, collection, storage and reutilisation of run off; and

(iii) by water recovery from wells after deep percolation beyond the root profile. (Para 9.18)

99. Many small farms and fragmented land parcels and often several different land uses—together compose a watershed, their presence must be accommodated within efficient watershed development and management techniques. In many situations, group action may be required to attain the desired objectives. (Para 9.19)

100. Improve technology will relate to crops—variety fertility, management, land development, water conservation, etc. In the end, millions of small, often illiterate farmers, who have little capital must learn to apply the tools of science to extract more food and ultimately a better quality of life from their hostile environment. Compromises must be found between short-term and long-term objectives. The challenge is great. (Para 9.20)

101. Timely completion of all from operations before the rains is essential. The earlier the sowing is done, the longer the period the crop has to grow and mature. Hence, the tillage operations should be completed before the onset of rains. In an inter-cropping system it is necessary to till or harrow immediately after the harvest of one of the component crops as otherwise weeds take over and the yield of longer duration component is drastically reduced. (Paras 9.29)

102. The various dry land research over the last six years have identified and/or fabricated several farming machinery. The costly implements could be supplied to farmers on hire service. (Para 9.30)

103. During the last 6-7 years, scientists in different regions have evaluated all the important crops generally grown in the area for their relative efficiency of production. On the basis of data obtained efficient varieties/crops have been identified for different regions of the country and these are now available for use by the extension machinery. The experience has been that change-over to improved crop varieties is a basic requirement to enable the growers to benefit fully from yield based inputs, fertiliser, available moisture, etc. (Para 9.31)

104. The farmers will have to be prepared to sow as soon as the seeding rain occurs. This can only be done if the land has already been tilled after the previous harvest. It is sometimes suggested that this tillage should be done after the harvest at a time convenient to the farmer. In drought prone areas, disturbing the top soil after the kharif harvest during periods of high temperature and high wind can lead to serious soil erosion. The tillage to be effective and, at the same time, not destructive will have to be done just after the harvest so that the land settles down before the temperature and wind increases. Alternatively the tillage will have to be done at a time shortly before the expected seeding rain so that erosion effects are minimal. (Para 9.33)

105. The most important contributor to the increased productivity of land in the drought prone areas is the utilisation of the land for a kharif crop wherever a kharif fallows, followed by a rabi programme, is the traditional practice. The analysis made by ICRISAT which we have reproduced gives the parameters for deciding which areas are suitable for a kharif sowing. The Committee would recommended that based on this analysis a kharif sowing shall be attempted at the seeding rain in all these areas in drought prone zones. (Para 9.35)

106. Special efforts should be made to enrich the organic matter content of drylands. All the organic wastes of plants, cattle dung, etc., should be incorporated into the soils as FYM or compost. The practice will improve the soil structure and their water holding capacities. (Para 9.40)

107. Whilst various types of weed control have been experimented upon in the coordinated research programme, a proper cost benefit analysis has not yet been done which can enable the extension organisation to effectively introduce a chemical weed control programme. It is rather unfortunate that the cost benefit criterion has not yet entered the experimentation. There are a number of operational research programmes being carried out in many large areas in the country under strict technical control. It is necessary that these operational research programmes go into a proper analysis of the cost benefit that can be attributed to weed control in lands similar to those found in drought prone areas. Particularly, as *vertisols* (black soils) and *alfisols* (red soils) predominate, experimentation should now be done for these two types of soils in varying depth conditions immediately. The Committee would recommend an early examination of the weed control cost benefit as it has no doubt at all that in drought prone areas,

with all good cultural practices, unless weed control is effectively done, substantial part of productivity will be lost. (Paras 9.42 and 9.43)

108. Not only would consistent rainy season cropping often not be profitable, it would probably endanger the profitability of the more important post-rainy season crop. We, therefore, emphasise strongly the importance of breeding for high yield potential post-rainy season sorghums for these and similar regions. (Para 9.50)

109. For extension and implementation purposes it is convenient to divide the system for farming into two parts: (i) soil and water management technique; and (ii) cropping patterns and agronomic practice. Soil and water management designed to control run off to dispose of excess water and to minimise erosion frequently including direction of cultivation have to be planned and implemented on a whole-watershed basis since guidance of water from plot to plot is crucial. On the other hand, cropping pattern decision and agronomic practices should be adapted to the watershed topography, only if the benefit of such group action are sufficient. (Para 9.53)

110. In actual field level experimentation, the farm pond has been found useful under vertisol conditions. The Committee will recommend that the present policy of supporting a farm pond system in the vertisols in the low rainfall areas may continue. The actual cost per hectare of the system is not such that one should wait for the further field experience and hold back the national priorities. If necessary, adaptive research can be carried out on a sufficient sampling basis by State Department which may yet have some doubt on the subject. (Para 9.58)

111. The cost of broadbed and furrow system is not very high considering the crop advantages that appear to arise from the package of practices. Time taken for primary tillage is a very important aspect in drought prone areas where the rainfall pattern is extremely variant and the moisture accumulation in the soil for seed bed persists only for very short spells of time. It may, therefore, be worth considering by the extension organisations whether this additional expenditure should be undertaken or not. Anyhow there is definitely a case for adaptive research analysis in the medium and shallow vertisol areas. (Para 9.60)

112. Research and experiments by themselves are not enough to decide on detailed advice on either the crop patterns or improved agricultural practices for various zones of the country with various types of soils and rainfall pattern under the low rainfall group. A lot of adaptive research will have to be done by the State Agricultural

Departments in close association with the ICAR research stations with the technical support of agricultural university, to evolve the most profitable or most fool proof crop or mixed crop system and improved practices which can be recommended in micro regions in the states under different soil conditions in drought prone areas. The Committee recommends that necessary adaptive research should be organised quickly in the blocks, particularly having black soils. (Para 9.61)

113. Broad Bed and Furrows definitely have a benefit in the deep and medium vertisols situations. Compared to the cost of land shaping on this basis, the benefit are substantial. The broad bed and furrow system can be adopted in individual fields and need not necessarily be with adjustment of boundaries on a watershed basis. ICRISAT experimentation seems to prove that watershed based adoption of field boundaries to graded cultivation may result in only modest increase of gross returns. But this may not be sufficient to motivate farmers to exchange land on a voluntary basis. They have also pointed out that whereas water control on a watershed basis is desirable for drainage and run-off and irrigation control, the existing field boundaries can be respected. From the practical angle, however, for selling this strategy to the farmers, more rational research on the field under varying conditions is absolutely essential and the earlier it is undertaken it would be better. (Para 9.62)

Livestock Development

114. Arid areas are considered to be the best suited for sheep husbandry which is already an important source of livelihood for a large number of rural people. In semi-arid areas the total livestock is pretty large. They are poor milkers but good drought breeds. However, these cattle and buffalo breeds require further improvement of their potential for production. Sub-humid arid areas also have sufficient livestock resources, but it is their proper use and management that would determine the success of the programme for their development. In humid arid areas the resource endowment is the best. The productivity of cattle is low and efforts are necessary to develop them through improved breeding and management practices. (Paras 10.3, 10.4, 10.5 and 10.6)

115. Sheep as a specie is most suited for arid areas because of its close grazing habit and adaptability to the arid conditions. Expanding sheep population has, however, not only resulted in depletion of natural

vegetation in their home tracts but also on their migratory routes. Because of their close and selective grazing nature and their ability to utilise many weeds and bushes and to travel long distances in search of forage and water, sheep have often been levelled as the creators of the desertic conditions. In reality, it is not the sheep but the man who owns the sheep who is to be blamed for mis-management of the grazing land which has resulted in the desertic conditions. Controlled and judicious grazing practices on the desert land could prevent soil from erosion and the droppings collected on the fertile land over the years could eventually convert it to more fertile land. (Paras 10.12, 10.13 and 10.16)

116. Improvement in production and quality of wool and body weight due to cross-breeding, provision of a better health cover and adequate supply of feed and fodder is expected to provide higher returns. However, no reliable data are available on the economics of supplemental feeding of sheep during growing stages, breeding season, later part of gestation, location, etc. In our opinion, it is necessary for the purposes of planning sheep development programmes to have detailed information on these aspects. We, therefore, recommend that the Indian Council of Agricultural Research (ICAR) and Agricultural Universities should initiate without delay studies in this direction. (Para 10.17)

117. Crop husbandry in these areas with low total rainfall, is a gamble. All the farming communities, particularly small and marginal farmers, can better depend on sheep rearing as the main source of livelihood. (Para 10.19)

118. Cross breeding of superior local flocks with exotic rams for better yield of mutton and wool will result in the production of bigger animals with higher body weight having proportionately higher nutritional requirements. Unless, therefore, a strong fodder base is created, the potentiality of the crossbred animals cannot be fully harvested. (Para 10.19)

119. Having accepted a sheep rearing programme as an important part of drought prone area development the Committee would recommend that detailed planning of the programme as is being done in the IDA districts on the basis of further experience so far gathered and a comprehensive attack on the programme in the district through a duly constituted extension unit with the relevant technology should be immediately brought into effect in all the drought prone area districts considered to be good for sheep breeding. There must be continuous

monitoring and improvement of the scheme so that full benefit from the programme accrues to the sheep rearers. (Para 10.24)

120. Whilst performance in the IDA districts can be considered as better than in non-IDA district, it has to be noted that the recommended level of flock per 100 hectares is 400. This has not been reached so far anywhere. The Committee recommends that the organisation for the technical management of these units and the technical support to the sheep rearer groups within the units should be improved to bring about the level of 400 sheep per unit within the next two years. (Para 10.27)

121. Village based flocks must have additional pastures. This is very relevant in drought prone areas. The Committee has already pointed out how 1/3rd to half of the land-holdings, whether small, medium or big, are left fallow every year in the poor rainfall areas because of inability to cultivate them in time. An extension programme should be launched to put some of these general fallow lands under a permanent pasture cover with suitable cultivation practices to maximise fodder production within the holding. (Para 10.33)

122. In the desert areas we have to handle not only the village based flocks but also the flocks which are nomadic perennially and those nomadic for some months in the year. (Para 10.34)

123. Nomadism is the problem mainly of the desert areas. If a large 2000 hectare plot is developed with groundwater where available or in a 'khadin' in a suitable location, the pasture under good management can easily support throughout the year a flock of 4 sheep a hectare or 8000 for the pasture. (Para 10.35)

124. Considering the very large acreage that have been reserved for the base sheep breeding farms, the number of rams produced per year for distribution by the various farms seems to be strangely extremely limited. The Committee would request that an immediate study of the situation in these farms be made and the reasons why the available facilities have not resulted in much larger issue of rams for the field programme be investigated and the faults remedied quickly. Otherwise, the support for the large sheep breeding programme in the DPAP would never be forthcoming. (Para 10.45)

125. While recommended breeds of sheep are now available for arid and semi-arid of the country, such breeds are not yet available for humid region. It is, therefore, suggested that sheep development in humid areas should be brought about mainly through selective breeding in local breeds and introduction of exotic breed must wait or be done in stages by using half-breed rams. (Para 10.48)

126. In regard to sheep improvement programme of migratory flocks, it is essential to provide necessary facilities on the migratory routes like improved grazing, area availability of some conservative fodder, necessary inputs for sheep improvement like prophylactic vaccination and drenching, superior pure breeding rams, sheep shearing and wool and live animal marketing facilities. The sheep and wool extension centre should also have sufficient drinking water resources for human and animals. They may provide credit and banking facilities to the nomadic sheep farmers. The migration will be controlled by these centres through communication among different centres. (Para 10.51)

127. Majority of sheep under migration belong to Marwari and Jaisalmeri breeds which are good carpet wool breeds. It may be desirable to improve the wool quality for manufacturing superior carpets. (Para 10.53)

128. The desert development report of the National Commission on Agriculture has emphasised the need for the development of pastures for sheep rearing. They have recommended that wherever irrigation schemes exist and particularly in areas commandable with lifts from the Rajasthan Canal System and by natural flows, substantial pasture development under irrigation conditions should now be taken up. The Committee would reiterate this recommendation and ask for rapid action. (Para 10.55)

129. In the afforestation programmes that are now being taken up on a large scale, priority may be given to location tree fodder units wherever possible and wherever sheep flocks are in a large number. (Para 10.55)

130. One of the hazards which the sheep have to face to the lack of shade in summer. If tree fodder units can be spreadover sufficiently large areas on a scattered basis, they will give sufficient shade for sheep flocks which are nomadic in summer and even for village flocks which has shade difficulty in summer. (Para 10.55)

131. Although the importance of development of marketing facilities for wool and live animals and development of small scale wool based industry has been stressed earlier, it is further emphasised that such facilities must be organised both for the sedentarised and migratory flocks by the Government or the Cooperative Agencies as this will avoid profiteering by a number of intermediary agencies dealing with the marketing of live animals and wool. (Para 10.56)

132. The Central purchase of sheep from the cooperative and

slaughtering them at a modern abattour necessarily means a follow up in the deep freezing carcass and marketing the meat in frozen condition. Obviously, in such a centralised location near the area of the sheep flocks there will not be any substantial market for fresh meat. The Committee will recommend that a well thought out programme should be developed for one such centre with a minimum economic level of sheep to be slaughtered per day and a tie up made with large metropolitan consuming centres like Delhi, Calcutta, Madras and Bombay. (Para 10.57)

133. There will also have to be a well spread marketing organisation to push the sale of frozen meat to ordinary householders. In his context, the Committee would point out to the pioneering work done by the Fisheries Department of Karnataka in filleting of sea fish caught in Mangalore, transported in deep frozen conditions to a chain of retail centres in Bangalore for sale. By this and suitable promotion, substantial sea fish consumption has been developed in Bangalore. Such a network of retail centres with link up to the main production centres will have to be planned for mutton on a similar basis in the pilot scheme. (Para 10.57)

134. During migration, sheep from different areas mix up in the grazing zones and follow common migratory routes. Thus, one diseased flock may contaminate large areas of the grazing lands on its route causing serious threat to the other flocks grazing over those areas. As such, it is highly necessary to undertake routine prophylactic measures against the commonly occurring diseases. (Para 10.58)

135. Slaughter of goats for meat purposes should be increased so that the rate of growth of goat population may come down. The Committee has already indicated that in view of its habit it can cause damage to areas under afforestation. Suitable management systems should be devised to exercise greater control over their movement and feeding habits. (Para 10.63)

136. Breeding programme should be planned keeping in view the local agro-climatic conditions. (Para 10.69)

137. Identification of breeds, both exotic and indigenous suitable for the area has to be done, to develop their productive capacity. Improved indigenous breeds from other areas with similar agro-climatic conditions should be utilised for upgrading of local, non-descript stock in the villages under dryland farming conditions. (Para 10.73)

138. Any programme for rapid improvement of cattle wealth and

thereby the income from cattle would be most welcome addition to the poor economy of drought prone areas. Hence there is a need for rapid introduction of the crossbreeding programme. The Committee would, therefore, strongly recommend that the bases of exotic cow farm, breeding bull farm and frozen semen banks should be brought up to great efficiency immediately so that an active cattle development can take place in drought prone areas. (Para 10.74)

139. One of the reasons given for the slow pace of spread of frozen semen technology is the lack of canisters for holding liquid nitrogen to keep the frozen semen straws in conditions for insemination in the field. The Committee understand that the present demand far out-reaches available supplies in the country. The Ministry of Agriculture will have to take a close look at the present programmes of demand and supplies and solve the problem satisfactorily. Otherwise, this single factor may be a serious deterrent to the rapid growth of animal husbandry in the drought prone areas. (Para 10.75)

140. Murrah in Haryana and Mehsana and Surti in Gujarat are the high milk yielding breeds of buffaloes. These breeds have attained not only all India importance but also international recognition as important milk breeds of buffaloes. The following approaches should be followed for improvement of these breeds. Firstly, their genetic potential for milk production should be improved further through selection breeding in their native breeding tracts. Secondly, the sires of proven worth belonging to these breeds should be used for up-grading non-descript buffaloes in other areas through crossbreeding. Graded Murrahs are considered suitable to and are being distributed in arid and semi-arid tracts of drought prone areas. (Para 10.78)

141. The necessity for milk production enhancement being so great, all production potential should be actively exploited for obtaining the maximum possible use. This would require enlargement and strengthening of the existing programmes as also initiation of additional programmes. Carefully planned systematic breeding programmes including progeny testing of selected bulls should be undertaken for progressive genetic improvement of the stock. (Para 10.80)

142. At present most of the veterinary hospitals are poorly equipped, do not have modern aids for arriving at prompt and correct diagnosis of diseases and lack facilities for undertaking surgical operations. Even drugs for treatment of common ailments are in short supply. These problems are more acute in the drought prone areas. The

Committee would urge that wherever animal husbandry programme is taken up, immediate steps should be taken to provide animal health cover. (Para 10.81)

Pasture Development and Range Management

143. Pasture development in drought prone areas, apart from increasing fodder availability and thereby promoting development of animal husbandry, confers the benefit of providing grass cover on lands subject to wind and water erosion. Unless the livestock are fed adequately and with quality fodder to provide all the nutrients in required proportions, their productive potential is not realised in the form of increased production of milk and other animal products. Adequate production and good quality of fodder and grass thus becomes a pre-requisite for the success of animal husbandry programme, so vital to the economy in these areas. (Paras 11.1 and 11.3)

144. Notwithstanding the land resources constraint, these areas do offer considerable scope for pasture and fodder development on the available areas if the latest technology for fodder crops and pasture development evolved at the Central Arid Zone Research Institute, Jodhpur, the Indian Fodder Grassland Research Institute, Jhansi and other places is adopted appropriately. (Para 11.8)

145. Another important problem in the implementation of pasture development was lack of seeds of suitable grass species in adequate quantities. These were problems of adoption of these varieties. It is necessary to plan the pasture and fodder crops development properly and implement a package of technical recommendations within the watershed frame for the success of the programme. (Para 11.12)

146. A conscious policy fixing annual targets in the various states for an existing grassland development and marginal land development is the answer. The identification and allocation of areas should be based on the regional expectations of development of types of domestic animals and their quality as have been postulated in the recommendations of the National Commission on Agriculture. (Para 11.15)

147. For planned grassland development leading to intensive fodder production, the area has to be kept out of the nomadic grazing the scrub animals that goes on endlessly in all these lands. The nature of the soil in the grassland that have been identified will enable the

planners to decide which particular type of fencing will have to be used and what will be the minimum area of land that would be economically maintainable. This exercise will have to be done simultaneously by each state whilst identifying the grasslands. (Para 11.17)

148. The programme of identification of grasslands and intensive development can generally be followed without much difficulty in areas reasonably away from the village sites. Where such lands are close to the village and in the areas demarcated as grazing lands within the village boundary, the strategy of development will have to adapt itself to the people's need. (Para 11.18)

149. There is a temptation for the nomadic cattle and sheep breeders to drive their cattle and sheep over sand-dunes stabilisation systems under the garb of private rights. In the interest of the community's welfare, the Committee would recommend some legislative measures to ensure a complete fencing of all the land and ensuring and preventing direct grazing on such sand-dune stabilised areas. The grass will have to be harvested by manual labour and fed to the cattle and sheep. (Para 11.19)

150. Naturally, grassland development cannot be taken up all over the area identified for such development. It is recommended that it would be desirable to take up the development work initially in areas where reasonable accessibility to water facilities are available so that the stabilisation of the grasses and fodder can be accomplished quickly so as to demonstrate the benefit from the new method to the people before they lose patience with the reservation. (Para 11.20)

151. Both sheep and goat are part of the nomadic economy. The grasslands away from the village settlement that are developed either in the Government areas or reserve forest areas will have generally to be protected against indiscriminate grazing. (Para 11.24)

152. In nomadic sheep rearing, the problem of improvement of the breed through artificial insemination or direct cover becomes difficult unless the flocks can be brought together to a fixed place during the breeding season. These large grass reserves can be utilised as such centres for bringing together the sheep flocks of nomadic breeders at the time of breeding. (Para 11.24)

153. When the lambing takes place, the ewes and the lambs can also be kept in the settlement round the grassland with permission to utilise grasses inside the reserve. Thus, active improvement of breed can be done. There is scope for this approach, particularly, in the States of Rajasthan, Gujarat, Haryana and Maharashtra where sheep breeding

is even now sufficiently large. It can be usefully introduced in the Southern States to extend the flocks rapidly where mution breeds will be the order of the day. (Para 11.24)

154. Once organised grasslands are developed throughout the country, it will happen that for maximisation of yield there should be periodical harvest of the crop. There may be excess supply in certain parts of the season when the nomadic flocks can find natural ranges. It should be general practice to harvest such surpluses and maintain reserve in the large grasslands of the country for utilisation during serious droughts in the areas surrounding. The necessary technology for hay making with necessary equipment should be part of the grassland development programme. (Para 11.25)

155. Grassland development programme will have to be on a package basis, with a link up of research, extension, infrastructure development, input supply and control. (Para 11.26)

Horticulture Development

156. There is considerable scope for increasing horticultural crop production, particularly in Rajasthan in the large areas being served by the Bhakra and Rajasthan Canal Systems. Ganganagar District has already nearly 6,000 hectares under fruit, vegetables, etc. In fact, it has been established that wherever canal irrigation water and good quality water from other sources like wells and tubewells is available, almost all the fruits and vegetables for which climatic conditions are suitable can be grown. The extremely dry conditions enable the production of a fine a quality of papaya without the undesirable latex odour in its pulp. (Para 12.3)

157. With irrigation resources, commercial seed production of vegetable crops, e.g., lady finger, cucurbits, tomato, potato, juteseeds, chillies, brinjal, peas, cumin, coriander, etc., can be taken. Large scale production of vegetables for fresh market and for preservation factories also has enormous scope. Gardening of vegetables like cauliflower, tomato, potato, carrots, onion, garlic, etc., can be highly profitable. (Para 12.9)

158. Research work is in progress at the Central Arid Zone Research Institute, Jodhpur and Haryana Agricultural University, Hissar, to further identify the types of cultivars within these fruit crops which can withstand salinity without detrimental effects on heir productivity. The result of this research should be pursued further.

Some of the vegetable crops like spinach, beat, cabbage, brinjal and some root crops are tolerant to salinity. (Para 12.10)

159. In recent years, extensive, research has been carried out in Mexico, Israel, Australia and USA to increase horticultural production by efficient management of watersheds. In India, such work is in progress at the Central Arid Zone Research Institute, Jodhpur. Some of the indigenous plant types can be planted even without following this technique, e.g., *kair* (capparis decidua), cordia myza, custard apple, etc. Their productivity, will, however, increase if due consideration is also given to watershed management. (Para 12.12)

160. As in hot arid zone, the rainfall is not only very low but is confined to the period from July to September, with 9 to 21 rainy days out of 12 to 30 rainy days in the whole year. The fruit crops selected for cultivation in these regions must be such that their maximal growth period falls during the period of maximum water availability in the soil and low vapour pressure deficit in the atmosphere. (Para 12.13)

161. While selecting cultivars of a particular fruit tree, care should be taken to choose the early ripening ones so that they make maximum use of the residual soil water from the monsoon rains. (Para 12.13)

162. Among the vegetable crops, the most hardy types belong to the cucubataceous and selaraceous groups. Besides these, cowpea, gourd, early, cauliflower and okra are also sufficiently hardy. There is however, need to grow the drought hardy cultivars of these vegetable crops for rainfed production. (Para 12.14)

163. In vegetable crops also, optimum production is possible by adopting techniques of moisture conservation and run-off concentration. (Para 12.19)

164. Considering the marginal nature of the land in many cases, and the non-availability of adequate moisture and the risk involved in successfully raising foodgrain crops, great importance would have to be placed on opportunities to diversify rural economies away from crop production, to the extent possible, into activities that are less dependent on the vagaries of rainfall. Horticulture is one of the excellent opportunities which could provide a greater income to the farmers in such lands which are not good for crop production. The Committee would strongly urge that horticulture should be taken up as an integral part of the package approach to the development in the drought prone and desert areas. All essential steps would have to be taken. Extension support is the first essential item. This would not, however, be enough by itself unless suitable varieties are identified

seeds and cultivars provided when needed. (Paras 12.24 and 12.25)

Afforestation

165. At present, areas classified under permanent pastures, cultivable wastes, barren, uncultivated land and forests are overgrazed and denuded. Hence, not only the development but protection and management of the forest and plant cover also assume considerable importance. It is necessary to provide for the requirements of fuel and fodder so that the people are not tempted to cut trees indiscriminately and inhibit the process of afforestation. (Para 13.5)

166. The programme of tree planting has to be taken up on areas in and around agricultural fields and other areas where wood lands cannot be created. Planting can be carried out (i) on and along bunds and rises, (ii) marginal or peripheral bunds, (iii) field and property boundaries, (iv) village paths, (v) fore-shores of tanks, (vi) irrigation channels, (vii) institutions like schools, hospitals, panchayat bhavans, places of worship, etc., (viii) banks of small streams and any other available place. (Para 13.12)

167. It is necessary to educate the farmers about the importance of tree planting on farm land. As the first step towards farm forestry, the farmers can confine their activities to grow their own timber, fuel and fodder trees along field bunds and marginal land where cultivation is uneconomical and not possible but the soil allows it. (Para 13.13)

168. All over the drought prone areas of the country, the farmers leave a third to a half of their land fallow every year, whether big or small, because they cannot possibly cultivate the entire land. It has been recommended that they may put part of their land under permanent intensive pastures and take a subsidiary occupation of Animal Husbandry. There is a case for putting part of the land under free lands and plant trees. (Para 13.16)

169. Suitable species of different regions of India as also the improved techniques of afforestation have since been complied in the Forest Research Institute Publication entitled *Handbook of Afforestation Techniques*. The selection of species suitable for a particular area would necessarily have to be governed by the following considerations:

(i) objective of planting, viz., fuel, small timber, fencing, bioaesthetic, erosion control, top feed production, etc.; and

(ii) locality factors, viz., climatic, topographic and biotic parameters.

The other criteria for selection of tree species are (a) farmers' preference, (b) deep root system, (c) light down, (d) bird repellent, (e) ease of establishment, (f) fast growth, (g) resistance to drought/forest/fire, (h) multiple use, coppicing, adaptability and compatibility, etc. The Committee would strongly recommend that this programme should be taken up as a massive programme and should be backed with full political support. (Paras 13.17 and 13.18)

170. In every Indian village, traditionally a portion of the land was reserved for the village forest. This was common property to be managed by the village elders for the benefit of all the villagers. The first to be affected by the rush for forest material by the expanding population was the village forests. Except in the very interior areas, village forests are now bare earth wherever the land has not been encroached upon. Rehabilitation has to start here. Considering the magnitude of requirements, the village towards farm forestry, the farmers can confine their activities to grow their own timber, fuel and fodder trees along field bunds and marginal land where cultivation is uneconomical and not possible but the soil allows it. (Para 13.15)

171. Trees are planted close and regularly pruned into bush form so that leaves and twigs are maximised instead of timber. Some fuelwood will be available annually in the pruning of the twigs. In the interest of social justice, it is suggested that the proper landless families near the forests may be allowed half a hectare each of such land and helped to grow the fodder trees or Tassar culture or lac growing. The latter two will be beneficial mainly to the tribal who naturally do Tassar culture and Lac culture now on forest trees. It is necessary, therefore, to divide the programme of degraded forests between fuelwood plantations by the forest departments and trees for leaf formation for Tassar, Lac and fodder by the landless families allotted right on trees on land for the purpose. (Para 13.29)

172. The fuelwood plantation in degraded forests is to be harvested after 15 years at the start because the land is of poor quality having lost all nutrients. But future cuts can be once in 10 years because the land would have regained its fertility in the first rotation of 15 years. Thus a plantation of 4.2 million hectares per year less one million in farm forestry per year in a 15 year rotation will take 48 million hectares in the first round tapering off to 32 million hectares after 25 years from

start. If part of the plantations can be irrigated, area required will go down further. Technology will surely find ways and means of increasing productivity meanwhile, to link demand with supply. For the leaf programme it is annual harvesting of leaves. It is suggested that a programme of 5 lakh hectares per year may be taken up in the next twenty years. This will over time help 20 million poor labour families near the forests to get a decent living. (Para 13.30)

173. Everyday trees are not necessarily trees with only fuel value. Trees yielding many varieties of minor forest produce and trees giving fruits on which the tribal population live and also earn some money by collection, are also being devastated. One of the main objectives of the tribal development programmes is to ensure that these benefits are not lost to the tribal but augmented. So in all these plantations it should be a rule that trees giving minor forest produce like mahua, karanj, neem, etc. and fruit trees like mango, tamarind, jack and others are suitably interspersed. (Para 13.31)

174. Mainly large scale plantation of eucalyptus should be avoided because they upset the ecological balance of fauna and flora very badly. (Para 13.31)

175. Intensive fodder development is necessary if the devastation of forest areas and plantations by all types of cattle is to be avoided. (Para 13.32)

176. The following programmes are already in operation and have to be intensified on a proper judgement of the development need:-

(i) When farmers keep good milch cattle or crossbred sheep or exotic pigs, they must be persuaded to put a part of their land under intensive fodder tree cultivation. This development is already taking place on a large scale in Gujarat, Punjab and Haryana and needs intensification in the other States; and

(ii) In the Drought Prone Areas, it has been explained that a third to a half of the land and in desert areas much more is left uncultivated in each year because of the rainfall pattern and pressure of time. A part of the land can go under fuelwood and a part put under permanent fodder tree. (Para 13.32)

177. During the Sixth Plan large scale afforestation will be going on in social forestry including village and panchayat lands and degraded forests. If the community interests can be sought and maintained by the forest department in these programmes it should not

be difficult to introduce a temporary tongiyas cultivation programme in these areas without any fear of the lands going out of the control of the forest department. (Para 13.33)

178. Tamil Nadu has initiated a programme of growing fodder in all the areas of development where the tree cover has not yet shaded the forest lands. They also allow the village cattle nearby to graze these areas on payment of a very reasonable fee. It is suggested that if they can give preference to the poorer families owning sheep and cattle and particularly those who have taken to improvement of their breeds, it may give substantial benefit to the poorer sections towards their economic improvement. Other States can also follow this very useful approach to fodder addition for the villages near the reserve forests and commercial forests. (Para 13.34)

179. It is necessary to put through the basic concept of a National institute with sufficient capacity at once. A necessary start of our massive programme of social forestry will depend entirely on the speed at which we get this base laid and recruit the necessary order of staff. (Para 13.35)

180. Forest Service has traditionally been one where all their staff at all levels have been trained to the job after selection to the service. There are not enough training colleges at present to train all those that have to be added to the staff in a crash programme. This problem of manpower requires immediate attention. (Para 13.35)

Sand Dunes Stabilisation in Arid Areas

181. Stabilisation of sand dunes is the most important necessity in the hot arid zones primarily for checking the growth of desertic conditions and protecting productive agricultural lands in the neighbouring areas from the wrath of moving sands. (Para 14.2)

182. Efforts in sand dunes stabilisation, if they have to be effective, have therefore to be carried out in the wider context of scientific management of the total land resources in the region. (Para 14.8)

183. Vegetative cover is the only answer for stabilising of sand dunes. (Para 14.11)

184. The first priority for sand dune stabilisation is obviously in areas surroundings villages, townships and fertile lands where the sand dunes are threatening to engulf the area. The extent of sand dunes of this nature will not be so substantial that a phased programme of sand dune stabilisation over the next ten years with state investment cannot

answer the problem. (Para 14.15)

185. On a priority basis a programme of action for stabilisation of sand dunes which may cause difficulties should be taken up on phased basis. The land use survey which is being carried out by Central Arid Zone Research Institution (CAZRI), will be able to identify the priority sand dunes areas. These dunes, it is often found, are not on lands completely in the control of Government but also covers existing ryotwari tracts. The pattern is mixed. Sand dune stabilisation has to be done on a watershed basis. Any programme, therefore, will have to include both government and private lands. (Para 14.15)

186. Sand dunes stabilisation gives large areas which can be usefully put under pastures or small timber and can be expected to give returns on a commercially viable basis. The Committee suggests that two types of approach would be useful. In taking up large scale programmes of such sand dune stabilisation on the principle now followed for afforestation of panchayat lands, sand dune stabilisation of areas, selected comprising both government and private lands, can be put under the sand dune stabilisation organisation which will do the entire investment and development of the area. The return from havesting of the usufruct when it is ripe will go to the government from the government lands and on the private lands a sharing formula can be developed. It is suggested that a 50 : 50 sharing will be reasonable. (Para 14.15)

187. If the community approach is not possible in any area because of factions, a master plan for sand dune stabilisation can be worked out with those who are willing to agree to do the necessary stabilisation work on their individual fields. If the lack of agreement by any of the farmers prevents work on his lands and if the work is absolutely essential to prevent deterioration of the rest of the work, some statutory provisions can be made for compulsory execution and recovery of investment. The soil conservation act which already provides for such works can be invoked wherever available. The ARDC and now the proposed National Bank for Agriculture and Rural Development (NABARD) have suitable programmes of refinancing which can be availed of for this purpose if an integrated large scale programme is taken up. (Para 14.15)

188. As regards the Rajasthan Canal Area, all shifting dunes in command area must be stabilised by planting over with grass to prevent sand casting of arable land. (Para 14.16)

189. Grazing of livestock on dunes should be restricted so as not to

disturb the soil but people may be allowed to cut grass on payment of moderate fees. (Para 14.16)

190. In the canal cultivated area suitable shelter belts and wind breaks should be established to minimise the effect of hot winds and reduce sand castings. (Para 14.16)

191. Advantage should be taken of spare water in the early stages of development in command area for growing trees on a massive scale. These programmes should receive the top most priority in the Rajasthan Canal Area.

192. Incidentally, it has come to the Committee's notice that a tree (Leuoacena Leucucephala) popularly known as 'IPIL' in Philippines and SHEMOO in Thailand has got great potential not only as a supplying fodder and shelter but also fuelwood. This tree is prolific producer of leaves, flowers, pods, buds and and twigs, all of which are relished by the cattle. The annual yield of dry fodder is 6 to 10 tonnes per acre, depending on the quality of the soil and irrigation facility. Its leaves and tender buds can be used as vegetables, its seed can be ground and the flour used for making bread. It gives a very good yield of fuelwood. The Committee would recommend that this specie may be tried in the Rajasthan Canal Areas and in such other areas where underground water is known to exist. (Paras 14.17 and 14.18)

Solar Energy and Wind Power Utilisation

193. The research in utilising solar energy and wind power for replacing the diminishing sources of energy is national issue. It will be noticed that quite a lot of research is now going on. Before the research can be applied in the field more proper cost—benefit studies will have to be done on location specific studies so that the technology can be suitably given to the people for adoption. The Committee would therefore, recommend that in all these researches in development of equipment and in running of systems for utilisation of solar energy and wind power, the research should define clearly limitations of use of the equipment and the cost-benefit of the utilisation. (Para 15.23)

194. The equipment so far designed for cooking and for providing hot water for family use is well within the means of a family with modest means in the rural areas. The Central Arid Zone Research Institute (CAZRI) will have to develop brochures explaining this and giving the cost-benefit data so that the extension workers can straight away adopt this programme in the rural areas. (Para 15.25)

195. Hot water will be available during the day. In hill areas and in the desert areas also, it is a commodity most welcome during the day for bathing in winter. Of course, this facility will be used more by middle class and that too in the semi urban and urban areas. A suitable brochure may be developed by the CAZRI for this purpose also for utilising by extension workers. (Para 15.26)

196. Use of solar energy can be suitably designed to provide for drying facilities. There may be many uses for such drying facilities in the rural economy. Where this will be useful will have to be studied and suitable brochures developed by CAZRI. (Para 15.27)

197. Wind power is spasmodic and at present will probably be economic only in lifting water to a tank or a reservoir. Urban water supply schemes and minor irrigation schemes can possibly be designed utilising wind power. The parameters have yet to be developed. Whichever organisation is attending to this research, will have to develop suitable brochures giving the cost benefit and also explaining the limitations so that the extension organisations can see whether they are adaptable for their local problems. (Para 15.28)

Strategy for Transfer of Technology

198. The major problem is the transfer of appropriate technology to the people in the specific watershed for promoting rational use of land, water and other natural resources. Effective transfer of appropriate technology for watershed development would involve the following activities:-

(i) ascertaining the present level of technology in the related sectors;
(ii) identifying the type of technology needed and suited for the felt needs of the population of the watershed in general;
(iii) based on such feed-back, need for adoption or adaptation of available technology for improving the productivity of the Area and preventing the ecological deterioration;
(iv) testing the suitability of new specific technology in different agro-physical and climatic regions requiring a large number of adaptive field trials and operational research project under different geographical and socio-economic conditions; and
(v) Strengthening the linkages between research and field personnel. (Paras 16.1 and 16.3).

199. It has to be noted that the development of appropriate technology for the drought prone areas require an effective feed-back mechanism. The research has also to give priority to the development of low cost technology. A careful analysis of the methods of agriculture, animal husbandry, etc. in these areas might indicate that a few modifications in the existing practices could yield better results instead of introducing new innovations which may not only be costly but may also require lot of efforts before the farmer could be persuaded to take them up. (Para 16.5)

200. Uni-disciplinary research now generally prevalent in the Agricultural Universities and parallel research being carried on in various institutions—Central and State—in various aspects of the sciences has to be brought together in multi-disciplinary applied research programme in order to solve the specific problems of drought prone areas. The establishment of regional research centres on a multi-disciplinary basis is essential. (Para 16.5)

201. What are the important steps necessary for transferring appropriate technology to rural areas, particularly the drought prone areas. The obvious answer is the field extension and farmers' training, supply of information, literature, audio-visual education, field demonstrations, etc. Training of extension workers would also be necessary. (Para 16.8)

202. The most distinguishing characteristics of the new methodology is that the Village Level Workers (VLW) and the Agricultural Extension Officers are utilised in an intensive time-bound management system under a fixed programme of training and visits to the farmers field regularly every fortnight. The training has a direct focus on specific agricultural practices and recommendations related directly to farm operation during a given fortnight. (Para 16.10)

203. The new Agricultural Extension methodology aims at ensuring transfer of know-how available at the Agricultural Research Stations to the farmers fields through an effective time-bound management system. This is being achieved through a systematic schedule of training of Extension Workers, to equip them with the latest know-how. The transfer of technology from Extension Workers to the farmers is ensured through a fixed programme of visits every fortnight. The methodology followed in the existing set up can be adopted in the DPAP areas also but what would be essential is that the extension personnel working in these areas must be provided training in all the disciplines for which the area has the best potential and

support is called for. (Para 16.12)

204. The technical capacity of the VLW in the programme is limited to agricultural development only. On the other hand in the watershed management approach which is basic in DPAP the main thrust is firstly in restoring ecological balance and then maximising soil and water conservation for increasing crop productivity. The technical expertise for doing this work has to be spelt out carefully. (Para 16.13)

205. The planning and execution of the soil and water conservation programme for the Government and community lands should be done by a suitable organisation in the Project. This work obviously cannot be done under the present T&V programme. For this, the Committee suggests the following approach. Once priority watersheds have been identified in the Project area for watershed management technical teams of the soil and water conservation experts in the project technical group must prepare the soil and water conservation programme for the Government and community lands with such help as may be required from the higher technical echelons for the individual watersheds. This plan must be implemented in full in the first year of the watershed programme as without this protection to the higher reaches, the farmers programme will not be fully productive. (Para 16.14)

206. The soil conservation organisation in the District should be given the responsibility to get the work done on schedule. The funds should be provided by the DPAP. (Para 16.14)

207. The technical team of the project helped by such higher level expertise as is necessary will have to decide for each watershed the particular pattern to be followed. (Para 16.15)

208. The landshaping programme on the holdings of all the farmers participating should be completed in the off season before the start of the second cropping season. The technical support for this will have to come from the soil and water conservation experts in the project, helped by the VLWs who suitably trained in advance will follow the T&V method to get the programme implemented in time. (Para 16.15)

209. Where a change of cropping is essential in any holding to prevent wrong use and consequential soil deterioration, the technical experts in the project should identify the holdings and the changes necessary. The VLWs should then be used in the T&V programme to get the change done by persuasion. (Para 16.17)

210. In the T&V method there is a back up by a Technical Group

which trains the VLWs every fortnight during the cropping season for the programme to be put across in the field in the next fortnight. This back up technical group with a base experimental area is crucial for watershed programme. (Para 16.17)

211. Besides the technical disciplines involved in the T&V, a soil and a water specialist will have to be included. It is preferable that this group is based at the project centre, for each DPAP project area. (Para 16.17)

212. The base area should be a suitable watershed of the same size as the watersheds chosen in the project and should be close to the project centre. In this watershed the technical group will personally supervise all the aspects of the intended programme that they are going to introduce during the year in the project. The base will be a demonstration centre for the project and a training centre for the field personnel. Higher level technical experts in the district must visit these demonstration areas and correct mistakes and solve special area problems that may arise. Selection of such back up areas should be done carefully so that substantial people's backing in the watersheds is available and the farmers are prepared to experiment. Such watersheds should get all the subsidies and help that demonstration centres get under the state plan so that this will be additional attraction for people's participation in a new venture with some risk. (Para 16.17)

213. The technical team back stopping the watershed programme will have to decide for each watershed the present status of available technology suitable as a first step to improving the traditional cultivation practices and landuse patterns by marginal changes to improve the productivity and prevent deterioration of the ecology. (Para 16.19)

214. The most important stage in transfer of technology will be the testing of the suitability of specific technology in different agro-physical and climatic regions to that introduction of the most modern technology can be done in the location specific condition. This requires a large number of operational research projects follow up by adaptive field trials. (Para 16.20)

215. It is necessary for the ICAR to expand the national demonstration concept to include a large number of national demonstrations of the latest technology for handling the watershed approach in drought prone areas. (Para 16.20)

216. The ICAR may examine early how best the lab-to-land programme can be modified to suit the requirements of a watershed

approach. (Para 16.21)

217. Education of individual farmers about the right crop to grow on his field and the correct agronomic practices along with the minimum soil conservation and water conservation practices on his holding should be the main plank of the T&V programme in the initial stage. (Para 16.22)

218. Operational research programmes in large watersheds should now be taken up by the ICAR in the various DPAP zones so that the technologists may refine and improve upon the package approach to make it location specific to the various DPAP zones in the country. The operational research project will be a necessary back up to the national demonstration programme. (Para 16.23)

219. The Government of India provide assistance to the State Governments through the centrally sponsored schemes to strengthen the efforts of the states in the transfer of appropriate technology to the rural areas. The Committee would strongly recommend that the assistance provided under this scheme should be available for extension support in the drought prone areas. (Para 16.24 and 16.25)

220. The Central element in the strategy for development of the drought prone areas should be the process of improving the capacity of rural people to control their environment by motivating them to make maximum utilisation of their own capabilities and the local resources. For long term development of drought prone areas, the first attempt should be to create awareness and consciousness among the people of the efficacy of both short-term and long-term measures. (Para 16.31)

221. At the Planning stage priority should be given for the assessment of villager's needs and their priorities. The administration and technologists might think that the people have destroyed the ecological balance by their short-sightedness. But they should also realise that they are creating a disequilibrium in ignoring the problem of their survival and suggesting of long gestation plans. (Para 16.33)

222. If people's participation has to be enlisted, such interventions to which the villagers will rationally respond have to be identified, short gestation income generating programme without further deterioration of the ecology for the people in the watershed have to be started and only then the long-term conservation or regenerative programmes can be pushed ahead. (Para 16.34)

223. There is need to discuss at the level of operations details of the micro-watershed plan with the residents of the watersheds to avoid any mutual conflicts and secure their active participation. This could

be done either through general meetings of all the residents or through the local panchayat or watershed cooperative, if it is formed. (Para 16.35)

224. Under the watershed approach, every piece of land requires some special treatment whether it belongs to a big holder of small holder, though the big holders may not qualify for subsidy. The land of the big holders has to be treated not because they belong to power group, but because it is a technical necessity for the development of the watershed. (Para 16.36)

225. We cannot think of excluding programmes for the landless in the watershed development programme—If the marginal or surplus lands are being distributed among the landless, the watershed project should provide for the development of pastures or horticulture on these lands, with guaranteed employment in secondary and tertiary sectors during the waiting period. This should also be specifically provided as part of the plan to achieve a participatory process. (Para 16.37)

226. The watershed budget should have adequate provision for the extension education programmes of the people of the area before the watershed programme is undertaken. (Para 16.38)

227. The long-term objective of development of the drought prone areas should formulate some plan for educating the children and youth of the area so that when they grow up they understand their responsibilities as a citizen for mitigating the effect of drought. (Para 16.39)

Nomads and Nomadism in Desert Areas

228. Because of the severe sociological tensions created by the nomads, whether pastoral nomads or artisan nomads or non-descript, there is a general cry that nomads should be sedentarised. At the same time, it is often argued that artisan nomads like *gadoliya* lohars are not amenable to sedentarisation. The Committee would take the view that nomadic communities will accept sedentarisation and modify their economy provided the society can give them a firm base for livelihood which is better than what they are earning today. The economic attraction will prevail in all human motivations. (Para 17.20)

229. In the Chapter on "Livestock Development" the Committee has already explained how gradually nomadic sheep breeders can be brought to a limited number of centres in the ranges for the breeding and lambing season without any serious difficulties to them. Gradually,

when they come to such centres for nearly 8 months in the year, the sedentarisation will automatically follow. Therefore, their movement outside will then be limited to a few months in the year to exploit large grass ranges available. When the community is so gathered, all the advantages of a sedentarisation, a society should be given to them by the State. (Para 17.21)

230. Today with communications expanding and established, artisan systems developing in reasonably approachable urban centres, many communities who use the artisan nomads may no longer find them necessary. Thus, over time this will be a dying race unless we now take steps to utilise the skills that are available inn the artisans for the benefit of themselves and the society. (Para 17.22)

231. Before the artisan nomads die out by sheer force of economics, it is desirable to bring together into groups under a village industry development project in a convenient area close to available markets under the strategy explained in the report of the Committee on "Village and Cottage Industries". Selection of centres and persuading nomadic groups to concentrate there will be infructuous unless the necessary raw material supply, credit and marketing facilities are simultaneously imposed on the centre. Training them for greater skills is also a part of village industry development. (Para 17.22)

Organisational and Financial Arrangements

232. The Committee has recommended in its report on "Organisation of Administrative and Financial Structure for Backward Area Development". What it considers to be appropriate organisational and financial arrangements for realising the full potential of the area and executing a comprehensive development programme embracing all activities—developmental, social services, infrastructure, etc. The Committee would, therefore, reiterate that the recommendations made by it in its report on "Organisation of Administrative and Financial Structure of Backward Area Development" covering "planning processes and decentralisation" methodology of Central and State Plan allocations, organisational set-up for plan implementation, personnel policies, financial and budgetary control, etc., are eminently suited for the development of the drought prone areas and should be implemented as early as possible. (Paras 18.12 and 18.13)

233. There should be a District Planning and Coordination Cell under the Chairmanship of the Collector, to work out a proper

programme and secure the best development of resources particularly in respect of such schemes and programmes which cut across the boundaries of more than one IDP. (Para 18.14)

234. An Integrated Project Level Authority consisting of two or three blocks should be set up by an executive order. (Para 18.14)

235. The Block Development Officer, or his equivalent, would function as an Executive Officer under the Integrated Development Project Authority (IDPA) and all beneficiary Oriented programmes would be implemented by the Block Administration under the overall superintendence and direction of the IDP Authority. (Para 18.41)

236. Apart from the high level Steering Committee which will guide implementation of all the programmes, a Coordination Cell has been suggested at the State headquarters not only to monitor the progress but also to ensure that the funds earmarked for the development of these areas are not divested by the departmental heads to other areas. (Para 18.14)

237. The Committee would strongly recommend that each State should have an interdisciplinary land authority/board for planning in major watersheds and giving guidance to the lower level organisation in the planning, execution and implementation of the programmes on micro watershed basis. (Para 18.15)

238. The existing departments at the state level like agriculture, forest, horticulture, etc., are concerned with their sectoral activities. What is essential is an organisation at the state level which can ensure preparation of integrated projects on watershed development, guide their implementation and monitor the progress with reference to the overall objectives. (Para 18.15)

239. The Committee would strongly urge that as a counterpart of the State Board, the Central Government in the Ministry of Agriculture must also set up a National Landuse Board/Authority. (Para 18.16)

240. Expertise in various disciplines, which constitute the key component of planning and implementation of programmes on watershed approach are located in the Department of Agriculture and in the Department of Agricultural Education and Research under the Ministry of Agriculture. As it is essential that there is complete coordination and agreement between various disciplines which has to provide input to the development activities in drought prone areas, the Committee would strongly urge the constitution of a Standing Multi-Disciplinary Committee with its own secretariat to guide project preparation, supervise implementation and provide necessary technical

and research support, etc. (Para 18.17)

241. The present procedure is that at the request of the State Governments, the Central Government sends the Teams to assess the damage of the drought affected areas. The Committee would strongly recommend that a representative of the Division dealing with the drought prone area programme should invariably be included in the Central Team to assess the quantum of funds to be made available to the States and once schemes are sanctioned and approved whether for creation of permanent assets or for providing relief, these should be prepared and executed in consultation and under the supervision of the Integrated Development Project Authority. (Para 18.18)

242. The authority in the project would be in a far better position to decide as to the type of works which should be undertaken immediately to provide relief to the affected people. It would use these funds not only for providing relief to the drought affected but also get part of their own programmes for the benefit of the area with the help of these funds. The Committee is of the view that if such a system could be streamlined and operationalised, there would be better utility for funds made available for drought relief, in such areas which have been identified as chronically drought affected. (Para 18.18)

NATIONAL COMMITTEE ON THE DEVELOPMENT OF BACKWARD AREAS, 1978 — REPORT ON DEVELOPMENT OF NORTH EASTERN REGION November 30, 1978 — November 12, 1981[1]

Chairman Shri B. Sivaraman, Member, Planning Commission

Members Shri Som Dutt; Prof. Mrinal Datta Chaudhary (ceased to be member w.e.f. November 30, 1978), Shri S.S. Marathe (ceased to be member w.e.f. November 30, 1978), Shri Ranchor Prasad; Shri Ramakrishanayya; Shri K.P.A. Menon; Shri R.M. Honavar; (ceased to be member w.e.f. January 31, 1981); Shri S.A. Dave; Dr. Y. Nayudamma; Shri Anand Sarup; Dr. B.D. Sharma; Shri Suresh Mathur; Dr. D.M. Nanyundappa; Shri S.M. Ghosh.

M. Secy. Shri Nitin Desai

Appointment

The Government have been pursuing certain policies and programmes in regard to the development of backward areas since the Fourth Five Years Plan. It is now necessary to review the working of these various programmes and to set out a suitable strategy or strategies for the development of Backward Areas in the context of the priorities and objectives set out in the draft 1979-83 plan. The Planning Commission have, therefore, decided to set up a High Level Committee to formulate appropriate strategy or strategies for effectively tackling the problems of Backward Areas vide its Resolution No. PC(P)17/NCDBA/78-MLP dated November 30, 1978.

1. Planning Commission, Government of India, New Delhi, 1981, xiii + 67 p.

Terms of Reference

(i) To examine the validity of the various concepts of backwardness underlying the definitions in use for present policy purposes and recommend the criteria by which backward areas should be identified;

(ii) To review the working of:

(a) the existing plans for dealing with the general development problems of backward areas like Tribal Sub-Plans, Plans for Hill Areas, etc., and

(b) the existing schemes for stimulating industrial development in backward areas such as the schemes for concessional finance, investment subsidy, transport subsidy, sales tax concessions, etc., similar schemes in the agricultural and allied fields like DPAP, and general measures for tackling the problems of poverty and unemployment with a view to find out their efficacy in the removal of backwardness; and

(iii) To recommend an appropriate strategy or strategies for effectively tackling the problem of backward areas, classified, if necessary, according to areas, causes or prescribed remedies.

Contents

Summary of Conclusions and Recommendations; Introduction; Characteristic Features of the Region; Strategy of Development; Administrative Structure; Jhum Cultivation; Horticulture; Plantations; Forestry; Animal Husbandry; Handlooms and Sericulture; Industry and Minerals; Transport and Power; Annexures Chapter 2 – 2.1 to 2.2; Chapter 6 – 6.1 to 6.2; Chapter 9 – 9.1 to 9.3; Chapter 11 – 11.1 to 11.2; Chapter 12 – 12.1.

Recommendations

Introduction

1. The North Eastern Region, comprising of the States of Assam, Manipur, Meghalaya, Nagaland and Tripura and the Union Territories of Arunachal Pradesh and Mizoram, does not fall into a separate

category of backwardness. Much of the region will be covered under one or the other category of fundamental backwardness. Specifically three types of fundamental backwardness are found in the region, viz., areas of tribal concentration, hill areas and chronically flood affected areas. (Para 1.3)

2. As far as industrial backwardness goes, the whole of the north-east has been categorised as industrially backwards as per the National Committee's Report on Industrial Dispersal. (Para 1.3)

Characteristic Features of the Region

3. The first and most marked characteristic feature of this region is the low density of population in all areas other than Assam and Tripura. The very low densities in many parts of the region are attributable to the nature of the terrain. The second marked characteristic of the population of this region is its rapid rate of growth which has tended to be substantially higher than the national averages. The third important characteristics of the population of this area is the high proportions of scheduled tribes. (Paras 2.8, 2.9, 2.11 and 2.12)

4. Considering the fact that the total tribal population of the area is only 4.35 million, there are a large number of relatively small tribes. Many of the tribes cut across not merely State boundaries, but also international boundaries. Thus, there is a great deal of heterogeneity of population within the area. (Para 2.14)

5. The ability of the tribal community to benefit from the job opportunities generated through development process is substantially greater in the north-east than in the other tribal areas. There is a stock of educated youth who, if trained, can take up positions in development, administration, industrial projects, etc. (Para 2.14)

6. Production for self-consumption and subsistence is the basis for economic activity and calculations on market values are seldom the basis of decision on what and how to produce. In this connection when the system is opened to market forces the local tribals, even though they may be well educated, may not in fact benefit. (Para 2.15)

7. The processes of non-agricultural development generated in this area do not always benefit the tribals except in the limited area of government employment. (Para 2.16)

8. There are some tribal groups which have had long tradition of contact with the market economy and they are in a better position to cope with the opening up of their economies. There are, however,

many other groups which have lived a more isolated existence who may well lose out if they are exposed to uncontrolled market forces. These variations in the ability of different tribal communities to cope with a new economy have to be taken into account in any development strategy. (Para 2.17)

9. The high participation rates and the low rates of unemployment mean that there is very little employment slack to be taken up in the hill States. Because of this it has not always been possible to find labour for construction work in the region even at relatively high wages. But it may be noted that this may also be, to some extent, due to lack of organisation for mobilising labour. (Para 2.23)

10. Development plans in the hill areas of the north-east cannot be based on the assumption of an employment slack and the alternative employment generated by new developments in horticulture, plantations, animal husbandry, etc., must offer fairly high wages or returns per manday if they are to succeed. The possibility of shortage of candidates or technical and non-technical posts in development administration and in project must also be kept in mind. (Para 2.25)

11. The problems of development lie not in the lack of natural resources but in the large investment required for infrastructure development, the inadequacy of labour and the necessary skill needing an extensive programme of manpower development. (Para 2.26)

12. The hilly terrain of the north-eastern region and the pattern of land availability has led to two distinct systems of agriculture: (i) settled agriculture in the plains, valleys and gentler slopes and (ii) jhum (slash and burn) cultivation elsewhere. (Para 2.32)

13. The general practice in Jhum areas is that each village has a well-defined range of operation in which the jhum cycle as well as other activity like hunting and wood cutting are confined. Within this area land is allotted to each household on the basis of its capacity or its need, by a village level authority like village council or a chief, guided by village elders. (Paras 2.36 and 2.37)

14. The hilly terrain in of the north-eastern region offers ample scope for the development of horticulture and plantations. Animal husbandry is an important part of the traditional agricultural system. However, the pattern of animal husbandry in hill areas shows a significant difference from the plains and from the general all India pattern. In the traditional non-agricultural sectors of the dominant activities are handloom weaving, sericulture and handicrafts. In the

modern sector the level of development is limited. (Paras 2.43, 2.44 and 2.46)

15. From the point of view of infrastructure development the principal problem in the region is the inadequacy of communication facilities. (Para 2.48)

Strategy of Development

16. The north-eastern region is exceptionally rich in natural resources. The primary objective of development strategy must be to utilise these optimally and in a manner that maximises the benefits accruing to local people. This will require not merely additional investment in infrastructure and production facilities but also a programme of manpower development and measures to reorient the system of land tenure in the hill areas. (Para 3.2)

17. The main elements in the development programme for the north-east must be measures to control *jhuming*, improvements in co-op. husbandry in the flood prone valley, an animal husbandry programme oriented to local conditions, the tapping of the huge potential for horticulture, plantations on forestry, the promotion of sericulture and commercial handlooms, the development of modern industries in a manner that will maximise local impact and the improvement of communications. (Paras 3.3 to 3.47)

18. Most of the States and Union Territories in this region are too small to be able to sustain the full range of expenditure on education and training which is the charge of State Governments in the rest of the country. Hence the special role played by the North Eastern Council in this regard is crucial and should be strengthened. (Para 3.50)

19. Nation-wide leadership will be required to ensure that development is not hindered by lack of necessary technical and managerial personnel and attitudes of parochialism. It is not easy to get top quality personnel from the rest of the country without special incentives. The North Eastern Council can give the leadership in starting a dialogue and laying down the necessary norms in manpower recruitment and appointment for a possible aggressive development policy. The States/Union Territories which are members of the North Eastern Council must honour the consensus reached in the North Eastern Council. (Para 3.51)

20. A quickening of the pace of development in the hill areas of this region carried with it the risk of the tribal being exploited.

Protective and promotional measures to avoid this must be an integral part of the development strategy for this region. (Para 3.52)

21. Promotional measures to encourage train and assist trials, particularly the educated and urbanised ones, to utilise the opportunities for small industry, transport operations, trade and other services are equally important. What is required is a supporting structure for credit delivery, marketing raw material supply and technical assistance that can provide a well thought out package. (Para 3.53)

22. The traditional structures like Village Council can be used to secure the participation and involvements of people in the development effort. (Para 3.54)

Administrative Structure

23. The development strategy for this region will require substantial new developments in agriculture, animal husbandry, horticulture, plantations, etc. These developments will require the establishment of facilities for research, new training institutions of nurseries, breeding farms, etc. At the present stage the optimum size for many facilities would be beyond the requirements of individual States. In these cases the North Eastern Council can set up these facilities to serve several States thereby allowing these States to benefit from economies of scale. (Para 4.6)

24. The new developments to be promoted in different sectors will also require a close link up between basic research, adaptive research, field trials and extension effort. The North Eastern Council can do this in the form of pilot projects which when proved successful, can be emulated by the States. Thus, at the present stage of development the NEC should have the responsibility and the corresponding capability for high level technical supervision in fields like crop production, horticulture, plantations, animal husbandry, etc. (Para 4.7)

25. Once the regional facilities are set up in the region, the NEC Advisers must travel around in the region to see whether and how the facilities are being used, to build up local expertise in the State Governments and advise State Governments as to how best they can use the regional facilities. (Para 4.8)

26. The Planning Commission must try and ensure that there is no overlap or duplication in the NEC Plan and the plans of the individual

States. They must also ensure that the development thrusts initiated through the NEC are pursued by the States. In order to do this, the Planning Commission can use the expertise available in the NEC to keep itself informed about local developments. The peripatetic advisers of the NEC can provide the Planning Commission with an effective feedback to monitor the plan. Coordination can be improved if the Planning Commission nominates an officer to liaise with the NEC on a full time basis. (Para 4.9)

27. Permanent rights over settled land are increasingly being recognised and the movement from community to individual ownership has begun. However, the individual needs to be given a legal right to the land. The District Councils can play an important role in this since the authority over land tenure is vested in them. State Governments cannot pursue programmes for *jhum* control without such assistance from District Councils. (Para 4.19)

28. A large part of the forest area in the north-east is under the control of District Councils. However, these Councils do not have the technical staff to plan and manage these forests. A certain commonality of approach in silvicultural practices is necessary and, to ensure this, silvicultural control over District Council forests should be allowed to rest with the State Forest Departments. (Para 4.20)

Jhum Cultivation

29. There are many areas where the *jhum* cycle is much larger or much shorter than the average. Hence the strategy for *jhum* control cannot be based on the average figure for a large area, but must take into account the condition in each area. (Para 5.7)

30. There seems to be a discrepancy between picture of land tenure that emerges from discriptions of the tribal society of the region and the data thrown up by the NSS survey. This difference needs to be probed further. (Para 5.9)

31. The evaluation of the pilot project on jhum control programmes in Meghalaya and Arunachal Pradesh have brought out certain important points which needs to be taken into account in future programmes. The Committee would draw attention to certain aspects which should also be taken into account in future programmes.

(i) With the exception of the pilot schemes of the NEC, the jhum control programmes in the region do not seems to be based on the watershed approach;

(ii) Though most programmes offer some support in addition to the assistance for land shaping and other land conservation measures, none of the programmes seem to have a truly comprehensive and integrated package of services for the jhumia;

(iii) The problem of weeds and pests may well be greater in settled cultivation than in jhum cultivation. The package of practices recommended for jhum agriculture will have to take this into account; and

(iv) The food needs of the jhumia may not be met by the crops which would be taken up in settled cultivation and some dependence on outside sources for the same items will be there. The answer does not lie in undertaking settled cultivation with the same mix of crops as in jhuming but in a better public distribution system. The cropping pattern will have to be determined on the basis of productivity and economics.

The Committee also notes that the orientation of the measures taken up is basically towards jhum control, i.e., to the conversion of jhum to settled agriculture rather than to jhum improvements. The latter is equally important but practically no work seems to have been done. (Para 5.28 and 5.29)

32. The strategy for jhum control must distinguish between different areas on the basis of the extent to which the jhum cycle has shortened and ecological problems have arisen. On the basis of field surveys jhum areas should be put into three categories:

(i) Areas where the cycle is still above say, 10 years and where ecological problems are not yet acute. In these areas the emphasis should be on improving the productivity of jhum through better agronomic practices and improved varieties;

(ii) Areas where the cycle has fallen below say 5 years and where ecological problems are already acute. These areas should be taken up on a priority basis for conversion to settled cultivation within a period of 10 years; and

(iii) Other areas: These areas will probably face acute problems in the near future. Hence, in this case, the immediate measures may be for improving jhum but there should at the same time be a programmes for the gradual introduction of settled cultivation.

This programme may extend over a period of 20 years. (Para 5.30)

33. Each State/Union Territory should examine the jhum cycle situation in each of its villages and identify the three classes of villages for necessary action. Having done this an annulised programmes should be drawn up. The required finance may come from the provisions for jhum control, soil conservation, minor irrigation, IRD, etc. (Para 5.31)

34. Adaptative research on jhum cultivation in different areas as distinct from alternatives to jhuming in terms of settled agriculture is necessary. This particular aspect of agricultural research has not received sufficient attention so far and should be taken up on a priority basis by the ICAR research complex. The ICAR research complex take up such an operations research programme in various sub-regions. (Para 5.35)

35. In areas where settled cultivation is to be promoted, the principal criteria for the selection of a model in any local area must be the extent to which it raises productivity per unit of land and per manday of work. The conversion of Jhum lands to settled cultivations, whatever be the model chosen, must also take account of the nature of the land tenure system. The first problem that has to be tackled is that of giving the Jhumia permanent, heritable and transferable title to some part of the Jhum land. (Paras 5.38 and 5.39)

36. It is necessary to approach the problem on a community basis. The attempt should be to persuade all house holds in a village to change over to settled cultivation. This can be done through the good office of the village council or the tribal chief. The authority controlling the distribution of land should give individual households permanent heritable and transferable rights over the land brought by them under settled cultivation. The balance of the village lands, which will now no longer be required for cultivation can be converted into community forest under State Government ownership or, if that is not feasible, under the control of the village council. Such community approach will minimise the problems involved in moving from the existing system of land tenure to individual ownership. (Para 5.40)

37. It is necessary to provide the required draught power through power tillers and through a suitable re-orientation of the animal husbandry system. The farmers will also have to be trained for ploughing operations by the extension machinery which will have to be

strengthened for this purpose. (Para 5.41)

38. The planning of Jhum land conversion must take place on a watershed basis. Watershed management calls for scientific survey and investigation of each watershed by technical team. Since several hundred such investigations will be necessary, it is essential that technical capabilities for this purpose are built up quickly. (Para 5.42)

39. The implementation of Jhum control schemes has to be taken up on a project basis so that all related investments comprising outlays on soil conservation, agriculture extension, input subsidies, infrastructure, etc., are covered in the plan. The responsibility for implementation may rest with the project authority even though the technical control may be exercised by the respective technical hierarchies. (Para 5.43)

40. Facilities for adaptive research under varying agroclimatic conditions seems to be lacking. The responsibility for localised adaptive research must be gradually passed on to the State Governments. (Para 5.50)

41. Continuous technical guidance to the farmers will be required. It is, therefore, necessary that an effective extension system with at least one village level worker per village, one extension officer per 8-10 VLWs and suitable complement of subject matter specialists at district and sub-divisional levels be established in all the hill areas of the region. Areawise priorities for strengthening of extension must be laid down on the basis of the proposed development programmes. The extension staff must be in position one year earlier. The Group must be multi-disciplinary as required for the watershed approach. (Para 5.52)

42. The NEC must have a cell for propagating the watershed management approach. (Para 5.53)

43. There must be a smooth movement from pilot schemes, of the sort that have been taken up so far, to demonstration projects and, based on the demonstrations, a training programme for the field level staff of the State Governments. (Para 5.53)

Horticulture

44. A more aggressive programme of horticultural development is required. This will involve not merely paying attention to existing orchards but new developments. Cultivars from other areas in India in similar conditions have to be identified for different parts of the region. Bare areas in forest may also be suitable for intensive horticulture

development. Besides new fruits grown in similar conditions elsewhere can also be promoted, e.g., chickoo, durain, mangousten. (Para 6.13)

45. Horticultural research has to be aggressive now is the extension of the ICAR's research topographical and climatological conditions indicate that a particular fruit can be grown. (Para 6.14)

46. With regard to citrus, what is required now is the extension of the ICAR's research results to the field. This will require an extension machinery which is effectively linked to the research complex. This link at present stage of development may have to be provided by the NEC which should have a top level citrus expert on its staff, whose job will be to carry over established technologies to the various states where citrus development is possible. The relevant horticultural wings of states will need strengthening. (Para 6.15)

47. It would be desirable if the economics of alternative processing schemes for pineapple are studied carefully by the NEC. (Para 6.16)

48. The extension of horticulture in some parts of the North East will meet with some difficulties of transportation. In remote areas which are difficult of access, it may be possible to pursue the cultivation of nut trees, since in these the problem of deterioration of the fruit in transit does not arise. (Para 6.17)

49. The foundation of effective horticulture development is the available of suitable cultivars. It would be useful to undertake a survey of the material that has been distributed to see that has worked. Alongwith the process of identification of suitable cultivars, nurseries should be expanded to meet local demand so as to reduce the need to rely on purchase of planting material of doubtful quality from trade sources. (Para 6.18)

50. Given the required scale of operations the horticulture wing of the Agriculture Department will require substantial strengthening in all States. The extension effort will have to cover not merely the provision of planting material and subsidies but also export advice on plant protection and the maintenance of orchards. Moreover, some arrangements for adaptive research and data collection of state level will be necessary to provide a link between the regional facilities like ICAR Research Complex and the extension machinery. (Para 6.19)

51. The upgradation of horticulture in this region will have to be accompanied by effective marketing arrangements. What is required is an integrated structure of marketing and processing starting from some arrangements for primary collection (say through cooperatives),

processing, storage, and at the apex, an organisation that can undertake marketing outside the region in national and international markets. (Para 6.21)

52. All horticultural growers in the area can be brought within cooperative fold and linked to the processing unit. The possibility of introducing the two or three tier pattern for cooperativisation of growers and linking them with direct or regional level processing and marketing facilities may be worth examining. This may be done by the NEC. (Para 6.21)

53. The processing and storage operations will have to be designed on the basis of the specific requirements of the region. The climate of the region can also be used to advantage by having cool houses for cold storage in the higher altitudes and solar driers for drying fruit. (Para 6.22)

54. The potato crop in this region comes earlier than from anywhere else in India. Thus it has to compete with cold storage potatoes in the early season and has a price advantage. However, this particular aspect of potato marketing needs to be studied in greater detail by the NEC or NERAMAC. (Para 6.25)

55. The Centre's Potato Research Institute must have a station in north-east to develop early season potato for better storage and transport. This extension of area under potato needs to be pursued along with related investments in cold storage and marketing. This latter aspect of processing and marketing can be taken up by the Regional Agricultural Marketing Corporation. (Para 6.25)

56. Ginger production can be stepped up if facilities for preservation and dehydration of ginger are set up. (Para 6.26)

57. Vegetable seed production for national markets may be feasible even in the near future. The National Seeds Corporation should investigate the possibility of seed production in the area for the Indian market. (Para 6.27)

58. Large scale extension of vegetable production will depend entirely on the establishment of effective processing and marketing arrangements. This should be pursued since many of the hill vegetables can be produced in what is the off season in the plains. (Para 6.28)

59. So far we have not been able to utilise fabulous floral wealth for the benefit of the total people. To do this there is a need for a floriculture development centre to undertake extensive surveys to locate plant species of high floricultrue value an propagate the selected species for commercial purposes. A joint unit of the Botanical Survey

and the ICAR Research Complex should be located in this region. (Para 6.30)

Plantations

60. The development of plantation crops has been given a special place in the development strategy for the north-eastern region, particularly the hill areas. This is because this area offers great promise for crops such as tea, coffee and rubber and also because these tree crops are an ecological sound alternative to *jhum* cultivation. (Para 7.1)

61. An important constraint on the expansion of plantations is the labour intensive nature of the activity. Plantation development would require the diversion of workers from other agricultural activities. This would be facilitated if plantation development is linked with jhum control. Such an approach is also necessary if local fears that plantations development will lead to large scale immigration arc to be removed. (Paras 7.16 and 7.17)

62. The plantation development programme in this region also can be based on the smaller holder approach. Compact areas can be taken up for development by cooperation with each individual family being given the right to about 2 acres. The individual family would have the right of usufruct but would not have the right to alienate the land or convert it to some other use. This will require the development of special patta. The processing facilities require would be provided for one or more of these compact areas. (Para 7.19)

63. The District Councils can play an important role in plantation development by organising the extension of plantation area on their lands. They can form cooperatives and can give rights to individuals as has been suggested in the case of corporations. (Para 7.23)

64. Rapid development will require an effective coordination machinery at State level and the responsibility for plantation development must be clearly assigned to a particular department. The approach to plantation development outlined earlier will also require the establishment of a corporation in most cases. In many of the States, this has already been done. In order to support the Stets the NEC in its organisation should have a technical and managerial group to assist the State Departments responsible for plantations as well as the plantation corporations. Coffee, Tea and Rubber Boards should have extension arrangements in the region. (Para 7.2)

Forestry

65. The pre-investment survey should identify areas with low stock medium stock and high stock both within and outside the reserved forests. This is necessary if suitable priorities are to be established on an area-wise basis for the planning of afforestation and exploitation. (Para 8.5)

66. The pattern of ownership of village and district councils forests may be left as at present but silvicultural control may be transferred to the Forest Department. Working plans would be drawn up by the Department and at the time of harvest there would be a sharing of proceeds with the concerned village/district council. This approach of course requires a substantial strengthening of forest departments in the region and also an appreciative response from village and district councils. (Para 8.12)

67. The forests under village and district councils control provide fuel and buildings materials for the local population. Any programme to bring these under the silvicultural control of the forest department will have to be accompanied by a programme of Social Forestry to meet the essential requirements of the local population. In Jhum conversion schemes, the area released from jhuming can be used for this purpose. In other areas the need of the local population will have to be taken into account by the Forest Department in drawing up Working Plans. A similar approach is necessary to meet the fuel wood requirements of urban areas. (Para 8.13)

68. The density of population in some States/Union Territories is very low. This sparseness of population reduces the size of the working force and thus makes the exploitation of forest resources difficult. The NEC should study carefully the experience of the West Bengal Forest Department in the Darjeeling area so as to draw useful lessons for resolving difficulties because of, paucity of labour and transport difficulties. (Paras 8.14 and 8.15)

69. It may be desirable to consider the mechanisation of forestry operations in the north east. Such mechanisation will generate employment opportunities for educated youth and be economical at the relatively high wage rates prevalent in the region. (Para 8.16)

70. The provision of roads for forestry development will have to be limited to definite programmes for exploitation drawn up by the Forest Department, the Forestry Corporation or Forest based industrial units. (Para 8.17)

71. The problem of infrastructural development in forestry can be tackled if the infrastructural requirements are built into the scheme. The scheme should be drawn up in such a way that the cost of infrastructure, whether it be roads or ropeways or skyline crane can be recovered from the sale proceeds. If such commercially oriented schemes are prepared, they can be taken up by the financial institutions as bankable projects. Forestry exploitation plans can also be designed so as to take maximum advantage of the strategic roads which are being built in the remoter parts of the regions. (Para 8.18)

72. The approach to forestry development in this region cannot be based merely on the conventional approach which focusses attention on products like timber, plywood, fuel wood and pulping material. There are certain other activities which need to be integrated with forestry development plans. The more important of these are oak tasar culture, the cultivation of fodder trees, horticulture, development and the collection of medicinal plants. (Para 8.19)

Animal Husbandry

73. The starting point for the animal husbandry programmes must be a clear assessment of local requirements of local milk, eggs and meat. This assessment of requirements should be the basis for planning animal husbandry development. (Para 9.7)

74. The availability of breedable bulls from the regional farms is limited. With natural service the number of cows that could be covered would be limited and the cross-breeding target of 4 lakhs animals cannot probably be reached. Hence it is necessary that the frozen semen technology is extended as rapidly as is possible. (Para 9.12)

75. The Indian Council of Agricultural Research and the Assam Agricultural University must continue work on the utilisation of local forage crops and fodder trees. The programmes of social forestry and jhum control should include provision for fodder trees and fodder crops respectively. (Para 9.13)

76. The establishment of proper slaughter houses is essential if the meat economy of the region is to develop. Incidentally, a modern slaughter house will also allow the utilisation of by products like eases and blood meal. The latter in particular is very useful for animal food. (Para 9.16)

77. It is particularly important to pursue the programme of cross-breeding of beef cattle as soon as the bulls become available for

the proposed exotic beef cattle farms. (Para 9.17)

78. With regard to feed, the fodder, the local grasses and forage trees seems to have great potential. The ICAR has done some work in analysing these. This work should be used to devise appropriate feeding schedules for cattle, using these nutritious grasses and leaves as ingredients. (Para 9.18)

79. There is a large demand for Para 18 in the region and pigs are brought from outside into many of the hill States. At present, much of the spread between the cost of production and market price accrues to the trader who brings in pigs from outside. Piggery development will have to ensure that this income is realised by local farmer. It will also benefit consumers by lowering prices. (Para 9.21)

80. The markets for processed pork must be studied and the required facilities should be built into the main slaughter house. (Para 9.23)

81. The hill areas do not seem to be self-sufficient and pigs are brought in from the plains. One reason could be lack of effective arrangements for procurement of local supplies from rural areas to service urban markets. The shortage of pork and its high price make piggery a particularly attractive proposition. This will require a more rapid extension of exotic breeding and arrangements for processing and marketing. (Para 9.24)

82. The principal problem in the case of poultry is the lack of effective arrangements for the marketing of eggs and boiler meat. Though this has been suggested several times not much progress has been made. The local requirement for eggs may be somewhat limited because of the high levels of meat consumption. Hence any expansion in the pace of poultry development will require more effective marketing arrangements than what obtain at present. The market for eggs and poultry meat requires close study. This may be done by the NEC. (Para 9.26)

83. It is essential that the duckery centre in Tripura is developed and special attention is paid to duckery in the plains. (Para 9.28)

84. In this region the orientation of sheep husbandry may have to be towards meat and wool may be subordinate. (Para 9.28)

85. Goat development and goat breeding by crossing with exotics should also be pursued since goat meat will help to relieve the shortage of meat in the hill areas of the region. (Para 9.28)

86. Despite the very favourable position with regard to livestock availability, the hill areas of the region are not importers of meat.

There is clearly some major organisational failure underlying this phenomena. The Committee would suggest that one reason for this failure could be the lack of effective processing and marketing arrangements. As far as milk is concerned, something is being done as part of the Operation Flood Projects. The Committee would suggest that effective arrangements for procurement, processing and marketing of these products is an important as advances in productivity. Hence it would recommend that this matter be examined at a regional level by the NEC who may be asked to prepare a processing and marketing plan for livestock produce. (Para 9.30)

Handloom and Sericulture

Handlooms

87. The development of handlooms in the North Eastern Region will have to concentrate on commercialisation of local skills and designs. This would involve identification of a number of products which would have market potential within the region, in the rest of the country and also in the export markets. (Para 10.2)

88. The foundation of any effective programme of handloom development in the region must necessarily lie in a suitable organisational set-up. In this report on Village and Cottage Industries, the Committee has suggested a Group Centre approach for servicing clusters of artisans. The same approach is relevant for the development of the handloom sector in the conditions prevailing in the North-East. It should be possible to identify at least 50 such group centres in the different States and Union Territories. Once these are identified, package of measures comprising training, loom modernisation, design and product development and market linkage should be introduced to make each of the group centre viable and self-sustaining. (Para 10.3)

89. For the identification of group centres an important factor to be borne in mind will be the availability of weavers who will be interested in getting themselves trained in the operation of the newly introduced wider width in the looms. (Para 10.3)

90. The replacement of the loin loom by wider width looms may be the basis for the commercialisation of the handloom industry. But this has to be undertaken with a great deal of discretion and caution. Loin looms will continue to be appropriated for serving local markets, and inspite of the handicap of the narrow width of the cloth produced

has design advantages. Development Commissioner for Handlooms should take up special projects to find means of commercial exploitation of the loin loom tradition of this region. (Paras 10.3 and 10.4)

91. Given the constraints of space in the existing households, the common workshed approach is perhaps best suited for the introduction of these new types of looms. In the identified group centres over a period of five years about 50,000 new looms should be introduced in such common worksheds. (Para 10.5)

92. In all the identified group centres, training facilities will have to be set up. The approach should be similar to the training of carpet weavers in different parts of the country successfully taken up from 1975-76. The emphasis of these centres will be on training a sufficient number of master artisans, who in turn train other weavers in the area. Initially the production centres will primarily be training centres where a master artisans would impart training to selected local weavers in the cooperation of the new type of looms and the production of newly developed products. (Para 10.6)

93. The production centres organised on the workshed basis in the group centres would be attached to the already existing state level organisations for purposes of market support. This linkage has to be established from the inception so that these small production centres are not begged down with uncleared production. (Para 10.7)

94. It is necessary to forge links with the existing marketing organisations in the handloom sector for national level marketing of the production. The NEHHDC has already taken steps to open show rooms in the different parts of the country besides warehouses. The Committee would recommend that an important role should be played by All India Handloom Fabrics Marketing Cooperative Society which has a series of well-appointed show rooms all over the country. (Para 10.7)

95. Development Commissioner for Handlooms has already located weavers service centres with design sections at Gauhati, Imphal and Agartala. These will have to be strengthened particularly with reference to designing and training facilities. (Para 10.8)

96. The Government have already decided to set up an exclusive institute of handloom technology for the North-East which is most likely to be located at Gauhati. This Institute will have to play a very important role and carry out continuous research and development work. Both in regard to training and design development this institute

will have to coordinate with the organisations implementing the aforesaid project. (Para 10.8)

97. The distance involved and the difficult nature of the terrain push up the cost of yarn for the North-Eastern weavers. The Committee recommends that the present transport subsidy scheme should be operated on a much more basis as regards yarn. The various handloom corporations and apex societies already set up in the States together with the NEHHDC will have to play a more active role in the distribution of the year. (Para 10.9)

98. The NEHHDC should act as an overall coordinating agency for the development of the handlooms and handicrafts sector in the North-East. One of the problems of the handloom industry in the North-Eastern Region is the supply of yarn to the handloom weavers. The Corporation could supply the yarn upto the district level in the District Industries Centres. From these, the State's agencies can take out the responsibility for ensuring that yarn reaches the handloom weavers. A process house at Gauhati has been sanctioned, NEHHDC could extend this role to cover more and more processing facilities in different areas according to demand for processing both yarn and cloth. (Para 10.10)

99. As far as marketing is concerned, the State Corporations could concentrate on marketing in their own States while the NEHHDC would concentrate on the All India Market and for the States where such corporations have not been set up. (Para 10.10)

100. The NEHHDC in collaboration with the Regional Institute for Handloom Technology could associate itself with the technical training for weavers and management training for executives at different levels. Other activities of the Corporation would include facilities for warehousing supply of credit and acting as an apex organisation in the region. (Para 10.10)

Sericulture

101. In order to exploit the rich potential that exists for sericulture, it is necessary to chalk out the following programmes of action:

(i) Organised castor plantation in specific areas by identifying farmers who are willing to undertake eri plantation and silk worm rearing;

(ii) Development of infrastructural facilities by way of getting up grainages for supply of eri silk worm eggs to the eri rears, organising spinning activities on decentralised basis and helping in the marketing of eri yarn; and

(iii) Upgrading the existing research institution of Central Silk Board for undertaking applied research on eri culture in collaboration with State Level Agricultural Institutions.

The above programme of action is urgently called for as this sector remains untapped and has to be fully exploited for creation of employment and also for utilising the eri silk yarn for clothing needs in this area. (Para 10.13)

102. In order to step up production of Muga silk a number of important measures are called for:

(i) Area under Muga plantation should be substantially increased to make available the host plant for rearing activities;

(ii) Muga plantation which is undertaken in the forest areas should be developed on economic scale of plantation as has been done in the case of tropical arjun plantation so that rearing activities are facilitated;

(iii) A package of incentives should be provided to the Muga rearers and a scheme on the lines of the Inter-State Tasar Project for increasing muga silk production should be implemented by Central Silk Board under the Centrally Sponsored Schemes; and

(iv) Activities for the raw material bank for muga raw silk opened recently by Central Silk Board should be stepped up and arrangement should be made to ensure that the procurement of cocoons is directly from the rearers themselves and not from the middleman dealers. Further muga cocoons should be treated as minor forest produce and fair price should be assured to the rearers. Since muga rearers are part of the tribal community in the area, tribal development plan programmes should include specific projects for muga development. (Para 10.16)

103. The crucial elements in the strategy for the development of mulberry culture therefore have to be the rearing of high silk yielding variety of silk worm race and improvement of leaf yields by extension of high yielding varieties and appropriate agronomic practices. The Committee suggest for following:

(i) It should be examined that as to what are the varieties of mulberry which will grow profitably in this area and help in the process of increasing mulberry silk industry in this region;

(ii) Detailed trials of several varieties of silk worm, mono, bi and multivoltine should be tested out to find a suitable economic mix of varieties which can give three or four raising a year;

(iii) In order to popularise mulberry sericulture 10 pilot extension centres should be set up by Central Silk Board in this region;

(iv) Nucleus grainages of Central Silk Board should be established for production of seed cocoons and supply of commercial eggs to the rearers. As a subsequent measure the State Governments should be helped to set up grainages for production of commercial layings;

(v) As far as possible even from the beginning the improved techniques of the rearing of mulberry worm successfully adopted in Karnataka, Andhra Pradesh and Tamil Nadu should be introduced in this Region also; and

(vi) Arrangements for marketing of cocoons reeling of cocoons and supply of raw silk to the weaving centres should be undertaken.

(Para 10.17 and 10.18)

104. With regard to Oak tasar, the Committee recommends that Oak plantation should form part of the forestry programmes in this region and extension facilities should be provided to increase the area under oak plantation. (Para 10.22)

105. In Oak tasar culture, production of seed cocoons is inadequate due to low effective rate of rearing and high sex-ratio for preparation of commercial layings. Most cocoons produced are used for laying preparation. For preparation of layings, seed cocoons are subjected to a period of artificial hibernation, i.e., preservation in cool environment. A more precise and efficient method, i.e., preservation of the seed cocoons in the cold storage should be adopted. The problem of irregular emergence can be solved to a large extent by finding out the required temperature or seed preservation. Supply of seed cocoons can be increased considerably when optimum conditions for their preservation are established. (Para 10.23)

106. Oak tasar worm shows a tendency of continuous degeneration affecting the vigour of the worm as well as fertility. Pure parent stocks of A. pernyi and A. reylei need to be maintained in large, numbers, so that fresh hybrids can be obtained every year. The rearing of parent

stocks can be intensified at the Parent Stock stations of Meghalaya and Manipur. Stocks of hybrids can be reared in controlled rearing houses to prevent degeneration. (Para 10.24)

107. Standardisation of reeling and boiling processes is essential in order to achieve a production of uniform and quality reeled yarn. (Para 10.26)

Industry and Minerals

108. From the point of view of medium and large industry the most promising resources are the forest wealth of the region and the substantial deposits of oil, coal and limestone. The development of horticulture and plantations can assist in the growth of small and medium agro-based industries. The growth of sericulture and the demand for yarn in the handloom sector provide a base for the development of textile industries. These along with a variety of small units for serving local consumption demands can provide the basis for a more rapid industrialisation of the area. (Para 11.4)

109. Given the difficulty in attracting manpower from outside and the lack of a sufficient number of adequately trained local persons, it may take decades to survey the resources of the area fully. It may be desirable to follow a slightly different approach in which, in the first instance, a large part of the region is covered by first approximation surveys. Thereafter, promising areas could be identified and priorities set for the more detailed ground based surveys. Detailed investigations can be taken up when the prospect for the exploitation of a surveyed deposit seems sufficiently. (Para 11.9)

110. There are possibilities for developing industries based essentially on local markets. The identification of these would have to be based on a careful survey of the present level of demand for manufactured consumer goods and intermediate goods in the region. The Committee is not aware of any such systematic study in this area. It would recommend that the NEC undertake such a study of the local demand for manufactured goods, the manner in which this is being met, the extent to which the local demand can be met by local units, the types of units, that can be set up for this purpose, the optimum scale and investment for such units, etc. (Para 11.10)

111. Action plans have been prepared by several DICs. These Action Plans also identify a certain number of industries for which there is, on the face of it, a potential for development. These reports

can provide a starting point for more detailed feasibility reports which should try and establish the feasibility and viability of the proposals and provide the basis for a bankable proposition. The feasibility reports may be commissioned by the promotional agencies of the State Governments like the Department of Industries and the Industrial Development Corporation. (Para 11.11)

112. In its Report on Industrial Dispersal and on Industrial Organisation, the Committee has recommended a three-tier structure for entrepreneurial development, the first tier being provided by DIC, the second by the State level promotional agencies and the third by a regional centre to be set up by the IDBI. In the north-east the dependence on the third tier may be quite substantial. Hence, the Committee would recommend that the IDBI should set up a regional entrepreneurship development centre in the north-east. Apart from actual training, this centre should also provide guidance to other 'EDP' Programmes by undertaking periodic evaluation of these programmes. The NEC can also play an important role in this task in several ways. Firstly, it can strengthen the expertise available within the region by organising training programmes for the staff of the State and District level industrial promotion organisations. Secondly, it can help the States in getting expertise from outside whenever it is required. Thirdly, it can assist the States in arranging for suitable exposure to working enterprises both within and outside the north-east region for the entrepreneurial trainees. (Para 11.14)

113. The development of entrepreneurship as well as the need for technical support during the construction and operation stage will require an effective institutional system. One possible approach would be to exchange personnel between the institutions in the north-east and their successful counterparts elsewhere in the country. The expert from elsewhere in the country would work in the north-east while the officer from the north-east works in the counterpart institution to gain the necessary experience. After a fixed period of, say two years, the expert on deputation can revert back and the officer from the north-east can return. Such an arrangement could help in building up the talent in local personnel. The NEC and the DC (SSI) would have to accept responsibility for such a programme. (Para 11.15)

114. In the north-east the need for exploiting local demand fully for purposes of industrial development is very great. Hence the DC (SSI) would have to pay particular regard to implement its responsibilities for ancilliarisation in an effective manner in this region. It must also

take the lead in ensuring that the demands arising from Central Government Organisations in the region are also met to the greatest extent possibly by local industry. (Para 11.16)

115. The uncertainties in the supply of raw materials from outside the region would have to be reduced firstly by the extension of the national distribution network of major suppliers like STC and SAIL in the region and secondly by a more vigorous policy of raw material support by State Governments. (Para 11.18)

Transport and Power

116. With regard to rail development the most important gap seems to be the limited capacity available to service the areas south of the Mikir Hills. A linkage with the rest of the country via the Brahmaputra Valley is essential. This would require that the entire section from Gauhati to Lumding and Southward would have to be upgraded and its capacity increased. Already its capacity is below requirements and will be even more so once the new lines into Manipur. Tripura and Mizoram become operational. The Committee would suggest that the proposal in this regard and other proposals for rail development in the region may be examined sympathetically keeping in mind the relaxation of investment criteria suggested by the National Transport Policy Committee. (Para 12.8)

117. With regard to road development at present stage further development in the north eastern region would have to be based on the specific needs of each project and programme. Moreover, given the large gap in requirements, every attempt must be made to locate projects and programmes in manner that minimise the need for additional infrastructure. Thus market oriented horticulture can be developed fast in areas clearly served by roads. Forest based industries can be located in forest areas which can be readily opened for exploitation. The resource available for road works may be stretched further if the standards of road construction are re-examined, in the light of area needs so as to identify economics in construction costs. (Para 12.14)

118. There will be areas where new opportunities have been identified and can be promoted if road transport is provided. The roads required for such purposes should be given priority in the general road development programme of the States, NEC and the Centre. (Para 12.15)

119. There is a programme for the construction of strategic roads and roads required for administrative purposes. The compulsions with regard to routes and alignments differ in these cases from development roads. However, there will be many cases where such administrative and strategic roads will help to exploit potential for development. (Para 12.15)

120. One possibility for extending the road network is to include road development as part of a productive scheme. A commercial forestry scheme can include the required road development within the forest area. These roads can be used for other purposes. A similar approach may be possible in other sectors, e.g., plantation. (Para 12.15)

121. The developments in horticulture plantations and other sectors would be difficult unless trucking services are available even in the interior. Special measures to promote road transport operations may be taken. This could take the form of concessional loans for freight transport operations or the extension of freight services. (Para 12.16)

122. The possibility of taking up water transport in some of the tributaries of the Brahmaputra has been identified and areas of potential have been identified. Further development of IWT in this region would relieve the pressure on the rail and road system and needs to be pursued. (Para 12.17)

123. The NEC has identified several areas where ropeways schemes could be taken up. These alternative models of transport can help to met requirements for large industrial or mining projects and would have to be considered mainly in the context of such developments. (Para 12.18)

124. A comprehensive and integrated area transport plan should be prepared for the region by the Planning Commission and the NEC. The progress of implementation of the area transport plan should be monitored by the Planning Commission. (Para 12.19)

125. With regard to the immense hydel potential of the region, what is required at this stage is detailed investigations and project preparations which, given the size of the projects, will naturally be a Central responsibility. (Para 12.23)

126. The extension of electricity to rural areas can play an important role in lift irrigation and in decentralised agro-processing. Hence the pace of rural electrification needs to be stepped up from the point of view of local development. REC's lendings in the north-eastern region should be placed in the lowest category, i.e., the category with the easiest terms of lending. (Para 12.24)

127. It is essential that the micro hydel potential in the remote hill areas of the north-east is investigated and if found to be feasible and economical, a shelf of such schemes is prepared. Schemes should be taken up on a priority basis where there are possibilities or agro-processing and primary processing of forest produce. The REC should support such viable micro hydel schemes. (Para 12.25)

NATIONAL COMMITTEE ON THE DEVELOPMENT OF BACKWARD AREAS, 1978 — REPORT ON DEVELOPMENT OF TRIBAL AREAS

November 30, 1978 — June 11, 1981[1]

Chairman Shri B. Sivaraman, Member, Planning Commission

Members Shri Som Dutt; Prof. Mrinal Dutt Chaudhary (ceased to be member w.e.f. November 30, 1978); Shri S.S. Marathe (ceased to be member w.e.f. November 30, 1978); Shri Ranchor Prasad; Shri Ramakrishanayya; Shri K.P.A. Menon; Shri R.M. Honavar (ceased to be member w.e.f. January 31, 1981); Dr. S.A. Dave; Dr. Y. Nayudamma; Shri Anand Sarup; Dr. B.D. Sharma; Shri Suresh Mathur; Dr. D.M. Nanjundappa; Shri S.M. Ghosh

M. Secy. Shri Nitin Desai

Appointment

The Government have been pursuing certain policies and programmes in regard to the development of backward areas since the Fourth Five Years Plan. It is now necessary to review the working of these various programmes and to set out a suitable strategy or strategies for the development of Backward Areas in the context of the priorities and objectives set out in the draft 1979-83 plan. The Planning Commission have, therefore, decided to set up a High Level Committee to formulate appropriate strategy or strategies for effectively tackling the problems of Backward Areas vide its Resolution No. PC(P)17/NCDBA/78-MLP dated November 30, 1978.

1. Planning Commission, Government of India, New Delhi, 1981, xxiv; 120 p.

Terms of Reference

(i) To examine the validity of the various concepts of backwardness underlying the definitions in use for present policy purposes and recommend the criteria by which backward areas should be identified.

(ii) To review the working of:

(a) the existing plans for dealing with the general development problems of backward areas like Tribal Sub-Plans, Plans for Hill Areas, etc.; and

(b) the existing schemes for stimulating industrial development in backward areas such as the schemes for concessional finance, investment subsidy, transport subsidy, sales tax concessions, etc., similar schemes in the agricultural and allied fields like DPAP, and general measures for tackling the problems of poverty and unemployment with a view to find out their efficacy in the removal of backwardness; and

(iii) To recommend an appropriate strategy or strategies for effectively tackling the problem of backward areas, classified, if necessary, according to areas, causes or prescribed remedies.

Contents

Summary of Conclusions and Recommendations; Introduction; General Characteristics of Scheduled Tribes; Strategy of Development; Review of Past and Ongoing Programmes; Constitutional Provisions; Forest and Tribal Economy; Land and the Tribals; Education; Co-operatives in Tribal Areas; Organisation of Administrative and Financial Structures; Acknowledgements; Annexures I to XXXI.

Recommendations

Introduction

1. Inspite of differences in problems between different zones there are a few common features of tribal economic and social life which merit consideration in formulating any development programme in tribal areas. (Para 1.7)

2. The tribal Sub-Plan approach aims at a comprehensive

development of the area with focus on the individual family. It, therefore, follows that the approach must necessarily include not only development programmes but also programmes aimed at providing some of the basic needs of the local people. (Para 1.13)

3. It is not desirable that non-tribals in the given area should be completely left out, particularly as some of the development programmes would be such as would have to be handled on an area approach with particular focus and emphasis on the tribals and other weaker sections in that particular pocket. Also, it has to be remembered that certain other weaker sections in the tribal areas, particularly scheduled castes, have symbiotic relationship with the scheduled tribes. (Para 1.14)

4. Alienation of land has continued and time bound programmes for identification and restoration of alienated lands have not yielded results. (Para 1.15)

5. Major tribal communities have not taken the benefit of the institutional infrastructure established. In many areas, the level of literacy has remained very low. (Para 1.17)

6. Effective and sensitive administration for tribal development was sought to be established as a part of the Sub-Plan strategy. Some frame has been created but there is a lack of effectiveness because a clear unity of command had not emerged. (Para 1.19)

General Characteristics of Scheduled Tribes

7. The tribal situation in the country presents a varied picture. Some States like those of the North-East have predominant tribal population, others like those of West-East Central belt have high tribal concentration and still other areas like those of Southern States, the tribal population form only a small percentage of the total population. (Para 2.1)

8. The spread of literacy was not uniform in all the States, literacy rate between Scheduled Tribes on the one hand and the general population on the other varied from State to State. (Para 2.6)

9. The livelihood base for tribals is, by and large agriculture and allied activities. The cultivators form 57.56 per cent of the total workers among Scheduled Tribes and Agricultural Labourers 33.04 per cent. (Para 2.10)

10. About 29 per cent Scheduled Tribe Cultivating households have holding of less than 2.5 acres as compared to 34.5 per cent of the

general population. The percentage of households land holding of 10 acres and above is about 20 per cent among Scheduled Tribes which in case of general population it is 22 per cent. (Para 2.12)

11. The tribal areas can be broadly divided into seven regions which have different agro-climatic and demographic characteristics:

(i) Central Southers Tribal Region,
(ii) Central Northern Tribal Region,
(iii) Western Tribal Region,
(iv) North-Eastern Tribal Region,
(v) North Western Tribal Region,
(vi) South Tribal Pocket, and
(vii) The Oceanic Groups (Para 2.15)

Strategy of Development

12. The strategy for tribal development should underline measures for building the inner strength of the community so that they are able to face, as quickly as possible, the new system on term of equality. In this frame, education and health services have to be given a high priority in the developmental profile of the tribal areas. They have to be accepted not only as necessary investment for faster economic growth but also as an effective protective device during the transitional phase. (Para 3.22)

13. The I.T.D.P. Plan envisaged identification of specific problems in the area and suggestion of specific measures for meeting these situation. The following are some of the aspects which are to be specially noted :

(a) Primitive Communities;
(b) Areas with distinctive economic activity like shifting cultivation;
(c) Areas with predominantly forest based economy;
(d) More backward sub-regions;
(e) Growing urban centres;
(f) Areas of influence of industrial and mining complexes, existing potential; and
(g) Other problem areas, if any. (Para 3.26)

14. The I.T.D.P. approach, could not be accommodated in a

'society' model which, by definition, was not capable of assuming the responsibility of the Government and must be satisfied with limited functions. Even the requirements of flexibility and adaption inherent in the Integrated Tribal Development Project approach could not be fully satisfied in a society. Similarly, a statutory authority was also unsuitable because of the need for clear delineation of powers even in their case as distinct from those of Government. The best and the only practical course was to establish the Integrated Tribal Development Projects by a resolution of Government, with clearly defined tasks in there respective areas covering all facets of social and economic life of the community. All issues coming in the way of achieving the goal had to be resolved as stipulated in the sub-plan strategy. (Para 3.27)

15. It has been observed that barring some States neither inter-disciplinary structure nor leadership has been effective. The strategy outlined envisaged a comprehensive development approach to be implemented on the basis of a 'Project Approach', aiming at an integrated development of the area, with special emphasis on the least advantaged, and to improve the productive and earning capacity of the poor in their existing activities or through promotion of new activities. The beneficiary oriented approach had to be fitted in as part of the area development plan. (Para 3.28)

16. The National Committee has gone in a great detail into the constitution, composition, functioning, delegation of power, both administrative and financial and suggested a set up for an integrated area development of administrative and Financial Structure for backward area development authority in the Report on 'Organisation of Administrative and Financial Structures for Backward Area'. This model is essentially based on the ITDP model envisaged in the Sub-Plan approach but not represents complexes. The Committee would recommend that the approach outlined in its report on 'Organisation of Administrative and Financial Structure for backward area development should be fully implemented in all sub-plan areas and all the ITDPs streamlined and restructured on the basis of suggestions therein. (Para 3.29)

17. In the tribal areas there are other weaker sections, particularly Scheduled Castes which have symbiotic relationship with the Scheduled Tribes. The Committee would, therefore, recommend that the criteria for the determination of the tribal Sub-Plan area should be revised to include Scheduled Caste population also. While delineating the Sub-Plan area, areas having 50 per cent Scheduled Tribe plus

Scheduled Castes population should be included under the Tribal Sub-Plan. (Paras 3.35 and 3.36)

18. The tribal areas are passing through a stage when the individual is facing the situation of basic conceptual change in relation to property ownership of natural resources, etc. the economic infrastructure, in this context, should comprise stabilisation of their *de facto* rights in a form acceptable in the new system. Preparation of land records, recognition of traditional rights in forests, regulation of markets and money lending, etc., fall in this category. The institutional infrastructure paves the way for growth and development of the community and the area in the changing situation. This includes extension service, financing institutions, local bodies, etc. The tribal communities are handicapped by their unfamiliarity with these institutions. Benefits accruing from such developmental efforts do not therefore generally reach them in due proportion. In order to prepare tribals to avail of the infrastructural facilities, these should be introduced gradually and in a manner so that the tribals could make use of them for improving their quality of life. The normal structure should be modified and designed so that they are within the comprehension of the tribals and they become active participants. The physical infrastructure comprises road network, electricity, etc. This infrastructure by itself cannot be sufficient condition for tribal development and unless it is linked to specific economic programmes suitably adapted for the benefit of tribals, it may result in back-lash effect. (Paras 3.38 and 3.39)

19. Inability to adapt programmes to the local needs is a serious problem. The extension agency is not familiar with the tribal situation and the well tried local practices may be ignored in favour of prescription evolved for more advanced areas. There is real paucity of adequate information base about these areas and their economy and suitable programmes in many important sectors still remain to be evolved. (Para 3.40)

20. The new programmes demand new skills, which could be different but not necessarily higher, than what the average tribal already possesses. Unless, therefore, there is deliberate and adequate effort and preparation, which is generally at present lacking, to train the tribals in the new skills, the new programmes may be beyond the capacity of the individual tribal to adopt. (Para 3.41)

21. Under all the developmental programmes involving subsidy and loans, the tribal has to undergo a variety of formalities wherein he has to sign legal documents concerning agreements, etc. These for-

malities are beyond his comprehension. We have therefore, recommended restructuring of the existing set up in our report on Organisation of Administrative and Financial Structure for Backward Area Development. These recommendations apply to all backward areas, including tribal areas. (Para 3.42)

22. There are some aspects of tribal life and culture which are not wholly compatible with the requirements of modern economy. One important fact of their life is the 'Pleasure Principle' he wishes to enjoy life in its full. He may be unwilling to accept the discipline of the new economic system. The tyranny of disciplined labour could be avoided by reworking the schedule of operations which may be more suitable to them rather than being dictated by the needs of the organisations. (Para 3.44)

23. It is necessary that the sociological dimension of the tribal situation are not only clearly understood but their implications in relation to economic programmes are also spelt out and programmes are suitably adapted and phased. (Para 3.45)

24. The traditional social customs have been exploited by the vested interests at a heavy cost of the tribal community. Effective measures in these areas through social education and voluntary effort are a pre-condition for a meaningful economic programme. (Para 3.46)

25. The sociological aspects of the tribal situation are not only relevant but also crucial in many respects. Suitable reorientation of planners and administrators may be necessary so that a problem solving approach is adopted and action plans become realistic. (Para 3.47)

26. In the absence of a clear profile of the tribal economy in the country, the problem of tribal development is often viewed in terms of the socio-economic situation of various tribals who had attracted the attention of anthropologists and administrators because of their primitiveness. With the quickening of pace of economic development and introduction of new elements in these areas, a number of problems of adjustments for these tribals have arisen. These are the groups, generally small in size, which require most careful consideration in the national economy and the service of devoted people as also a flexible human approach for solving their problems. (Para 3.48)

27. The exploiting elements, who do not contribute to the local economy, have to be put down with a heavy hand. Elimination of exploitation has to be a priority item on the agenda. (Para 3.53)

28. In the case of the small land holders and landless labourers, a policy of 'restraint and support' is to be evolved. The illegal and im-

proper alienation of land has to be undone and lands should be restored to their rightful owners. In any case, future alienation of land is to be put to a complete halt at any cost. (Para 3.54)

29. The working classes amongst the migrant communities have to be accepted as a partner in the area development programme subject to the condition that they should not be allowed to corner the major share in the new opportunity. (Para 3.55)

30. The symbiotic relationship between certain groups and tribal communities has to be appreciated in realistic terms. While the element of exploitation has to be removed as a part of general strategy, the members of the scheduled caste and other communities at the same poor level need to be identified and helped to establish in alternative occupations and contribute to the growth of the local economy. (Para 3.56)

31. Programmes under the tribal sub-plans must have a definite shift towards family oriented programme with a clear target for each beneficiary group. In these programmes, the proportion of different needy communities other than the exploitative in the tribal area may be the guiding factor for fixing the number of beneficiaries in each group. (Para 3.57)

32. The members of the Scheduled Tribes may be assigned a share in proportion to their numbers with some weightage, say 10 per cent, the members of Scheduled Castes in proportion of their numbers and the balance being assigned to other people belonging to the weaker sections of the population. (Para 3.57)

33. Any distinction in the matter of grant of subsidies, etc. to the Scheduled Castes in the tribal Sub-Plan areas and in other backward areas would create an embarrassing situation. The Committee would leave it to the States to decide what concessions should be available to the Scheduled Castes in the backward areas. All that the Committee would recommend that the concessions available to the Scheduled Castes in the Tribal Sub-Plan areas should not be at a lesser level than are being extended to Scheduled Castes in other areas, particularly backward. (Para 3.58)

34. In any open ended scheme approach, there is the great danger that the other groups may take away the lion's share leaving the tribal Community where they are. This has happened in many schemes and even under the tribal development blocks. In this stipulation, the flow is that the extension agency can afford to be passive with no built in obligation to approach the members of the tribal communities. There-

fore, it is essential that the balance is maintained at all levels. The physical extension of and allocation of resources for any scheme must be subjected to strict criterion of the stipulated number of tribal families being benefited. (Para 3.59)

Review of Past and Ongoing Programmes

35. The Tribal Sub-Plan approach aims at a comprehensive development of the areas with a focus on the individual families. In such an approach, there are programmes like agriculture, horticulture, forestry, soil conservation, minor irrigation, etc., social welfare services, drinking water supply, appropriate infrastructural programmes, etc., which have got to be taken on an area basis. In other words, the approach has to be an 'Integrated Area Development Approach'. The Committee has already made its recommendations in this regard in its Report on 'Organisation of Administrative and Financial Structure of Backward Area Development'. (Para 4.20)

36. Administrative unpreparedness has appeared to be an important constraint in purposive utilisation of resources. There have been savings even in the limited resources allocation for the Sub-Plan areas and funds have not been fully utilised. Suitable arrangements for effective implementation are urgently required lest unregulated expenditure becomes counter productive. (Para 4.21)

37. The establishment of a single line of command, organic integration of the programmes in the field and an effective delegation of powers both financial and administrative to the project authorities, although agreed to in principle, remain to be fully implemented. In some States, even the first steps have not been taken. Again, the implementation of the programmes depends largely on quality of personnel. The Committee has found that a large number of posts in the key sectors are vacant in most tribal sub-plan areas. The Committee has dealt with this aspect in the Chapter dealing with the organisation of Administrative and Financial Structure. (Para 4.21)

38. Inability to adapt programmes to the local needs would appear to be another major problem. The extension agencies are not familiar with the tribals situation and the well tried local practices are often ignored in favour of prescriptions evolved for universal application. In the absence of adequate data base about the Tribal Sub-Plan area, suitable programmes in many important sectors still remain to be evolved. (Para 4.22)

39. There has been no conscious approach to train the tribals in the new skills which would be needed for new programmes. (Para 4.23)

40. It was expected that each Department would adapt its programmes with reference to the specific needs of the Sub-Plan area. This process has, however, been initiated, but its pace is very slow. The distinction between the sectoral programmes and the tribal development programmes addressed to specific groups is not always appreciated. The result is that achievements are not commensurate with the money spent. Preference for bigger programmes even though some of them may not be of direct relevance to the tribals, persists in most of the States. (Para 4.24)

41. Agriculture and allied programmes in these areas have so far followed the pattern adopted for the developed areas. Therefore, it has not touched even the fringe of the problem in these areas. Agriculture development programme, shifting cultivation, irrigation, animal husbandry and horticulture development would require special attention. Problems relating to agriculture and allied sectors, both in the hills and in drought affected areas, have been dealt with by the Committee in its Report on 'Development of Backward Hill Areas' and on 'Drought Prone Areas'. The Committee would urge that the various approaches suggested in the reports should be adopted for tribal development by the concerned Departments both in the States and Centre, and necessary steps taken to reorient existing programmes. (Para 4.27)

42. A comprehensive concept of qualitative improvement in the socio-economic status of the family with focus on women and children, is necessary. So far there have been no appriciable efforts of the Welfare needs of the tribal communities. This is an important task which should be taken up urgently if the economic development efforts have to become meaningful in these areas so as to bring about a total improvement in the quality of the life of the individual. (Para 4.30)

43. Apart from Education, health services, nutrition, social services, drinking water supply, etc., would also require adequate attention. Once the concept of a total development of area, as recommended by the Committee, is translated into action, this would have to be taken care of. The recommendations made by the Committee in its Report on Development of Backward Hill areas with regard to infrastructural development and in its report relating to the Development of Village and Cottage Industries, should also be suitably implemented in the tribal sub-plan areas, on the lines recommended therein. (Para 4.30)

Constitutional Provisions

44. The review of the Constitutional Provisions, clearly brings out that adequate powers have been given to the executive for making regulations having the effect of law so that the special responsibilities for tribal development can adequately be discharged. There are three alternatives for making a law for scheduled areas depending on the situation in each case:

(i) Legislation by Notification;
(ii) Legislation through Regulation; and
(iii) Normal legislation. (Para 5.42)

45. Even though the Constitution has made specific provision for the special needs of the communities and tribal areas, it gives further discretion to the executive to meet any contingency which may rise in relation to protection and advancement of the tribal communities. This discretion, however, is limited to Scheduled areas and Tribal areas only. In respect of tribal communities living outside these areas, it will be necessary to rely on the general laws. (Para 5.43)

46. It was visualised that certain laws of the State or Centre may need to be changed sometimes drastically. The Governor, therefore, has been given the power to make any changes in a low of State Legislature or the Parliament 'not withstanding anything in the Constitution'. In certain cases, it may be that the interests of the tribal communities may have already been adversely affected for reasons of omission or commission at some level. Fifth schedule, therefore, specifically makes a provision for giving retrospective effect to the Governors without any reference either to the Tribal Advisory Council or to the Union Government. Thus, the Constitution gives almost unlimited discretion to the executive for making any change in the law, should such a contingency arise. (Para 5.43)

47. A distinction has been made in the case of regulation making powers of the Governor compared to his powers to amend a law by notification. A regulation is required to be assented to by the President before it becomes applicable. The Governor is also obliged to consult the tribes Advisory Council before making any Regulation. Thus, the distinction between the Governors power to amend the laws and the power to make regulation is clear. (Para 5.44)

48. The Governor has wide powers to rectify the ill effects of any

law whatsoever, but when certain positive measures are to be taken, which may or may not affect an existing law, the Governor is to be guided by the Tribes Advisory Council and must seek approval of the President. It is significant that all these legal measures do not require the approval of the State Legislature or the Parliament. (Para 5.44)

49. The legislative powers of the Parliament and State Legislatives are defined under Articles 245, 246 and 248 and the three lists given in the seventh Scheduled indicate the manner and nature of their distribution. There is no entry in the three lists pertaining to either to the Scheduled Areas or the Scheduled Tribes. Therefore, any legislation in relation to these subjects fall within the purview of the Parliament in exercise of its residual powers under Article 248 (1) read with entry 57 in List I of Seventh Schedule. (Para 5.45)

50. The responsibility of the Union Government has been made clear by extending the executive power to giving of directions for preparation and execution of programme for tribal development and for good administration of the Scheduled Areas. These provisions are reinforced by making necessary financial provision for this purpose a charge on the Consolidated Fund of India. The Constitution provides for effective protection of tribal communities even by limiting, wherever necessary, the fundamental rights in important ways. Reservation in the services as also in the political system has been provided for. The Governor is given the special responsibility for peace and good governments of the Scheduled Areas and he is required to report to the President annually. A Special Officer is appointed under the Constitution to oversee the functioning of the safeguards under the Constitution and report to the President thereon. The Parliament is kept informed about the state of tribal development through his report. (Para 5.50)

51. Our review shows that the constitutional safeguards in relation to reservations of seats in the Parliament and the State Legislatures have been effective and continue to be fully provided for. The representation in services has been claiming due attention and the situation in this respect has been improving. There is a system of review of reservations at the highest level in the Central and State Governments. The Parliament and State Legislatures are also conscious about reservations. The Commissioner for scheduled castes and scheduled tribes makes a detailed and critical review of reservations in his report. The members of the service belonging to the Scheduled Castes and Scheduled Tribes can themselves approach the Commissioner

wherever necessary for enforcing their rights. (Para 5.51)

52. The Constitutional provisions in relation to the protection and development of tribal communities and administration of scheduled areas, however, have not been operationalised. Law provides the basis and the frame for all administrative action. But the regulation-making power under the Fifth Schedule has been used by the States to a very limited extent. (Para 5.52)

53. It has been held that it is the Parliament which can enact a law on tribal affairs. But no law has been passed so far by Parliament either for protection or for development of the Scheduled Tribes. Similarly, no regulation has been made for peace and good administration of the scheduled area, although there is a specific provision for this purpose under the Fifth Schedule and administration has continued to remain the weakest spot in tribal affairs. (Para 5.52)

54. The position in relation to economic programmes has also remained vague and was somewhat unsatisfactory before the Fifth Plan. The tribal sub-plans have, however, provided a frame for meaningful discussion and continuous review about the level of investments and the quality of programmes in various sectors. But the administrative apparatus which was envisaged as a part of the sub-plan strategy remains to be established. We consider that rising level of investment without effective protection and administration may by counter-productive in relation to the welfare and interests of tribal communities. (Para 5.53) .

55. The Central Government have issued guidelines from time to time about the need for effective protection, purposive implementation and good administration for the tribal areas. But the basic structure has remained unchanged. Even a realistic assessment of the emerging situation is not available to the Union Government in the absence of a purposive and reliable feed back although the Governor is expected to send an annual report on the administration of the Scheduled Areas. The Governor himself is handicapped by the fact that no one reports to him directly about the problems of the scheduled areas and the progress of development of tribal communities. His reports tend to present a mere narrative of the activities of the Tribal Welfare Department in the State. (Para 5.54)

56. The Constitution also envisages that the Special Officer (Commissioner for Scheduled Castes and Scheduled Tribes) shall investigate and report to the President on the working of Constitutional Safeguards. But the Commissioner is an external authority. He gives an

array of suggestions, year after year, only some of which may be picked up for special attention. (Para 5.54)

57. There is no mechanism within the system for internal appraisal and corrective measures on a continuing basis. Therefore, the President has not issued even a single direction to any State in the last thirty years exercising his powers to give directions for development of tribal communities under Article 339 (2) or for good administration of the Scheduled Areas under the Fifth Schedule. The basic reason is the lack of a systematic and continuous appraisal of the situation with reference to the clear policy frame and administrative goals which may be set in this regard. Thus, there is a critical gap in the Constitutional scheme which makes it virtually inoperative. This gap can be filled only if the executive keeps the Governor and the President informed about the situation in the tribal areas and the development of tribal communities. (Para 5.54)

58. The various Constitutional provisions relating to the administration of the Scheduled Areas are complementary to one another and provide a broad frame for action. A satisfactory plan of action has to be drawn up to operationalise all these elements in such a way that they function in unison. The basic elements which go to determine the quality of administration have to be clearly defined. (Para 5.55)

59. It is necessary that a clear programme should be worked out for regular appraisal of the administrative situation in the tribal areas, corrective measures taken by the States and the supporting financial provisions made for that purpose by the States and the Central Government under the first proviso to Article 275(i). (Para 5.55)

60. The overall responsibility for good administration of scheduled areas and protection and development of Scheduled areas and protection and development of Tribal communities rests with the Union Government. A system of regular dialogue at the national level similar to that of the Ministry of Agriculture (under the aegies of the Ministry of Home Affairs), therefore, should be immediately worked out. (Para 5.56)

61. So far as preparation of tribal sub-plans is concerned, it has now become a part of the normal planning process and the Planning Commission review programmes and priorities, sectoral allocations, actual programmes, etc., for the tribal areas as a part of annual State Plan and Five Year Plan exercise. But a parallel system is necessary for review of the administrative system and its performance in the Scheduled Areas and implementation of tribal development

ministrator, Collector and Tribal Development Commissioner. They should also be given adequate powers for enabling them to effectively guide the course of change and development in these areas. The working of the regulations for good administration of the Scheduled Areas should be specially reviewed in the Governor's 'Report'. (Para 5.64)

Forest and Tribal Economy

74. In the past few years, a comprehensive frame to which all aspects of forestry and tribal economy are fully reconciled has not yet emerged. There is a search for such an approach both amongst foresters and planners for tribal development. It is clear that the overall national interests, particularly ensuring ecological balance, must be paramount. Yet, within the parameters, as defined by national consideration, there are many alternative action plan possible which may have varying implications for the local tribal economy. (Para 6.10)

75. The rights in forests can be sustained only if there is a comprehensive frame for the protection, use and development of forests in which the community and the individual must assume the responsibility for creation of new forestry wealth and its protection. We do not agree with the approach of Dhebar Commission since they ignored these aspects and emphasised only the rights. The broad approach outlined by the National Commission on Agriculture will have to be followed. (Para 6.11)

76. The local tribal community, which has symbiotic relationship with the forests, should be accepted as partners in the local forestry development efforts in each area. Unless this promise is accepted and built into the system, it may not be possible to avoid conflicting situations at the local level. The best protective devise for the existing forests and the new additions is to create an interests of the local community in the forest wealth. (Para 6.12)

77. It is necessary to distinguish between the tribal communities who have a along tradition of symbiotic relationship and other agricultural groups for whom the forest is just a source for satisfying some of their needs. The relationship of the two is qualitatively different which should get reflected in the policy frame and developmental programmes for these areas. (Para 6.13)

78. The symbiosis between the tribal community and the forests should be re-established through suitable plans of development of these regions. (Para 6.14)

79. We are on the threshold of technological revolution in agriculture and landuse whose significance is not quite appreciated as yet. The new agricultural technology is inevitably leading towards higher specialisation in landuse. Now comparatively smaller areas can support bigger populations so far as food grains are concerned. The sub-marginal lands, which are being used for raising poorer grains or where cultivator has to remain satisfied with poor yields can be put to many better alternative uses which incidentally also help in restoring the ecological balance. (Para 6.15)

80. Today it is possible by choice of a suitable technology and production pattern that any piece of land, about a hectare or so, can make a family economically viable. The choice can be as wide ranging as the capital intensive coffee plantation on one hand, through plantation of fruit-bearing trees, host plants for tusar to plantation of fodder-trees, linked to animal husbandry and fuel-wood plantation on the other. Tusar cultivation with plantation of host trees is an important area of good potential for some regions. (Para 6.15)

81. The weaker sections of the community can provide necessary manpower to create tree wealth on marginal lands which, in quite a few cases, are still under State control. The experience of horticulture programme in Orissa shows that the cost of programme with individual ownership is likely to be moderate. The problem with an average person may be of sustenance for the period of his engagement in this activity. Methods can be found to provide financial support to the landless labourers or marginal cultivators for a limited period till he acquires the new resource-base and becomes viable. (Para 6.16)

82. A large programme of coffee plantation has been taken up in Andhra Pradesh with financial support from A.R.D.C. Each individual tribal is assigned a piece of land for plantation and he is provided technical and financial assistance. He has a right on the trees and their usufruct but he does not have the right of alienation. It is such groups of individuals interested in creation of new tree wealth as a part of their individual development plans that will get vitally interested in the development and protection of the forest. The planning for creation of this new tree wealth may also keep in view the requirements of the community of the region and of the national economy. It will thus be possible to have a frame in which the local needs, national priorities and economic well-being of individual tribal living in these areas are fully harmonised. (Para 6.16)

83. We are at a point where full implication of new technology

have not yet been appreciated and there is time when the landless and the weaker sections of the community particularly the tribals can be given a resource-base. It may be necessary that a strong organisation is created for this programme which may provide necessary technical support as also the financial resource for this programme which has a comparatively longer gestation period. The organisation may also organise in due course marketing with a view that the primary producer gets the maximum benefit. It will be necessary that the personal and social needs of the tribal producer are also fully provided for by this organisation so that the individual is not required to go to a money-lender which may mean syphoning off the benefit of new development through indebtedness. (Para 6.17)

84. The Plans of Integrated Tribal Development Projects and the Working Plans of forests, should be reviewed and suitably reformulated for achieving the balance in the development of the people and the forest. (Para 6.18)

85. The collection of minor forest produce has to be organise as an economic operation taking into account the market forces. It is only when the collection prices and the market prices are almost equal that the temptation for bye-passing the normal system can be curbed. There may be a notional reduction in the royalty of the State but it will be more than fully compensated by many other to the State by the fact that the total collection will be duly accounted for. (Para 6.23)

86. The trader and the contractor are primarily interested in maximising their profits from the operations during the period of their lease. This generally leads to over-exploitation of minor forest produce which may even be detrimental to the forests itself. Introduction of a system of rotation, closing each area for one year in four years has restored the normal production. (Para 6.24)

87. One of the important basic premises in any forest programme is to strengthen the resource-base and establish linkages with the long term interests of the local economy. This applies equally in the case of minor forest produce. It is, therefore, necessary that a systematic plan of action is worked out for minor forest produce. The middle-man in all forms, whether contractor, trader or agent, must be removed from the scene. (Para 6.25)

88. Minor forest produce should not be treated as a source of revenue to the State. It should provide maximum return to the tribal so that economic interest is created in the maintenance of forests with the possibility of substantial incomes accruing to the individual regularly

from its collection. (Para 6.25)

89. The price of minor forest produce should be remunerative and linked to the market price. (Para 6.25)

90. All leases for collection of minor forest produces should be given exclusively to Cooperative of tribals. (Para 6.25)

91. The Ministries of Agriculture and Home Affairs together should ensure that the entire trade in minor forest produce is organised through the co-operatives on monopoly basis and this new system is introduced with effect from the next working season. The necessary regulations or other legal support should be provided to make it effective. (Para 6.25)

92. A system of announcing support price for minor forest produce should be introduced so that the tribal may not be suddenly faced with the possibility of erosion of his income in some areas. The purchase of minor forest produce should be taken up by a State level or regional organisation through LAMPS. (Para 6.26)

93. A risk fund should be built up for meeting the contingency of a sudden slump in the market in one or more commodities. Since the size of operations in each State will be large, this should not create a serious problem. A contribution could also be made from tribal welfare fund for this purpose. If the trend in relation to some minor forest produce is a long term one, it should be possible to plan a gradual shift. The concerned ministries in the Central Government may support these operations through the network of LAMPS wherever necessary. The Ministry of Home Affairs should assume the nodal role in guiding the policies and monitoring the progress. (Para 6.29)

94. The tribal should not merely remain a collector of forest produce without any role in the maintenance of augmentation of resources. The extension programme for training of tribal collectors of minor forest produce particularly those engaged in tapping the trees should be taken up. (Para 6.27)

95. The LAMPS should assume a central role even in the maintenance of forest base. The training programmes for maintenance and scientific working of minor forest produce should be organised through the LAMPS. (Para 6.27)

96. In case of some forest produce the individual tribals may be given the right to collect from specified areas or trees so that their proper upkeep is ensured and the individual gets interests in their continued maintenance. This practice has been started in Andhra Pradesh for collection of gums from the reserved forests. Similarly, the host

plants are assigned to individuals under tusar programme in some States. This approach should be adopted whenever feasible. (Para 6.27)

97. A Comprehensive programme of identifying the various forest produce, assessing their potential and also feasibility of marketing and their alternative use, etc., should be formulated. The Forest Research Institute should take a head in this matter and direct suitably its research programme. It should provide guidance to the States in this matter on a continuing basis. (Para 6.28)

98. It is necessary that the first processing of minor forest produce is organised within the tribal area and through the Co-operative system. The main objective should be to retain maximum benefit from this activity within the local economy which should accrue to the primary collector. (Para 6.29)

99. The Co-operativisation of minor forest produce should be accorded a very high priority since this will give immediate additional income to the average tribal and will also be in the interest of development of the forests themselves. A time bound programme of 2 to 3 years should be prepared for establishing processing units for minor forest produce in the Cooperative sector within the tribal area. (Para 6.30)

100. A substantial programme of social forestry has been taken up recently which aims at providing for the needs of local community from the proposed tree-lands outside the reserve forests. (These new 'Social forests' may be managed by the community after they have got established.) They are expected to cater the various needs of the community like fuel-wood, timber for housing, agricultural implements, etc. (Para 6.32)

101. The social forestry programme and the tree culture programme will help substantially in restoring the balance. Nevertheless the social forestry programme is still in the early stages and its cost is comparatively high. The social forestry by itself may not fully meet the needs of the tribal economy since the relationship of the tribal economy with the forest is very intimate and far reaching. It will be necessary to review the plantation policy in the forest area as well in a larger frame. (Para 6.32)

102. The programme of forestry should make adequate provision for mixed plantations with the objective of providing the tribal community with their basic requirements and increasing production of minor forest produce which may help them to supplement their cash incomes. A minimum percentage of useful species in all plantations

should be fixed for each area taking into account their potential and the needs of the local economy. (Para 6.33)

103. It is necessary that Forestry Corporation concentrate on the poorer areas and ensure investment of substantial additional funds from financial institutions in these areas. (Para 6.26)

104. The forestry operations are not covered in many States by the provision of minimum wages for agricultural workers. In remote areas, the labourer is at the mercy of the forest contractors, his agents or the petty officials of the department. Even when a better wage employment may be available in some area, the local tribal may still be obliged to work on forestry programmes at the lower wages because he has to live in the area and maintain good relations with the forestry officials. The relationship of the forest labour and the employment agencies, therefore, are to a large extent exploitative, the advantage of which is taken by the middleman or it may get reflected in lower working expenses of the forest department. It is necessary that the forestry labourer in these regions should be ensured a reasonable wage taking into account the factors like arduous nature of the job and its casual and seasonal character. (Para 6.38)

105. No serious effort has been made so far even though in principle it has been accepted that the entire working of forest should be planned through the Co-operatives. Neglect of this aspect besides affecting the average tribal adversely, is against the long term interests of the forests. So long as the individual tribal remains a casual wage earner, he is bound to seek a firm base in agriculture or other activities which may lead ultimately to the denudation of the forest. (Para 6.39)

106. In view of the fact that forestry operations have widely fluctuating labour requirements during different seasons, it may be possible to provide regular employment only to a small proportion of total labour force even under intensive forestry management scheme. This inherent problem can be resolved by organising the forestry work through the Cooperatives. (Para 6.40)

107. The working of forests could be so organised that each member of the Cooperative be provided wage employment for a minimum number of days. (Para 6.40)

108. The Cooperative could organise labour teams for working even in the distant regions which may be outside the reach of an individual. Thus, regularity and predictibility of wage employment will help in stabilising the local economy. The Cooperative should be in a position to ensure a reasonable Wage for their labour. (Para 6.41)

109. In Gujarat and Maharashtra the forest labour cooperative societies are entitled to 20 per cent of the net profit from forestry operations which is arrived at after deducting the actual expenses according to the prescribed scales from the net sale proceeds. The same principle should be extended to all forestry operations in the country. (Para 6.41)

110. Each member of a Forest Workers Co-operative, who may put in qualifying number of mandays during a year, should be entitled to a share in the net profit. (Para 6.41)

111. Even in those areas where working is being done through the department or where Forestry Corporations have been established, forestry works should be executed entirely through the Forest Labour Cooperative Societies. The change-over to the working through the Cooperatives should be completed within a period of 2 to 3 years. (Para 6.41)

112. The forest department should assume the responsibility of organising the Forest Labour Co-operatives. (Para 6.41)

113. The organisation of forest labour in Cooperatives will enable the Department to associate them in the management and working of the forest which will also help in moving towards a more balanced development in these regions. I will, thus, be possible to re-establish a symbiotic relationship between the forest and the tribal economy. (Para 6.42)

114. In most of the States the tribals cultivating lands in the areas of Forest Village have full tenancy rights. However, in some States they still continue to hold lease for a limited period. It will be necessary that all these anomalies are removed without any further loss of time and a programme of development of these villages is taken by systematically. The forest department will, however, continue to have in many cases a special role in the development of these villages in view of their physical location. (Para 6.43)

115. Suitable programmes for development of erstwhile forest villages, therefore, should be prepared urgently and implemented, if necessary under the aegies of the forest department. They should particularly concentrate on tree-based economic activity. (Para 6.43)

116. The industrial units should be set up in the Cooperative sector so that there is sharing of net benefit between the forest labour and the persons employed in the processing unit. (Para 6.44)

117. In the highly capital intensive industries like paper. While interest of the State, the entrepreneur and labourer in the organised sector

are adequately taken care of, the forest labourer has to be satisfied with casual employment which is generally seasonal in character. Even in this case a fair deal can be given to the forest labourer if a programme for training them for higher skill jobs is taken up. (Para 6.45)

118. The leases for supply of raw materials from the forests should be given to the labour cooperatives. (Para 6.45)

119. There are signs of change even amongst the shifting cultivators, who are facing the problem of growing pressure of population and dwindling resources. In these areas if a viable alternative can be given to the tribal it may be acceptable. The areas where the cycle of shifting cultivation has got reduced below the critical period of 10 year or so should be taken up for tackling this problems on a priority basis. Special comprehensive plans for the concerned regions with problem of shifting cultivators as their focus, should be prepared. (Para 6.47)

120. The development of shifting cultivators should primary be within the area of their traditional habitat. (Para 6.48)

121. There should be a mixed programme of developing valley lands for permanent cultivation with provision of irrigation wherever possible, horticultural programmes on moderate slopes and forestry plantations on top lands. Animal husbandry, poultry and piggery should be provided as subsidiary occupations. (Para 6.48)

122. The broad approach of family based programmes should be followed in these areas in which the aim should be to make each individual economically viable with a suitable mix of economic activities and choice of tree crops. Each shifting cultivator group may be accepted as a unit under this approach so that suitable leadership can emerge from within and the programme can become self-sustaining. (Para 6.48)

123. It will have to be ensured that the lands set free from shifting cultivation are put under alternative use without any time lag so that the individuals in the group are not attracted to resume shifting cultivation at the slightest pretext. (Para 6.48)

124. Comprehensive micro plan for each group of cultivators should be prepared by inter-disciplinary teams which may be constituted exclusively for this purpose. (Para 6.48)

125. Necessary funds for implementation of this programmes should be the first charge in the resources earmarked for these areas from the relevant sectors under the tribal sub-plans. (Para 6.49)

126. An average tribal has a wealth of knowledge about the forests and their produce, wild life, etc. The forestry programme should be so

organised that full advantage can be taken of these skills. In certain cases it may be necessary to upgrade these skills and given them an understanding of the broader frame so that they can appreciate their role in the new perspective. The base, however, in all these cases should be the native skill of the individual in each areas. (Para 6.49)

127. The programme should be to upgrade their skill rather than superimpose unfamiliar methods which may be difficult for them to master in a short period. (Para 6.49)

128. A new climate of participation can be better engendered by voluntary organisations who can make a choice of persons for each area or task taking into account the precise requirements particularly on the human relation side. They are likely to adopt a problem solving approach rather than being bound by rules and procedures. There is, however, considerable reluctance to associate voluntary organisations in many States though commendable work has been done in some pockets where the State and the voluntary organisations have joined as partner in certain programmes. The work done by Bharat Agro-Industries Foundation is particularly note-worthy which has become a pace-setter in fodder-tree cultivation and improvement of cattle. Special effort should be made to encourage voluntary organisation in specific programmes in the remote forest regions. (Para 6.50)

129. The new approach in the forestry programme will require considerable reorientation of the officers and men of the forest department. These officers do acquire a good knowledge of the area through long association which officers of other departments including even tribal welfare may not have. (Para 6.51)

130. A relationship of authority and subservience is underlined and even considered necessary for smooth and efficient functioning of the system. The interests of the tribal community tend to be disregarded. This is one of the important contributing factors for the climate of distrust between the administration and the people in the tribal areas. The re-orientation of the forestry personnel is crucial and should be taken up urgently. (Para 6.51)

131. All officers and men at all levels must appreciate the symbiotic relationship between the forests and the tribal community. One cannot develop at the cost of the other. (Para 6.51)

132. All officers and men in the forest department should be given a good idea about the tribal life and their economy and interdependence between the development of the tribals and the forest. (Para 6.51)

133. All programmes of training to the officers, both at the point of entry and in-service, should have Forests and Tribal Development as important item. In courses leading to formal examination, full papers be introduced on this subject, in other cases capsule programmes, depending on the level and duration of each course may be prepared. (Para 6.51)

134. A tribal development unit should be established in the Forest Research Institute which should have a full faculty of tribal development comprising disciplines of tribal sociology, tribal economy and tribal administration. (Para 6.51)

Land and the Tribals

135. Various state governments have taken a number of measures from time to time for protecting tribal lands, particularly in the scheduled areas, some states even altogether prohibiting all transfers of tribal lands. But the total impact of all these measures has not been very significant (Para 7.21)

136. Sometimes even progressive measures, like those of land reforms, have adversely affected the tribal communities because those laws did not take into account the special situation in the tribal areas. (Para 7.21)

137. Many a legal provision have had adverse effect because of their faulty application or incongruous interpretation. (Para 7.21)

138. All transfers of land from tribals to non-tribals should be prohibited and prohibited effectively. (Para 7.21)

139. Where no law to prohibit land transfer exists, suitable law should be enacted immediately. Consequently, it will be necessary to critically examine the law and suitably chisel it with reference to the clear objectives set up in this regard and keeping in view the inherent limitations arising from the socio-economic situation. (Para 7.21)

140. The tribal generally has a high regard for the 'word' and believes that all others also have the same value. Therefore, he is prepared to put his thumb impression or sign any paper without any reservation. The articulate people are generally very careful in their dealings and they ensure that the property acquired by them is in accordance with the letter of the law which however may be circumvented in subtle ways. It is, therefore, necessary that oral evidence is placed on a higher pedestal and the law of evidence is amended so far it is applicable to the evidence of members of the scheduled tribes so as to

follow oral evidence to be adduced against all forms of documentary evidence including the registered documents. (Para 7.22)

141. In the scheduled areas in case of a dispute about the ownership of land, it should be presumed that the land belongs to the tribal unless proved otherwise. Therefore, the onus of proof that the land has been acquired by the individual in accordance with the provisions of law should be on the non-tribal holder of the law. (Para 7.22)

142. The procedure for advancing of loans, execution of agreements, etc., should be prescribed as to require the payment and formalities being completed in the 'open' where members of the village community should be present and attestation by one or more members of the community depending on the nature of agreement, should be made obligatory. Any violation of this rule should have the effect of making the transaction or agreement *ab-initio* null and void. (Para 7.23)

143. The special procedure so adopted for the tribal areas should be widely publicised. Once the broad outlines of a procedure are known to the people and its parameters clear, it will be difficult for any one to take undue advantage of the ignorance of the tribals. (Para 7.23)

144. Much of the trouble in relation to land titles also arises from the fact that the owner of the land has no document with him and the records prepared by the revenue officials is final. In the institution of tribal areas this puts the tribal to great disadvantage and he is at the mercy of the patwari. This situation needs to be corrected. Pass Book should be prescribed for keeping record of all lands including standing trees owned by a tribal, which should be kept by the tribal himself. (Para 7.24)

145. It should be made obligatory for the substance of any agreement or other legal formalities creating a charge on his land, directly or indirectly, to be recorded and duly authenticated in this Pass Book. No liability of any description whatsoever on tribal land should accrue if it is not recorded in the Pass Book. (Para 7.24)

146. The registration of all land transfers should be subject to prior verification by the registration authorities that the conditions of transfers contained in the law have been strictly complied with. (Para 7.24)

147. Many a time the spirit of the law is not fully appreciated by those responsible for their implementation. The rules made under these laws tend to emphasise the formal and procedural aspects only which results in their mechanical operation. Therefore, the rules in these important matters should be elaborate which should give a clear idea of

the basic objectives of the law and also indicate possible alternatives along with their implications for guidance of the executive officers. Detailed guidelines should also be given besides bare legal provisions and rules made thereunder. (Para 7.25)

148. It is necessary that rules should be framed, which should be exhaustic but in simple language as soon as law relating to transfer or partition of land is enacted. Where rules remain to be framed immediate action should be taken. Detailed guide-lines should also be issued to ensure that the basic objective of the concerned law is communicated to the officers responsible for their implementation. (Para 7.25)

149. The progress of cases relating to tribal lands is not satisfactory. The proceedings in Civil Courts is far too tardy and formal – technical. The law relating to all aspects of tribal lands should be simplified with a view that it is possible to dispense justice to the tribal rather than being satisfied with completing the technical requirements. (Para 7.26)

150. The jurisdiction of Civil Courts should be barred. In those States where Revenue Courts do not exist, special machinery should be created for this purpose. (Para 7.26)

151. The possibility of prolonging the proceedings by the interested parties should be removed by limiting the number of appeals and also the points in which intervention of higher authorities can be sought. (Para 7.26)

152. The officers should not be content with technical disposal of cases, the real facts being treated as inadmissible pieces of evidence. (Para 7.26)

153. The administration should forcefully appear on the side of the weak because the equations are heavily loaded against him in our present system. There should be a visual demonstration of the capability of law to unto injustice against the tribals. (Para 7.26)

154. The order of the revenue courts for restoration must be implemented within a time limit the responsibility for all necessary action in this regard being placed on the Project Administrator. (Para 7.26)

155. Continuous vigilance is needed all through, right from the points where the land changes hands to the final disposal of the dispute in the highest court. In case force is used against the tribal disturbing his possession or preventing him from taking back the rightful possession, administration must intervene, *suo-moto* if necessary, and the other party suitably chestised. (Para 7.27)

156. Occupation of tribal lands through deceit or use of force should be made a penal offence. (Para 7.27)

157. The trial of cases relating to preoccupation of tribal lands or reoccupation of lands restored should be tried by Executive Magistrates. Such cases should be made penal offence under the law. (Para 7.27)

158. Special legal assistance should be provided to the tribals in all cases relating to their land disputes. (Para 7.28)

159. The Project Administrator should come in the picture and ensure that all cases are brought to the court of law. (Para 7.28)

160. In all tribal areas, Standing Councils should be appointed who should take up, *inter alia,* all cases of land disputes in which tribal is a party. (Para 7.28)

161. A convention should also develop that service of lawyers as Standing Counsels for protection of tribal interests will be taken into account while making selection for Government Pleaders and other assignment in the Judiciary. (Para 7.28)

162. The Special Counsel should be responsible for bringing to the notice of the Deputy Commissioner and the Project Administrator all cases of judgements in which the spirit of the law might not have been honoured so that immediate corrective measures can be taken. (Para 7.28)

163. There should be a constant review of the judicial pronouncement to ensure that no technical flaw is taken advantage of by the interested groups in these proceedings and the corrective measures are immediately taken. (Para 7.28)

164. While general measures for identification and restoration of alienated land may be taken throughout the tribal region, areas with possible high incidence of land alienation should be organised. Special teams comprising revenue officers and representatives of development administration should be constituted who may take up the task of identification and disposal of cases simultaneously. (Para 7.29)

165. There should be a time-bound programme for identification of critical areas, assessment of the problem of land alienation and the final disposal of cases. A period of two years should be the outer limit for this programme in view of its crucial importance. (Para 7.29)

166. It would be necessary as also practical that all illegal and irregular transfer in the last forty years or less, i.e. after the year 1940, should be identified and necessary steps taken to restore them to their rightful owners. The law of limitation should be suitably amended for

this purpose. (Para 7.30)

167. The individual tribal is under continuous pressure of a variety of forces which ultimately result in the loss of his only capital base, the agricultural land. Therefore, it is necessary that all those forces which individual tribals are facing incessantly are identified, understood and countered suitably, otherwise the legal measures taken by the States will continue to be inadequate and ineffective. (Para 7.31)

168. In view of the new situation where alienation is now in favour of stronger sections amongst the tribal community, it will be necessary that the transfer of land as between members of the tribal community themselves is also regulated. Suitable law or regulation should be enacted for this purpose. (Para 7.32)

169. A strategy has to be worked out so that he is not forced to borrow at usurious rates of interest from the money-lender who readily comes to his help since he can finally lay his hand on his land. We would discuss at length the urgent need for making the cooperative credit system throught the LAMPS effective without any further delay. (Para 7.33)

170. The consumption credit linked to marketing of minor forest produce and other economic programme should get the highest priority. (Para 7.33)

171. It will also be necessary that all existing debts are assessed and scaled down following the principles of *den dupat*. (Para 7.33)

172. If the tribal has a liability, it should be taken over by the LAMPS so that the link between the money-lender and the tribal is broken and a new relationship gets established with the Cooperative System. This should be the primary task of Tribal Development Project Authority and all manpower resources of the State should be mustered to complete this within a period of a year or so. This operation should be organised on a campaign basis so that this issue is solved once for all. (Para 7.33)

173. Those who want to move to an alternative occupation may be suitably assisted as a part of the general tribal development programme. However, it should also be appreciated that the schemes for occupational mobility do not result in unregulated transfer of property guided merely by personal consideration adversely affecting the economy of the community particularly of the weaker sections amongst them. (Para 7.34)

174. It is necessary that the reduction of the size of holdings below viability level is prevented to stabilise the economy of the tribal at the

margin both by positive measures of assistance and regulation of fragmentation. (Para 7.35)

175. The benefits of new technology should be made available to the vulnerable groups and they should be enabled to put their land to optimum use according to its potential. (Para 7.35)

176. A law prohibiting fragmentation of land below viability level should be enacted. Viability levels should be determined keeping in view the quality of land, level of technology and the socio-economic situation in each area. Village Committees may be constituted under this law which should be made responsible for working out mutual adjustments of lands in cases of likely partition for any reason whatsoever. (Para 7.35)

177. The transfers of lands as between members of the tribal communities themselves should also be regulated with a view to prevent holdings from becoming non-viable. (Para 7.35)

178. In case a member of the scheduled tribes proposes to dispose of his land, because he may wish to migrate from the village or move to an alternative occupation, the co-partners and other eligible tribal landless labourers and marginal farmers should be given the right of pre-emption. In many a tribal community such a practice is already prevalent and has the sanction of tradition. (Para 7.36)

179. It will also be necessary to work out a scheme for the temporary management of land on behalf of those persons who may be in distress. This needs to be reinforced in the wake of growing individualism and new opportunities which are becoming available to section of the people as a part of tribal development programmes. (Para 7.36)

180. There may be some tribals who may not be able to cultivate their lands for the time being on account of some problems, personal, social or economic. They should be suitably assisted to regain command of their lands after the obligation is discharged or when they are again in a position to manage their lands. (Para 7.36)

181. There should be a scheme for financing purchase of land by landless and marginal tribal land-holders, should they have an opportunity in pursuance of the above policy fame. The loan should be soft and returnable in 10 to 15 years depending on the quality of land and the general economic situation in each area. (Para 7.37)

182. In case a tribal is required to sell his land for unavoidable reasons and no eligible tribal comes forward to purchase it, the State should purchase the land and assign it to other tribals on easy terms.

Para 7.37)

183. In many states, substantial areas have been allotted for cultivation from deforested lands. In many cases, illegally occupied lands have also been settled in favour of encroachers. A cautions and pragmatic policy in this important matter will go a long way to help the tribal economy. All available land should be allotted exclusively to tribal landless labourers and marginal landholders. Only if no eligible tribal is available it should be allotted to other landless agricultural labourers. (Para 7.38)

184. On no account should bigger land owners be allowed to acquire more lands from de-forested lands since it would ultimately lead to transfer of land in some form at some other point. (Para 7.38)

185. Much of the de-forested land may not be capable of being developed as good agricultural land. Nevertheless, now that appropriate technology is available which can enable an individual becoming viable almost on any piece of land of an acre or so, suitable programmes should be prepared based on specific economic activity like horticulture, tussar rearing or animal husbandry. In case the land is fit for agriculture, suitable assistance should be given for land development, improved agricultural practices, etc., soon after its allotment. (Para 7.39)

186. An integrated programme, aimed at establishing the economy of tribals located at the margin, should be prepared in each area. It should include debt redemption, taking over of liabilities already incurred, provision of credit for consumption and social purposes, wherever necessary. The credit should be a part of a specific production programme for each family so designed as to enable him to discharge the old and the current liability on time and make him economically viable in the long run. (Para 7.39)

187. A cautious approach, should be adopted in the planning of programmes for the vulnerable group. In the first instance, all schemes should be within an integrated planning frame which should be prepared at the block and project level. Secondary, high cost technology should be avoided in the initial state. Thirdly, in all these programmes the forward and backward linkages as also coordination between the different departments should be worked out very carefully. (Para 7.40)

188. A comprehensive landuse plan should be prepared immediately in all villages where land has been allotted in the recent past or is likely to be allotted in future. A programme for development of

land for agriculture or utilisation for other purpose like the horticulture, tussar, animal husbandry, etc., should be given to the individual as soon as the land is allotted so that he can become economically viable within a reasonable period. (Para 7.41)

189. Identification of alienated land, its restoration and establishment of a new economic frame should be taken up almost simultaneously. The legal framework should also to be strengthened to provide a firm base for this action programme. (Para 7.41)

190. The new economy has to be built on the basis of family-wise programmes. These families have to be organised in viable groups as has been envisaged in the growth centre and cluster approach suggested by us for general adoption for development of backward areas. There should be a continuous review of progress made in the execution of this programme at the Project and the State level. (Para 7.41)

Education

191. The problem of educational development in tribal areas is quite complex. The educational authorities and others sometimes tend to over simplify the issue by partial analysis of the problem and generally conclude the discussion with solutions which may be either too idealistic or too expensive. There are no short cuts to effective administrative and a situation of organisational failure cannot be corrected merely by providing higher capital investments. Therefore, it is necessary that comprehensive review of the reasons for the present state of education in the tribal areas is made and a package of schemes for educational development is prepared. (Para 8.6)

192. There is increasing uniformity even in the reading material at elementary level with the central production of text books and guidance from higher levels in the form of model curricula, guide books, etc. The text-books, therefore, may contain material which may be largely unfamiliar to the child. Learning in this situation becomes a burden with no relevance to his environment. The problem of language makes the situation still worse. Eventhough it has been accepted that teaching in the early classes should be through the mother tongue of the child, no satisfactory arrangements have been made in most cases. The child learns by rote without much understanding. The child misses the opportunity of developing the faculty of conceptualisation which is essential for higher learning particularly in mathematics and science. (Para 8.8)

193. A large majority of children in the elementary schools are not able to proceed beyond the lower primary classes. The defects in the educational system become contributing factors to the differential growth of education amongst different tribes and areas. (Para 8.9)

194. When educated youth are not able to move out, they find it difficult to adjust. Even thought the number of such persons is very small, they create a bad example. Youth boys get alienated from their families and traditional occupations. Thus they become maladjusted in their society. This is a national problem but the tribal communities are being required to face it even before a real beginning has been made in education. This has made some of them indifferent even to elementary education and the enrolment continues to be low in class three onwards notwithstanding the spread of educational institutions. (Para 8.10)

195. Education must assume a key role during the present phase of tribal development and must be conceived in comprehensive terms to cover all aspects of community life where they come in touch with the new system. (Para 8.11)

196. The most important aspect of education in tribal areas has to be that the community should be enabled to have a clear perspective of their relationship with the modern system. (Para 8.11)

197. Education must be meaningful to the people. This was the central theme of basic education in which the children learnt by doing and drew upon the experience in their ordinary life. (Para 8.12)

198. Education in the elementary schools should be location specific. A child who may spend eight years in a school should come out better equipped for life in the village. The curriculum should be suitably restructured so as to have elements of agriculture, forestry, animal husbandry, cottage industry, and so on. The teaching of subjects should be relatable to specific problems. They come to the student naturally in his studies of life sciences. The student should get an idea of the various institutions which are relevant to the rural economy. This should be a part of his social study course. (Para 8.12)

199. The choice of subjects at the Middle and High school levels should be provided keeping in view the local needs. (Para 8.13)

200. The tribal children show a greater promise in agriculture. It will be useful if agriculture and such other subjects are introduced as independent subjects at the High and Higher Secondary levels. Specialisation, however, should not be so narrow as may deter the student from pursuing higher studies in general institutions. (Para 8.13)

201. A programme of "citizen education" with a comprehensive

frame covering the needs of all sections of the tribal population is necessary which should basically aim at protecting the community from a sudden cultural shock and enable to it to graduate through the transitional phase without any erosion of their economic base. (Para 8.15)

202. Broadly speaking "citizen education" should comprise, *inter alia* following elements:

(i) a basic understanding about the heritage of our country;
(ii) the institutional infrastructure, particularly those institutions, which come in contact with the individual;
(iii) the rights and duties of a citizen;
(iv) the important channels for redressal of grievances;
(v) the expected code of conduct of citizen in different situation contrasting it with the traditional spontaneous responses of an individual or the community;
(vi) a better understanding of the economic process, the regulations about exchange economy and handling of money;
(vii) the basic difference between the traditional economic frame and the modern frame, particularly the value of the written tradition in contrast to the oral tradition;
(viii) the role and functioning of cooperative and other financing agencies;
(ix) an understanding of the agricultural extension services emphasising the approach rather than the content; and
(x) a greater awareness about the achievement of science and technology with special reference to his own surroundings.

(Para 8.16)

203. The precise content of the citizen education programme should be decided taking into account the present stage of each community. The programme should be built around the local tradition and should emerge as an organic whole drawing upon the tribals' own world view and should gradually help him to have a better understanding of the new system. Highest emphasis should be laid on the areas which are of day-to-day concern to him like the points of contact with the authority and methods of getting relief on various counts. (Para 8.17)

204. Planning of education infrastructure should be adapted to the existing distribution of population with the clear objectives of provid-

ing universal coverage to children by the school system and also provide an effective citizen education to the community. (Para 8.20)

205. There should be a local school in all hamlets which may admit children in class one and at the most up to class two. This local school should be a part of the formal education system. It should have a local person i.e. a person belonging to the hamlet preferably a woman as the teacher. The first problem in the backward areas will be to find a suitable person for this job. Since the condition that the individual must belong to the hamlet is crucial, it is the qualification which should be kept flexible. Any person willing to work as a teacher and who may have necessary aptitude irrespective of his own educational qualifications should be selected for this assignment. He would be given necessary training if he may not have formal education so that he can run the school for the children in the age group 5—7. At the next stage, there should be a lower primary school up to class 3 or 4 with two to three local school as feeder institutions. This L.P. school may be linked to a Sevashram. The children in these classes will be grown up and may not find it difficult to live as resident scholars. The Sevashram should also cater to the day scholars for those villages in the areas from where children may be able to walk to the institution. The day scholars should also be provided mid-day meals, a pair of school uniform, books, etc., so that there is no pressure for admission to the Sevashram. (Para 8.21)

206. A group elementary schools including local schools are treated as a unit for elementary education in the tribal areas. A group of 5 to 6 schools may constitute an Elementary School Complex. One of the schools, preferably a middle school, may be designated as the focal school of the complex. A senior teacher may be responsible for the management of all institutions in the complex. He may be given one extra hand to make day-to-day arrangements in case of absence of a teacher from his duty. The teachers in the complex may be selected in such a way that the group may have persons with aptitude in mathematics, science, language, fine arts and physical education. While each teacher may continue to work in his school, he should be in constant touch with other teachers in the complex and help them maintain good standard in his special subject. The focal school in the complex may be specially developed. It may have a small library and a science laboratory. Children and teachers from all constituent institutions in the complex may meet once a week in each school by rotation. This day may be used for common academic programme, exchange of notes amongst the teachers, citizen education and sports. This get together

will give an opportunity to the local community for active participation in the education of their children as also self-education. The elementary School complex, thus can develop as an institution for complete education of the entire community by the family of teachers under a common leadership. (Paras 8.22 and 8.23)

207. In the more advanced areas with larger villages, it may be possible to follow the general pattern of primary schools and middle schools. The proportion of middle to primary school should be gradually increased so that the educational facilities to all children up to the age of 14 becomes universal. In the first stage, each group of five primary schools should have one middle school. The schools should also cater to the educational needs of the non-student youth who may have missed the opportunity of attending school. (Para 8.24)

208. The structural imbalance at the higher secondary level should also be corrected gradually. (Para 8.25)

209. It will be necessary that in all educational programmes, particularly in the award of stipends and provision of hostel facilities, preference is given to students belonging to educationally backward tribal communities. The criteria for award of scholarships, stipends and admission to the hostel should be suitably changed subject to other eligibility conditions like distance of educational institutions from student's residence. Once fixed quota of seats are assigned to different communities on the basis of their respective numbers, the students from comparatively advanced communities will get in on the basis of merit while those belonging to the backward communities will get admitted if they satisfy the eligibility conditions. It is, therefore, necessary that the assistance programme in education are now addressed to those groups and areas which have been left far behind. (Para 8.28)

210. Even though, general assistance may continue for all communities, special schemes on a more liberal scale should be prepared for the more backward areas and more backward communities. Unless a suitable differential is built into the educational assistance scheme the gap will continue to grow and the process of educational spread may not pick up. (Para 8.28)

211. The level of literacy of a community and of an area, therefore, should be accepted as an important criterion for special assistance programme. The low literacy blocks, and now literacy regions within each block, should be identified. Similarly, the communities at low literacy level should also be identified in each state for special assistance. Those blocks which are at less than half the general literacy

level of the state may be treated as backward. Similarly, communities at less than half the level of literacy of tribal communities in that state may be considered backward. (Para 8.29)

212. The literacy among the women is particularly very low. Therefore, a special programme should be prepared for girls of those communities where the level of literacy amongst women is very low. The assistance in the case of the most backward communities should be substantial, right from the primary classes. This should continue at the middle school and higher secondary levels. (Para 8.29)

213. The residential institutions also need a second look. In the more sparsely populated areas, the residential institutions like Ashram Schools and hostels should be treated as an integral part of the institutional infrastructure for universal coverage. (Para 8.30)

214. The admission to hostels should be provided on universal basis to students living beyond a specified distance from primary/middle/higher secondary schools so that all those who want to pursue their studies are not denied the opportunity simply because there is no institution in their neighbourhood. This will also be a more economical alternative to opening of institutions in the remote areas where initially the number of students is likely to be small. (Para 8.30)

215. In the advanced areas, residential institutions should cater to selected children who are likely to make a grade in higher education. (Para 8.30)

216. In view of the fact that wide disparities have appeared in education, the Central Government should work out a scheme of assisting the States to cover the entire education programme for tribals including scholarships, stipends, hostels and Ashram Schools with differential and higher assistance for the more backward communities and areas. The assistance for this programme may be provided to help the states to achieve this objective within the next 10 to 15 years. (Para 8.31)

217. The increasing base of better qualified persons can be used for making good the deficiency in certain subjects by selective recruitments. Mathematics is an important part of elementary education. Science has now been introduced in the curriculum of the primary schools. But suitable arrangements have not been made for their teaching. Teaching in these classes requires greater skills. Therefore, graduates in Science and Mathematics could be specially inducted in the tribal areas through special recruitment. In every Elementary School Complex there should be one teacher each with background in

Mathematics and Science. The command of a language is essential for higher education. It is, therefore, necessary that one of the teachers in each Elementary School Complex should be qualified in the local dialects so as to help the students in regional languages. Such selective induction of teachers with background in Mathematics and Science will help in improving the quality of instruction in the elementary schools and provide a firm base for higher education. (Para 8.33)

218. Teaching in classes I and II should be through the mother tongue. The text-books should be accordingly planned to formulate transition from the local dialect to the regional language at the stage of class three. The teaching in the early classes should be so organised that children may get acclamatised to the translation by careful use of the local and regional language together. The appointment of local teachers in the local schools suggested earlier will meet the particular problem satisfactorily. A policy of recruitment of teachers at other levels also from the local areas will help in this process. (Para 8.34)

219. Measures may be necessary for improving the quality of personnel who are already working in these areas. Many of them are not even trained. Some of them may have been recruited with lower qualifications. (Para 8.35)

220. The school system, needs to be adjusted both in terms of its timing and its vacation. Busy agricultural period should be declared as holidays. (Para 8.36)

221. One of the important reasons for low enrolment of girls in the tribal areas is the lack of relevance of education for their roles and responsibility. If education could be made more relevant to the felt needs of the community and aspirations of the people, the girls' attendance may improve and improve substantially. (Para 8.38)

222. Even though there are inhibitions in the tribal area to send a girl to a boys school yet the presence of a lady in an institution can be added attractions to the girls. If the lady teachers could also give special instruction in useful arts, the attendance may improve. Husband wife teams may be appointed in Sevashram schools on voluntary basis without insisting on the qualifications of the lady teacher. (Para 8.39)

223. Distance is the most inhibiting factor in the girls' education. A girl may be attracted to a school within the hamlet but if she is required to go out to a distant school it may become a problem particularly in the early stages when there may be only a few girls, even one or two, who may be eligible to join a school. Once the number of girls increases, they may get together and attend even distant institutions. The

spread of educational institutions itself may help in improving the attendance of girls. The opening of pre-primary institutions with husband-wife teams as suggested above, will also improve the situation. (Paras 8.39 and 8.40)

224. The number of girls institutions however, has not increased and their needs has been relegated to a secondary position. Since distant adversely affects girls' enrolment, it is necessary that residential facilities for girls is provided on a more liberal scale than is warranted by their proportion amongst students in general. There should be at least one girls hostel in each tribal development block to begin with. It may be in the form of an Ashram School in the more backward blocks in which girls studying in higher classes may also be provided residential accommodation. (Para 8.41)

225. In blocks where girls education has picked up hostels for senior classes may be established. (Para 8.41)

226. Even though the general level of literacy amongst the women is generally low it will be necessary to adopt differential incentives for different communities and areas for girls education. (Para 8.41)

227. Girls in elementary schools may be provided with a pair of uniforms. The rate of scholarships for girls at all levels should be higher. (Para 8.41)

228. Special stipends may be given to those coming for training in various institutions, both short-term and long-term. (Para 8.41)

229. Arrangement should be made for fine arts, music, etc., in all girls' hostels and at least one selected High School in each project. (Para 8.41)

230. In view of the sparseness of population and poor communications, it is essential that the first supervisory point should be as near the institutions as possible. We have suggested the establishment of Elementary School Complexes with the head master of the middle school or the upper primary school, as the case may be, as the head. The Head Master of the school complex, therefore, should be given full responsibility for administration within the area of the jurisdiction of the complex and other isolated institutions, if any, outside the complex. (Para 8.43)

231. A distinction may be made between academic supervision and administrative control at the elementary school complex level. As far as possible only one organisation may be responsible for the administration of the all education institutions and exercise full control over them. But so far as academic supervision is concerned, it must be

unequivocally the responsibility of the education department and it should be ensured that this responsibility is properly discharged by them. (Para 8.44)

232. The preparation of syllabus, its adaptation and preparation of reading material, etc., should be the responsibility of the Education Department. The policies in this regard should be common for the tribal areas with suitable adaptation. (Para 8.45)

233. There should be a Joint Board for tribal education at the state level with Commissioner. Tribal Development or Secretary, Tribal Welfare as the Chairman and Secretary Education, Director of Public Instruction, Director Social Welfare, Director Tribal Welfare as Members. This Board should have the overall responsibility for monitoring progress of education, maintaining of standards, adaptation of programmes and for improving the quality and content of instruction and personnel. (Para 8.45)

234. A closer supervision should be exercised at the district or the project level depending on the conditions of each area. A committee may be constituted comprising Project Administrator, District Education Officer, Tribal Welfare Officer, Panchayat Officer. This Committee should report to the Joint Board at the state level. (Para 8.45)

235. The norms of technical and administrative supervision should be clearly spelt out. The Education Department should ensure that each institution is inspected once in six months by the first supervisory officer. There should be a higher level check of the standard of education in each institution the method of teaching, etc., by the Education Department once in three years. The Project Level Committee should prepare a quarterly resume of the inspection at the first supervisory and higher levels and submit it to the state level Joint Board. The Board should ensure that the necessary follow up action is taken in the case of specific problems brought out in the inspections. (Para 8.46)

Cooperatives in Tribal Areas

236. A tribal requires a package of services, the main components of which are credit for production as well as consumption, supply of seeds and other agricultural inputs and consumer goods and marketing of produce, both agricultural and minor forest. These activities constitute the major areas of exploitation of the tribals. LAMPS, if they have to be effective, have to be streamlined and restructured to provide for the following services:

(i) Provision of short, medium and long-term credit for agricultural purposes;

(ii) Provision of inputs of agriculture like fertiliser, seeds, insecticides, agricultural implements and machinery;

(iii) Provision of essential domestic requirements like foodgrains, cloth, salt, sugar, vegetable oil, kerosene, matches, tobacco, soap, etc., against the member's entitlement under the cash component of the scale of finance or against a limit specifically sanctioned for meeting his consumption needs;

(iv) Provision of technical advice and guidance needed for modernising agriculture and allied activities;

(v) Marketing of agricultural produce or products of allied activities like dairying poultry keeping, etc.;

(vi) Marketing of minor forest produce;

(vii) Provision of credit for expenses incurred to meet certain social obligations in birth, marriage or death ceremonies;

(viii) Primary processing of minor forest produce, which will provide employment and additional income to members; and

(ix) Promotion of thrift. (Para 9.13)

237. The entire package of services of the LAMPS should be available, in addition to the Scheduled Tribe, to every other poor family in the tribal sub-plan area, identified on the basis of normal criterion. (Para 9.14)

238. The LAMPS should be the only cooperative organisation in the tribal sub-plan area to handle short, medium and long-term loans for rural development. Their services in the matter of provision of credit should, therefore, be available to all participating members in the cooperative on the same lines as is available elsewhere with primary agricultural cooperatives. (Para 9.14)

239. The more affluent sections also need for input services for farm husbandry and technical advice and guidance and this should be available to them from the LAMPS. Essential domestic requirements should be available in the LAMPS specially for the benefits of the poorer sections. Sophisticated goods should not be normally maintained in the LAMPS and, if they are, they should be on a commercial basis. (Para 9.14)

240. If the viability concept is properly analysed, it will be found that it is only a block level organisation which can, over time, provide the necessary competence in the LAMPS to render all these services.

The Committee, therefore, recommends that LAMPS shall be organised only on the basis of one LAMP per block in the tribal sub-plan area. Necessary action may be taken to introduce this form of LAMPS in all the blocks in the tribal sub-plan area within a reasonable period of time which the Committee suggests may be not more than three years. (Para 9.17)

241. One centre for services at the block level does not meet the requirement of a service centre close to the client in a cooperative movement. The Bawa Committee had specifically recommended that a block level LAMPS shall have sufficient number of branches in order to cater to the rural families at places to their place of living. A branch to cover a population of roughly 10,000 to 20,000 has been suggested. The Committee endorses this recommendation. The branch will have to be suitably located taking into consideration both the population and the area of operation and in areas with scattered population, it may have to serve a population of less than 10,000. (Para 9.18)

242. The staff at the branch level need not have the high-level expertise as at the block level. They will have to carry out instructions from the head of office and should be in a position to follow orders and maintain the relative accounts. The number and the type of expertise at the branch level will certainly depend upon the level of business that the branch has to undertake. Broadly, it can be assumed the Head of Office at the Branch would be of the quality and capacity now found in LAMPS of 10,000 population. (Para 9.18)

243. The Committee urges the Centre/State Governments to make vigorous efforts immediately to develop LAMPS. (Para 9.19)

244. There should be a time bound programme supported by technical assistance from the State Governments, and where necessary, by financial aid from the State Cooperative Banks and the State Governments to vitalise and develop LAMPS so that they are in a position to discharge the functions expected of them. (Para 9.21)

245. The Committee endorses the recommendations of the Committee to Review Arrangements for Institutional Credit for Agriculture and Rural Development (CRAFICARD) that–

> "There should be two categories of membership of societies— one exclusively reserved for the weaker sections distinguished by the lower rate of share capital prescribed for them and the other earmarked for those contributing share capital at the usual rate. Everyone of these two categories of members should be supplied

with a pass book in two different colours containing all relevant details. This is to facilitate statistical reporting and analysis, and not to dilute the rights of the members belonging to the weaker sections. The entries in pass book should conform to the entries in the land register and other books of account of the society and the Validity of entries should be ensured by prompt authentification by the concerned official of the Society."

The Committee would only suggest that in the LAMPS the pass books given to the weaker sections may be divided into three classes—A for Scheduled Tribes, B for Scheduled Castes and C for other weaker sections so that statistical analysis in the tribal sub-plan can be done more effectively. Further, the pass book issued for the non-weaker sections may have a sub-group under classification A for Scheduled Tribes of the more affluent. This is necessary for proper analysis of the benefits given to Scheduled Tribes as a class. These sub-divisions should be maintained in the LAMPS registers. (Para 9.22)

246. In the tribal sub-plan, it has been provided that all members of Scheduled Tribes will be entitled to get 50 per cent of the share capital as grant-in-aid and 50 per cent as loan from the sub-plan funds. The Committee would recommend that for the other sections also 50 per cent of the share capital should be given in the form of grant-in-aid and 50 per cent as loan from the sub-plan funds. (Para 9.23)

247. The recommendations of the CRAICARD on the entries in the pass book are limited to the credit functions of a cooperative. LAMPS have multifarious functions and services to render to their clientale. The pass book should reflect all these services and the limits to which the member would get these services from the LAMPS. (Para 9.24)

248. For the first five years the cost of the organisation both at the headquarters of the LAMPS and in the branches shall be paid for by the sub-plan funds, on a telescopic scale. The Committee is well aware that this policy will mean a reasonable allocation of funds from the sub-plan provisions; but considering the importance of this service in bringing the tribal and the poorer sections out of the clutches of exploitative forces, this expenditure is basic for further development of tribal areas. The situation may be reviewed after five years and if, in particular backward areas where population is scarce and distances large, need for continuing the contribution on a tampering scale exists, the problem may be examined by the Tribal Welfare Department of the

State and remedies developed. (Para 9.25)

249. The LAMPS as envisaged by us require a high level of technical competence and management ability to set the scheme working. The Committee, therefore, recommends that the first five years when the sub-plan allocations provided the necessary funds for management expenditure in order to ensure proper performance and development of the area, it is desirable that the project officer of the I.T.D.P. will be the Chairman in the block under his Project. This will enable a suitable tie-up between the technical services and the credit services and also enable a suitable orientations of area programmes to lead to greater productivity in the area and larger business to the LAMPS. The situation may be examined after a period of five years to see whether non-official Chairman can be inducted at that stage. Even when a non-official Chairman is inducted, it is desirable that the head of the management (Managing Director) of LAMPS is given the same status as in a Farmers Service Society so that his financial discretion is suitably protected. (Para 9.26)

250. Training of the non-officials to take charge of the Cooperative system in due course, has to be an essential part of the development of tribal sub-plan areas. The cooperative movement had initiated a training programme for inclusion of cooperative principles to aspiring members of cooperative and local leadership and it will be necessary to have a similar training programme suitably adopted for the tribal areas, particularly to train the Scheduled Tribe members and leaders in the cooperative and other principles embodied in the LAMPS and how this is to benefit the population. (Para 9.27)

251. A suitable member of the Scheduled Tribe (non-official) be nominated as the Vice-Chairman of the LAMPS and in order to train him in the working he should be given some specific sectors of the LAMPS operations to handle, under the overall guidance of the Chairman. In the training courses for non-officials, such vice-chairman should be given intensive training. (Para 9.27)

252. LAMPS have to be assisted by a number of experts in various disciplines and also competent accounts and clerical staff. A separate cadre should be organised in each State for proper administration of the LAMPS which should draw its personnel, to start with, from the concerned Departments. (Para 9.28)

253. Simultaneously with the induction of officers and staff, on a limited deputation basis, from the various departmental cadres, there should be a conscious attempt to make direct recruitment to this cadre

so that in course of time the cadre stands on its own feet. The problem of stagnation would also arise even in the case of those recruited directly. A solution would have to be found for this problem by opening avenues of promotion for them in the higher organisations relating to their flow of work. (Para 9.29)

254. A proper exercise should be carried out by the Project authority as to the requirements of the officers and staff in the LAMPS and its branches keeping in view its work load and the functions. (Para 9.30)

255. The Board of Directors of the LAMPS should have other important official functionaries connected with the various organisations related with the work as well as an adequate representation of non-officials. Two-third of the non-official representation should be from the Scheduled Tribes. (Para 9.32)

256. LAMP is to take out the Scheduled Tribe members and other weaker sections of the area, from the clutches of the money-lender. All the services now being rendered by the money-lender are being looked after by the LAMPS. If no action is taken to see that dues if any legitimately due to the money-lender from the member of the LAMPS is suitably paid off, any development that takes place in the economy of the member will only result in the money-lender maintaining his clutches and taking away all the profit. Some method will have to be found for absorbing debts due from the member of the money-lender. (Para 9.33)

257. Various debt redemption laws have been passed by the various states to free the weaker sections and particularly scheduled tribes from the clutches of the money-lender, particularly in the matter of extortionate claims as against actuals given. There is the provision for courts at local level to initiate debt redemption processes and after taking evidence bring down the claims to what is decided as legitimate. For effective relief, there has to be two conditions (a) the courts will have to be local and it will be necessary to bring back the old revenue courts which dealt with these problems. It is also necessary to keep the civil courts out of this jurisdiction, (b) Oral evidence will have to be allowed against any documentary evidence as was the practice in the old agency areas of the Madras province. Both these may require drastic changes in the debt redemption, and debt regulation Acts of the various States. The Committee will recommend that immediately the relevant laws should be examined in order to amend them suitably to make these two recommendations valid. Having done this, it is necessary to

carry out an operation on a war-footing to bring down the debts to reasonable levels of all the members of the weaker sections under the LAMPS. Having done this, the debt should be taken over by the LAMPS under its account and the money-lender paid off. Similarly, the cooperative loans should be paid off and brought within the LAMPS account. For the funds required for both, provision will be made under the sub-plan funds. (Para 9.34)

258. When the cooperative movement in the TDA was originally examined, certain experiments were done in such take over of existing debts. Studies made in the Dhudi-areas under the Banawasi Sewa Ashram in Mirzapur, U.P. has shown that normally these debts are of very small amount for a family. Yet, their extortionate power is tremendous when in the hands of the money-lender. The Committee would, therefore, suggest that if the necessary action is taken for debt redemption, the amount required for take over, will not be very substantial. (Para 9.34)

259. The LAMPS after take over of the liabilities of its members will have to initiate suitable programme of development for its members to enable them not only to repay the debt taken over by the LAMPS in suitable instalments but also repay the production loans that will be necessary to the member for increasing his productivity. (Para 9.35)

260. Simultaneously with the debt regulation there has to be an aggressive development programme involving the families of the weaker sections. This necessitates that the project authority should simultaneously prepare the programme of action and see that it is implemented. (Para 9.35)

261. As regards the requirements for social purposes, these are only a few times in the life of a scheduled tribes family and if there can be provision to give the loan when required and take it back in instalments, suitably fixed, the tribal will escape the clutches of the money-lender in one of the sectors where he is most exploited. The consumption credit system must provide for a running account during the year where he gets his requirements on credit and pays back with produce as and when he collects the same. As regards the social purpose loan, it can be similarly paid back by his produce provided a suitable time frame is fixed for the return. The Committee would point out that calling this system a consumption credit purveyance is not strictly correct if the modalities of the system are examined closely. The tribal requires the credit during the year in order to keep him active. In looking

after his consumption needs it is ensured that he can actively pursue his activity and produce the necessary product either in minor forest produce or agricultural produce for discharging his liabilities. (Para 9.36)

262. As consumption requirement of the family during the year will be repaid to the LAMPS by bringing minor forest produce and other produce and the like to the LAMPS, an estimate should be made at the beginning of each year for each member as to what would be his consumption credit requirements and what would be his repayment capacity. Normally, the repayment capacity should be taken as about 1/3 to 1/2 of the amount of minor forest produce that the family is expected to gather and other produce which he may be bringing to the market. (Para 9.37)

263. As regards the consumption credit for social purposes, an overall limit should be fixed for each social performance in the area and that limit should not be exceeded for any reason. The limits may not be as high as those suggested by the Committee on consumption Credit for general purposes. Whatever it be, these limits will have to be decided preferably for the project area by the project authority and followed by the LAMPS. (Para 9.37)

264. The repayment of this loan should be distributed over a period of years as may be found convenient in the area keeping in view the possible surpluses of minor forest produce and other products which the families would be able to get, provided fair price is given. (Para 9.37)

265. The Committee would emphasise that the need for a NABARD type of operation for rural development having been accepted in the national scheme, till such an organisation comes into being, the recommendation of the CRAF ICARD that methods must be found by the Reserve Bank of India for meeting the responsibilities of NABARD till it comes into operation, should be accepted by the Reserve Bank of India and necessary action taken to fill this gap in the credit requirements for the LAMPS. If it happens that this will need any statutory amendment and there will be a time lag, the Committee recommends that till the Reserve Bank of India takes over, funds must be found from the sub-plan allocation. (Para 9.38)

266. A conscious effort should be made by the LAMPS management to see that only such essential items as are mostly needed by the tribals and the poorer section of the community are handled by them on priority basis and only after those needs have been met, they may un-

dertake distribution of non-essential items to tribals and other members provided it is economical. The Committee would like to make it clear that in recommending this approach, it is not the intention of the Committee that non-tribal members should not be provided their requirements. All that it is emphasising is that a judicious approach should be brought about in the stocking of consumer goods and the priority should be for such goods as are needed mostly by the tribal and other weaker sections of the population. (Para 9.39)

267. It is only when LAMPS give tribal a reasonable price for his produce that he would be enthused and have the necessary confidence in LAMPS and would be induced to sell his surplus produce to the LAMPS. It is equally essential for the LAMPS in their own interest to provide this facility as this is one source which would enable the tribals to repay the various types of loans which LAMPS would be advancing to them. (Para 9.40)

268. The entire system of credit and development is to be properly worked in the sub-plan areas, fixing of a fair price for commodities brought to the LAMPS by its members, is the most essential part of the operation. This price should be such that a trader or middlemen with a profit motive will not be able to overbid. At the same time, it is necessary that the organisation improves its handling and checks its leakages so that by paying such a price it does not lose in the market. The attempt to cover inefficiency by mulcting the buyer or the seller must stop. Otherwise, the system will collapse. (Para 9.42)

269. The Committee does not recommend any change in the existing linkage of the LAMPS for credit purpose and the present practice of linking them either to the District Cooperative Banks or with the Lead Commercial Banks should continue. These institutions would, however, have to ensure adequate and smooth flow of funds to LAMPS and provide the necessary guidance, supervision and also do the monitoring, etc. (Para 9.45)

270. LAMPS should be made the agents of the LDBs of that area invariably to survey long term credit in the LAMPS area of operation. No parallel primary land development bank should be allowed to have any operation in the same area. (Para 9.45)

271. The Project Authority should assess the requirements of inputs of various LAMPS under its jurisdiction and pass them on to the District or the Sub-District agency which handles supply of these inputs. As stated earlier, the inputs should be made available to the LAMPS for distribution to its members on a consignment and commis-

sion basis and all expenses incurred thereon, whether transportation, storage, etc., must be borne by the supply agency. (Para 9.46)

272. It would be the duty of the Project Authority and the Block Development Agency to provide the technical and extension support to all the programmes undertaken therein. There would have to be a complete liaison between the Block Development Agency and the LAMPS in this regard. The Committee is not in favour of recommending separate extension and technical staff in the LAMPS. (Para 9.47)

273. The Committee would recommend that whichever be the apex organisation for a particular item of produce and which is entrusted with this responsibility in the state must undertake to lift all the goods purchased by LAMPS at the price fixed by it. (Para 9.48)

274. A market intelligence cell must be set up in each of these State level bodies not only to fix a reasonable price for produce but also to enable it to market the produce, where needed. This apex body should also assess the local needs in respect of the produce which may be surplus in the production season but may later be required by local population for its own consumption. (Para 9.49)

275. It would not be possible for the LAMPS to establish direct contact either with the secondary or the apex level organisations. It would be the responsibility of the Project Authority to establish these linkages and ensure that these arrangements work smoothly. (Para 9.50)

276. The State/District level Agencies would require adequate transportation facilities for sending stocks of agricultural inputs and consumer goods to LAMPS and for collection of agricultural and minor forest produce procured by them for marketing in the internal and external markets. The number of vehicles required by these agencies would depend upon its turn over. The Committee would, therefore, strongly urge that any assistance in regard to transportation should only be to the Secondary and Apex level organisation for collecting produce from LAMPS and for supplying requirements of the LAMPS. As soon as these reach the Block Headquarter, internal distribution within the Block should be done by bullock carts etc. (Para 9.51)

277. Branches of LAMPS require godown facilities depending upon the area of operation, the capacity of the godown to be constructed may vary. The branches of LAMPS could have a small godown where as LAMPS should have a sufficiently big godown. (Para 9.52)

278. At the state level, a Review and Implementation Committee should be set up under the Chairmanship of Tribal Commissioner and consisting of representatives of all concerned organisations at the State level to take stock of progress made in implementation of various schemes and providing further direction. (Para 9.53)

Organisation of Administrative and Financial Structures

279. The report of the National Committee on the Organisation of Administrative and Financial Structures for backward areas development covers all the aspects so far as tribal area is concerned as these would get classified as "backward". (Para 10.1)

280. The Project approach, with necessary modifications with regard to administrative and financial autonomy, should be implemented in the tribal areas. (Para 10.2)

281. The Committee has also dealt with in the relevant chapter (Chapter 8) of this report on Organisation of Administrative and Financial Structures, the methodology of plan allocations to backward areas, including tribal areas, budget provisions, special project fund for local planning, placing of funds with the project authorities, delegation of adequate powers, unused funds, etc. (Para 10.5)

282. Good administration of tribal areas is the key to success in tribal development, particularly during the transitional phases, when the economy may undergo structural change and the community may face enormous challenges. The level of administration should be assessed and the Centre should provide suitable assistance for raising the level of administration of the tribal areas to that of other areas within a reasonable time. (Para 10.7)

283. The Finance Commission may be specifically asked to go into the question of grants-in-aid to the States for good administration of scheduled areas and development of tribal communities. Pending the availability of the findings of the Finance Commission, as and when such a reference is made, the Committee would urge that:

(i) Special Central Assistance for the tribal sub-plan areas should gradually increase till all the elements envisaged in the plan get fully operationalised;

(ii) The cost of incentive to be given to the personnel posted in the tribal sub-plan areas recommended by the Committee as also any other strengthening of the administration to bring it to a minimum norm should be given by the Government of India as a part of its annual grants-in-aid to the State Government; and

(iii) Assistance to the States for tribal welfare programme in the State Plan sector, which is being separately shown in the Central Grant under Gadgil formula, should be specifically assessed and made non-divertible. (Para 10.11)

284. It has to be admitted that Tribal Areas suffer from certain disabilities like lack of housing, educational, medical facilities, etc. Consequently, there is strong disinclination on the part of the Government officials to serve in these areas. The National Committee has dealt with the personnel aspects in Chapter 7 of its report on Organisation of Administrative and Financial Structures. The Seminar on Tribal Development in Bhubaneshwar also went into this question in great detail, and recommended the following measures to attract suitable personnel to serve in the tribal areas:

(i) The places of postings in tribal areas should be graded on the basis of accessibility, availability of social services, etc. and suitable special pay should be given to persons posted there;

(ii) Scholarships to enable children of such persons as are posted in places without a Middle School or a High School should be given, subject to a maximum of two children;

(iii) Free housing should be provided to all personnel working in the tribal areas. In case, residential accommodation is not available, suitable compensatory allowance should be given;

(iv) Long term benefit should be given to persons rendering satisfactory service of 5 years or more in the tribal areas in the shape of higher pension and gratuity on retirement;

(v) Preference should be given to the personnel who have worked in the Tribal areas in the selection for foreign assignments/ training abroad and awards of fellowships, etc.;

(vi) All personnel of the State and the All India services should be obliged to serve in the tribal areas within five years of their initial entry into service;

(vii) Personnel serving in the Tribal areas should be encouraged to learn recognised tribal dialects for which training facilities should be provided. Those who undergo such training and attain required proficiency should be given lump-sum monetary rewards;

(viii) Special care should be taken for selecting the right type of personnel for service in the Tribal areas particularly at the level of Block Development Officers, Project technical heads and Project Director. Their tenure in a Project should be for a minimum period of 3 years and it would be fair to give them postings at good places on completion of such tenure in tribal areas; and

(ix) The Central Government should provide special funds under Article 275(i) of the Constitution for raising the level of Administration in the Tribal areas and the measures suggested above should qualify for such assistance.

The Committee is in full agreement with the above recommendations and would strongly urge their acceptance by the Union/State Governments. (Para 10.12)

24

NATIONAL COMMITTEE ON THE DEVELOPMENT OF BACKWARD AREAS, 1978 — REPORT ON GENERAL ISSUES RELATING TO BACKWARD AREAS DEVELOPMENT

November 30, 1978 — November 30, 1981[1]

Chairman Shri B. Sivaraman, Member, Planning Commission

Members Shri Som Dutt; Prof. Mrinal Datta Chaudhary (ceased to be member w.e.f. November 30, 1978); Shri S.S. Marathe (ceased to member w.e.f., November 30, 1978); Shri Ranchor Prasad; Shri Ramakrishanayya; Shri K.P.A. Menon; Shri R.M. Honavar (ceased to be member w.e.f. January 31, 1981); Dr. S.A. Dave; Dr. Y Nayudamma; Shri Anand Sarup; Dr. B.D. Sharma; Shri Suresh Mathur; Dr. D.M. Nanjundappa; Shri S.M. Ghosh

M. Secy. Shri Nitin Desai

Appointment

The Government have been pursuing certain policies and programmes in regard to the development of backward areas since the Fourth Five Years Plan. It is now necessary to review the working of these various programmes and to set out a suitable strategy or strategies for the development of Backward Areas in the context of the priorities and objectives set out in the draft 1979-83 plan. The Planning Commission have, therefore, decided to set up a High Level Committee to formulate appropriate strategy or strategies for effectively tackling the problems of Backward Areas vide its Resolution No. PC(P)17/NCDBA/78-MLP dated November 30, 1978.

---

1. Planning Commission, Government of India, New Delhi, 1982, xv + 135 p.

Terms of Reference

(i) To examine the validity of the various concepts of backwardness underlying the definitions in use for present policy purposes and recommend the criteria by which backward areas should be identified.

(ii) To review the working of:

(a) the existing plans for dealing with the general development problems of backward areas like Tribal Sub-Plans, Plans for Hill Areas, etc.; and

(b) the existing schemes for stimulating industrial development in backward areas such as the schemes for concessional finance, investment subsidy, transport subsidy, sales tax concessions, etc., similar schemes in the agricultural and allied fields like DPAP, and general measures for tackling the problems of poverty and unemployment with a view to find out their efficacy in the removal of backwardness; and

(iii) To recommend an appropriate strategy or strategies of effectively tackling the problem of backward areas, classified, if necessary, according to areas, causes or prescribed remedies.

Contents

Summary of Conclusions and Recommendations; Introduction; Past Approaches to the Problems of Backwardness; Evaluation of Rural Development Programmes; Concept of Backwardness; Criteria and Strategy of Backward Area Development; Industrial Development of Backward Area; Statistical Base for Local Planning; Focal Point—An Area-cum-Beneficiary Oriented Approach; Growth Centre as the Catalyst of Area Development; Credit; Rural Marketing; Organisation and Administration; *Annexures* 1.1 to 1.9; Chapter 4 – 4.1; Chapter 6 – 6.1 and 6.2; Chapter 7 – 7.1; Chapter 8 – 8.1; Chapter 9 – 9.1; Chapter 11 – 11.1 to 11.6.

Recommendations

Introduction

Past Approaches to the Problems of Backwardness

1. The problem of regional balance and of backwardness has

attracted the attention of planners. The problem has sometimes been seen in terms of inter-state disparities though there is also a recognition that there are many disparities within each state also. The emphasis has been on backwardness in terms of economic performance though the impact of historical and social factors on economic matters has been recognised. A clear concept of backwardness seems to be missing and the term is used in a more or less in vague sense to designate areas that do not seem to be benefiting adequately from general development measures. The more concrete steps taken involve mainly special schemes like the subsidies for industry of the social area development programmes. Many of these special schemes are more palliatives that fail to tackle the root of the problems of backwardness. What seems to be missing is the recognition that most backward areas have a potential for growth which can be tapped if certain special initiatives are taken. The important task of planning for backward areas is to identify what these special initiatives are in each type of backward area. (Para 2.19)

Evaluation of Rural Development Programmes

2. Various physical surveys were supposed to have been carried out as a prelude to the schemes but have, in general, not been carried out. (Paras 3.11 and 3.16)

3. Although block level lists of small farmers, marginal farmers and agricultural labourers, have not usually been kept, the studies did not find major leakages in terms of subsidies and credits going to ineligible families. The range of leakages in terms of proportion of misclassified beneficiaries was usually less than 20 per cent. (Para 3.17)

4. Leakages can be reduced if the required lists of SF, MF and AL kept updated at the block level. (Para 3.17)

5. Initial expenses amounted to 50 to 75 per cent of the subsidy component of loan-subsidy depending on the beneficiary's status as SF, MF or AL. It was found that since preliminary expenses were always substantial many beneficiaries had to resort to high interest personal loans to cover these expenses. Non-pecuniary costs of the certification process included the resultant delays as well as loan rejections arising from minor errors that are prone to be found in certificates. The prescription of such certification is also an obvious invitation to corruption. (Para 3.20)

6. It is difficult to avoid documentation entirely but the

maintenance of updated lists would also minimise the necessity for different kinds of certificates. A reduction in the number of documents required would also reduce the volume of travel and other expenses. (Para 3.20)

7. The vast majority of beneficiaries in the livestock linked schemes were found in villages with better transportation linkages. (Para 3.21)

8. Many of the programmes have not been as successful as expected because of the lack of integrated planning of related facilities and coordination between the different agencies involved. The evaluation studies seem to indicate that existing arrangements for coordination and integrated planning at the local level are not very effective. Improvements in arrangements for local planning and coordination are essential if the special programmes are to succeed. (Para 3.77)

9. One important aspect of coordination is the link between beneficiary oriented schemes and area development measures. The evaluations bring out the importance of the infrastructure in ensuring that beneficiaries can take full advantage of the schemes directed at them. Deficiencies in infrastructure arises not merely from the lack of financial resources but also from shortage of personnel. Hence, there is a vital need to link up beneficiaries oriented schemes with area development measures and the provision of infrastructure. (Para 3.78)

10. There have been many deficiencies in the support systems. The correct technical advice has often not been given. Critical elements like marketing support have been missing in some cases. Arrangements for technology transfer like farmers training have not been very effective. (Para 3.79)

11. Systematic efforts to spread the impact of programmes on the interior are necessary if the special programmes are to achieve their purpose. (Para 3.80)

12. There is a general tendency in plan programmes to concentrate on new investments and not pay sufficient attention to the maintenance of past investments. This feature has been brought out by the evaluations of the special programmes also. It would be useful if the repair of deteriorated facilities and the maintenance of existing assets become an integral part of the planning process. It may be possible to use the Food for Work Programme for this purpose. (Para 3.81)

13. The procedures which the beneficiary have to follow to obtain

assistance are very complex and need some simplification. The assumed economics of the schemes meant for beneficiaries participated also needs to be cross-checked and reviewed from time to time. (Para 3.82)

Concept of Backwardness

14. There are no absolute standards of "backwardness" as there are not such standards for 'development'. Hence the concept is relative one and in the ranking of areas, as perceived by people, all but the ones at the top are seen to be 'relatively backward'. The root of the problem lies in the lack of clarity on the concept of backwardness and its relevance for the processes of planned development. In multi-tier democracy it is also necessary that there should be some degree of consensus behind the specific definitions used to make the concept operational. (Paras 4.3 and 4.5)

15. Backward areas must have a potential for development and there must be some reasons for supposing that by detailed planning, administrative and financial support the productivity of the areas can be raised. This presumes that the area has potential for growth which at present has not been dealt with satisfactorily. Where there is no potential for growth, the answer, as already indicated in past plans, lies in out-migration. Thus for purposes of planning, the areas identified as backward must have three key characteristics:

(a) They must have potential for development;
(b) There must be some inhibiting factor which prevents this potential from being realised; and
(c) There must be a need for special programme to remove or mitigate the inhibiting factor and realise the full potential for development. (Para 4.7)

16. The concept of backwardness that the National Committee considers relevant for planned development is that an area is backward if it is in need of special measures, in order to utilise its development potential to the full. In this context, special measures are not merely a question of finance but will involve directional departures or changes in the complex of policies, programmes, technologies, and institutional arrangements in the various sections of development (Para 4.7)

17. The index based approach require specification of the

following:

(i) A set of basic indicators;

(ii) A procedure for weighting or aggregating so that these indicators can be reduced to a single measures; and

(iii) A cut-off point below which areas are to be considered backward.

The principal problem with the index based approach is that there is a great deal of arbitrariness at each one of the three stages. This arbitrariness leaves much scope for disputation. (Para 4.12 and 4.14)

18. From the point of view of the Committee there is a difficulty in the type of indicators chosen. Generally these indicators reflect the results of a development process rather than the casual factors which led to the present situation. The Committee has suggested a concept of backwardness which requires the identification of areas in need of special measures to alleviate the constraints on development. It is not all clear that the types of socio-economic variables used in the index-based exercises reflect this orientation. The aggregation of a variety of indicators into a single measure poses many difficulties. Since the choice of indicators does not necessarily reflect a prior analysis of relevant factors, there is as yet not acceptable method of aggregation. (Para 4.16 and 4.17)

19. The index-based approach does not classify districts into problem categories and in fact further analysis is required in order to do this. There is also no indication that those below the cut-off are all developable and have the requisite potential. (Para 4.20)

20. Poverty and unemployment may be manifestations of backwardness but are certainly not causative factors. There are areas which have to be treated as backward even though they do not show a high poverty percentage or rate of unemployment. (Para 4.22)

21. With regard to estimates of domestic product at district/ block level, some rudimentary calculations are possible. However, the usefulness of such income estimates is open to question. The income generated in an area is not the same as the income accruing. At a block or district level the difference between these two concepts can be quite substantial. (Para 4.23)

22. It has been suggested that instead of using an overall index it may be easier to define sectoral indices to identify backwardness with respect to specific sectors of development, e.g., agricultural

backwardness, industrial backwardness, educational backwardness, etc. The Committee feels that such sectoral indicators would also have to face the problem of identifying relevant indicators, aggregating them and defining cut-off points unless there happens to be the same single indicator and a well-defined norm on which there is a fair measure of agreement. (Para 4.24)

23. The Committee feels that the present position with regard to data availability and the development of methodologies is such that an index-based approach to the identification of backward area cannot be recommended. Such an approach will not be able to take into account all the relevant factors in an objective manner and the subjective judgements regarding the choice of indicators, weighting patterns and cutoff points will be open to extensive disputation. (Para 4.25)

24. The term 'problem areas' has to be understood in the context of the concept of backwardness indicated by the Committee. The specificity of technological possibilities, variations in the sectoral mix of economic activity, differences in infrastructure requirements and difficulties in the participation of local people in the economic activities, will to some extent, be found in almost any area. However, there are certain areas where these problems are of an order that requires special measures. In this sense backwardness as defined in the problem area approach is also a matter of degree. The usefulness of the problem area approach lies in the fact that it avoids aggregating very different types of areas into one generalised category labelled 'backward'. The problem area approach is constructive in the sense that the process of defining and identifying backward areas itself suggests the nature of the remedies that have to be applied. (Paras 4.27 to 4.30)

25. The National Committee would recommend that the following types of problem areas be treated as backward for purpose of planning.

(i) Chronically drought prone areas;
(ii) Desert areas;
(iii) Tribal areas;
(iv) Hill areas;
(v) Chronically flood affected areas; and
(vi) Coastal areas affected by salinity.

These six categories can be viewed as six types of fundamental backwardness. In this sense an area may suffer from the handicap of more than one type of fundamental backwardness. (Para 4.35)

26. The six types of fundamental backwardness identified will help to identify the areas where suitable area specific development strategies can give results. However, there is one constraint which can make this difficult. This arises from the prevalence of feudal elements in production relations. The main characteristics of feudalism is that the fruits of labour go to the people at the top and as a result, the vast mass of people at the bottom have no incentive to change. Hence directional change and area specific strategies will have no effect unless the overall fundamental defect of feudal social structure is corrected. (Para 4.37)

27. There are many areas where the potential for development is not realised because administrative systems are poorly developed and indifferently staffed. The Committee recognises the gravity of this problem but for backwardness as a further type of backwardness. (Para 4.38)

28. The Committee has also considered the problem of industrial dispersal and in that context identified certain areas as being in need of special measures to promote industrialisation. It is a matter of history and cannot be lined up straightaway with an index of local potential of human endeavour. It is in a class by itself and remedies have to be sought, not in area development schemes, but in the creation of a commercial and industrial environment in a dispersed network of growth centres. (Para 4.40)

Criteria and Strategy for Backward Area Development

29. The Committee has dealt with the development problems of these areas and suggested remedies in separate reports. These recommendations should form the basis for action in these areas. (Para 5.2)

30. There are some areas which can fall into more than one category of backwardness. For example, there is an extensive overlap between tribal and hill areas particularly in the north-east. There is also some overlap between tribal and drought prone areas, e.g., in south-east Rajasthan. In these cases the appropriate strategy has to be to combine the remedies suggested for both types of areas. (Para 5.3)

Industrial Development of Backward Areas

31. The salient features of the specific recommendations of the Committee for operationalising the strategy for industrial dispersal are listed below:

(i) The cut-off criterion for the selection of centres for the development of medium and large industry would be that they should have a population of at least 50,000 and that they should be situated at a minimum distance from an existing industrial centres. For this purpose "existing industrial centres" should be all towns/urban agglomerations with an employment in non-household manufacturing of over 10,000. The minimum distance should be 150 km. for centres with an employment of over 150 thousand, 100 kms. for centres with an employment of 50–150 thousand, 75 km. for centres with an employment of 25–50 thousand and 50 km. for centres with an employment of 10–25 thousand;

(ii) 100 such centres should be selected out of all eligible towns for development in the Sixth Plan;

(iii) Each growth centre should be managed by an Industrial Development Authority which would have the charter to development and provide the necessary infrastructural support as well as to mobilise funds from institutions like IDBI, HUDCO, etc.;

(iv) For institutions like IDBI, HUDCO, etc., to play an effective role, it would be desirable that appropriate financial support to these institutions is assured during the plan period;

(v) State Governments should undertake to provide the requisite infrastructural facilities at these selected locations and to orient their own promotional efforts in the same direction. Urban Development programmes may be used in these centres on a priority basis; and

(vi) The schemes of Central capital subsidy, concerning finance and income-tax concessions may continue for the Sixth Plan period for all small industries located outside the cut-off areas specified under recommendation (i) whether located in a growth centre or not. The infrastructural support the Committee will be recommending for each growth centre will not be available for industries which may come outside such growth centres. (Para 6.6)

32. The Committee accepts that the spill over effects of a centre outside state may be somewhat lower than in the State itself and some modifications of the distances may be acceptable. A shorter distance accepted by general consensus among the states for such a situation, may be used for determining ineligible areas in a state because of the effects of existing centres outside the states. (Para 6.8)

33. The cut-off distances recommended by the Committee reflect a judgement which the Committee considers valid. The main argument advanced by states is for a shorter distance. The Committee is prepared to accept a shorter distance criteria provided the distance is not made so short that our objective of industrial dispersal is in all the backward areas of the country is thereby not reached within a foreseeable future. (Para 6.9)

34. The Committee has defined existing centres on the basis of the level of employment in non-household manufacturing as per the 1971 census. It has been argued that non-household manufacturing includes large number of workers and in small scale manufacturing units whose spread effects are likely to be much less than that of large factories. Hence it has been suggested that the cut-off distances applicable to centres where the major part of employment is in tiny units should be somewhat lower. The Committee feels that there is some validity in this argument. (Para 6.10)

35. The transport subsidy scheme in its present state does not seem to be very effective as is clear from the very low level of disbursements. Hence the National Committee is of the view that an alternative approach is required to meet the problem of high transport costs and uncertain availability of raw materials in remote areas. (Para 6.25)

36. The Committee would suggest that transport subsidy scheme should be linked up with the improved arrangements for raw material supply. The Committee has recommended that establishment of a state level supply and marketing corporation for supporting small and village industries. In the view of the Committee, these corporations should be responsible for much of the raw material supply from outside the regions. (Para 6.27)

37. The Committee would recommend that, for the controlled or canalised raw material, the transport subsidy should be calculated on the basis of the lowest cost of transportation from the actual supply point to the concerned depot of the support organisation. (Para 6.27)

38. The transport subsidy on raw materials on items other than

canalised and controlled material, as also the supplies obtained directly by industrial enterprises in the eligible areas should be paid on the following basis:

(i) The source of supply may be deemed to be Delhi for eligible areas in J&K and Himachal Pradesh, Lucknow for eligible areas in U.P. and Calcutta for eligible areas in the north-east, Sikkim and West Bengal or the actual supply point if it is nearer;

(ii) For a certain distance from the deemed or actual source of supply no subsidy should be payable. This cut-off distance will have to vary for the different eligible areas and may be determined after closer study by the Ministry of Industrial Development. This same subsidy may also determine the proportion of transport costs for movement beyond the cut-off distance which would be subsidised; and

(iii) Through road movement should be supported and the norms for permissible road haulage and costs may be determined by the Ministry of Industrial Development. (Para 6.28)

39. With regard to the regions to be covered the Committee would recommend the inclusion of the Darjeeling district of West Bengal to the present list. (Para 6.29)

40. The Committee would not recommend any change in the class of eligible units or the quantum of the subsidy. However, the subsidy should also cover coal and petroleum products but in this case it should be calculated on the basis of the costs of transportation beyond the specified rail head only. (Para 6.29)

41. In the case of Andaman and Nicobar Islands and Lakhshadweep, port charges, should be included in the calculation of transports costs. (Para 6.29)

42. Apart from the transport subsidy, the Committee would recommend that more stock yards and depots should be established in the remote regions in which the transport subsidy is applicable for the supply of raw-materials by public sector organisations like the SAIL, STC, NSIC, etc. (Para 6.30)

43. Till such time as more stock yards are established the costs of transportation upto district headquarters should be absorbed in the national system. (Para 6.30)

44. An assessment of the raw material requirements in the

backward regions should be prepared by the Ministry of Industries who should then pursue the matter with the concerned Central Organisations for ensuring the necessary supplies. (Para 6.30)

45. The Committee would suggest that in any pricing system for commodities produced or marketed through the public sector, a degree of freight subsidisation on supplies to remote areas would be worthwhile. (Para 6.31)

46. A subsidy on the transport costs of sending products out of the region may be of some relevance mainly for some small and village industries. In these cases the transport subsidy on the movement of output may be paid to the official organisations which offer marketing support to small and village industries. The principles underlying such a subsidy may be as follows:

(i) The destination of output may be deemed to be Delhi for eligible areas in J&K and Himachal Pradesh, Lucknow and for eligible areas in U.P. and Calcutta for eligible areas in the north-east, Sikkim and West Bengal or the actual destination whichever is the nearer;

(ii) For a certain distance upto the deemed or actual destination no subsidy should be payable. This cut-off distance would have to vary for different eligible areas and may be determined after clear study by the Ministry of Industrial also determine the proportion of transport costs for movements beyond the cut-off distance which would be subsidised; and

(iii) Through road movement should be supported and the norms for permission road haulage and costs may be determined by the Ministry of Industrial Development. (Para 6.32)

47. Irrespective of a transport subsidy, improving the transport infrastructure in the remote regions is a necessary prerequisite for industrialisation. The development of new roads bridges or other transport facilities that shorten the distance to the national road and rail network may have a more significant impact on the costs of transport for a wide range of industries. (Para 6.33)

48. A scheme to subsidise trucking operations in remote regions may be considered. This could take the form of loans on concessional terms for the purchase of trucks, provided these trucks are based in these areas. The growth of locally based truck fleets would improve the availability of transport facilities, which may be of greater

consequence particularly for small industries or low-weight/high volume industries. (Para 6.34)

49. The Committee would recommend that the freight rates from the remote regions as presently identified for the transport subsidy scheme, to the nearest metropolitan areas should be set at a concessional level. (Para 6.35)

50. The National Committee recognises that the State Governments will wish to promote industrial development in all areas within their territorial boundaries. The Committee would however, suggest that the State Governments cannot plead for central schemes for industrialisation of backward areas if their own actions work against the orientation of these central schemes. Once a certain consensus on the concept and definition of industrially backward areas is reached, then the Central and State Governments must work together to promote industrial development in the identified areas. Hence the State Government schemes must also reflect the same geographical orientation as the Central schemes. They must build in a preference in their own schemes of concession for the areas identified as industrially backward for the central schemes. (Para 6.42)

Statistical Base for Local Planning

51. These exercises in local planning for backward area development cannot be undertaken in any effective manner if the data base for such planning is not built up. (Para 7.1)

52. With regard to crop statistics the coverage of horticultural crops and minor crops, which may be important in some areas needs to be improved. The classification of non-cropped areas needs further refinement and elaboration and categories like "barren and uncultivable lands" have to be defined more precisely, since new developments in technology may well make many of these areas usable for production purposes. These refinements and elaboration in the classification of non-cropped area may be particularly important in backward areas. (Para 7.5)

53. From the point of view of local planning the principle deficiency in the system for estimating yields lies in the fact that the estimates as presently made may not be valid at the block level. It will, therefore, be necessary to supplement present arrangements by a special coverage at block level of important crops in that block. (Para 7.6)

54. The sample surveys for yields estimates presently exclude many agricultural activities like horticulture, animal husbandry, fisheries, etc. Hence measures to obtain estimates of yields will be required for these activities at block level. (Para 7.7)

55. There is a quinquennial census which provides comprehensive data on livestock, agricultural machinery, implements, etc. These data can and should be processed at the block level to provide a base for animal husbandry statistics. At present these datas are collected on a household basis but are not being tabulated in a manner which shows distribution of livestock assets by household categories. This is an important element in local planning and should be covered in the tabulation programmes. (Para 7.10)

56. There is an elaborate scheme of farm surveys which collects detailed data on cost structure, input use, etc. At the block level, a supplemental effort at analysing the techno-economics of major agricultural activities in the block will have to be made by the district statistical system. (Para 7.11)

57. Unit level information must be stored in a readily retrievable form so that the schedules are easily reprocessed to obtain information in a different format if required. The primary data must be stored in two sets of cards/discs/tape decks. One of these should be accessible to all Central and State Governments Departments and organisations, research workers and academicians so that they can reprocess primary data in the manner required for their analysis. The Committee understands that this has been accepted for NSS data. The principle should be extended to all data sources. (Para 7.13)

58. In the industrial sector comprehensive data is not available even for the number of units let alone for magnitudes like production, input use and employment. Moreover, the system of enquiry lacks coherence in that there is an overlap between some systems and a total exclusion of certain sectors. (Para 7.14)

59. The data from the Factory Act Records and Economic Consensus of 1977 and 1980 can be tabulated block-wise. This should be done and the lists and estimates emerging from this should be compared with the lists maintained by the IDC and by local offices of bodies like the Handloom Directorate, Coir Board, etc., so as to construct a complete sample frame. (Para 7.15)

60. The Committee would recommend that the DIC and the project group for village industries should carry out regular surveys of units in their area to collect data on raw material requirements,

marketing problems, labour requirements, etc. The surveys can concentrate on the major sectors in the block and district. This can be organised on a census basis if the number of units is not very large and on a sample basis otherwise. (Para 7.16)

61. Local agencies like the DIC and the project group for village industries must undertake techno-economic studies of this nature for a few sectors of importance within this area. Management institutes and other academic bodies must be used in a systematic way for this purpose. (Para 7.17)

62. The data system for the service sector is particularly weak except where the service activity is in the public sector. These enterprises will also be covered in the Economic Census and it would be desirable to institute some system of sample surveys and techno-economic studies for these sectors as has been suggested for small and village industries. (Para 7.18)

63. It would be desirable to ensure that as and when the household card system in a project area is complete, the relevant data are transmitted to the agencies responsible for the census/sample enquires. (Para 7.19)

64. The data system suggested above rests on four censuses : the Population Census, the agricultural Census, the Livestock Census and the Economic Census. These provide the bedrock on which the rest of the system is constructed. It is essential that the concepts and definitions used in these censuses are consistent and stable from census to census. (Para 7.20)

65. It is necessary that the tabulation plans for all census based enquiries be modified to provide block level table. (Para 7.21)

66. The State level organisations like the Statistical bureau have their own statistical staff. At present much of the time of this State Statistical Staff is used to undertake survey on a matching sample basis with the NSS. In a sense they are duplicating the work done by the NSS, by now the size of the central sample in the NSS is large enough to provide valid estimates at State or sub-region level and there is no real need for a matching State sample. The State Governments resources are better utilised to fill in the gaps in the data system for local planning. (Para 7.22)

67. The staff required for field work is available. However, all of this staff is not under unified control. What is required for the effective use of this staff is co-ordination. This can and should be done by the District Statistical Officer who is in position, at present, in most

districts. (Para 7.23)

68. The work to be done has to be assigned to the different field workers on the basis of an agreed work plan. The basis for this must be a plan which specify the items of data to be collected and the proposed coverage of enterprises or households in the block and the district. This must be done by the district planning authority, the project authority, the DIC and other planning agencies in consultation with the District Statistical Officer. (Para 7.23)

69. The decentralisation of processing capabilities is very important if data is to be made available in good time. Moreover, the ready availability of processing facilities at local level will encourage a more constructive use of statistical data in local planning. Hence there should be a data processing set-up attached to the D.S.O. (Para 7.25)

70. The planning agencies at block/project/district level will have to obtain data from the various agencies involved and put them together in the form of a statistical abstract. This abstract should cover not just the general economic data but also the statistics generated as part of the administrative process. In many states this is being done at the district level. The National Committee would recommend the same should be done at block and project level. (Para 7.26)

Focal Point — An Area-Cum-Beneficiary Oriented Approach

71. A closer link is required between infrastructure development and programmes which are feasible in the area and further between these programmes and the capacity of the families to absorb the technology. It is this tie up between the family-wise approach and the area approach that has to be established at the focal points. (Para 8.13)

72. Such an approach, has to be as close to the beneficiaries as possible. The appropriate level has to be a cluster of villages, with a population of 15,000—20,000, where plans would be implemented and family-wise contacts built up. It is in this context that the Committee is recommending a focal point approach to take care of both the beneficiary and the area-oriented needs. (Para 8.14)

73. The selection of the village as a focal point will have to be done very carefully. Broadly speaking, the Committee would suggest that the village so selected should be reasonably big village, it should be centrally-located geographically and its activities should cover as far as possible, within a radius of 5 kms. (Para 8.16)

74. The Committee considers that each focal point should have

certain rural infrastructure facilities, depending on the potential identified, both for agricultural and non-agricultural activities. The focal point should also provide the necessary economic and social services to the rural community. (Para 8.17)

75. Integrated Rural Development Programme should be implemented through the establishment and development of focal points (growth centres) in a planned manner so that the village is, as far as possible, more than 10 km. from such a focal point. In this manner, the planning process will be brought nearer to the field and the schemes will be more relevant to the problems and potentialities of the selected areas and its people. In such cluster, one village should be developed as a focal point. (Para 8.17)

76. It would be the duty of the Project Authority to ensure that the rural development programmes of the cluster are not implemented as a separate programme with its own chain of command but are linked and coordinated with other Block level programmes as necessary. (Para 8.19)

77. The Committee would, emphasise that it is essential that whatever be the programme, necessary support must be available to the focal point from the Block level. If this requires some strengthening of particular discipline, this will have to be under taken. (Para 8.20)

78. A comprehensive resource survey is generally regarded as the first stage of assessing the potential for development. The resources survey should aim at and be limited to such of the resources which can be developed with the technology at present available, the manpower in the area and the skill available and the state of the infrastructure and the administrative competence that is also available to translate potential into increasing the gross product. Identification of the resources that are to be studied in some depth for preparation of the plan for the Block is, therefore, to be the first exercise. The Committee recommends that this process should be carried out by the peripatetic team having a detailed dialogue first with the project level advisory group, helped by the administration at the project and the block level helped by higher level technical experts. (Para 8.21)

79. The initial exercise will have to be based on development of the area by the people. Exogenous development by entrepreneurship and skills from outside the area should be reserved for a later part of the planning process. The planning group will then organise survey of these resources only in the first run, on the basis of such statistical information as is readily available. Too much time should not be taken

in getting into details of village-wise statistics at this stage. (Para 8.22)

80. The experience of the actual working of the schemes in many parts of the country shows that the essential requirement of dovetailing a viable area programme with the family-wise approach has not received sufficient attention so far, may be because a workable methodology has not yet developed. The Committee is of the view that unless a methodology is prescribed which is understood by the field level organisations of the various development administrations and their respective role clearly defined in the process, this tie up cannot take place. (Para 8.25)

81. The initial remuneration of the families, their occupation and income for the bench mark survey will be relevant to all types of methodology for their development. This exercise will take time. Hence programmes should be phased over a period of five years. Any attempt to rush this time phase will be counter productive at the end. (Para 8.26)

82. Having decided on a quinquennial time frame for the family-wise approach, a haphazard identification of one-fifth of the families in a block each year will also not be desirable. The Committee would recommend that five foci, suitably placed in important villages in the block, and sufficiently dispersed over the area of the block, may be selected for starting the family-wise assessment. For each of these regions, the family-wise study and link up of the programme will have to be phased over a five year period. (Para 8.27)

83. Before, members of the family can be asked the question as to what development programmes they will adopt, there has to be sufficient dialogue between the planners and the people to explain what sort of programmes available. (Para 8.28)

84. The planning group having identified the type of development programmes which are suitable of the area, it is necessary to examine whether there are already nucleii of various programmes in the block. Where there are no nucleii of such programmes, pilot programmes will have to be established as demonstration centres in the block. (Para 8.29)

85. Simultaneously with the preparation of the block programmes and enumeration of the families and their capacity, a parallel demonstration programme of the various developmental approaches available and considered suitable in the area should be started. (Para 8.29)

86. The planning process will be a continuous one, refining the

family-wise approach as programmes are demonstrated and families adopt them. One should not wait for perfection before starting the link up between family-wise approach and the area programmes, in each block in each of the mandals there must be some programme or the other considered suitable for the area which are already in operation and showing results. (Para 8.30)

87. There are certain programmes already in the plan which develop certain infrastructure in the area which can be availed of for development of various classes of families in the area. (Para 8.32)

88. The general development programmes in the area will have a definite role in giving greater income opportunities to all classes of the population. In the family-wise approach, the planning group should take this into consideration and see how much of the families which were not given a link up with a development programme during the year can be benefited by the area programme. It will then be their duty to enumerate such families who will benefit and see that the extension organisation attends to them and that they get the required benefit. (Para 8.32)

89. The path that the Committee has recommended tries to adjust the programme at each stage with the facilities that are available at that point of time.

The sequence of action is as follows:

(a) development programmes which are already understood in the areas and are suitably demonstrated, should be linked up with the family approach;
(b) general schemes of development which automatically lead to the development of families within the ambit of the schemes are to be identified and the beneficiaries listed and their requirements ensured;
(c) simultaneously, tightening of the effectiveness of the input supplies including credit and the health and pest control measures so as to give necessary coverage to every family in the rural areas covered by the programme; and
(d) demonstrating new programmes in the Block first and then enumerating families for coverage in different clusters. (Para 8.33)

90. By merely training the available block staff in the statistical exercise, it should be possible without any large expenditure to

complete the family wise survey and fill up the forms in a matter of two months. If the planning authorities choose the lean season, it is easy to depute the various developmental staff, particularly the village level workers and agriculture staff for completing this exercise. Any additional expenditure on stationery, transport, etc., should be a part of the plan expenditure. (Para 8.34)

91. All our area programmes were started with the objective of developing the production potential of the area on the basis of the introduction of new technology and provision of suitable institutional, infrastructural etc., facilities. The planning group will have to provide for the development of all the families in the area considered suitable for a programme or programmes. The Committee emphasised that what they are seeking is development of the area as a whole by utilising the resources of the area and not merely a selective development of the poorer sections only. (Para 8.34)

92. Today, the agricultural labour and rural labour suffer from having to sell their wages in a buyers market. The general growth that can be initiated and should be initiated will create the sellers market for labour which only will give a bargaining position to the agricultural labour and hence higher wages. (Para 8.34)

93. Some additional support would be necessary for surveys, both area and family-wise, planning, provision of infrastructure, etc. Ordinarily it should be a part of the budget of the Block and there should be no difficulty in taking care of this expenditure from the various special grants which are being made available to the Block. In any case, the Committee has earlier recommended in its report on "Organisation of Administrative and Financial Structures for Backward Area Development" that Rs. 5 lakhs per annum should be given to each of the Blocks in the backward areas, as per a phased programme. The Committee feels that with this money as well as the money available under IRD and other programmes, it should be possible for the Project Authority to build up 5 focal point centres in each Block. (Para 8.35)

Growth Centre as the Catalyst of Area Development

94. The Committee has suggested measures for increasing productivity and utilising fully the development potential for backward areas and also for achieving a reasonable distribution of benefits towards the goal of social justice. This frame leaves out a sector of opportunities for the semi-skilled and highly skilled population and

educated youth in the areas of fundamental backwardness which is available in the general growth of the nation in various fields of development. (Para 9.1)

95. In most of the large projects located in backward areas neither the direct involvement in the construction of these projects nor the secondary and tertiary growth opportunities could be availed of to any large extent by the people of the backward areas round about. Further, there has been no complementary growth in other sectors of the economy as we normally expect. The Committee has noted with much concern this gap between the possible opportunities and the availing of the opportunities by the surrounding population. The Committee has tried to see if bridging of this gap is possible. The broad conclusion is that this is possible provided very substantial support, planning and implementation of various infrastructure and aid programmes are carried out by the State administration. (Para 9.3)

96. Broadly speaking, we can foresee five major types of development which would create growth centres with the substantial potential for generating all round development in the backward areas surrounding the projects and amongst the people of the area. There are:

(i) Industrial complexes;
(ii) Growing urban complex;
(iii) Raw material exploitation (forest and minerals and industries based thereon);
(iv) Large Irrigation Projects; and
(v) Hydel and Thermal Projects.

The type of secondary and tertiary potential generated and the measured required to ensure that this potential is used for the development of the backward area will vary from case to case. (Paras 9.4 and 9.5)

97. The construction phase of the project has many opportunities for suitable entrepreneurs to avail of the employment and earning opportunities. The construction itself generates secondary and tertiary growth in the infrastructure creation and the service supports required. A continuous monitoring of demand will have to be made and steps taken to train the local people to avail of the opportunities. (Paras 9.6, 9.7 and 9.8)

98. Besides, the project plan, a large secondary plan for training of manpower and its absorption has to be made. The responsibility for

doing this must rest with the district planning centre working in association with the project. (Para 9.8)

99. Large scale ancillary industrial development providing materials required for the construction of the project and for the housing can well be developed in these backward areas following the guidelines that have been given in the report of the Committee on "Industrial Dispersal". These industries will have to be nurtured from the start in ensuring the ancilliarisation of the demand of the project. (Para 9.9)

100. The new road structure leads to opportunities for developing sub-growth centres which themselves will then generate secondary and tertiary employment in the surrounding areas. Such sub-growth centres where a large number of people will be gathered will require various amenities and services. Proper town planning in the beginning itself for the sub-growth centres will save a lot of trouble later on. Thus town planning and town development will have to be linked up to the growth centre approach. (Para 9.10)

101. Supply and services for the large population that will congregate at the project and at the sub-growth centres will require consumer goods and various services. Unless there is sufficient planning of the production of the necessary consumer goods as far as possible in the surrounding areas and for training people for taking up the service occupations that are available, the general experience has been that opportunities are grabbed by generally more forward people from other areas of the State or outside. (Para 9.11)

102. Transport service give a lot of opportunities for self-employment of educated unemployed youth. These opportunities are of a fairly remunerative kind. (Para 9.12)

103. Entrepreneur identification, their training, credit and technical advice that may be needed have all to be laid down by the state. (Para 9.12)

104. The development of the area to be irrigated by the project itself calls for tremendous amount of detailed planning of opportunities and how to avail of them. Mere detailed work in localising programmes and projects in agriculture and connected subsidiary occupations will itself absorb a large number of planning and executing personnel. Agricultural development in the vast areas that would be irrigated will need marketing facilities, credit and transport for moving the surplus production to outside markets. Unless this is planned in advance and the facilities are provided, agricultural

development and development of other subsidiary occupations will not progress satisfactorily. (Paras 9.13 and Para 9.14)

105. In the report on 'Industrial Dispersal', the Committee has already given an idea of the developmental opportunities arising from the construction and running of the industrial complexes.

(a) Opportunities for direct employment in the construction and operational phase of the industries that will be located in the industrial complex;

(b) A rapidly growing town attracts a large number of people in direct employment in the industries located there and the secondary and tertiary growth. This will generate large demand for consumer goods supplies and various domestic services;

(c) The educational requirements of an industrial growth centre would be much more than in a hydel or irrigation project. Similarly, medical facilities will be of a higher order. Unless the necessary infrastructure for both of the right quality is built up the growth centre will not develop and hence further development will not take place; and

(d) Transport and communication services will be tremendously important in an industrial growth centre. (Para 9.17)

106. The general experience is that wherever projects are developed in backward areas, normally local people do not get a look in either for employment or for marketing their goods at reasonable prices. The linkages between such projects and opportunities for local people to avail of them will need a planning and implemen- tation organisation. (Para 9.19)

107. The funds provided in the project for rehabilitation can be used in constructive way to promote area development and to strengthen the linkages between the project and the surrounding area. The present approach which sees rehabilitation largely as a matter of compensation should give way to a more positive approach which combines rehabilitation of the displaced families with area development. (Para 9.20)

Credit

108. The National Committee endorses the recommendations of the CRAFICARD in regard to credit arrangements for integrated

agricultural and rural development programmes and would strongly urge that the improvements and the streamlining recommended by the CRAFICARD, once accepted by Government, should be implemented speedily, and, on priority basis, on the backward areas. (Para 10.3)

109. There are certain special features of the backward areas like the tribal areas, development of village and cottage industries, small scale industries sector, for which the National Committee had made certain recommendations/in its reports on these subjects. The recommendation suggestions made by the National Committee are supplementary to the general recommendations made by the CRAFICARD. These recommendation and the CRAFICARD recommendations have to be knit together to evolve an appropriate credit structure in the backward areas of the country for agriculture and rural development. (Para 10.4)

Rural Marketing

110. The objectives of an efficient rural marketing system are:

(a) to enable the primary producers to get the best price;
(b) to provide facilities for lifting of produce which the producers are willing to sell at a reasonable price;
(c) to reduce the price spread between the primary producers and ultimate consumers; and
(d) to make available all products of farm origin to consumers at a reasonable price without impairing the quality of the produce. (Para 11.4)

111. Notwithstanding all the efforts taken and investments made so far in organising and developing the assembling markets, roughly one-fifth of the marketable surplus in the case of food crops and half to the three fourths in the case of commercial crops do not seem to be coming to the assembling market at all. There has so far been no concerted efforts for development of marketing infrastructure in most of the States. (Para 11.9)

112. The Ministry of Rural Reconstruction should look into the question of levy of market fees and give general guidance as to what should constitute a reasonable market fees which should provide adequate income not only to cover the running cost but also essential developmental facilities including internal roads, which limits the producers using the markets. (Para 11.14)

113. Any amount of efforts to increase the productivity of the backward areas would be infructuous unless the producer is assured of an incentive return on his produce. What is thus needed is that a regulated market should not be far away from the village. It will be ideal if this facility could be treated at a place as near as possible and in general within a radius of 5 kms. a distance negotiable by foot or cart within an hour. (Paras 11.16 and 11.7)

114. The Committee would, recommend that wherever focal point approach is adopted, priority should be given either to convert the "shandy" where existing into a regulated market or where no stand or *haat* exists to set-up a new regulated market. (Para 11.18)

115. The National Commission on Agriculture had recommended certain minimum facilities, to start with, in these sub-markets and assembly markets which are indicated below: (Para 56.1.2)

(i) Physical facilities for grading, weighing and storage should be available in the market;

(ii) There should be an agency which should take charge of the cultivator's produce, advance him money for his immediate needs, process the produce, arrange for further marketing at the next point and then make final payment;

(iii) An alternative of personal dealing and disposal should also be available to the cultivator;

(iv) There should be means of communication for market information i.e. Posts and Telegraph Office with a provision for telephone;

(v) Shops selling production inputs and domestic necessities should be available to the producer in the localities where markets are situated; and

(vi) Facility of inter-village and intra-village road communication should exist in the proposed market area.

The Committee would endorse the above recommendations as it considers that these are the minimum facilities required.

116. The Committee would suggest that in the backward areas, there should be at least one regulated market in each project to which the assembly and sub-markets could be linked. It would also suggest that steps should be taken immediately, where necessary, to notify the commodities which have not yet been covered under the market legislation, particularly cash crops, livestock, livestock products, fruits

and vegetables. (Para 11.9)

117. The *shandies/haats*, which are to be developed either as assembly markets or sub-markets, and majority of which are likely to be below the level of taluka headquarters, would require to be treated on special footing by providing necessary finances to improve their physical facilities and working capital. These assembling markets and sub-markets may not be able to devote necessary funds for providing physical facilities in the initial stages. (Para 11.20)

118. The Committee would strongly urge that all State Governments should create a "Market Development Fund" to which the market Committees in the State should contribute a certain percentage of market revenue and the State Governments contribute matching grants. With this Fund and the assistance available from the Central Government it could be possible to develop existing *shandies/haats* into assembling maintain too many purchasing points of their Year Plan. (Para 11.21)

119. The Committee would also recommend that the present procurement agencies like the Food Corporation of India, the Jute Corporation of India and the Cotton Corporation of India, etc., should strengthen their relationship with cooperative structure and encourage them to perform this purchasing activity rather than maintain too many purchasing points of their own. (Para 11.24)

120. The endeavour of the State Government should be to develop the cooperative marketing structure and its apex organisations so as to make them more effective tools in building up an efficient rural marketing system, and strengthen the functional bonds between the apex bodies at the State level and the concerned national institutions, wherever they exist. (Para 11.24)

121. The Committee would recommend licensing of all market functionaries compulsorily without exception. Also in view of the limited service rendered brokers should be phased out from the market; they could be persuaded to become commission agents. The weighing of produce should be done by the market committees. Only produce graded and weighed should be handled over to the commission agents according to the choice of the producers/sellers. The practice of commission agent making payment to the producer-seller is not a sound practice and a system of payment through banks located in all regulated markets has to be popularised. (Para 11.25)

122. Commodities have to be stored at farm level before marketing at market level at processing plants and at the level of wholesale and

retail trading. The Committee would recommend that improved methods of storage at the farmer's level should be popularised. (Paras 11.26 and 11.27)

123. There is need for special efforts to construct storages in rural areas i.e. at each of the assembly or sub-market centres suitably linking them with the storage facilities at the wholesale and terminal markets. This is quite important in the case of backward areas. (Para 11.28)

124. It is essential that, depending on the production potential and the need for sale, each Integrated Development Authority should be sure that adequate cold storage facilities are available at some of the selected points. (Para 11.28)

125. The Committee would strongly urge that the Agricultural Committees and the Cooperative Societies, particularly at the focal points must take in hand the primary processing of the important commodities produced in these areas. (Para 11.30)

126. As regards the agro-processing industries, the Committee would invite attention to its detailed recommendations in regard to the development of agro-processing industries in Para 8.53 to 8.56 of its report on "Industrial Dispersal". An agro-processing unit is best located at a central point of production of the particular agricultural produce. The regulated and other markets can play a very important role in this regard. What the Committee would suggest is to organise the necessary agro-processing industries at the market yard or nearby which is the collecting centre for the produce. The recommendation made in the report referred to earlier need to be pursued. (Para 11.31)

Organisation and Administration

127. The effective implementation of the strategy for the development of backward areas will require substantial strengthening and streamlining of administration as well as changes in the modalities of financing and implementation of development projects. The National Committee recognised the importance of this aspect and therefore dealt with it in its very first report on Organisation of Administrative and Financial Structures for Backward Areas Development. (Para 12.1)

128. The Committee would emphasise that effective administration is the key to rapid development in backward areas. The crucial elements that determine the success of administration are effective co-ordination, the quality of personnel and clarity in the relative role of

administration and institutions. (Para 12.20)

129. The National Committee in its report on the organisation of administrative and financial structure for backward areas development has suggested a certain approach to planning and implementation. It has indicated that the essential requirement at planning and administration at the areas must be as follows:

(a) It must offer coordination of the political, administrative and local institutions for determining the programme of development for the area and the manner in which it can be implemented, thus enabling direct interaction between citizens, panchayati-raj bodies, non-official agencies like cooperatives and implementing agencies;

(b) It must bring together all the administrative operations at the areas level under effective coordination and a minimum effective control of a single agency to be able to effectively counteract the powerful forces of centralisation and fragmented decision-making, associated with vertical administrative hierarchies dealing with separate segments of the economy;

(c) It must provide an effective mechanism for formulating a programme of development based upon the local resources, needs and expectations of the people;

(d) It must interact with the existing institutions and local bodies and bring an administrative cohesion in these bodies by persuasion and get an agreed participation in the development programme with specific responsibility for their part in the programme; and

(e) It must clearly lay down a programme of work for the participating agencies which would be made responsible for the proper execution of their respective assignments.

In pursuance of this approach the Committee has suggested a project approach on the pattern of the integrated tribal development project for the total development of the project areas. (Paras 12.21 and 12.22)

130. The Committee has made certain specific recommendations to meet the problem of personnel in backward areas. The recommendations of the Committee involve a resort to a measure of compulsion as well as grant of incentives and provision of facilities. The Committee in its report has noted with regret that a culture seems to be developing in the country with those who have got into the

administrative and technical field that they are entitled to the best that country can give and that they should not be asked to move to backward areas. There are of course, problems of incentives and facilities but the important point is that the country has right to expect exertion from the development staff and technologists. A sociological pressure has to arise so that needs of backward areas can be met. It is equally important that the Governments and States strictly ensure that posting of officers and staff to the backward areas based on logical approach are not cancelled, whatever be the pressure, political or otherwise. (Para 12.28)

131. The Committee has noted with regret that politics has started playing a very crucial role in the matter of transfer and postings. There is a need to restore discipline in the administrative machinery so that the transfers are not circumvented by officials through the help of politicians. Existing government instructions in this regard must be implemented. (Para 12.28)

132. Coordination is a management problem. The essential needs of coordination are:-

(i) The coordination must have a bird's eye view of the whole complex and broadly understand interplay of the several parts in the functioning of the system;

(ii) When systems are large, each functional component should be given full freedom to work with decentralised authority to the head in charge of the function;

(iii) The coordinator should not treat himself as an expert in any of the functions and over-rule the head incharge of the functions, but bring out the problem at the coordination level for a consensus; and

(iv) The coordinator does not impose decisions but arrives at an acceptable concensus in which he will have to take a guiding role on the basis of his understanding of the inter-play of the functions in the system. (Para 12.32)

133. The most important thing is that coordination is not merely a matter of systems. It will require an ability in each officer to see himself as part of a local team. It will also require skillful management of people by the head of the coordination system, whether he be a project officer or the chairman of a coordination committee. These things can come about not merely by the institution of systems but by the gradual evolution of working practices. (Para 12.33)

25

NATIONAL COMMITTEE ON THE DEVELOPMENT OF BACKWARD AREAS, 1978 — REPORT ON INDUSTRIAL DISPERSAL
November 30, 1978 — October 25, 1980[1]

Chairman Shri B. Sivaraman, Member, Planning Commission

Members Shri Som Dutt, Prof. Mrinal Datta Chaudhary (ceased to be member w.e.f. November 30, 1978); Shri S.S. Marathe (ceased to be member w.e.f. November 30, 1978); Shri Ranchor Prasad; Shri Ramakrishanayya; Shri K.P.A. Menon, Shri R.M. Honavar (ceased to be member w.e.f. January 31, 1981); Shri S.A. Dave; Dr. Y. Nayudamma; Shri Anand Sarup; Dr. B.D. Sharma; Shri Suresh Mathur; Dr. D.M. Nanjundappa; Shri S.M. Ghosh

M. Secy. Shri Nitin Desai

Appointment

The Government have been pursuing certain policies and programmes in regard to the development of backward areas since the Fourth Five Years Plan. It is now necessary to review the working of these various programmes and to set out a suitable strategy or strategies for the development of Backward Areas in the context of the priorities and objectives set out in the draft 1979-83 plan. The Planning Commission have, therefore, decided to set up a High Level Committee to formulate appropriate strategy or strategies for effectively tackling the problems of Backward Areas vide its Resolution No. PC(P)17/NCDBA/78-MLP dated November 30, 1978.

1. Planning Commission, Government of India, New Delhi, 1980, 98 p.

Terms of Reference

(i) To examine the validity of the various concepts of backwardness underlying the definitions in use for present policy purposes and recommend the criteria by which backward areas should be identified.

(ii) To review the working of:

(a) the existing plans for dealing with the general development problems of backward areas like Tribal Sub-Plans, Plans for Hill Areas, etc., and

(b) the existing schemes for stimulating industrial development in backward areas such as the schemes for concessional finance, investment subsidy, transport subsidy, sales tax concessions, etc., similar schemes in the agricultural and allied fields like DPAP, and general measures for tackling the problems of poverty and unemployment with a view to find out their efficacy in the removal of backwardness; and

(iii) To recommend an appropriate strategy or strategies for effectively tackling the problem of backward areas, classified, if necessary, according to areas, causes of or prescribed remedies.

Contents

Summary of Conclusions and Recommendations; Introduction; Historical Evolution; Development of Policy for Industrial Dispersal; Evaluation of Policy and Programmes for Industrial Dispersal; Industrialisation and Employment; Industrialisation and Urbanisation; Policy Recommendations for Medium and Large Industries; Policy Recommendations for Small Industries, Ancilliary Industries and Agro-Industries; Impact of Industrial Development; Annexures from 1.1 to VII.3 and Tables from 2.1 to 8.3.

Recommendations

Introduction

1. The problem of industrial backwardness should be approached from the point of view of the strategies required to encourage industrial dispersal away from existing centres to new centres in in-

dustrially backward areas. (Para 1.2)

Historical Evolution

2. There is no reason for supposing that the existing pattern of industrial locations in optimal and the objective of policy must be to correct these irrationalities. (Para 2.19)

Development of Policy for Industrial Dispersal

3. In a broad sense the Central Government has a crucial and overall responsibility in the regulation and development of industry so as to achieve national objectives. (Para 3.1)

4. The Government has always evinced an interest in encouraging industrialisation of backward areas and several very promising approaches have been outlined in the plans. However, many of the promising approaches towards dispersal of industries have not in fact been pursued. (Para 3.19)

Evaluation of Policy for Industrial Dispersal

5. The benefits of the Central Investment subsidy and concessional finance have accrued to a small number of districts, mostly in the west or south. The bulk of the districts which have received substantial benefit are in States/UTs which were not classified as industrially backward by the Pande Working Group. Most of these districts are in close proximity to relatively developed industrial centre. (Paras 4.20 and 4.24)

6. Neither on a population nor on an area basis did backward districts get as much of finance from all-India term lending institutions as non-backward districts. (Para 4.22)

7. The availability of concessional finance and subsidy has been a significant motivating factor in persuading entrepreneurs to locate their units in backward districts. (Para 4.25)

8. The availability of industrial infrastructure and nearness to markets in developed centres seems to be a major factor determining location for medium and large units. (Para 4.25)

9. The bulk of the employment is of local labour. Skilled labour often comes from outside. (Para 4.25)

10. Entrepreneurship for medium and large units generally comes

from outside the area, but small entrepreneurs are mostly local. (Para 4.25)

11. The bulk of the direct benefit of Central public investment has accrued to industrially backward states. (Para 4.28)

12. Licensing policy is a negative instrument and cannot by itself promote industrial development in industrially backward areas. I can at most impose certain restraints on the pace of expansion in developed areas and thereby make it easier to attract entrepreneurs to industrially backward areas. (Para 4.32)

13. With a few exceptions, the industrial estates programme has not helped to relocate industries away from developed areas to new centres. (Para 4.42)

Industrialisation and Employment

14. It is absolutely essential that the employment benefits from new manufacturing activity promoted in backward areas should accrue to persons from those areas and that the secondary/tertiary benefits that flow out of industrial development and the high wages obtainable in the development are availed of by local entrepreneurs and local labour. (Para 5.1)

15. Backward areas suffer from the fact that growth impulses from centres of modern manufacturing have not percolated down. It is necessary to generate growth impulses within these areas. (Para 5.2)

16. The high level of earnings in modern manufacturing can generate demands for agricultural produce and other consumer goods which can stimulate agricultural production, small industries, trading and other service activity. (Para 5.3)

17. Modern manufacturing employment can stimulate growth impulses by the upgradation of local skills. (Para 5.4)

18. The influx of industry generates further growth impulses through the development of ancillary units. (Para 5.5)

19. The services developed for industry can make it easier to undertake development in other sectors. (Para 5.6)

Industrialisation and Urbanisation

20. A certain degree of concentration is inevitable in the location of industrial activity. Public policy cannot ignore the advantages of agglomeration and hence the aim of policy must be to develop viable in-

dustrial growth centres in backward regions. (Paras 6.1 and 6.2)

21. The natural tendency of industry to congregate together at certain locations implies that there is an intimate link between industrialisation and urbanisation. (Para 6.4)

22. The experience of over seven decades proves that the formidable attraction of existing centres can be countered if an appropriate mix of infrastructure and entrepreneurship is made available at new centres. (Para 6.7)

23. Planning for industrialisation and urbanisation have to go together. A programme to disperse industries to new centres, the programme to develop medium sized towns and the objective of controlling metropolitan congestion are complementary to each other. (Para 6.9)

Policy Recommendations for Medium and Large Industry

24. The essential elements of a policy for industrial dispersal are first the need to direct industrial dispersal policies at a sufficient distance from existing centres, second, the importancc of infrastructure development and the third need for coordinated effort. (Para 7.1)

25. Industrial dispersal policy should encourage the location of industry in suitable growth centres with due weightage for such growth centres in the States which are industrially backward. (Para 7.6)

26. The cost of providing the infrastructure will have to be minimised by selecting growth centre which are already sufficiently urbanised and have a good level of work of the infrastructure already in position. An existing urban centre with a population of 50,000 or more (as per the 1971 census) will have quite an amount of the necessary infrastructure. Provided urban centres with reasonable existing facilities are selected it should be possible to develop 100 new industrial centres during the next 10 year period. (Para 7.7)

27. Three criteria should be used for the selection of eligible centres :

(i) They should have a population of 50,000 or more as per the 1971 census;

(ii) They should have less than 10,000 workers in non-household manufacturing as per the 1971 census; and

(iii) They should not be near existing centres. "Existing Centres" may be defined as all centres with a level of employment in non-household manufacturing exceeding 10,000. Nearness may be defined in terms of the following cut-off distance from each category of existing centres:

Level of employment in non-household manufacturing in existing centres	Cut-off distance beyond which new centres should be chosen
Over 150 thousand	150 kms.
50—150 thousand	100 kms.
25— 50 thousand	75 kms.
10— 25 thousand	50 kms.

(Paras 7.9 to 7.11)

28. Starting with 100 eligible centres during this plan period and watching their pace of development there may be scope for increasing the number of such growth centres during the next plan period. (Para 7.14)

29. The 100 selected centres may be distributed between the industrially development and industrially backward states in the ratio 30 : 70. For this purpose developed states may be defined on the basis of the value added per capita in manufacturing in 1975-76 being above the national average. On this basis Gujarat, Haryana, Maharashtra, Karnataka, Punjab, Tamil Nadu and West Bengal may be considered industrially more developed states. Ten centres out of the 70 for the backward areas can be allotted to the hill states of Jammu and Kashmir and Himachal Pradesh, the north-east states (excluding Assam) and Union Territories. The balance may be distributed within each category, the share of each state being proportional to the area and population (with equal weights for both). (Paras 7.13 and 7.15)

30. The precise selection and phasing of development may be left to the states though the selection would have to fulfil the criteria of eligibility. (Para 7.15)

31. States may be permitted to select centres with a population size less than 50,000 within their allotment if this is necessary in the interest of regional balance or from the point of view of economising infrastructure costs. (Para 7.15)

32. Without vigorous efforts on the part of State Governments the preference in favour of backward states may not amount much. (Para 7.16)

33. An Industrial Development Authority (IRA) should be set up

for each selected centre. (Para 7.18)

34. The essential features of the IDA's should be as follows:

(i) They should have the jurisdical authority to receive grants from the Central and State Governments and to borrow from other sources;
(ii) They should be delegated with all the authority required for planning, promotion and management of the Centre; and
(iii) They should have on their governing council field representatives of all authorities involved in the issue of sanctions and registration. (Para 7.18)

35. At the state level a coordination committee under the chairmanship of the Chief Secretary should secure the required degree of inter-departmental co-ordination and also monitor the performance of the IDAS. (Para 7.19)

36. In industrially backward areas investments in infrastructure may have to precede demand. (Para 7.20)

37. With regard to power supply the crucial requirement is not so much the location of generation points in backward regions but the upgradation of transmission and distribution systems and the assurance of power supply at least in the selected growth centres. The responsibility for ensuring this will rest with the State Electricity Boards. (Para 7.21)

38. Some investment in transport may be required in remote regions or for short link stretches. Another aspect that has to be taken care of is the provision of regular service for passenger and freight transport. The responsibility for this rests with the Central Government (Railway Board and National Highway Organisation) and the State Governments. (Para 7.22)

39. Upgradation of telecommunication facilities in the selected centres will be necessary and must be accorded priority in the telecommunication plan. (Para 7.23)

40. The development of industrial areas and industrial estates in the selected centres will be the responsibility of the IDA. (Para 7.24)

41. The IDA should undertake those aspects of housing and urban development that arise directly from the growth of industries, e.g., township development commuter facilities. (Para 7.25)

42. The IDA should be authorised to undertake water supply development wherever necessary. (Para 7.26)

43. The funds required for area development and the provision of minimum facilities will have to be borrowed. To enable the IDA to do this it will have to be provided with seed money at the rate of 20 per cent for that part of the total expenditure which is recoverable and 100 per cent for the non-recoverable component. The seed money shall be found 75 per cent from the Central funds and 25 per cent from state funds. Whenever a commercially viable scheme is worked out the necessary support should be provided at the required level. (Paras 7.28 and 7.29)

44. Apart from the expenditure incurred directly by the IDA, there will be some items which will be provided for separately in the State and Central Plan, e.g., telecommunications, major roads, electricity supply, etc. The requirements of growth centres will have to be given priority in these provisions. (Para 7.28)

45. The IDA should work on a commercial basis and make investments according to necessity, so that the return from entrepreneurs flows in, a regular manner. (Para 7.30)

46. The most important part of the plan will be the preparation of a master plan. If such a plan is prepared the financing of the project should be the responsibility of the IDBI and should be undertaken by them on a direct finance basis. The Plan will have to make due provision for funding the IDBI for this new enterprise on a sufficient basis. (Para 7.30)

47. The requirement of industrial dispersal will be better met if the coverage of the central subsidy scheme is modified so that it is applicable only to areas which are not 'near' existing industrial centres. For this purpose, 'existing centre' and proximity can be defined as for the selection of growth centres, i.e. 'existing centres' are all towns/urban agglomerations with a level of employment in non-household manufacturing of 10,000 or more as per the 1971 census and proximity is defined is terms of the following cut off distance:

Level of employment in non-household manufacturing in existing centres	Cut-off distance beyond which Central subsidy and concessional finance should be applicable
Over 150 thousand	150 kms.
50—150 thousand	100 kms.
25— 50 thousand	75 kms.
10— 25 thousand	50 kms.

The coverage is not restricted to the selected centres but the whole area beyond the cut-off distances. (Para 7.32)

48. The geographical coverage of the central subsidy and concessional finance schemes should be the same. (Para 7.33)

49. There is a provision in the existing schemes for selectivity in the application of subsidies for large projects. This selectivity provision is unnecessary since there is a ceiling on the amounts given by way of subsidy or concessional finance. (Para 7.35)

50. The concession under Section 80 HH of the Income Tax Act should be available to units set up in areas outside the area of influence of existing industrial centres as defined in the recommendations for the central subsidy and concessional finance scheme. (Para 7.37)

51. It is necessary to bring rationality into the various subsidies offered by State Governments to induce industries to locate themselves in the State. One suggestion offered is that the various states' subsidies should be linked up only with the locational approach in the Central subsidy and concessional finance scheme. (Para 7.38)

52. The Pilot Plan Subsidy introduced by some states appears to be unnecessary if the present subsidy system continues and infrastructure at the selected growth centres is build up quickly. (Para 7.40)

53. The nucleus plant approach outlined in the Industrial Policy Resolution of July, 1980 can be used in the industrially backward areas as identified in the recommendations regarding the Central Subsidy and Concessional Finance Scheme. Notlessthan 50 growth centres should be developed through the nucleus plant approach in these areas, preferably in the next five years and in any case within ten years. In addition a substantial majority of the nucleus units along with their small units must be located in the industrially backward states identified by the NCDBA. (Para 7.42)

Policy Recommendations for Small Industries, Ancillary Industries and Agro-Industries

54. The promotion of small scale units in industrially backward areas can reduce the costs of generating manufacturing employment to a substantial extent. They may also be more suitable for local entrepreneurs than larger units. Hence it is necessary to take special measures to ensure their dispersal to backward regions. (Para 8.5)

55. Apart from the loans from commercial banks and general advisory functions (which may be of limited value), the coverage of small scale units by the official support system is poor. (Para 8.8)

56. Existing industrial estates in the selected growth centers should be rehabilitated. Those growth centres which do not have industrial estates should be provided with one. In addition, 100 new industrial estates should be developed in centres away from the growth centres, in the industrially backward areas. The infrastructure planning and development of these 100 industrial estates will be coordinated and the land and shed development financed through DIC. (Para 8.16)

57. The DIC concept, suitably modified is the correct answer for a covering organisation to meet the most important requirements of small industries which are:

(a) Market intelligence and marketing aids;
(b) Help in getting through the various controls and sanctions necessary for the establishment of new industry;
(c) Credit for fixed and working capital;
(d) Raw materials supply at reasonable rates not much above the wholesale rates at which large and medium industries manage to get the raw materials; and
(e) Common service facilities close by so that repair and maintenance jobs, finishing, testing, etc., can be done quickly and efficiently at reasonable charges. (Para 8.17)

58. The DIC will have to help in tying up the requirements of the state purchase organisations with organised production in the small industries under its control. (Para 8.18)

59. A link-up between consumer cooperatives and super markets on the one hand and small scale units in industrially backward areas should be secured through the DIC. (Para 8.19)

60. A good part of the stores and spares requirements of Central Ministries and associated organisations can be obtained through tied small industries in industrially backward areas through the DIC. (Para 8.20)

61. Raw material dumps should be established at growth centres/industrial estates for major industrial raw materials like steel, non-ferrous metals, plastic raw materials, basic chemicals, etc. These dumps should be managed by the IDAs in the growth centres and the DICs in other industrial estates. (Para 8.23)

62. Central and State agencies responsible for raw material supply should accept that the requirements of small scale units in backward areas will be a first charge on available supplies. (Para 8.23)

63. The number of branch centres of the SISI in industrially backward areas must be increased to at least 50 so that access to technical assistance services is improved. The extension agencies should work in close collaboration with the DIC so that an entrepreneur is provided with continuous guidance from the first project idea to its realisation and through the teething problems in early years. (Para 8.24)

64. The outreach of SFCs to small scale units is limited. It is necessary that SFC operations in backward districts should cover a much larger number of units. If necessary additional branch offices of SFC may be set up for this purpose. The credit managers of the DIC must ensure that the finance requirements of small units, particularly those set up by new entrepreneurs are adequately covered. (Para 8.26)

65. It is essential that the system for obtaining the required sanctions and clearances is simplified so that the number of these that are required is minimised and the authority to issue these is decentralised planning of this tie-up. (Para 2.27)

66. The rehabilitation of existing industrial estates and the development of new estates will have to involve, among other things, the promotion of tied ancillaries to large public and private sector units. The DICs will have to do the basic planning of this tie-up. (Para 8.29)

67. Existing public and private sector units can support tied ancillaries at new centres. (Para 8.42)

68. Public enterprises should make payment for purchase from ancillary units within 30 days of delivery. The responsibility for monitoring performance in this regard should lie with the state level committees. (Para 8.44)

69. Out of the existing and additional requirements of public sector units there should be a diversion of Rs. 20 crores per year in purchases from tied ancillaries in industrially backward areas. This can support 200 new units per year or 1000 over five years. At ten per estate it can support 100 new industrial estates. Another Rs. 10 crores of diversion per year can look after the rehabilitation of old estates and units. (Para 8.45)

70. The Governments directions on ancillaries has been carried out in the breach. The ministries can play a more effective role in carrying out the policy directives of government *suo moto* without producing from an outside body. (Paras 8.45)

71. There is a large field of small industries where location is guided by the local market and needs. These can be divided into two

classes (a) maintenance, repair and service units, and (b) agro-processing industries. These two sets of industries can be developed by any state by a careful check of raw material supply and the type of maintenance, etc., support that is needed. It is also possible for a state to generate new centres for such industrial development by first activising the agrarian revolution towards greater production of what are called cash crops. (Para 8.46)

72. There will be potential for the development of repair for agricultural equipment in many backward areas. One of the tasks of the DIC can be the development of such centres by suitable linkages between the local educated youth and the markets of the spare parts. Planning of these units and continuous monitoring of their needs can be an essential part of the project level IRD planning and implementation group in backward areas. The development of agro-servicing workshops and service development can also be linked with the focal point approach. (Paras 8.47 to 8.49)

73. There is a danger of over-provision of repair and maintenance facilities leading to underutilisation. Hence the planning and development of this sector has to be a careful exercise taking into account a fair estimate of demand. The first step will be to upgrade existing facilities of this kind to the higher levels required, bringing in new entrants only when the additional need has been clearly established. (Para 8.50)

74. In project area planning in backward areas; it should be possible to plan the development of small scale agro-processing units in the project or block area in a time phase to suit the expanding production and consumption demand. The semiprocessing units will naturally be located close to the collection points. Preferably these units are best located at the focal points. (Para 8.51)

75. The potential for the development of cash crops in backward areas is substantial. This can provide the base for large scale agro-processing units. For these industries, the DIC can deal with the major role of identifying industrial opportunities and organising entrepreneurship. However, the responsibility for tying up draw material production and marketing must rest with the district planning and implementation organisation. (Para 8.53)

76. The regulated market system can provide an organisational framework for developing agro-processing industries. (Para 8.55)

77. As a first move towards effective development of agro-processing units in backward areas it is necessary to establish fully ef-

fective Regulated Markets with professional supervision covering the most important cash crops (which could include food crops) in the area. (Para 8.55)

78. The Regulated Market Committee should:

(a) organise and run the agro-processing industry and thereby support the market to give a fair price to the farmer; or
(b) be a major partner in the venture and give share to the farmers who generally use the market yard and run a joint agro-processing industry providing the expert management to the venture and stabilising the price to the producer. (Para 8.56)

Impact of Industrial Development

79. The programme to stimulate industrial development in new centres must be accompanied by systematic measures to maximise local impact. (Para 9.1)

80. It should be the responsibility of the state administration to identify the skills that are necessary, the extent to which they are not available locally and the manner in which local people should be trained to fill these gaps. (Para 9.1)

81. In backward areas the present obligation on public sector units to recruit through the local exchange should be maintained, and the possibility of extending such an obligation to medium and large private units which go to the new growth centres should be considered wherever these units are to receive special concessions. (Para 9.6)

82. The district ITI must adjust its curriculum to the requirements of the district industries and industries in neighbouring districts. (Para 9.6)

83. Practical experience will have to be provided in the training course in established industries in the state and outside. A system should be established in the Central Ministry concerned to do this systematically not only in the case of ITI trained people but also in the multifarious fields left uncovered by ITI and where practical experience is more valued by the Industry. At the state level the coordinating body should be the State Industrial Promotion Organisation. The field level requirements and problems should be studied and reported by the IDA for growth centres and by the DIC for requirements outside the growth centres. (Para 9.6)

84. The IDBI should be responsible for regular concurrent

analysis of the selection process for EDP programmes in different states so that the results of experience are taken into account in the identification and solution of entrepreneur. (Para 9.16)

85. The potential sources of entrepreneurship that can be tapped are:

(i) People who already have an industrial background either having run an industry which is close to the field selected or who have worked at lower levels in industry;
(ii) People from traditional trading families;
(iii) Technicians and professionals; and
(iv) Others.

Entrepreneurs from these classes should be available even in backward areas. Entrepreneurial promotion should be extended to attract persons from backward areas who have migrated out for lack of opportunity. (Paras 9.12 and 9.17)

86. The training of entrepreneurs is an important aspect of the programmes :

(i) In backward areas the state should be prepared to give help to the trainees in the form of suitable accommodation and stipend. (Para 9.18)
(ii) At the end of the training period, the selected applicant must be given a blueprint of the industry he wants to start. A good consultancy aid to assist in this is vital and should be obtained by the training organisation at its expense. (Para 9.19)
(iii) There should be close coordination between the training organisation and the state industries development organisation. (Para 9.20)
(iv) Continuous technical guidance and consultancy assistance during the period of operation is as important and the promotional organisation must provide for the same. (Para 9.20)

87. Entrepreneurial development and training should be undertaken in regional centres catering to more than one state. These regional centres should be organised and run by the IDBI. Whilst establishing the centres and running them may be a charge on the developmental role of the IDBI, the stipend of the trainees will have to be contributed by the States sponsoring them. (Para 9.21)

88. Regarding the provision of finance to entrepreneurs in backward areas the following aids are the minimum required :

(i) Margin money for small industries will have to be lower in backward areas. The Committee would recommend that it may be set at 20 per cent of which 15 per cent will be available from the subsidy and the balance 5 per cent will have to be found by the entrepreneurs. The flow of subsidy and institutional resources to the entrepreneur must match with the flow of expenditure and there should be a suitable provision to cover pre-investment expenses also;

(ii) Margin money for working capital will have to be lower and should not exceed 50 per cent of the normal requirement as specified by the monetary authorities. In addition both term loans and production loans must be available as a package from the institutions so that eternal wrangle on security can be overcome;

(iii) Both types of credit must be adequate for smooth operation. There must be regional body of arbiters in which the state promotion organisation, representatives of the SISI and the main banks of the area must be involved; and

(iv) Some arrangement will have to be developed to see that the enterprise gets paid in full promptly for the supplies to other industries and the public sector. (Para 9.24)

89. Entrepreneurship for medium and large industries in the new growth centres is likely to come from the public sector or from private sector units situated elsewhere. At the start itself such units should select people from the area with the necessary qualifications and on merit and train them for higher level posts in the mother factory. These persons should be seconded to similar level posts in the mother plant. When the new venture goes on stream, the old hands at this level in the mother plant should be deputed for a two or three year spell at the new plant and the trainees absorbed in old plant in those posts on the understanding that after two or three years, they will take over at the new plant and the deputationists will return to the mother plant. (Para 9.26)

90. It is essential that the Labour Department of the State Government exercise vigilance in the matter of labour relations and set up a well staffed office at all new growth centres. This office should be responsible not merely for conciliation after disputes have arisen but

also for monitoring and anticipating problems so that preventive action can be taken. (Para 9.27)

91. Industrialisation generates a potential for consumer goods and services because of the high wages paid to labour. This secondary and tertiary growth has to be directed to the areas surrounding the growth centres. The responsibility for exploiting this opportunity will be a coordination problem. It is suggested that this may be done by the district planning centre working in coordination with the IDA, the DIC and the IRD project authorities, if any, in the region. (Para 9.29)

26

NATIONAL COMMITTEE ON THE DEVELOPMENT OF BACKWARD AREAS, 1978 — REPORT ON INDUSTRIAL ORGANISATION November 30, 1978 — November, 1981[1]

Chairman	Shri B. Sivaraman, Member, Planning Commission
Members	Shri Som Dutt; Prof. Mrinal Datta Chaudhary (ceased to be member w.e.f. November 30, 1978); Shri S.S. Marathe (ceased to be member w.e.f. November 30, 1978); Shri Ranchor Prasad; Shri Ramakrishanayya; Shri K.P.A. Menon; Shri R.M. Honavar (ceased to be member w.e.f. January 31, 1981); Dr. S.A. Dave; Dr. Y Nayudamma; Shri Anand Sarup; Dr. B.D. Sharma; Shri Suresh Mathur; Dr. D.M. Nanjundappa; Shri S.M. Ghosh
M. Secy.	Shri Nitin Desai

Appointment

The Government have been pursuing certain policies and programmes in regard to the development of backward areas since the Fourth Five Years Plan. It is now necessary to review the working of these various programmes and to set out a suitable strategy or strategies for the development of Backward Areas in the context of the priorities and objectives set out in the draft 1979-83 plan. The Planning Commission have, therefore, decided to set up a High Level Committee to formulate appropriate strategy or strategies for effectively tackling the problems of Backward Areas vide its Resolution No. PC(P)17/NCDBA/78-MLP dated November 30, 1978.

1. Planning Commission, Government of India, New Delhi, 1981, ix + 26 p.

Terms of Reference

(i) To examine the validity of the various concepts of backwardness underlying the definitions in use for present policy purposes and recommend the criteria by which backward areas should be identified.

(ii) To review the working of:

(a) the existing plans for dealing with the general development problems of backward areas like Tribal Sub-Plans, Plans for Hill Areas, etc.; and

(b) the existing schemes for stimulating industrial development in backward areas such as the schemes for concessional finance, investment subsidy, transport subsidy, sales tax concessions, etc., similar schemes in the agricultural and allied fields like DPAP, and general measures for tackling the problems of poverty and unemployment with a view to find out their efficacy in the removal of backwardness; and

(iii) To recommend an appropriate strategy or strategies of effectively tackling the problem of backward areas, classified, if necessary, according to areas, causes or prescribed remedies.

Contents

Summary of Conclusions and Recommendations; Introduction; Small Industries Development Organisation; Small Industry Service Institute; State Level Industrial Organisation; State Level Corporation; District Industries Centres; Industrial Development Authority; District Supply and Marketing Societies; Planning and Coordination; An Overview; Annexure 6.1 : DIC Programme — Physical Achievements.

Recommendations

Introduction

1. A Central organisation is no more capable of supporting the promotion and development of the so many types of industries that can be usefully promoted in the present economy. It is now necessary that the States take over the basic responsibility for the development and

encouragement of small industries. But this responsibility cannot be discharged effectively without the active cooperation and an umbrella role on the part of the central organisation created for the development and support of industry. (Para 1.4)

Small Industries Development Organisation

2. Considering the role envisaged for the SIDO in its franchise, the present organisation is not sufficient to discharge the role. (Para 2.9)

3. Because many States, particularly those backward in industrialisation have not yet taken up their allotted responsibility for development of small industries in their States, the SIDO with its hierarchies of organisation is trying to get down to the entrepreneur in the field and develop small industries in the States directly. As a result, their overall role of policy development and interacting with the Ministries and Organisations which both lay down policies and create necessary infrastructure does leave a lot to be desired. (Para 2.9)

4. The SIDO should keep to and develop on effective role in policy development and guidance and technical development and guidance on All India basis. (Para 2.9)

5. The Economic Division of SIDO should improve the monitoring system and lay down the all India policies for monitoring. At the same time, bulk of the actual monitoring in the field and reporting will have to be undertaken by the vast extension organisation that is now being developed in the field for development of small industries. (Para 2.10)

6. The Economic Adviser (SIDO) must *suo moto* take up important sectors of small industrial development for examination and advise without waiting for somebody to ask. (Para 2.10)

7. Wherever project profiles have been issued by SIDO, it is necessary for the Economic Adviser's Division to do some periodical checks to see how far the presumptions work out in the field and what modifications may have to be adopted by the Technical Advisers to make the profiles more acceptable and more realistic and useful. (Para 2.10)

8. The Committee would recommend that the primary responsibility for identifying and dealing with sickness should be that of the Directorate of Industries in the State. The problem may be referred to SIDO if it cannot be tackled at the State level. (Para 2.11)

9. An integrated system involving the Block Industries Officers, District Industries Centres, the Directorate of Industries and SIDO should be evolved as to ensure that the data for small scale industries is comparable in range and reliability to the data that is available for medium and large industries with the DGTD. (Para 2.12)

10. The functions of Industrial Advisers should be defined as follows:

(i) Helping the State level and regional small industries development organisations to keep abreast with latest developments in technology;
(ii) Monitoring (a) technological developments and (b) changes in the pattern of demand in order to identify new opportunities for development and modernisation and emerging problem areas; and
(iii) Continuously monitoring the changing balance of advantage between large and small industries and seeking changes in policy in favour of small industries. (Para 2.14)

11. A part of the time at regional meetings of SIDO should be used for a wider meeting which should include officers of the concerned Directorates of Industry, DGTD, IDBI and concerned financial institutions. Every attempt should be made to ensure that the best available technical expertise in the country whether it be in the public or private sector is used at these quarterly meetings. (Para 2.15)

12. A regular flow of published material from SIDO would also help in this task of maintaining the level of technical knowledge in the lower echelons which are involved in direct contact with industries. (Para 2.15)

13. These should be a scheme to second officers of SIDO for operational duties in industrial plants on a regular basis so as to ensure that they remain aware of conditions at the shop floor and enterprise level. (Para 2.16)

14. It is necessary to ensure that there is a back up consultancy scheme to allow SIDO to obtain the services of outside experts. (Para 2.17)

15. The work of the Industrial Advisers may be so organised as to group products with substantial growth potential in a rational manner between the Advisers. If necessary, the number of posts of Industrial Advisers in SIDO should be increased. There should be specialists

under the Industrial Adviser dealing with the specific items. Every attempt should be made to ensure that the SIDO has sufficient expertise within organisation at least for the small number of items with high potential. (Para 2.18)

16. There should be a greater interaction between SIDO and DGTD in matters like demand appraisal, technology assessment, etc. The operational interaction between SIDO and DGTD should take place not merely at the top level of the Development Commissioner or the Industrial Adviser but also lower down in the hierarchy. (Para 2.19)

17. The Directorate of Industries in the States must take the lead in identifying areas/industries where there is need for modernisation, initiate action and monitor progress. (Para 2.21)

18. The Directorate of Industries should acquire the services of a Project Manager for the scheme, taking every care, to ensure that this Manager has the required technical and managerial competence. (Para 2.21)

19. When a modernisation programme is sufficiently large the responsibility for implementation may be passed on to the relevant District Industries Centre. (Para 2.21)

20. The role of the Central organisation in the modernisation programme must be to support the Directorate of Industries by way of advice, finance and facilities. (Para 2.21)

21. Modernisation be a part of function of each Industrial Adviser and not of just one who is so designated. (Para 2.22)

22. The project based approach for modernisation schemes could also be followed wherever there is some potential for intensive development of a new type of small industry in a concentrated area. (Para 2.23)

23. The role of SIDO in monitoring implementation of the ancilliarisation scheme should be considerably strengthened. (Para 2.25)

24. The Industrial Adviser (Ancilliaries) should undertake independent studies on the progress of ancilliarisation in specific public sector projects. He must be allowed to look into the structure of operations and purchase programmes in public sector projects to identify the scope for ancilliarisation. (Para 2.26)

25. There should be a High Level Committee to lay down specific targets for individual enterprises under the scheme and to monitor progress. This Committee should be serviced by the Industrial Adviser (Ancilliaries) and his organisation. It should include the Secretary

(Industrial Development), the Development Commissioner (SSI) and the Secretary of the concerned administrative Ministry. (Para 2.27)

26. The Government Director on the Board of Public Enterprises should be specifically charged with the responsibilities of ensuring that the scheme of ancilliarisation is implemented sincerely. The Industrial Adviser (Ancilliaries) should use the services of the Government Director for tackling specific problems in the response of the parent enterprise to the agreed ancilliarisation scheme. (Para 2.28)

27. The potential for ancilliarisation in large projects, whether public or private, which are subject to licensing control must be identified by Industrial Adviser (Ancilliaries). (Para 2.30)

28. The production of ancilliarisable items must be left out of the licences which must also contain the conditions that a certain percentage of purchases should come from ancilliaries. (Para 2.30)

29. It must be the responsibility of the Industrial Adviser (Ancilliaries) to ensure that the requisite efforts are forthcoming from the State Government concerned. (Para 2.31)

30. There should be a Deputy Adviser (Industrial Estates) under the Industrial Adviser (Ancilliaries) who will have to ensure that the two programmes for industrial estates and for ancilliary development are adequately coordinated. (Para 2.32)

31. It is essential that SIDO should be associated with the processes of allocation of imported and controlled raw materials to ensure that the requirements of small industries particularly those in backward areas are fully met. (Para 2.33)

32. The Small Industries Board should be made more effective by proper bringing up of problems by the Ministry to the Board as and when opportunities arise. The Board can also utilise its standing committee approach to deal with particular problems of small industries which are crucial at the time. It is not necessary to give a statutory status to the Board. (Para 2.34)

Small Industry Service Institute

33. The number of SISIs, Branch SISIs, etc., located in industrially less developed area should be increased to at least 50. (Para 3.2)

34. The industries which cannot be covered by the DIC, should be provided the requisite technical expertise by the regional SISI, Branch SISI or Industrial Extension Centre. (Para 3.3)

35. The SISIs should not be thought of as intermediary units

between the DIC and the Central Organisation but as organisations which will complement the DICs. What is required is a balanced distribution of technical expertise between the DIC and the SISI. (Para 3.3)

36. The pattern of distribution of expertise between the DIC and the SISI cannot be uniform and will vary from State to State and even district to district. It is clear that this approach will require a clear coordination of the staffing pattern and work programme of the DICs and the concerned SISI. (Para 3.5)

37. The present arrangements for coordination between SIDO and the SISI and between the SISIs and the State Governments do not need any substantial modifications. However, the staffing pattern of SISI must be coordinated with the technical expertise built up in the DICs by the State Government so as to avoid unnecessary duplication. (Para 3.7)

38. Operational coordination between the DICs and the concerned SISI be secured by periodic meetings of the concerned officers of the two organisations. This meeting may be called by the concerned SISI who may provide the Secretariat for this purpose. However, the meeting would be chaired by the Director of Industries so as to ensure effective participation and decision-making by the State Government. (Para 3.8)

39. There should be periodic survey of the requirements of technical expertise in each SISI to be undertaken by SIDO and posts should be rearranged according to need by the DC(SSI) on the basis of the discussions at the regional meetings. (Para 3.9)

40. In order to avoid too great a frequency of transfers the requirements should be assessed on a fairly long-term basis and a post should be assigned to SISI only when the corresponding expertise is likely to be required for 3–5 years. Shorter term requirements could be met by making *ad-hoc* arrangements. (Para 3.10)

State Level Industrial Administration

41. The nature of the State Governments' responsibilities require both a departmental structure as part of the government and a technical wing to advise the State Government and oversee field level implementation. (Para 4.3)

42. The primary responsibility of the Department of Industries will be for planning and policy formulation. (Para 4.5)

43. The Department of Industries will consist primarily of Secretariat staff though it should have an Economic Adviser to provide analytical guidance on planning and policy formulation. (Para 4.6)

44. The expertise of the State Government in the field of industrial development will be located mainly in the Directorate of Industries. (Para 4.6)

45. The primary focus of the Directorate of Industries will be on small industry development since the responsibilities of the State Government in this area are far greater than in the field of medium and large industries. (Para 4.7)

46. The Directorate of Industries must have a strong technical division. The level of expertise in this division should be such as to advise the technical officers in the DICs promptly and effectively on the various problems that arise in the field. They should also be capable of rendering advice to the State industries departments in technical matters relating to the field which they handle. (Para 4.8)

47. The technical competence of the Directorate of Industries will have to cover the requirements of the modernisation and ancilliarisation programmes. (Para 4.9)

48. The Directorate of Industries will need a strong economic, statistics and monitoring wing. This wing will be responsible for techno-economic analysis and advising the State Government on project economics and on policies. They will have to undertake periodic evaluations of specific programmes and policies. (Para 4.10)

49. Besides technical support and economic advice, operational functions will also have to be covered in the organisational structure of the Directorate of Industries. (Para 4.11)

50. Though the primary responsibility for coordination will rest with the State Department of Industries, it will be necessary to make provision for a planning wing in the Directorate also so as to provide the required technical support to the Department. (Para 4.12)

51. The Directorate of Industries should be headed by a senior officer equivalent in rank to a Commissioner. (Para 4.13)

52. The Directorate will need high quality technical staff and hence must be given sufficient flexibility to recruit the best talent available. (Para 4.13)

53. The orientation of Directorate of Industries has to shift from regulatory and rationing functions towards industrial promotion and development particularly with regard to small industries. (Para 4.14)

54. Along with the enlargement of the scope of functions of the

Directorate of Industries, there is equally a necessity for specific decentralisation of decision-making powers and even financial powers and supply powers to the DICs and the lower range where necessary. (Para 4.16)

55. Till the backward States are able to take over their responsibility in full through effective organisations, SIDO and the SISI along with consultancy organisations like the ITCOs should play a direct role in developing small industries in the State, but in a way where they develop and carry such organisations with them instead of trying to do everything directly themselves. (Para 4.17)

State Level Corporations

56. Lending by SFCs in the industrially less developed States must increase more rapidly than the average so that the share of these States in SFC lending goes up. (Para 5.5)

57. The SFCs must concentrate on a larger proportion of this lending to small units in backward areas. (Para 5.5)

58. The accessibility to SFCs for entrepreneurs in backward areas must improve and for this purpose Branch Offices of the SFC must be opened in all the industrial growth centres taken up for development. (Para 5.5)

59. The composite, loan scheme should be run through the DIC and SFC. The authority to sanction the loan would rest with the DIC, as an agent of the SFC. The SFC in turn should be eligible for refinance from the IDBI for the amounts disbursed. The required amendments in the Charters of the SFC and the IDBI would have to be made. (Para 5.6)

60. The limit for the composite loan should be raised to Rs. 50,000 and be kept under review so that it can be increased suitably as prices rise. (Para 5.6)

61. Sanctions for projects requiring between Rs. 50 thousand and Rs. 2 lakhs should be available at local level from the local office of the SFC for the term loan and the concerned commercial bank branch for the working capital loan. The DIC should be responsible for tying up the total requirements of the units in these cases though the formal sanctioning authority may remain with the lending institutions. (Para 5.7)

62. The Committee has recommended that the primary responsibility for planning and implementing infrastructure

development plans must rest with the Industrial Development Authority set up for each growth centre. With this approach the Infrastructure Development Corporations' functions become that of a civil contractor to the Industrial Development Authority. (Para 5.10)

63. Promotion of medium and large industries involve a variety of activities like keeping track of prospective entrepreneurs and contacting when they are in the process of firming up a project, running a public relations campaign to bring out the advantages of specific locations in backward areas, a well organised effort to convince the entrepreneurs as soon as he shows interest, assisting the entrepreneurs in obtaining the required clearance from the Central and State Government providing an 'after sales service' in the form of trouble shooting assistance, etc. The organisational framework for doing this can take the form of a corporation or a Cell in the Directorate of Industries. (Para 5.13)

64. The technical expertise required at DIC level may be developed, in the first instance, in the industry level corporations set up by the Sate Governments. Where the industry has to be promoted on a substantial scale in any district, the project manager should be placed in the DIC. These corporations can also continue with their other activities, viz., direct investment in producing enterprises and promotion of medium scale units. (Para 5.14)

65. Regional development corporations or target-group oriented corporations will not have the requisite level of technical expertise and hence the Committee would not recommend any exclusive reliance on these corporations for promoting small industries in industrially backward areas or amongst economically weaker sections. (Para 5.15)

66. If the promotional orientation of the technical consultancy organisations set up by the all-India financial institutions is increased, these organisations can also help to provide back-up technical advice for the DICs. (Para 5.16)

District Industries Centre

67. The shortfalls in DIC performance are attributable to some extent, to the fact that they are still in early stage of development and face some teething problems. However, there are some functions which seem to be assigned to the DIC which need to be tackled at a higher level if they are to be effectively performed, e.g., market intelligence and research. Even for other functions the DICs need

higher level support. (Para 6.21)

68. The role of the DIC in the allocations of infrastructural facilities does not seem to be recognised in the standard staffing pattern proposed. (Para 6.22)

69. The linkages between the DIC and existing organisations, particularly in the field of village and cottage industries are not very effective. (Para 6.23)

70. The DICs can play a very useful role if too much is not expected of them. The DICs have to be a part of a multi-faceted set up involving several agencies at the field level. In such a situation they cannot be held responsible for every aspect of in dustrial development. (Para 6.25)

71. The foundation of the DIC concept is the notion that, at a field level, the entrepreneur should have to deal with a single organisation. This is also the one element in the DIC concept that seems to be universally appreciated. (Para 6.26)

72. There should not be any difficulty in delegating decision-making powers to the DIC with regard to registration as a small scale unit or as a supplier for the government, certification of requirements of imports and scarce materials and sanctions and disbursal of subsidies, incentives, etc. With regard to the other items the role of the DIC may be recommendatory. (Para 6.26)

73. The multiplicity of agencies at field level cannot be eliminated altogether. In this situation, it may be desirable to introduce the concept of a programme package. In this concept the Directorate of Industries prepares a complete programme of development for a specific industry and indicates precisely the responsibility of all concerned field level agencies. The DIC implements the programme and oversees and facilitates the activities which have to be undertaken by other agencies. (Para 6.27)

74. It should be the responsibility of the State Directors of Industries to prepare such a package for all project managers in the DCIs under their control. Similarly, the SISIs must prepare a package for the industries which they are expected to service. (Para 6.27)

75. Even if the DIC can provide assistance to the entrepreneur in getting quick decisions from other agencies, the service provided is considered valuable by entrepreneur. This recommendatory role of the DIC can be made effective if certain key areas are staffed on a deputation basis by officers from the present related decision-making organisations. (Para 6.28)

76. The role of the DIC in raw material supply and marketing would have to be somewhat peripheral. (Para 6.29)

77. The DIC should continue to play an important role in the planning and management of industrial infrastructure. (Para 6.31)

78. The possibility of sanctioning water and power connections upto a certain limit should rest with the DICs. (Para 6.31)

79. The DIC should be the primary point of contact for technical advice on the establishment of new projects or on problem faced by existing units. (Para 6.32)

80. The concept of "guided entrepreneurship" is relevant for backward areas. The guidance will have to cover not merely technical discipline but also finance, marketing, purchase and inventory management, labour management, etc. All the required support comes within the concept of the DIC but in backward areas the guidance will have to be more comprehensive and thorough. (Para 6.32)

81. The wide role of the DIC requires that the General Manager should be a person of high quality. (Para 6.32)

82. There is a continuing obligation to advice and inform the entrepreneur about technical advances, new opportunities, emerging problems, etc. Sick units have to be identified and put back on their feet. In these cases the DIC apparatus is the correct instrument. (Para 6.33)

83. The responsibility of the DICs in the area of ancilliary development is for the field level implementation of centrally determined and accepted ancilliary development plans. (Para 6.35)

84. The DIC will have to be the principal field agency for the purposes of entrepreneurial selection and training. (Para 6.36)

85. The Committee envisages a three tier system for entrepreneurial development. For relatively simple projects the training could be provided at the DIC itself. At the next level the DIC may refer the case to the Directorate of Industries and the training may be organised by one of the State level promotional corporations or by a specialised agency set up for the purpose. A third level of entrepreneurial training will be run by national organisations like IDBI. (Para 6.36)

86. For purposes of coordination the DIC should link up with the district planning centre. This planning centre will prepare the district plan taking account of the infrastructure identified in the Action Plan, which the DIC must follow. (Para 6.37)

87. The Action Plan of the DIC will also form the basis for the identification of secondary and tertiary opportunities. This must be

done by the district planning centre. (Para 6.38)

88. With regard to functional managers the role envisaged for the DIC would suggest the need for a manager (planning, monitoring and economic investigation), manager (credit), manager (raw materials and marketing) and manager (village industries). These managers would deal with the operational responsibilities of the DIC in their respective fields. Other operational functions would be handled by the General Manager and lower level staff. (Para 6.40)

89. The concept of a project manager who will be a technical person but with enough experience to provide guidance on other matters is appropriate for the requirements "guided entrepreneurship". In each DIC there should be 3-4 project managers each one covering a well-defined set of industries. (Para 6.41)

90. Besides the project manager for specified industries the DIC may also need a miscellaneous expert to liaise with SISI/SIDO and direct entrepreneurs to the correct source for technical advice. (Para 6.41)

91. The DIC cannot restrict its presence in the district headquarters and will require a field staff. The industries extension officers at block level and the industrial specialist at project level will deal with general problems and function as the eyes and ears of the DIC in the field. (Para 6.42)

Industrial Development Authority (IDA)

92. The IDA should have the juridical authority to receive grants from the Central and State Governments and to borrow from other sources. The most suitable arrangement for purpose may be a company set up under the Companies Act. (Para 7.2(i))

93. The IDA should be delegated with all the authority required for planning, promotion and management of the growth centre. (Para 7.2(ii))

94. The IDA should have on its governing council field representatives of all authorities involved in the issue of sanction and registration. Wherever feasible, the authority to issue these sanctions or registration should be delegated to IDA. (Para 7.2(iii))

95. The IDA should include representatives of technical and financial institutions. (Para 7.2(iv))

96. The IDA should have a board of directors consisting only of officials. (Para 7.2(v))

97. A change in the chief executive should only be made in consultation with the IDBI which is expected to provide the loan finance required by the IDA. (Para 7.2(v))

98. The IDA is envisaged primarily as an infrastructure development and promotional agency. In this sense it will differ from the DIC whose primary focus of attention is on technical advice and consultancy. However, for technical advice it must coordinate with the DIC/SISI/SIDO machinery and must be in a position to direct the entrepreneur to the right technical agency. (Para 7.4)

99. The IDA should be headed by a senior officer. It will need a staff of planners, engineers and industrial promotion executives. (Para 7.5)

100. As far as execution of works is concerned, the IDA can rely on existing organisations like the infrastructure corporations or failing that on contractors. It need not build up an elaborate civil engineering capability. (Para 7.5)

District Supply and Marketing Societies

101. Raw material supply, inventory management and marketing are complex managerial functions which may not have much in common with activities like research and extension. Because of this, the establishment of a District supply and Marketing Society for this purpose is recommended. (Para 8.4)

102. The proposed DSMS is expected to be run on commercial lines and should get its credit requirements from the banking system. (Para 8.4)

103. Small industries require a variety of raw materials. Some of these will be subject to statutory control and for this the present system of certification and sponsorship by the Directorate of Industries/DIC would continue. In this process the assessment of requirements would have to be done by the technical hierarchy of the DIC who would also be responsible for checking and monitoring supplies. The power to grant the required certificate of requirements should be delegated to the DIC. However, for these as well as for other raw materials the responsibility for obtaining supplies, holding stocks and making deliveries would rest with the DSMS. (Para 8.5)

104. The DSMS must not restrict the activities to centrally allocated raw material. It must also undertake the responsibility for identifying and arranging supplies of local raw materials. (Para 8.6)

105. In the case of raw materials to be obtained from the other districts and from outside districts the State level organisation will have to coordinate. (Para 8.9)

106. A State level organisation is expected to attend to the thousands of small requirements at the district level and meet them in time. It is this work which a district organisation has to perform. (Para 8.9)

107. When the district level organisation will straigtaway take up the work of supporting small industries or leave it to the existing state level organisation till a sufficient business develops is a matter entirely for the States to decide and time its operations. (Para 8.10)

108. The DSMS would act as purchase agents for the public sector organisations and procure small industry output locally. The State or Central authority that is responsible for placing orders should pass on responsibilities to the DSMS to the extent required. The exact nature of the arrangement will vary from case to case, but the essential point is that there would be a direct relationship between the purchase organisation and the DSMS. (Para 8.11)

109. The DSMS will need a back up at state level for linkages with other state level and central organisations both for raw material procurement and marketing. Hence, the establishment of State level Corporation for this purpose is recommended. (Para 8.12)

Planning and Coordination

110. The Cell for Backward Area Development in the Ministry of Industrial Development be strengthened so that it can participate in other decisions effecting industrial development in backward areas. The analytical capability of this Cell should be built up so that it can intervene effectively in appropriate forums like the Planning Commission, Public Investment Board, the Licensing Committee, etc. (Para 9.2)

111. It must be the responsibility of the Secretary, Industries to ensure that this Cell is consulted on all decisions which are likely to affect the possibilities of industrialisation in the backward areas. (Para 9.2)

112. Vertical coordination between agencies not linked together hierarchical relationship for example the DIC and SISIs/SIDOs would have to be taken care of through regional meetings. (Para 9.5)

113. As far as horizontal coordination is concerned, what is

required is the Coordination Committee at the district, state and central level. (Para 9.5)

114. At the district level, the Committee should be headed by the District Collector/Magistrate and include the General Managers of the DIC and IDA field representatives of the lead bank and the SFC, representative of the integrated rural development projects in the area, the district planning group, the local ITI, etc. (Para 9.5)

115. At the state level, the Coordination Committee should be headed by the Chief Secretary and include representatives of all the concerned State Departments as well as representatives of the Khadi and Village Industries Board, the concerned all India Commodity Board, the IDBI, the SISI and the State Corporations. (Para 9.5)

116. At the Central level the responsibility for coordination would have to be exercised by the Ministry of Industrial Development. (Para 9.5)

117. With regard to monitoring and evaluation of programmes and schemes, the responsibility should rest clearly with the DIC at the district level, the Directorate of Industries at the State level and the backward areas development Cell in the Ministry of Industrial Development at the Central level. (Para 9.6)

Labour Training

118. The primary responsibility for providing facilities for labour training rests with the Directorates of Employment and Training. However, the DIC and the IDA have to play a role in identifying training requirements at the local level. (Para 10.7)

119. In many cases, training may have to be provided outside the local area in which case the Directorate of Industries would have to be the agency responsible for making the necessary arrangements. (Para 10.7)

27

NATIONAL COMMITTEE ON THE DEVELOPMENT OF BACKWARD AREAS, 1978 — REPORT ON ORGANISATION OF ADMINISTRATIVE AND FINANCIAL STRUCTURE FOR BACKWARD AREA DEVELOPMENT

November 30, 1978 — September 27, 1980[1]

Chairman Shri B. Sivaraman, Member, Planning Commission

Members Shri Som Dutt; Prof. Mrinal Datta Chaudhary, (ceased to be member w.e.f. November 30, 1978); Shri S.S. Marathe, (ceased to be member w.e.f. November 30, 1978); Shri Ranchor Prasad; Shri Ramakrishanayya; Shri K.P.A. Menon; Shri R.M. Honavar, (ceased to be member w.e.f. January 31, 1981); Dr. S.A. Dave; Dr. Y Nayudamma; Shri Anand Sarup; Dr. B.D. Sharma; Shri Suresh Mathur; Dr. D.M. Nanjundappa; Shri S.M. Ghosh

M. Secy. Shri Nitin Desai

Appointment

The Government have been pursuing certain policies and programmes in regard to the development of backward areas since the Fourth Five Years Plan. It is now necessary to review the working of these various programmes and to set out a suitable strategy or strategies for the development of Backward Areas in the context of the priorities and objectives set out in the draft 1979-83 plan. The Planning Commission have, therefore, decided to set up a High Level Committee to formulate appropriate strategy or strategies for effectively tackling the problems of Backward Areas vide its Resolution No. PC(P)17/NCDBA/78-MLP

1. Planning Commission, Government of India, New Delhi, 1980, (i) + viii + 79 p.

dated November 30, 1978.

Terms of Reference

(i) To examine the validity of the various concepts of backwardness underlying the definitions in use for present policy purposes and recommend the criteria by which backward areas should be identified.

(ii) To review the working of:

(a) the existing plans for dealing with the general development problems of backward areas like Tribal Sub-Plans, Plans for Hill Areas, etc.; and

(b) the existing schemes for stimulating industrial development in backward areas such as the schemes for concessional finance, investment subsidy, transport subsidy, sales tax concessions, etc., similar schemes in the agricultural and allied fields like DPAP, and general measures for tackling the problems of poverty and unemployment with a view to find out their efficacy in the removal of backwardness; and

(iii) To recommend an appropriate strategy or strategies of effectively tackling the problem of backward areas, classified, if necessary, according to areas, causes or prescribed remedies.

Contents

Summary of Recommendations; Introduction; Concept and Approach towards development of backward areas; Planning processes and decentralisation of planning; Methodology of Central and State plan allocations ; Identification of beneficiaries; Organisational set-up for planning and implementation; Personnel policies; Financing and budgetary control; People's participation and promotion of voluntary organisation; Acknowledgements; Appendices I to IX.

Recommendations

Concept and Approach

1. The objective should be to initiate all-round growth, utilising the full potential of the area with the help and participation of the

people of the area. (Para 2.1)

2. Considering the problems and the differing conditions, any approach towards the development of backward area must aim at realising their full potential, with special emphasis on the least advantaged. The aim should be to improve the quality of life of the people in backward areas. (Para 2.12)

3. The emphasis on the needs of the least advantaged groups should involve the following:

(i) improvement of productivity and earning capacity of the poor in their existing activities;
(ii) promotion of new activities to absorb the surplus labour force of poor house holds;
(iii) training the traditional workers in improved technology and methods to make their efforts more remunerative; and
(iv) training, particularly of younger household members to undertake new activities. (Para 2.13)

4. The actual contents of the programme would depend upon the conditions prevailing in the areas concerned, but, by and large, subject to their suitability, following activities would be appropriate for achieving the goals in view:

(i) Agriculture and allied activities;
(ii) Irrigation;
(iii) Soil conservation and water management;
(iv) Animal husbandry and poultry;
(v) Fisheries;
(vi) Forestry;
(vii) Processing of agricultural produce;
(viii) Organising input supply, credit and marketing;
(ix) Village, Cottage, tiny and small industries;
(x) Training of local youth and upgrading of skills of local population;
(xi) Developmental infrastructure; and
(xii) Social services —
(a) safe drinking water supply
(b) health (including family planning and nutrition)
(c) education
(d) housing

(e) sanitation
(f) local transport
(g) social welfare. (Para 2.14)

5. The Block should be taken as a 'unit' for planning and development. (Para 2.160

Planning Process and Decentralisation of Planning

6. The block being the 'Unit' for planning and development, integrated area development programmes should be implemented through a project approach on the Integrated Tribal Development Project (ITDP) pattern, covering 2 to 3 blocks, depending on the local conditions and situation. (Para 3.1)

7. It is to be ensured that the Block plan does not become a lone and truncated exercise and must be closely coordinated with planning at the District and State levels.

8. In order to ensure that necessary direction and guidance on major policy issues connected with the development of backward areas, particularly in block level planning and implementation, is available, there should be a high-powered steering committee at the State level under the Chairmanship of the Chief Minister and consisting of the Ministers for the key sectors in rural development such as Agriculture, Industry, Health, Education, Irrigation, etc., as Members. A senior officer of the rank of Commissioner should be Secretary of this Steering Committee. (Para 3.15)

9. The Block Level Plans and surveys should be initially carried out by a Block Level Planning Team consisting of the Block Development Officer and other technical and related staff available in the Block, assisted by surveyors, recruited on temporary basis to collect information about the households. (Para 3.20)

10. A District Planning Cell for the backward areas would have to be created. It is not necessary to provide whole-time technical specialists since the existing technical staff should be in a position to provide the necessary technical expertise for collecting of data and formulation of plans for the District. (Para 3.20)

11. The existing Technical Cells which have already grown during the Fifth Plan for strengthening the planning machinery at State level should provide necessary technical and secretarial support. In the case of such states as have not so for set up those cells, steps should be

taken to set them up immediately. There should be a separate unit in the Department responsible for plan implementation to monitor and analyse variations in the levels of development in backward areas in the State and act as a "nodal" point for integration of backward area plans in the State Plan. (Para 3.20)

Methodology of Central and State Plan Allocations

12. In order to ensure that necessary resources are provided both by the Central and State Governments to achieve the objective of integrated rural development of backward areas, it is essential to earmark the resources, out of the planned resources, separately for the development of the backward areas. (Para 4.2)

13. It is not enough merely to lay down that adequate funds must be made available for the development of backward areas. Governmental approaches and reflexes should be such as to convince the people that the Government of the day is really intent upon improving their lot and the Backward areas would get their due share out of the national kitty and it is not their better-off brothers who would prosper at their cost. Therefore, the concept of a "Sub-Plan for the development of backward areas" should be introduced, both at the National and the State levels. (Para 4.5)

14. As regards the methodology, it is recommended that the total State Plan outlay, including Central assistance available under the Gadgil and IATP formulae, which forms part of the State Plan, should first be divided into divisible and non-divisible portions. Care will have to be taken to ensue that no attempt is made to inflate the non-divisible pool and only such items, as are really not divisible, should be included in the non-divisible pool. It should also be ensured that allocations already earmarked for backward areas and classes like hill areas, tribal areas, etc., are not reduced; in fact, there should be a gradual increase every year in the overall resources earmarked for such areas. (Paras 4.12 and 4.13)

15. The divisible resources should be worked out on the basis of the following: (a) Calculate non-divisible resources intended for such items as are for the benefit of the whole State and are not susceptible to any division between the backward and non-backward areas, (b) Calculate what is already earmarked for such areas and classes as are backward like hill, tribals, arid and semi-arid areas, etc., with a suitable progressive increase every year; and (c) excluding (a) and (b), the

remaining State Plan resources would be regarded as divisible.

16. After giving careful, consideration to what should be the most equitable formula for dividing the divisible outlays, it is recommended that the State Plan outlays for the backward areas should be worked out on the basis of 50 per cent of the population and 50 per cent of the area comprising the backward areas. (Paras 4.12 and 4.13)

17. Once the State Sub-Plan and the total outlay for the backward areas has been determined the provision for such schemes such as, power, major and medium irrigation projects would be taken out as addition to the project or projects where the schemes are located. The remaining Plan provision would then be disaggregated on the basis of a project or a District where the whole District is declared as backward. There are going to be disparities even within the backward areas which are, comparatively speaking, somewhat more backward. For this disaggregation, it is recommended that this should be done on the basis of weightage of 50 per cent of population, 30 per cent of the area and 20 per cent of income generated. As indices of income generation are not likely to be readily available, it is suggested that till such time as reliable indices become available for giving weightage to the less backward areas, disaggregation may be done on the basis of 50 per cent of population and 50 per cent of the area. (Para 4.17)

18. It is suggested that the Central Ministries may, carry out a careful exercise and determine which of their schemes are of universal nature and can be divided between the backward and non-backward areas. (Para 4.19)

19. As has been suggested in the case of the State Plan, it is recommended that each Ministry should work out a list of schemes which they consider can be classified as divisible. Once this exercise has been carried out, the total outlay available for such divisible schemes should be apportioned between backward and non-backward areas of the country on the basis of weightage of 50 per cent for population and 50 per cent for area in the backward regions of the country. Ideally, of course, the best formula would be to work out allocations for the backward areas on the basis of 50 per cent for population, 30 per cent for area and 30 per cent for income generated in the backward areas. (Para 4.20)

20. In respect of Central schemes where sharing is on the basis of 50 per cent grant from the Central Government, it should be ensured that matching grants are always available from the Central Ministries where State Governments have made provision for these schemes in

the backward areas.

21. Under "Integrated Rural Development Programme", where the accent is on weaker sections, the Ministry of Rural Reconstruction has laid down criteria for defining beneficiaries and procedure of identification. These are good enough for identifying beneficiaries for the beneficiary oriented programmes and selection of the poorest from among those who are so identified. (Para 5.7)

22. In the absence of any precise statistical data, income estimation of an individual can at best be done either on the statement of the individual or on the basis of the information given by the village Sarpanch, etc. It is here that the crux of the situation lies. Such an approach is open to abuse and can lead to a misdirection of benefits. What precautions should be taken if any scientific attempt to collect statistical data about incomes, etc., is to be avoided? The only solution would appear to be involve the people themselves. Data so collected should be analysed in a public forum in the village, cross-checking with a large public participation. (Para 5.8)

Organisational set up for Planning and Implementation

23. The concept of planning for development and its execution, as a time bound programme, will require a well-considered counter-part Administrative input. Whilst the various hierarchical administrations and institutions and local bodies must be responsible for the perfection of their own systems of delivery, the overall command must be able to coordinate the programmes and distribute responsibility to the various parts. It must also have a minimum administrative control over the various field level organisations to get agreed programmes effectively, implemented. This is more so in backward and rural areas where the gap between intention and implementation is particularly large because of hierarchical weaknesses. Such a system has necessarily to be based on an area-approach. (Para 6.2)

24. Broadly speaking, the planning and development administration at the area level must ensure a coordination of the political, administrative and local institutions, bring together all the administrative operations at the area level under effective coordination, and provide and effective mechanism for formulation of programmes of development, based on local resources, needs and expectation of the people, and interaction with the existing institutions and local bodies, and bring an administrative cohesion in these bodies by persuasion and be in a

position to clearly lay down a programme of work for the participating agencies which could be made responsible for the proper execution of their respective assignments. (Para 6.3)

25. A strong multi-disciplinary leadership at the project level will have to be conceived. Whatever name this organisation is given and whatever task is entrusted to it for comprehensive development, it will have to address itself at every moment about its efficacy in crucial areas. Some of its essential features have to be a fairly wide delegation of authority, both in terms of finances and personnel, day-to-day administrative control over all related functionaries, irrespective of the department to which they belong, flexibility in budgetary and accounting procedures, etc. (Para 6.29)

26. Considering the fact that the new strategy envisages a comprehensive development approach, what has to be aimed is not the creation of a new organisation but suitable restructuring and remoulding of the existing set up. The administrative set up for integrated rural development should be area based, which built-in-multi-purpose characteristics for a well defined area. The set up should cover all rural development activities which should function in a coordinated way. In other words, the set up would largely be an entity comprising of the existing administrative units in the given area, with such innovations and modifications as are necessary to achieve the end in view. (Para 6.31)

27. A comprehensive development project is envisaged to be implemented on the basis of a "Project Approach" on the pattern of the Integrated Tribal Development Project for the total development of the project area. This project should cover the entire non-regulatory administrative apparatus in the project area. Each Project will consist of two or three identified backward blocks, depending upon the needs and size of the area. Situations can arise where a district may have only one such project or more than one project. (Paras 6.34 to 6.37)

28. Flexibility in original constitution, adaptability to every changing situation, adequate delegation of powers are some of the essential requirements which have to be satisfied by any formal structure of an IDP. The best course would be to set up an appropriate authority by an executive order of the State Government. The executive order should clearly lay down the delegation of powers so that there is no time lag between the formal constitution of an authority and its effective functioning. An authority created by an executive order will have the advantage of avoiding the creation of a separate legal entity. The developmental programmes through such an agency should be con-

ceived as comprising the totality of programmes under all sectors. (Para 6.41)

29. The authority would be responsible for: (i) planning, direction and monitoring of all programmes in the Blocks within its jurisdiction, (ii) exercise such powers as are considered necessary to ensure not only coordination of the work of all the departmental officers in the Project but also be in a position to have such control as would enable it to issue directives and take work from them. All officers in the Project would be directly under the day to day administrative control of the Chief Executive Officer. It has, however, to be ensured that the technical supervision and guidance from the concerned Departments should continue, as hitherto, and is not diluted in any way. (Para 6.43)

30. The Block Development Officer or his equivalent, would function as the Executive Officer under IDPA so far as the Block is concerned. All beneficiary-oriented programmes would also be implemented by the Block administration under the overall superintendence and direction of the IDP Authority, Peoples' associations and Voluntary organisations should be given fullest opportunity to plan and implement the programmes. (Para 6.44)

31. The block level planning and the project level implementation would require coordination at a somewhat higher level in order to work out a proper plan and secure the best deployment of resources. This has to be done at the District level. It is, therefore, suggested that the Collector should be the Chairman for all projects located in his district. (Para 6.45)

32. At the District Level there should be Advisory Committee for Planning, Coordinating, Monitoring and Implementation. (Para 6.46)

33. In the light of the set up suggested by the Committee, under which planning and implementation will be taken up by the project authority and the coordination by the District Planning and Coordination Cell, a view would have to be taken whether there is any need for the existing agencies, namely, SFDA, DPAP, etc., to continue as a separate entity or get merged with the District Monitoring and Coordination Cell at the District level. (Para 6.47)

34. Apart from the Steering Committee under 'Planning' which will guide the implementation of all programmes in the backward areas in the State, it would be necessary to have a coordination cell at the State Headquarters not only to monitor reprogress by various development Departments but also to exercise the necessary budgetary control and to ensure that Plan allocations made for the development of back-

ward areas are not diverted to any other area. This Cell must necessarily be attached to the Department dealing with Planning. (Para 6.48)

35. An officer of the rank of Additional Secretary/Joint Secretary in the Ministry of Rural Reconstruction should be designated as Director General, Development of Backward Areas. His duties would be to monitor and evaluate the progress in the implementation of various programmes. He would also coordinate with the other concerned Ministries about the release of funds, etc., like tribal development with Home Ministry, Rural Health with Health Ministry, Education with Education Ministry and drinking water with Ministry of Works and Housing. (Para 6.49)

36. The developmental activities and functions in the District should be grouped into a number of broad specialisation. These include, depending upon the need: (1) Planning, monitoring and evaluation, (2) Agriculture and allied sectors, (3) Forestry, (4) Engineering Services, (5) Health Services, (6) Social Services and (7) Industry and Employment. Each broad group may be headed at the District level by an except in a sub-specialisation which may be the most important for the area. (Paras 6.50 and 6.51)

37. In an integrated area development approach, it would be useful, to have integration of specialised functions within the same broad discipline under the charge of a sufficiently senior officer, each incharge of a broad specialisation. All sub-specialisations within each broad specialisation should be under unified command of the head of the Branch. The functions at lower levels would need to be made broad-based and redefined. (Para 6.52)

38. Since the Collector or the District Magistrate would be Chairman of all the project authorities located in the District, it would be essential to provide a separate cell to coordinate and monitor the implementation of programmes in various projects at the District level. (Para 6.54)

39. Relationship of the Integrated Development Project Authority and the Panchayati Raj Institutions has been defined in paras 6.62 to 6.65. (Paras 6.62 to 6.65)

Personnel Policies

40. The backward areas, in particular tribals inaccessible hills and desert areas suffer from some special disabilities because of their special problems. Some of these are: (i) lack of special services like

education, health, (ii) many of these areas are still unhealthy; (ii) communications generally are not well developed; (iv) housing facilities are conspicuous by their absence in the interior areas; and (v) most areas lack minimum amenities which are available in towns. In view of the considerable disparity in the availability of social services like education and health indifferent areas and spiralling prices which makes it difficult for fixed income groups to keep to the expected standards of living, transfers and postings, in effect, have come to be a part of the reward and punishment system in personnel administration. This is not a happy situation. Elements of punishment which have crept in must be eliminated by suitable built in elements of compensation. (Paras 7.2 and 7.3)

41. Large number of development posts in the backward areas are lying vacant. (Para 7.5)

42. More and more efforts would have to be made both at the political and administrative levels as well as in the educational institutions wherein younger generation entering the State services would have to realise that their responsibility lies more in serving their less fortunate brethren though it may lead to more effort and discomfort on their part. (Paras 7.6 and 7.7)

43. The problem of personnel can be generally divided into three parts:

(i) Personnel at higher level, generally belonging to all-India services or higher State services;
(ii) Personnel at the district level belonging to State services or junior levels in all-India services; and
(iii) Personnel in local cadres.

The problem in each category is different and calls for a different solution. (Para 7.8)

44. A suitable system should be devised to ensure that the selection of officers is based with a view to posting such of them in backward areas as could take up the challenge of difficult work and who have the requisite sensitivity, aptitude, training, etc., and the selection should be institutionalised at all levels. (Para 7.9 (i))

45. Steps should be taken to amends the service rules to make it compulsory for each future direct entrant to service for at least three years in the areas which are specifically identified as backward. (Para 7.9 (ii))

46. As far as possible, barring perhaps the senior administrative and supervisory posts, where experienced officers would be necessary, direct recruits, after suitable training, should be posted to the backward areas. They should not be kept for more than 3 to 5 years in the backward areas and an incentive should be offered to them after completion of their tenure in the backward areas by giving them a posting to a station of their own choice. (Para 7.9 (iii))

47. It should be ensured that the first posting on promotion is to the backward areas. In case of their reluctance or difference, service rules should be so amended as to deny them the promotions for a requisite period leading to loss of seniority. The incentive of giving them a station of their choice after serving the backward areas should also be available to them. (Para 7.9 (iv))

48. Field level and other similarly placed workers should be recruited from within the project area to the extent possible, if not possible, it should at least be made districtwise for such lower cadres. (Para 7.9 (v))

49. Travelling allowance rules should be suitably amended to provide incentive to the personnel to move on foot or on cycle in remote areas. (Para 7.9 (vi))

50. Officers posted to backward areas should be allowed special study leave over and above their normal entitlement, to undertake study work or research work in academic institutions in these fields. (Para 7.9 (vii))

51. State Governments should give topmost priority in existing Plan programmes and make specific provisions for housing accommodation in the backward areas, particularly at the block and project level. Funds should also be provided for office accommodation wherever it is not available at present. (Para 7.9 (viii and ix))

52. Adequate higher level educational and health facilities must be provided at least at the District headquarters. (Para 7.9 (x))

53. Efforts should be made to establish Central Schools so that the children of staff working in backward areas not suffer when they get posted in the areas where the medium of instruction is in a different language. (Para 7.9 (xi))

54. Field officers should be allowed the use of departmental vehicles for carrying patients to such hospitals where specialist treatment is available in case the existing medical facilities at the posting base are not adequate. (Para 7.9 (xii))

55. Newly recruited Medical Officers should be posted to the

backward areas and it should be made a condition of their service at the time of recruitment. (Para 7.9 (xiii))

56. Once a policy is laid down for posting the officers and staff and posting orders issued in accordance with this policy, this should not be cancelled or postponed, save in exceptional circumstances. (Para 7.11)

57. It is quite possible that the rationalisation of organisational structure and personnel in each project area may reveal considerable spare capacity in the organisations. This can be used for the additional work load likely to be created by the new developmental effort. Much spare capacity may particularly be available at lower levels because each organisation at present is trying to reach the field level through an independent hierarchy. On the other hand, higher level technical expertise may not be available. Each functionary may be looking to the district or the regional level for guidance in its respective field. The technical officers working in the project area should be on the regular strength of the respective cadres. There should be no deputation of officers to the project authorities. The requirement of additional personnel in the IDP area should be met by suitably upgrading departmental posts adding to the regular cadre strength of the concerned departments at an appropriate level. (Para 7.12)

58. In the absence of proper evaluation and follow up programmes, training in a number of cases has got routinised. Each Institution and each State appears to be moving in isolation. Training programmes for officers are sporadic and are not followed in all cases. The whole training programmes for backward areas needs to be reviewed and reinforced at the national and state levels. (Para 7.13)

59. Officers working in backward areas, particularly in tribal and hill areas, are many a time not conversant with the local language. This results in a deep gulf between the administration and people. Therefore, proficiency in the major tribal languages should be insisted upon in case of all officers posted in tribal and hill areas. A cash award of Rs. 5,000 should be given to every officers who attains the required proficiency. Tribal Research Institutes in States should make arrangements to impart training in tribal languages and have a proper standard for judging the proficiency of officers. Major dialect in the tribal areas should be treated on the same basis as tribal languages. (Para 7.14)

60. Incentives by themselves will not be sufficient. There should be an element of compulsion for learning tribal dialect. Every individual, who joins a local cadre, should be expected to learn the local

dialect within a period of one year. This should be incorporated as a condition of his appointment. Failure to learn the dialect should automatically result in termination of his service. Officers belonging to State and all India Cadre posted to these areas should also be expected to learn the local dialect within one year. In case of failure to do so, an adverse entry in their character roll should be made and further increments may be stopped. (Para 7.15)

Financing and Budgetary Control

61. For expeditious development effort, in the backward areas, a mechanism has to be evolved so that the adverse effect of the financial year ending at an inconvenient time in the working season and the time lag in allocation which results in the loss of full agricultural season in these areas can be remedied. (Para 8.3)

62. The existing procedures are so time consuming that by the time the field functionaries are in a position to execute them, the year is out. The departmental heads are naturally anxious to utilise the funds allotted to their departments and this results in their diverting the funds to programmes for which these were not originally intended. A mechanism has, therefore, to be devised not only to cut down the delays in issuing the sanctions and allocation of funds but also to ensure that adequate powers are available at the field level and reappropriations, if any, are not done to benefit the non-backward areas out of the funds intended for the backward areas. (Para 8.6)

63. The following budgetary approach for bringing in greater local involvement in the planning and implementation process for backward area development is recommended. The main objective, the Committee is seeking, is to gradually transfer to the planning and implementation unit at the project level larger and larger amounts every year which will be amenable to their control in planning their own area development. Another objective that the Committee has before it is to ensure that the intention to divert divisible developmental budget for the benefit of every project area in the backward area really gets translated in implementation and the funds so promised in the Plan and the budget at the beginning of the year do not get diverted to the non-backward areas. The methodology, the Committee has suggested may not be fully acceptable to every State because of the present constraints and its budgeting methodology. It is hoped that sufficient changes will be brought in by every State in their budget methodology to ensure that

the two basic objectives, the Committee has in view, are achieved.

(i) Under each major demand for the various development departments, a minor head shall be provided taking out the divisible share under each type of backwardness. There should be a convention that such funds shown against any type of backwardness are not reappropriated to any of the other heads in either the minor or the major head of the concerned department;

(ii) There shall be a major demand for each type of fundamental backwardness, for example tribal, hill, drought prone, desert, chronically flood-affected and coastal areas effected by salinity which may be accepted as categorisable as backward. Under this budget will be brought together –

(a) the annual amounts under the sub-plan of the various departments to be transferred for local planning, as recommended in paragraph 8.14;

(b) the special funds allocated in the State budget and in the Centrally-sponsored budget for ameliorating the conditions in that category of backward areas; and

(c) the proposed special additive of Rs. 5 lakhs which will be available for local planning and implementation, under each block of a project area, under that type of backwardness.

(iii) The disaggregated budget provision indicated under the minor heads of the major demands, as expendable under each type of backwardness, would continue to be operated upon by appropriate administrative departments in the normal way. A convention will be established that the department will have no authority to reappropriate the funds earmarked for the development of backward areas whether within the backward areas or to other non-backward areas without specific approval of the State Department incharge of monitoring and policy formulation for development of backward areas;

(iv) The Controlling officers of the administrative departments will have the responsibility of preparation of budget estimates, submission of revised estimates, etc. Disaggregated provision under the minor head under each class of backwardness will naturally have several sub-sectors relating to various plan programmes of the departments in the backward areas. The administrative departments should have the power to reappropriate funds within each project area under the broad type of backward area from one sub-sector to another sub-sector so as to ensure that overall surrender of funds, the project area is entitled to, is avoided as far as possible; and

(v) The planning and implementation organisation at the block level and the district level will have to formulate the integrated development plan for the allocations under the minor heads for the various types of backwardness, alongwith supporting or modifying plans fully under the control of the project authority for which funds are provided under items (b) and (c) of paragraph (ii) above. The intention is that gradually a rapport will be established between the development departments and local planning to orient the departmental plans to fit in with local aspirations and requirements in the interest of maximising development and helping the poorer sections. (Para 8.13)

64. Even though the divisible part of the State Plan is allocated to the projects, the sheer inertia of ongoing programmes will leave very little scope to the local planning group to adjust the funding to local requirements or an integrated development approach at the local level. Special steps will, therefore, have to be taken to force gradually a discretionary allocation to the local planning and implementation group to enable them to bring in local planning of greater and greater magnitude gradually. In the first year of the Plan, it may not be possible for the States to adjust their budgets to allow for this local diversion. But from the second year onwards, starting with 10 per cent of divisible amount and gradually increasing by 10 per cent each year and reaching 40 per cent in the fifth year, out of the divisible allocation, these amounts will be given to the Project Authority for planning and implementation of local programmes, best suited to their needs. (Para 8.14)

65. The Committee would recommend that 25 per cent of the departmental outlay covering the expenditure in the first quarter of the new financial year based on the budget provisions made by the department concerned and approved by the State Legislature may be released immediately the budget is approved by the State Legislature to the

Authority, without waiting for the formal sanctions to be issued by the concerned departments. This would enable the Authorities to maintain the continuity of the ongoing approved programmes without any interruption and would not have to await the receipt of formal sanctions from the concerned departments. Issue of formal sanction does take time. This procedure would avoid loss of any working season. In case there is delay in issue of sanctions for more than three months, more funds could be released, in advance, for the second quarter. (Para 8.16)

66. The Project Authority should be given powers to sanction any new scheme from the proposed project fund for local planning on the advice of the Board of Management and subject to the conditions enumerated therein. (Para 8.17)

67. As regards the funds administered by the concerned Departments, the IDP authority is in due course expected to prepare its own programmes and plans, which should be sent to the concerned Department after due approval by the Local Board of Management. Once the scheme and programmes have been approved by the competent authority at the State level, the IDP authority should be given the total outlay relatable to project areas for all the schemes approved therefor. They would, of course, have to be given policy guidelines by the State in preparing programmes to be undertaken by them but they should have complete freedom and flexibility to work out their own priorities. (Para 8.19)

68. The best course to avoid lapse of savings would be: (i) efforts should be made by the Coordinating Administrative Departments in the State to enjoin on the Project authorities to utilise the funds placed at their disposal for the purpose for which they are intended and a close watch kept on the savings with a view to fixing up responsibility, (ii) 50 per cent of the savings in a particular area may be allowed to the project authority as an addition to their next year's budgetary allocations, it necessary, through a supplementary grant, and (ii) intersectoral adjustments to avoid savings. (Para 8.23)

69. As development of backward areas has to be expedited, the Committee is of the view that a special allocation of Rs. 5 lakhs per year for each block in a project area for the Plan period should be available as a special additive. The Committee also appreciates that a new project approach cannot to imposed all over the country as one time operation. In order to enable the States to adjust their organisational planning and implementation structure to the new requirements the project approach will have to be phased for the five years of the

Plan period. It is suggested that about 600 blocks may be taken up in the first year and the programme phased to absorb all the backward blocks by the fifth year of the Plan. The Committee will try to work out some of these details as is possible in the final report. (Para 8.25)

70. The size of the investment in each of the Integrated Development Projects would need to be determined once the State and Central Sub-Plans for development of backward areas are ready. It has already been suggested that at least 10 per cent of the sectoral outlay in each Department for the development of backward areas should be made available to the Project authorities for taking up programmes suited to the local needs. It has also been recommended that at least 25 per cent of the budgetary outlay should be made available as Ways & Means Advance to each Project in order to avoid the likelihood of delay in routing the outlays through the State Governments and their merger with the general resource flow at the IDP level. While the Committee has not favoured the idea of a project authority being registered as a society, it is not opposed to the Project Authority being registered as a society for the limited purpose of receiving this Ways & Means Advance for a specified programme from the Central or State organisations in case it is found that it is not possible to provide such a Ways & Means Advance or to create a Nucleus Fund with project authorities because of the budgetary requirements. (Para 8.27)

71. The size of the outlay for each of the IDPs should be decided after careful discussion of the total Sub-Plan outlay for the development of backward areas. Disaggregation should not follow a rough or ready or *ad-hoc* formula. The level of investment in each IDP should depend on the level and potential for development and requirement of the project, as determined by the project authorities.

72. A strong accounting cell would seem to be a must at the project level. This Cell should not only be responsible for primary account keeping but devise a reporting system which satisfies the sectoral authorities. It should also advise the project authorities on financial matters and help them in monitoring the flow of funds from different authorities and in regulating it below the project level. (Para 8.29)

People's Participation and Promotion of Voluntary Agencies

73. The Task Force on 'Voluntary Participation in Rural Development' has spelt out the planning, fiscal and administrative frame for the involvement of voluntary agencies. It has also recommended that

voluntary agencies can help in the following fields: (a) preparation of meaningful plans of rural development, particularly these where the families have to be involved in their own uplift; (b) voluntary agencies can take responsibility and implement a part or whole of an integrated development programmes in the area. The Committee fully endorses the frame of action and fiscal and administrative support. (Paras 9.2 and 9.3)

74. Too much emphasis on general academic consultancies for preparation of such integrated plans may be abandoned. Only bodies with field experience in performance of programmes may be inducted for this purpose. (Para 9.4)

75. Experimentation in integrated rural planning involving families has been adopted in several parts of the country. Of these, the 'Uttar Merur' frame, further refined, appears to be best suited for our purpose. (Para 9.5)

76. Voluntary agencies which can handle a comprehensive integrated area and familywise programme are few in the country and where available have to be nurtured. (Para 9.6)

77. Taking the most obvious felt need of an area, a dedicated voluntary agency, given the lead, can gradually develop an all-round approach. This is a slow process and cannot be pushed, but the approach will bring out the various socio-economic problems to the forefront and activise the administration to find the correct remedies. (Para 9.7)

78. Popular organisations are of two kinds, the statutory like Panchayati Raj and the voluntary and *ad-hoc* like a group of farmers doing joint cultivation for producing cash crops requiring high investment. The Asoka Mehta Committee on Panchayati Raj has analysed the strength and the weaknesses of the Panchayati Raj system and has come to the conclusion that if our objective is the improvement of weaker sections of the community, Panchayati Raj has to be supervised by both social audit and performance audit and the responsibility for the performance audit should be with the group selected from the weaker sections. The arguments of the Asoka Mehta Committee bring out the basic conflict between the "Haves" and the "Havenots" in rural areas. Extending the argument, any voluntary organisation of "Haves" and "Havenots" together for balanced development is going to be counter-productive. What may be attempted will be small homogenous peoples groups, on a functional basis, of weaker sections only, linked to well defined simple functions like village industries, animal husbandry, etc. (Para 9.8)

79. The best methodology would be to identify small homogenous groups of people and then weld them into a voluntary group. Steps should be taken by the block organisation to identify small homogenous groups whose needs and requirements as well as social position are same. Once these groups are identified, they should be encouraged and motivated to form their organisations and to elect from among themselves their group leaders. (Paras 9.11 and 9.12)

80. Identification of group leaders by the people participating in the groups, whether elected or selected, should be left to the discretion of the members of the group. Arrangements would, however, have to be made to train them in properly equipped institution. On completion of their training, which, to start with, should not exceed one month or so, these group leaders would function as leaders of these groups and be responsible for highlighting their members' aspirations, needs and requirements. (Para 9.13)

81. Group leaders should promote the formation of their Members' Organisation(s)/association(s) at the 'block' level, where planning and implementation is to be actually done. These organisations, at the block level, should be properly constituted bodies as per the legal requirements. We would thus have at a sufficiently higher level a proper peoples organisation which will be responsible for planning and implementing programmes, formulated by it for all the families covered by the block. (Para 9.14)

82. The standard system adopted in our country is to provide subsidies to individual beneficiaries, grant-in-aid for infrastructural development and financial support to voluntary organisations for supplementing their resources. There should be clear-cut guidelines for the grant of subsidies to individuals. These are outlined in para 9.19. (Paras 9.16 and 9.19)

83. Grant-in-aid for infrastructural development has been an essential feature of the strategy of community development or rural welfare. By providing a part of the expenditure in the shape of grant-in-aid, the intention is to involve the community and given them a feeling of participation. Experience in such cases has not been very happy because of a variety of short-comings and drawbacks of the existing system. It must be accepted that infrastructural development and other developmental programme in a given area should be regarded by any enlightened Government, committed to the welfare of masses as a must. Most problems arise because of the imposition of the programmes from above. Suggestions in this regard are incorporated in para 9.20. (Para 9.20)

NATIONAL COMMITTEE ON THE DEVELOPMENT OF BACKWARD AREAS, 1978 — REPORT ON VILLAGE AND COTTAGE INDUSTRIES, November 30, 1978 — March 28, 1981[1]

Chairman Shri B. Sivaraman, Member, Planning Commission

Members Shri Som Dutt; Prof. Mrinal Datta Chaudhary (ceased to be member w.e.f. November 30, 1978); Shri S.S. Marathe (ceased to be member w.e.f. January 31, 1978); Shri Ranchor Prasad; Shri Ramakrishanayya; Shri K.P.A. Menon; Shri R.M. Honavar (ceased to be member w.e.f. January 31, 1981); Dr. S.A. Dave; Dr. Y. Nayudamma; Shri Anand Sarup; Dr. B.D. Sharma; Shri Suresh Mathur; Dr. D.M. Nanjundappa

M. Secy. Shri Nitin Desai

Appointment

The Government have been pursuing certain policies and programmes in regard to the development of backward areas since the Fourth Five Years Plan. It is now necessary to review the working of these various programmes and to set out a suitable strategy or strategies for the development of Backward Areas in the context of the priorities and objectives set out in the draft 1979-83 plan. The Planning Commission have, therefore, decided to set up a High Level Committee to formulate appropriate strategy or strategies for effectively tackling the problems of Backward Areas vide its Resolution No. PC(P)17/NCDBA/78-MLP dated November 30, 1978.

Terms of Reference

(i) To examine the validity of the various concepts of backward-

1. Planning Commission, Government of India, New Delhi, 1981, 69 p.

ness underlying the definitions in use for present policy purposes and recommend the criteria by which backward areas should be identified.

(ii) To review the working of:

(a) the existing plans for dealing with the general development problems of backward areas like Tribal Sub-Plans, Plans for Hill Areas, etc.; and

(b) the existing schemes for stimulating industrial development in backward areas such as the schemes for concessional finance, investment subsidy, transport subsidy, sales tax concessions, etc., similar schemes in the agricultural and allied fields like DPAP, and general measures for tackling the problems of poverty and unemployment with a view to find out their efficacy in the removal of backwardness; and

(iii) To recommend an appropriate strategy or strategies for effectively tackling the problems of backward areas, classified, if necessary, according to areas, causes or prescribed remedies.

Contents

Summary of Conclusions and Recommendations; Introduction; Present Status and Problems; Organisations Operating in the field of Village and Cottage Industries; The Strategy of Development of Village and Cottage Industries; Raw Material; Marketing; Technological Development; Training; Organisational Structures; Annexures I to XII.

Recommendations

Introduction

1. For providing gainful and productive avenues of employment to the growing labour force and relieve unemployment and under-employment in rural backward areas, a massive programme of industrialisation in the shape of village and cottage industries would have to be launched. This assumes added significance in the face of limited opportunities in the agricultural pursuits and for putting a check to the large scale migration to urban areas. The dispersed character of the village and cottage industries facilitate the utilisation of scattered resources of the rural backward area. (Para 1.3)

Present Status and Problems

2. In the context of backward areas development, because of the various inherent limitations to the growth of the organised industries sector in these areas and because of the insufficient potentialities of agricultural development and the migration to urban areas where opportunities are already limited, the importance of the unorganised sector is significant. In addition, on account of the predominantly rural character of the backward areas, the promotion of village and cottage industries assume a very significant role. (Para 2.4)

3. In our economic situation, with scarcity of capital and abundance of labour, our choice naturally has to be biased towards techniques making use of capital-saving or labour-intensive techniques. The techniques chosen need to take full cognisance of spread effect, need to protect employment, enhance productivity, develop skills and meet the needs of local consumption. However, in any such adoption, economic viability needs to be in the forefront. (Para 2.13)

4. Efforts should be directed towards upgradation of technology so that the artisans move out of their poverty trap at the earliest and their dependents enjoy ever increasing living standards. (Para 2.14)

5. The criterion of economic viability does not mean that subsidies can be dispensed with. Subsidies will be necessary to expand village and cottage industries particularly in the earlier stages. (Para 2.15)

6. In the existing set up for the unorganised sector the available technology is not fully utilised, productivity is quite low and much of the value added is syphoned off by exploitative middlemen. (Para 2.27)

7. The practical course is to introduce modernisation of techniques and improve the skills and make the worker capable of enhancing his productivity and his earnings so as to enable him to meet at least the basic necessities of life and come out of the clutches of poverty within reasonable time. (Para 2.27)

8. The artisan himself finds against odds at each level of his operations, be it the purchase of raw materials, the marketing of the products, the arrangement of credit, access to institution cover, etc. His weak sustaining and bargaining power is exploited by all and sundry, naturally to his utter disadvantage. (Para 2.27)

9. It is not enough that the value added is improved, but that, a larger portion of it reaches the worker. (Para 2.27)

10. There is a pattern of regional concentration in various household industries because of the historical growth process.

(Para 2.28)

11. The statistical picture of employment in household industries shows an alarming decline even after allowing for definitional changes. Backward areas will be the natural victims of this decline where their ability to attract modern industry, which replaces many of these declining activities, is limited. Hence protection and promotion of village and cottage industries becomes an important element in any strategy for backward area development. (Para 2.38)

12. Public policy must take into account the low level of earnings and the exploitation in this sector. Hence policy must be directed not merely at preserving these industries but at upgrading them in terms of technology so that earnings of artisans can be pushed above the poverty line. (Para 2.38)

Organisations Operating in the Field of Village and Cottage Industries

13. Khadi and Village Industries Commission (KVIC) is the premier organisation charged with the responsibility of developing and promoting cottage and village industries. The other important organisations concerned are All India Handloom Board, Central Silk Board. All India Handicrafts Board and Coir Board. (Para 3.1)

14. The organisation structure of KVIC suffers from certain deficiencies. The prime among these are lack of proper coordination between the KVIC and the State Board, lack of involvement of the State Government in the programmes of the Khadi and Village industries, the fact that the majority of the field level agencies are not appropriately equipped and KVIC has been able to cover through its programmes only a small number of artisans. (Para 3.10)

15. Organisations like National Small Industries Corporation, Forest Corporations and the like have also been contributing towards the meaningful development of village and cottage industries. (Para 3.36)

The Strategy of Development of Village and Cottage Industries

16. The basic expectation in the Plans is to develop the Village and Cottage Industries so as to provide greater and more remunerative employment to the increasing number of labour participants that the population increases is throwing up. The stated objective has not been achieved. The reason is not far to seek. The problem has not been

studied in any depth and remedies have not been sought. (Para 4.1)

17. The Village and Cottage Industries, except handlooms, sericulture, handicrafts, coir, minor forest produce, etc., have been treated as, more or less, the preserve of the Khadi and Village Industries Commission. Having given them the franchise, nobody else appears to have taken any significant steps to enable the Commission to fulfil its role or complement its work by their own effort to develop the sector. (Para 4.2)

18. The Khadi and Village Industries Commission has been suffering for long years by a running controversy on the limits of mechanisation. The arguments continue. Meanwhile the number of those seeking a living in this sector is obviously dwindling. (Para 4.2)

19. In the running controversy over how much labour intensity is to be maintained and how much mechanisation is to be allowed, the artisan is being forced to continue the traditional labour intensive approach which involves drudgery, sometimes of the entire family, with a small return in value added for the time employed. (Para 4.3)

20. On the question of flight of artisans from their traditional pursuits one can venture a good guess that the processes involving drudgery without adequate returns, act as the basic retarding force. If this tendency is to be reversed, such processes will have to be suitably mechanised. (Para 4.4)

21. The Committee has no hesitation in recommending that the primary approach in the strategy should be to evolve a suitable mix of the manual and the mechanical for each of the traditional industries so that those parts of the operation which involve heavy drudgery and expenditure of time, without adequate value added for the time spent, are suitably mechanised. Thereby, the artisan and his family can use their time better in those parts of the process where their skill comes into operation and the return in value for time spent is reasonable and at least a living wage is assured. It is this intermediate technology, wherein skill is retained and upgraded, which has got to be developed consciously and quickly. The Committee recommends that this should be the key strategy for reversing the diminishing returns in employment from this sector. (Para 4.4)

22. It is the fashion for any body supporting village and cottage industry to add almost invariably as a rider that the approach should be labour intensive and mechanisation should be frowned upon. The Committee wish to point out that the justification for village and cottage industries is not only the employment generation but the resultant im-

provement in quality of the consumer goods thereby produced. This is the most significant factor which distinguishes the artisan production from the machine made uniformity and gives the greater justification for this sector to survive. (Para 4.5)

23. The present position is that the artisan spends a lot of his time in drudgery and repetitive operations which can well be performed by machines thereby making time for putting in the skill in the finishing of the goods and enhancing the quality aspects. If this can be achieved without putting people off the industry, it will be the right strategy. (Para 4.5)

24. The Committee wants to emphasise that those taking of labour intensity do create an impression in the field workers that mechanisation of any sort is a taboo. There has to be greater precision in what we mean. (Para 4.5)

25. Because of the drudgery and the low return for the time spent, village and cottage industries are fast losing their attraction for not only the present generation of artisans but preventing the new generation from seeking a livelihood in this sector. (Para 4.6)

26. In case drudgery and fatigue are suitably reduced and the production becomes available in larger quantities, the absorption of the products would depend on the viable growth impulses generated in the economy. The perspective indicates hope on that front. (Para 4.7)

27. If the quality of the finished goods is improved and the necessary policy supports for the village and cottage industries are introduced, there is no reason to fear that this sector cannot find its due share in the commodity markets. (Para 4.8)

28. Intermediate technology of a suitable mix will have to be introduced immediately if we are to reverse the present tendency of deterioration in the sector. The approach is not only economically justifiable from the employment angle but also imperative for survival of the sector. (Para 1.8)

29. Within the framework of the growing economy, the increasing demand for consumer goods would involve many new articles of consumption. This segment of the demand can safely be syphoned off to the sectors of production using intermediate technology. These new lines of production opportunities will certainly attract the younger generation who may not like to pursue the traditional line but accept greater mechanisation which gives them better earnings. (Para 4.9)

30. The broad support required is as follows:-

(a) Continuous updating of the technology and moving towards higher productivity per unit by supporting research and development of intermediate technology which has low capital/output and capital/labour ratios;
(b) Providing the training, design and market intelligence organisations so as to change the production lines from those for the purely local market to those can develop larger markets;
(c) Developing the necessary markets organisations to collect and market the produce on a fair commission basis;
(d) Raw material supply for the industry at a fair price in small lots so that the enterprise need not have to invest large sums in inventories;
(e) Improvement of the tools of the trade so that the artisan is able to get the best tools that the latest technology can provide; and
(f) Finding the necessary credit for the individual and the area to make the entire organisation work. (Para 4.12)

31. The KVIC has grown over more than twenty years and developed its own inertia. In the judgement of the Committee any drastic changes in the working of this organisation will take a long time to be effective. As time is an important factor in the problem, the Committee is certain that beyond enabling the KVIC to play a more effective part, the main responsibility for rapid development of this sector has to be squarely placed with the State Government. The role of the All India Boards can only be complementary as they lack field approach. (Para 4.14)

32. The question of satisfying the preferences of the ultimate buyer of the products needs specific focus and attention through the development of designs, patterns, input supply, standardisation and marketing. (Para 4.15)

33. Steps have to be taken to evolve urgently the structure for carrying out the intermediate technology on a crash basis. There has to be a clear division of the research responsibility and a coordination structure for bringing the scientists and technologists and the users together for development reporting, monitoring of performance and extension to the field for effective solutions. (Para 4.16)

34. A rapid change of equipment, technology and training of the millions of artisans in the field to enable them to utilise the technology requires a vast hierarchy of field level experts supported by a pyramid of higher expertise and a large number of training units and organisa-

tions. (Para 4.17)

35. The Committee suggests that in the Sixth Plan we may concentrate on the following industries:

> Food and tobacco products; edible and non-edible oils; beverages; textiles (khadi, cotton handlooms and manufacture of garments); leather, footwear and repair of footwear; major carpentry sectors; ferrous; non-ferrous metals; major items of production in non-metallic mineral products; sericulture and tassar culture; carpet making and woollen garments. (Para 4.17)

36. Even within the selected industries, there is a need for selectivity in groups for development. The production units in village and collage industries are generally family units with the following basic requirements:

(a) Getting raw material in small quantities at a fair price in small lots through out the year so that the investment in inventories is minimal;
(b) Getting technical guidance in new technology and maintenance of this equipment at fair rates and promptly;
(c) Prompt marketing of his goods so that he can rotate his funds for raw material purchase and also meet his consumption needs by the value added; and
(d) Getting the necessary credit at fair rates of interest for all these operations. (Para 4.18)

37. What is wanted is a covering organisation which can perform these functions for the individual family and replace the money-lender trader by a helpful and effective organisation. Such a covering organisation must also be economical. (Para 4.18)

38. The strategy should concentrate on a group approach for each of the selected industries. (Para 4.18)

39. The service unit for the group will have to be located at a convenient centre within the area. (Para 4.19)

40. The basic strategy suggested by the Committee involves three crucial elements: first upgradation of technologies to ensure using standard and quality production, second a covering organisation to provide the required support for raw material supply, marketing, credit and technology and finally a group approach to ensure viability. (Para 4.20)

41. The Committee would like to focus attention on the utter lack of a machinery to transform policies into effective action. The need for an effective thinking and acting centre analysing the parts for action and for further policy decisions is very desirable. This body should not involve itself in the execution but be a Brains Trust. (Para 4.20)

Raw Materials

42. Whatever be the covering organisation assigned with the functions of buying and holding the stocks for dispersal, it is necessary to make suitable institutional arrangements for finding the needed funds on a priority basis at favourable rates of interest. (Para 5.5)

43. The policy and operational framework for provision of raw materials to the whole lot of artisans, dispersed over wide areas, is not in tune with the requirements. As at present, hardly any regulation exists whereby the raw materials trade is obliged to make available to the artisan, even the locally available raw materials, at reasonable prices. Price to the artisan is most important and it has to be viable. The Committee would like to stress this aspect of the problem. (Para 5.15)

44. The wide dispersal of artisans and their weak financial position necessitates that their small requirements of raw materials need to be made available at the needed time and at their doorsteps. (Para 5.16)

45. At the grass root level, it is desirable for a start to provide raw materials to the artisan through the proposed Group Centre Approach. (Para 5.17)

46. The Group Centre would help the proposed IDPA (Integrated Development Project Authority) in assessing the detailed requirements of various raw materials and in also subsequently checking on the proper use of the raw materials. (Para 5.17)

47. The Group Centre would be the effective delivery point for the supply of raw materials to the individual artisans. The supply of raw materials to the Group Centres would be from the district level agencies. (Para 5.17)

48. At the district level, the Committee recommends the formation of a DSMS (District Supply and Marketing Society) which would be given the responsibility for the procurement of the raw materials. (Para 5.18)

49. DSMS is to be run on a commercially viable basis. (Para 5.18)

50. The credit requirements of DSMS can be met through commercial and cooperative banks. State Governments can help by provid-

ing appropriate margin money and treat the same as a development expenditure. (Para 5.18)

51. DSMS should keep a proper rapport with DIC for optimal use of facilities. (Para 5.18)

52. The Committee recommends the utilisation of the services of LAMPS by DSMS. (Para 5.19)

53. The activities of DSMS would be hampered without a suitable link up agency at the state level. The Committee recommends that this state level agency be called SRIDC (State Rural Industries Development Corporation) and be responsible for handling all the raw materials problems of the village and cottage industries. (Para 5.20)

54. Village and Cottage Industries and also the small scale industries suffer from the shortage of raw materials supply at reasonable prices. As such the Committee recommends that a common organisation should handle the raw materials problems at the district and state levels. (Para 5.21)

55. The Committee recommends that requirements of village and cottage industries get the priority treatment and should become the first charge in that no cut be made in the amounts needed by these industries. (Para 5.22)

56. The district and state level organisations would take sometime to develop. Meanwhile in some industries like Khadi, Handloom, etc., some system of raw material supply already exists. The Committee would recommend that these systems should be continued and streamlined till the effective coming into being of the proposed organisations. (Para 5.23)

57. The Committee recommends that in case of forest based raw materials, the forest department should be responsible for delivering the materials at royalties plus transport to the DSMS from the nearest departmental depot, at the needed points. (Para 5.24)

58. The Committee recommends the continuous monitoring of the process of availability of raw materials at the field level and its proper utilisation in production. (Para 5.25)

Marketing

59. The essential element of mass marketing is that items demanded by the consumer should be available where the consumer demand exists. This necessitates having a wide network of retail outlets. Such networks are available through the outlets of KVIC, hand-

icrafts and handloom boards, super bazars, etc., are very limited and are hardly in tune with the requirements. (Para 6.8)

60. There are many reasons for poor efficiency in the existing marketing arrangements, more important being the inadaptability of the production to the needs in terms of attitudes, tastes and preference of known markets; lack of quality control and non-standardisation of the product, limited size of local exploitable market; competition from the organised sector or substitute products; lack of market intelligence and lack of constructive advertising. (Para 5.10)

61. The artisans are, by tradition and circumstances, production-oriented and not market-oriented. (Para 6.10)

62. The marketing of village and cottage industry products has to reflect modern trends. The marketing system for village and cottage industries must be as equally organised and sophisticated as that in the organised sector. (Para 6.13)

63. The village and cottage sector must produce a product which in designs, quality and price can compete with organised sector output. (Para 6.14)

64. The product must be available where and when the consumer normally purchases it. (Para 6.15)

65. For each product a strong brand image should be built up and projected through advertising in mass media and other promotional measures. (Para 6.16)

66. To give a boost to marketing, a link up between the supply of raw materials and marketing should be maintained. (Para 6.20)

67. Broadly, it may be assumed that an assurance of lifting 50 per cent of the product from the artisan would give him great relief. The balance of the 50 per cent may be left to him to meet his own personal needs and for marketing to the demand of his clients in the local markets at hand. (Para 6.20)

68. Identification of markets, other than the local, would obviously have to be entrusted to some agency. At the district level the function can be rightly undertaken by the DSMS. (Para 6.21)

69. The proposed agency at the State level, viz., State Rural Industries Development Corporation (SRIDC) would be the right agency to undertaken the functions at that level. (Para 6.21)

70. The Committee has elsewhere recommended a separate raw material and marketing organisation to cover village and cottage industries. For technical support and training, other organisations of a hierarchical nature starting from the group unit have also been recom-

mended. If these recommendations are accepted, the role of the rural marketing centre will be purely one of maintaining a suitable display and marketing centres at the urban level for all types of village industries. The Committee would recommend that the operation of the RMC may be limited to this particularised service for the village and cottage industry. (Para 6.22)

71. The Committee would recommend that all existing structures should become multi-disciplinary centres and sell such other products which can be profitably handled. But for the products of other organisations and other group units covered by the marketing chain, the rural marketing centres should preferably act as agents for sale. (Para 6.23)

72. The responsibility for maintaining quality of goods, studying the consumer market and putting in the right type of goods at the urban centres should be the responsibility of the DSMS where intensive development is contemplated. (Para 6.23)

73. Where new rural marketing centres have to be developed, it is desirable that from the beginning they are developed as multi-commodity display and sales centres. They should be placed squarely under the DSMS. (Para 6.24)

74. The Committee wants to make it clear that one sale centre in an urban market may not be enough for pushing the entire production of village industries to market. Existing private retail shops should in any case be fully brought in the chain of distribution. (Para 6.24)

75. The artisan at present not being able to hold back the goods has to go to the middleman trader who does the effective distribution for the festival seasons. The marketing organisation will have to take over this important role. (Para 6.25)

76. Strategy of marketing cover must have facilities for storage to keep goods in condition till the festival season and push the wares in the ready markets. (Para 6.25)

77. A suitable linkage with Government purchases can yield an assured market for the produce of the village and cottage industries. (Para 6.26)

78. The artisans wares will be accepted by the marketing organisation only if it fulfils the basic standards laid down for the goods by the organisation. There should be no compromise in this matter. (Para 6.27)

79. The Committee suggests that a neutral body for resolving dis-

putes about quality may be set up, by DIC for each district, comprising of technical experts who will be relevant to the problem. The decisions of these technical groups will be binding on both parties. (Para 6.27)

80. To push the goods and clear the goods quickly from stocks and enthuse the artisan to produce more the strategy should be for a lower price during the off-season. (Para 6.28)

81. There has to be some organisation which studies the market patterns and changing tastes and then prepares the specifications for new types of goods that have to be produced. This responsibility can be spread between the Central Government and the State Governments. The district marketing organisation and the state marketing organisation can draw the standards for purchase of goods from the artisans on their assessment of the market. (Para 6.29)

82. The whole focus to the development of village and cottage industries need to be market-oriented and commercial and not sheer production-oriented, and should ensure fair wage to the artisan. (Para 6.30)

83. The Committee recommends that in the initial stages marketing through advertisement will have to be a service to be rendered by the State organisations for the development of village and cottage industries. A subsidised service for this purpose will be fully justified. This of course will have to be linked up with the capacity of the chain of organisations to produce the quality and quantity required in the market. (Para 6.31)

84. If a proper marketing strategy is evolved, it should be possible to sell the products of village and cottage industries in new and distant markets in the country. The States will have to take the initial lead in developing such covering organisations for the industries most prevalent in the State. The Centre's contribution will be provision of marketing intelligence, training institutions, design development and suitable guidance to the States in improving their marketing strategies. (Para 6.32)

85. Many products of the village and cottage industries are finding special markets in foreign countries and Committee recommends full tapping of such potential markets. (Para 6.32)

Technological Development

86. The Technological Development in the Village and Cottage

Industries need to be geared to –

(i) enable the artisan in every village industry to avail oι the technological developments already made and the improved equipment that is available;

(ii) improve technology in order to mechanise such portion of the production chain in each industry which involves substantial drudgery and in return gives very little recompense in money for time spent; and

(iii) find out intermediate technology with greater mechanisation of certain common services in the production chain so that the production unit of the artisan adopting the system and supported by the necessary cover can improve his productivity. The minimum aim in productivity increase per unit is suggested as a quadruplicate increase before the end of the century and the maximum that can be absorbed in the economy has been shown to be as much as 16 times. (Para 7.6)

87. A close look at any village industry with a view to developing the technology will show that the problem is a multi-disciplinary one. There are very few technological research centres in the country which can handle a multi-disciplinary problem. The national laboratories mainly are uni-disciplinary bodies though a few of them have got the capacity in particular sectors to look at more than one discipline. It is necessary first of all to identify the various national institutes and research and technology bodies which can support the intermediate technology development for village and cottage industries. This can only be done at the national level. This postulates a national organisation which can study the basic problem and identify the necessary institutes. Having done this, the problems and suggestions that come up from the field from the various technical groups will have to be analysed and direction given to the research and development programmes in each of the village industries. (Para 7.12)

88. The experience in the field of KVIC and others shows that even though the equipment has already been designed which improves productivity of the artisan and the artisan is prepared to accept the equipment and there are provisions for training, there is no structure for producing the new equipment and supplying them in large quantities. A suitable organisation will, therefore, have to be developed for

assessing the demand and farming out the work. (Para 7.13)

89. The equipment needed by the artisans can be produced at different levels. In some cases the production at the level of individual artisan or a group of artisans may be possible. In others, the production may have to be assigned to small scale and medium scale sector of the industry. Yet in some other sectors, like leather technology, the desirability of producing the machines in the large scale sector may be necessary. (Para 7.14)

90. For each of the three stages of the development of technology indicated, the artisan has to be trained for adopting the improved technology. (Para 7.15)

91. Most of the technicians are not fully aware of the technology improvements that are going on in their sectors. There has to be an organisation for suitable inservice training for such technicians and technologists. (Para 7.16)

Training

92. Under TRYSEM, each district in the country should have at least one composite training centre. (Para 8.18)

93. New training centres of the composite type need to be set up in remote and inaccessible areas, hilly and tribal areas on a priority basis. (Para 8.19)

94. Financing of training infrastructure, whether old or new, should be done on 100 per cent basis by the Central Government. This is the only way we can build up at least one well-equipped composite training centre in each district of the country to meet the very large demand that the recommendations would entail for centres to be located in remote and inaccessible areas, hilly and tribal areas, and areas predominantly inhabited by members of the scheduled castes. (Para 8.20)

95. For course of less than one month's duration the stipend should be fixed at Rs. 5 per day. (Para 8.21)

96. For all training programmes, the cost of travel to and from the training institution should be allowed to be funded from the scheme. (Para 8.22)

97. Training patterns under different Ministries should be treated as patterns approved under TRYSEM also. Expenditure on such trades should be allowed to be incurred according to such pattern. (Para 8.23)

98. Provision of an improved took kit is one of the important factors in raising the productivity of a rural artisan. TRYSEM has no such provision. It is recommended that this crucial element should be built in an integral part of the scheme. (Para 8.24)

99. Provision of subsidy needs to be made for TRYSEM projects to be launched on a cooperative or community basis. (Para 8.25)

100. There is a need to include training of trainers or for strengthening the infrastructure relating to trainers' training institutions. (Para 8.26)

101. It is necessary to subsidise the interest rate, so that the effective rate charged from the rural artisans does not exceed the DRI interest rates. (Para 8.27)

102. There should be appropriate schemes for share capital participation in rural industries marketing, setting up of rural marketing and service centres and improvement of village *mandies* and *haats*. (Para 8.28)

103. The introduction of existing technology and the best equipment available has to be made to lakhs and lakhs of artisans in the country. Obviously, our usual methods of training centres will not answer the situation. The Committee, therefore, recommends that the approach should be to select master artisans in the industry who are acquainted with the equipment and the technology to be located in each group under the group approach for training the artisans in the group over a period of time by peripatetic handling. The Committee would suggest that the approach may be for the master artisan to first of all demonstrate the available technology with the best equipment possible at the growth centres of the group. (Para 8.39)

104. Each of the apex organisation responsible for selected village industries should pay attention to first of all identify the technology and the equipment that is now available and pursue pilot project of master artisan training of groups of artisans and establish the necessary norms. (Para 8.39)

105. The introduction of mechanisation to avoid drudgery will have to be on a common basis for those parts of the operation preferably at the group centre or in a number of suitably located centres within the group. The artisans to handle these machines will have to be trained at common training centres. (Para 8.40)

106. The master artisans selected on the basis of the existing technology are to be first trained in the new equipment and then used as the

guide on a peripatetic basis in the groups selected for the introduction of the new technology. In the initial stages, this will have to be done on a pilot basis and then the future master artisans for training can be identified within these pilot groups and sent for training to other areas. (Para 8.41)

107. All the group technicians should be suitably trained in the existing technology and further trained in the intermediate technology which may be developed from time to time. (Para 8.42)

108. Higher levels of technicians and administrative staff will have to be given management and familiarised with marketing practices, etc. All this will have to be in various training centres which will have to be identified by the DICs with the help of the State authorities. (Para 8.43)

109. If backward areas have to be developed, artisans may have to be developed in new areas wherever the need exists or the raw materials exist. For this, the Committee would suggest that the group approach would be the right approach for this training. Wherever, the new skill is to be introduced, a group of artisans should be selected and their training should be undertaken at a common training-cum-production centre. (Para 8.44)

110. The training centres and the use of training-cum-production centres should be ultimately adapted to the requirements of the particular situation. (Para 8.44)

111. The TRYSEM scheme for training unemployed rural educated youth is suitable for adoption to the training-programmes for village industries. (Para 8.45)

112. The various facilities given in TRYSEM scheme for training centres, trainers, subsidies for artisans, supply of equipment and allowance for wastage should be suitably adapted to each of the village industries and the scales suitably fixed in detailed consultation between the apex organisation for the industry and the Ministry running the TRYSEM programmes. The Committee would suggest that once this is done, the TRYSEM scheme should be automatically extended to such groups under the village industries training programme. (Para 8.45)

113. The Committee would point out that once the training and the equipment is passed on to the artisan he becomes a self-employed unit with much higher level of productivity and is, generally, able to go above the poverty line. The nation's expenditure on the training of one such artisan is a very small amount considering that we are achieving

the national objective of putting the family above the poverty line. (Para 8.46)

114. The Committee recommends that it may be desirable to bring into the training system the whole family in the house through peripatetic master artisan approach. (Para 8.47)

Organisational Structure

115. For each of the selected industries, the State will have to establish a Technical Hierarchy whose task will be to:-

(i) Provide technical support to the artisans in the Group Centre for the known technology and also organise the change over of the artisans to the equipment and accessories, established and already introduced in the known technology, on a time phase so as to cover all the artisans in the Group Centre within a decade;

(ii) organise the upgradation of the training of the artisans in the Group Centre to enable them to qualify and adopt the innovations established for his benefit and to organise the training of the artisans in such established and new technologies, wherever necessary;

(iii) ensure the quality of the production in the Group Centre in accordance with the standards and specifications laid down for the marketing through the field technicians and supervision of higher staff;

(vi) draw up standards and specifications to ensure the above concept and also introduce quality certifying arrangements through the District Industries Centre or such other alternative organisations as might be set up;

(v) advise on product and design development and provision of adequate support towards this;

(vi) establish pilot schemes and provide technical supervision for the introduction of intermediate technology, already established and tested;

(vii) advise the research and development organisation at the Centre on the various operations in the industry in the present technology which entail drudgery and call for suitable mechanisation of the operations; and

(viii) wherever a new technology has been established for the mechanisation of the drudgery part or other improvements, introduce the same through a common service organisation at the Group Centre. (Para 9.4)

116. Except in Handlooms, and to some extent in Sericulture, such a hierarchy does not exist now. Each state will have to organise their own hierarchies. The State level group will have to be highly trained so that the technical and training aspects can be covered adequately. Depending on the number of group centres, identified and covered in a selected industry, and its spread thereof, intermediate level or levels of technical support to the field level expert will have to be spelt out. In the initial stages, when the number of group centres in selected industries is not large, the State may make use of the common hierarchy for these industries. (Para 9.5)

117. The Committee would strongly recommend that there should be a Directorate of Rural Industries in each State which should have a technical hierarchy, and also provide market intelligence and support for marketing in the state as well as outside the state. Whether there should be only one. Directorate of Rural Industries covering all cottage, village and small industries relevant to the rural industries is a matter which is left to the state to decide keeping in view the requirements of the workload. (Para 9.6)

118. Whatever be the set up, it would be essential to ensure that the proposed Directorate of Rural Industries or such other Directorates as States may like to continue should have necessary linkages established with the existing national organisations, wherever available. (Para 9.6)

119. It would also be necessary to have some sort of technical support at the District level as it would not be possible to reach the Group Centres and provide the necessary technical cover in the field directly from the Headquarters. How it should be done is best left to each State to decide. The Committee would only suggest that the existing organisation of District Industries Centre or any other organisation which may be set up in lieu thereof or in a modified form should perhaps provide the nucleus at the District level to provide the support in the field which should trickle down from the State level technical hierarchy. (Para 9.6)

120. The National Committee in its report on "Organisation of Administrative and Financial Structures in Backward Area Develop-

ment" has recommended a comprehensive area development approach in backward area with emphasis on improvement of productivity and earning capacity of each family, promotion of new activities to absorb the surplus labour power of the poor households, training of traditional workers in improved technology and training of younger household members to undertake new activities. The proposed integrated development project authority would be responsible, among other things, for planning, direction and monitoring of all programmes in the project and blocks within its jurisdiction. All officers in the project which should include an Industries Extension Officer in the Block and an Industries Development Officer in the Project Team, would be directly under the day to day administrative control of the Chief Executive Officer of the Integrated Development Project Authority. The Group Centre approach for the development of village and cottage industries as well as a 'focal point' concept for services which would be an integral part of rural development, will be directly under the overall planning, coordination and supervision of the Integrated Development Project Authority. Actual implementation of programmes will be vested with the technical hierarchies for the various industries. (Paras 9.7, 9.8 and 9.11)

121. The proposed Group Centre would be an integral part of the Integrated Development Project Authority for planning, administration and monitoring. It would, of course, have the group technician incharge of each Group but the same would function under the overall control and direction of the IDP authority. The technical control of the Group Technician will be with the relevant technical hierarchy in that State.

122. The relation between the IDP Authority and the technical hierarchies will have to be closer than that between a Department and the Authority.

123. The Committee would strongly recommend that the availability of an Industries Extension Officer at the Block level is integral part of the entire approach and that this post, wherever it does not exist at present, must be provided immediately. (Para 9.12)

124. The Committee suggests that whereas in the fundamentally backward areas their recommendation for an integrated project approach is necessary, in the other areas the project support can be organised conveniently for each industry at a suitable area level which may be different for different industries. This project level organisation

will be fed by the Block Industries Extension Officer who is now a necessity in each Block. The District organisation is anyhow common to both fundamentally backward blocks and other blocks. (Para 9.14)

125. The Committee suggests that where the KVIC has already got a group centre in operation, they should take the responsibility for expanding the group sufficiently to make it viable and absorb more and more artisans in their group. The KVIC approach is multi-industrial and we should not lose this good point in our approach to rural industrialisation. (Para 9.15)

126. The Committee expects that the KVIC will be enabled to start a number of group projects in new areas through suitable voluntary groups and cover them with their organisation. Such groups will naturally be multi-industrial with khadi as an essential element. (Para 9.15)

127. The Committee feels that the marketing cover of the KVIC for village and cottage industries at present is very modest and if they seek to organise this structure for raw material and marketing cover for all the old and new group they will handle, it will be a long time process. The Committee will, therefore, recommend that the KVIC should accept the raw material and marketing cover being developed by the State in its operations. Only khadi will be their special privilege as nobody else has the expertise. (Para 9.15)

128. The Committee recommends that the officer(s) dealing with village and cottage industries in the District set up should be a member of Executive Committee of the District Supply and Marketing Organisation. Further, it may be judicious to keep the DSMS as a society registered under the Societies Registration Act and to keep the Board of such a society as a managerials expert group with a General Manager and a Group of Experts including the Officer dealing with village and cottage industries of the District Industries Centre, the Chief Executive Officer, or his nominee, of the IDPA, in the District, representatives of the credit institutions, preferably the Lead Bank and the Cooperative Banks. The Collector should be the Chairman of the Society. He can then bring in the coordination at the integration level. (Para 9.22)

129. Till the DSMS and SSMS are organised and start working in all the districts smoothly, it is obviously not desirable to immediately transfer the raw material supply responsibility of the KVIC, Handicrafts Board and the handloom organisation to the DSMS or the

SSMS. Ultimately, one organisation handling raw material supply at the decentralised level of the district and group will be the most economic and it is desirable to work for this objective. The transition from the existing organisations to the common organisation will have to be worked out in each States according to the competence developed in the DSMS and SSMS. The Committee is, however, clear in its mind that khadi being a specialised item will continue to be handled by the KVIC. (Para 9.23)

130. The technical hierarchy for each industry has to assess the requirement of equipment and accessories for their time phased programme of improving the quality and quantitative productivity in their industry. The Committee recommends that this hierarchy should be responsible for assessing the demand and placing the demand with firm orders on a time delivery basis with the District Supply and Marketing Society. This Society with the help of District technical hierarchy should organise the industries in the district which can manufacture the requirements. (Para 9.37)

131. The Committee recommends strongly that the TRYSEM scheme should cover artisans and technicians even if the trainees are drawn from existing artisan groups. (Para 9.45)

132. On the organisation side, the Committee recommends the following types of training:

(i) the group technicians to be trained in management practices;
(ii) The Block Industries Officer to be trained in the general problems of Village and Cottage Industries and Organisation;
(iii) The staff of the DSMS at various levels to be trained in the intricacies and art of marketing and managing raw-material inventories; and
(iv) The higher level experts in technology and administration in District Technology Hierarchies, IRD, State level planners and managers, to be trained in group education like the one followed for Command Area Development so that each understands his role in the common task.

Items (i) and (ii) above can and should be organised by the District Organisations. Item (iii) will have to be organised by the State in Marketing Management institutions. Item (iv) will also have to be organised by the State in Management Institutes and the like. The Sixth Plan at present does not contain the necessary provisions for this large scale training programme either at the Centre or at the State. The Committee recommends that the dimensions of a workable programme should be assessed and the problem settled between the State and Centre by suitable allocations every year in their plans. (Para 9.46)

133. The Committee suggests that there should be a National Board of Research and Technology for the Development of Rural Industries which should be set up as an autonomous organisation on the same lines as NCERT, etc. The functions of this Board should be:

(i) identify the lines of research to be followed for the various Village and Cottage Industries in avoiding drudgery and bringing in a suitable intermediate technology to improve quality and more than quadruple the output per artisan;

(ii) Farm out the items of research so identified on a priority basis to the Research Institute who can be expected to give results;

(iii) Check progress in the research programmes and take corrective action to pull up laggards and change horses, if necessary; and

(iv) Provide funds for the research scheme out of the Block grant given to them by the Department of Science and Technology. This Board should be given a "Block Grant" every year for funding the research programmes. (Para 9.47)

134. The State Government, would have to play a leading role in directing, monitoring and coordinating various aspects relating to the development of rural industries in the State as a whole. The Committee would strongly recommend that as, coordination with a large number of departments like Power, Excise, Finance, Planning, etc., would be necessary, one Department, whether a separate or an existing one, must be entrusted with the responsibility for the development of rural industries in each State. (Para 9.49)

135. The Committee recommend that all matters relating to khadi, village and cottage industries should be handled by one Ministry/Department at the Centre. The proposed National Board, on Research and Technology for the development of rural industries should also be located under this Ministry/Department. (Para 9.51)

136. The Committee recommends the following Organisational tie-up

Organisational Tie–up for Village and Cottage Industries

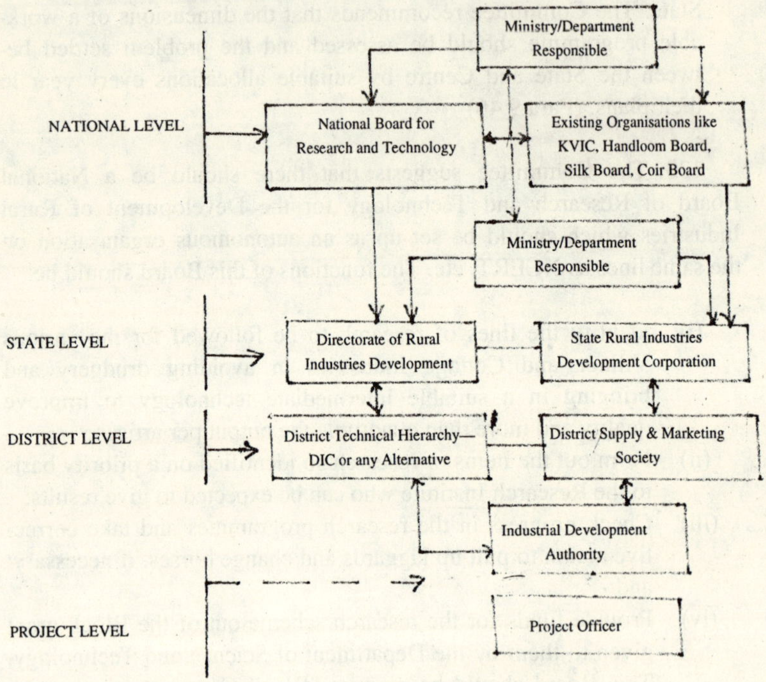

HIGH LEVEL SALT ENQUIRY COMMITTEE, 1978 — REPORT[1]

Chairman Smt. Abha Maiti replaced by Shri Lovraj Kumar

Members Shri S.C. Aggarwal; Shri T. Bhattacharyya; Shri E.P.W. De Costa; Shri M.M. Gurunath; Shri J.S. Iyer; Shri R. Jayaraman; Dr. D.J. Mehta; Shri K. Neelakantan replaced Shri A. Ramji; Shri Rasik Lal Mehta; Shri M. Bahl replaced Shri I. Mahadevan and was replaced by Shri S.K. Sarkar; Shri M.G. Shah; Shri T. Thangavelu.

M. Secy. Shri K.L. Sahni

Appointment

The problems effecting the salt industry in the country and the need for a detailed study of the industry have been engaging the attention of the Government of India for some time. Government have, therefore, decided to appoints a High Level Committee to undertake a comprehensive review of the problems facing the salt industry and to suggest suitable measures for the development of the salt industry. So the Government of India, the Department of Industrial Development in the Ministry of Industry appointed the High Level Salt Enquiry Committee vide its resolution No. 02012/4/76-Salt dated November 30, 1978.

Contents

Summary of Conclusions and Recommendations; The Scope of the Study; General; Demand of Salt; Present Production of Salt, Production of Salt Required to meet Projected Demand and Potential for Increasing Production; Distribution of Salt-Zonal Scheme, Storage and Retail Distribution and the Use of Salt Golahs in Calcutta; Costs and

---

1. Delhi, Controller of Publications, 1985, 345 p.

Prices; System of Licensing of Salt Works, Exemption upto the Limit of 10 acres, Salt Cess Fund, Operation of the Salt Cess Act, Code of Principles for Assistance from the Salt Cess Fund; Progress in Research and Development, Model Salt Farms, Research Stations and Regional Quality Control Laboratories; Specification and Standards; The Role of the Public Sector; Labour and Employment; Recovery of by-products; The Functoning of Cooperative Salt Works and Measures for Promoting the Formation of Cooperatives; The Revised Functions and Organisation of the Salt Department; Signature of Chairman and other Members of the Committee; Note of Dissent by Shri K.L. Sahni; Note of Dissent by Shri S.C. Aggarwal; Annexures I to IX.

Terms of Reference

(i) to assess the demand of salt for human consumption, industrial purposes and exports during the next ten year period;

(ii) to assess the potential for production of salt and to recommend measures to maximise production;

(iii) to make a study of costs and prices and recommend fixation of fair ex-works prices of salt for different regions;

(iv) to review the present zonal scheme for distribution of salt for human consumption (including iodised salt and with special reference to movement of salt by sea to West Bengal);

(v) to review the present arrangements for public storage and retail distribution of salt and to recommend improvements;

(vi) to consider the feasibility of freight equalisation for salt;

(vii) to review the operation of the Salt Cess Act, the Salt Cess Rules and the Code of Principles for cess assistance by way of loans and grants in order to ensure equitable benefits to all the salt producing regions;

(viii) to review other levels on salt production in different States in order to achieve uniformity to the extent possible;

(ix) to review the system of licensing of salt works including the present exemption upto the limit of 10 acres;

(x) to review the functioning of cooperative salt works and to suggest measures for promoting the formation of cooperatives in the field;

(xi) to review labour and employment situation in the salt industry and propose measures for fixation of wages and labour welfare;

(xii) to review and re-defined the role of public sector in the salt industry;

(xiii) to recommend measures for better quality control and upgrading the standard of indigenous salt to international standards;

(xiv) to review the progress of research and development of model salt farms including the operation of marine salt farms, research stations and regional quality control laboratories;

(xv) to consider the need for import of salt and to recommended measures for export promotion;

(xvi) to review the progress of salt based chemicals and recovery of by products from bitterns and propose measures for encouraging the establishment of marine chemical industry;

(xvii) to review the working of Salt Department and examine the feasibility of decentralisation of salt industry; and

(xviii) to consider any other matter proposed by the salt industry or the State Governments and to make appropriate recommendations thereon.

Recommendations

Demand of Salt (Chapter III)

1. The domestic demand of salt is expected to increase from 6.70 million tonnes in 1980 to 7.82 million tonnes in 1985 of which 0.24 million tonnes is of iodised salt in the presently notified goitre endemic areas : this could increase to 0.73 million tonnes if all the goitre endemic areas are notified. This domestic demand is expected to increase to 8.84 million tonnes in 1988.

The current level of exports of 0.29 million tonnes is expected to increase to 0.40 million tonnes in 1985 and to 0.45 million tonnes in 1980. (Paras 3.9.2 and 3.9.3)

Projected Deficit (Chapter IV)

2. While the current level of production is adequate to meet the current year's demand, the projected demand in 1988 will require an increase in the domestic production of 2.3 million tonnes. (Para 4.20.1)

Potential for Increasing Production (Chapter IV)

3. The domestic production can be increased by preventing

wastage by the washing away by improving warehousing and transportation of almost 1.0 million tonnes facilitating the adoption of improved technology which is expected to lead to increasc in production of atleast 10 per cent equivalent to 0.70 million tonnes and possibly to 1.40 million tonnes by improving the availability of labour and equipment an increase in the utilisation of areas already licensed to the extent of 50 per cent of the unutilised area can lead to an additional production of 3.0 million tonnes there is potential for further increasing the production of salt by undertaking salt manufacture in approximately 139,790 acres of saline land not yet under salt cultivation and a number of other uptapped sources such as brine springs in the North-Eastern States. (Paras 4.1, 4.7, 4.8, 4.9, 4.13, 4.20.2, 4.20.3 and 4.20.5)

Technological Improvements Feasible (Chapter IV)

4. The types of the technological improvements that appear attractive in each salt producing region have been summarised. (Paras 4.7.1 to 4.7.10)

Provision of Power and Fuels in the Dry Season (Chapter IV)

5. Increase in the production of salt has been hampered by restrictions imposed by certain State Governments in the supply of power and fuels without taking into account the seasonal character of the industry : the seasonal character of the industry must be recognised and adequate supply of power and fuels must be ensured to salt produces in the dry season. (Para 4.12)

Insurance of Salt Works (Chapter IV)

6. The feasibility of formulating a scheme of insurance against salt losses arising from such factors as unseasonal rainfall cyclones and other natural calamities that are clearly outside the control of salt producers, should be studied by the Salt Department with the assistance of the General Insurance Corporation. (Para 4.14)

Promotion of Salt Manufacture in Salt Deficit Areas Far Away from Salt Surplus Areas (Chapter IV)

7. The viability of exploiting the sources of salt in areas such as North-Eastern State and West Bengal which are far away from the

traditional sources of supply of salt and which suffer from frequent interruptions in the supply of salt due to difficulties in transportation of this essential commodity over long distances, should be studied immediately.

The Geological Survey of India should undertake a rapid industrial survey of these sources of salt and the Salt Department should ensure that these surveys are undertaken in the shortest possible time and the requisite funds are released promptly. (Paras 4.11, 4.13 and 4.20.5)

Iodised Salt and Iodisation Plants (Chapter IV)

8. The supply of iodised salt even in the currently notified goitre endemic areas which do not include a number of other goitre endemic areas, is barely half the assessed demand. Poor utilisation of capacity of iodisation plants and their sub-optimal location in relation to the disposition of demand and transportation problems combined with a failure to take measures to ensure that only iodised salt is available in the notified areas, has led to this avoidable situation. In many other countries all edible salt is iodised.

Messrs Hindustan Salt must immediately obtain specialist advice from the domestic manufacturers of iodisation plants to rectify the deficiencies in its iodisation plants so as to achieve capacity operation rapidly.

There should be no restriction on the erection of iodisation plants in the private, joint or public sector nor is there any need to be unduly strict in regard to the choice of the locations or technology.

The subsidy available from the Ministry of Health for the production of iodised salt can be confined to the production from plant owned by the Central and State Governments.

The State Civil Supplies Officers in the notified goitre endemic areas should be provided with standard sample testing kits to be developed by the CS&MCRI to ensure that only iodised salt is received and sold in the market. These officers should also be trained in the use of the simple submersion process and small standard submersion process units (that should be developed by the CS&MCRI) to assist in converting non-iodised salt seized in the market to iodised salt.

The despatch of iodised salt from Calcutta to the North-Eastern States should be expedited by placing this movement immediately in Category B. (Paras 4.16 and 4.20.7)

Fortified Salt (Chapter IV)

9. The Central and State Public Sector plants should actively promote the production and sale of fortified salts. (Para 4.17)

Imported Salt (Chapter IV)

10. Imported rock salt should be used only for Ayurvedic and Unani medicines. (Para 4.18)

Exports (Chapter IV)

11. There could be a large and remunerative exports of salt. Studies in this regard have been tardy. The State Trading Corporation in consultation with the Salt Department and the States of Gujarat and Tamil Nadu should immediately undertake studies on how viable exports can be increased rapidly and ensure that facilities such as increased rate of unloading and loading of salt, provision of barges, telecommunication facilities in exporting ports, are provided promptly. (Para 4.19)

Movement of Salt from Salt Works to Rail Heads (Chapter V)

12. Construction and maintenance of roads must be accelerated to facilitate the movement of salt from salt works to rail heads. (Para 5.1)

Movement of Salt from Salt Works to Ports (Chapter V)

13. An adequate number of barges and better communication and navigation facilities must be provided to improve the movement of salt from producers in the West Coast and the Salt Department and the State Governments concerned must take effective steps to provide these facilities. (Para 5.2)

Movement of Salt from Salt Works and from Rail Sidings (Chapter V)

14. Significant cost savings can be effected through rail movement by the provision of rail sidings wherever these are established as cost effective. The Salt Department and the railway authorities must jointly prepare detailed studies and surveys so that an effective

programme is formulated and implemented. (Para 5.3)

Movement of Loose Salt (Chapter V)

15. Movement of loose salt for edible purposes by road in certain circumstances facilitate transportation and reduce costs. Therefore, it may be permitted, but the Salt Department must specify the precautions that must be taken in such matters as wrapping in polyethylene, tarpaulins, etc., to ensure that no contamination takes place by external dust. Consequential modifications should be made in Salt Manuals. (Para 5.4)

Rail Movement of Salt (Chapter V)

16. Serious shortfalls have taken place in the planned rail movement of salt and specially serious in this is the very large shortfall in the movement of iodised salt. Cost effective detailed plans of the movement of salt by rail, road, coastal shipping and river craft have yet to be formulated with some degree of precision and the formulation of such a study and the preparation of a proper plan, are urgent. (Paras 5.6 and 5.8)

Measures to Improve Rail Movement (Chapter V)

17. Railway wagons must be allotted directly to the State Governments in accordance with their assessed requirements in category B and category C with their nominated wholesalers and distributors acting on their behalf of these States so desire. But no change in the destination booked in accordance with the instructions of the State Government should be accepted by the railway authorities without the specific authorisation of the State Government.

Till such time that all rail movement of iodised salt from its sources of supply is adequate to meet the full requirement or till further iodisation plants are established the movement of iodised salt from Calcutta should be placed in Category B. (Para 5.10.1)

Rail wagons for category D and E traffic must be allotted only after fully satisfactory allocations are made for category B and C movements (even in respect of after hours or holiday loadings). (Para 5.10.2)

The Salt Department and the Railway authorities in consultation with the State Governments should jointly work out a detailed programmes of the movement of salt (both iodised and non-iodised salt) indicating:

- additional rail sidings that are feasible and will facilitate the movement of salt from the salt works;
- nomination of loading stations that will facilitate the quick movement of salt and result in overall cost savings to consumers as also the additional facilities (platforms, etc.) that must be provided in such loading station;
- the routes on which full or partial rake movements are acceptable and the facilities for this that must be provided in the identified loading stations;
- the feasibility of utilising open wagons suitably covered by tarpaulins in fair weather months to supplement the transportation of salt in covered wagons;
- transhipment points that cannot be avoided and facilities that will have to be provided so that transhipment can proceed smoothly;
- assessment of wagons required for the movement of salt from each salt producing area to meet the projected demand atleast five years ahead;
- a detailed movement plan for each year for each zone (and for the next five years) subdivided into the plan for each quarter (taking into account the need to create stocks in centres of consumption to cover likely shortfalls in railway movement arising from movement restrictions on certain sections imposed in certain months) and meetings held every quarter to which State Government representatives must be invited to review the progress achieved in meetings the previous quarter's plan and the adjustments that need to be made in the plan of the following quarter; and
- a review of zonal plans and achievements atleast once every six months with the Railway Board to identify deficiencies so that the Railway Board can find suitable solutions.

The Salt Department and the Railway authorities must constantly keep under review the possibility of relaxing (in due course removing) restrictions on the movement of salt by rail from the salt producing areas in the South to West Bengal and the North-Eastern States where there appears to be a preference for the types of salt available from these sources. (Paras 5.10.3 and 5.10.4)

Measures to Improve Coastal Movement of Salt by Ships (Chapter V)

18. Bunching of vessels arrival in Calcutta must be avoided by closer coordination with the Directorate General of Shipping. Storage in Haldia Port and distribution of salt from there should be encouraged. Direct jetty loading of salt into coastal vessels should be arranged. (Para 5.11)

Present System of Price Control (Chapter VI)

19. The present control on prices is restricted to the quantity imported in Calcutta by sea. This has averaged about 222,000 tonnes/year and is equivalent to about 3 per cent of the total domestic consumption of the country. The price of this salt at source is 11.2 per cent to 12.8 per cent of the delivered cost of salt in Calcutta. The price actually charged in the last three years has substantially cxceeded the controlled price and no legal action has been taken against the salt manufacturers who have continued to contravene the Essential Commodities Act, 1955 which notified the controlled price of this salt in 1977. (Paras 6.1 and 6.5)

Study of Costs (Chapter VI)

20. There are large variations in the cost of production of salt within each salt producing region and between regions arising from such factors as the source of brine, duration of the season, yield of salt from brine, which are either largely or wholly outside the control of salt producers.

The cost of production in salt works of 100 acres tends to be high because of the higher cess paid and high wages: the cost of production of cooperative salt work is also high because of high wages.

In the circumstances, it is found infeasible to fix a fair price or fair prices for the salt manufactured in each salt producing area or sub-area leave alone for each of the several thousand individual salt producers. (Paras 6.2 and 6.3)

Present Sales Realisation (Chapter VI)

21. There is considerable variation in the sales realisation. To an

extent, this is found to be due to the poor financial capacity of certain salt works to hold substantial stocks as a result, of which these salt works have to sell their production quickly thereby realising lower prices. Difficulties in regard to transportation also affect the sales realisation of salt works. (Para 6.4)

Margins between Ex-works and F.O.R. Price (Chapter VI)

22. Analyses of the price build-up show that the margin between ex-works prices and F.O.R. prices is excessive. There is evidence that this results from the high premium on the allotment of rail wagons. (Para 6.6)

Wholesale and Retail Prices (Chapter VI)

23. Although many State Governments have complained of the erratic movement in wholesale and retail price in their consuming centres, few State Governments keep proper records of these movements. From such data as the Committee was able to collect, the margin between low and high retail prices is high in the North-Eastern States and Bihar. The general trend in the movement of these prices indicates that prices start to increase just before the onset of the monsoon which hampers smooth rail transportation; large fluctuations leading to excessive prices exist in areas to which the transportation of salt is difficult. (Para 6.7)

24. An analysis of wholesale and retail margins in these States shows that these are clearly excessive and in relation to these the excess margin realised in ex-works sales by salt manufacturers is insignificant. (Para 6.9)

Excessive Margins between Ex-Works and F.O.R. Prices and in Wholesale and Retail Prices (Chapter VI)

25. Thus, the analyses carried out by the Committee indicate that excessive margins exist in the ex-Works-F.O.R. price build up and in wholesale and retail prices. These excessive margins can be curbed to reach fair levels by:

– the Salt Department initiating a price surveillance system to advise all States Governments the fair price at which purchases can be made from different production areas and actively assist the State Government in purchasing salt at fair prices. The Salt Department must be specially vigilant to ensure that no form of cartelisation takes place and that salt producers do not take advantage of temporary situations of difficulty arising from shortage of wagons and the lack of adequate stocks in consuming areas;

- allotting rail wagons only to the State Governments for the movement of salt purchased by the State Governments or the wholesalers so authorised by the State Governments and not permitting any change in the destination of these wagons nominated by the State Governments without their prior approval;
- much greater vigilance by the State Governments in scrutinising purchase prices and margins charged by the wholesalers selected by them (and in the selection of wholesalers on the basis of their past performance);
- the State Governments stipulating the minimum level of stocks that wholesalers must maintain in nominated consuming centres: this minimum level must be fixed in consultation with the Salt Department and the railway authorities so that they take into account the problems affecting the transportation of salt from producing areas to the consuming centres. The analysis carried out by the Committee indicates that this is specially important in East and North East Bihar, all the North-Eastern States and West Bengal and that the level of stocks that should be maintained in the key consuming centres in these States should be equivalent to four months consumption; and
- contractual arrangements between the State Governments and the wholesalers/distributors selected by them that the latter will ensure that retail price will not exceed the ceiling figures mutually agreed as reasonable for the various consuming centres combined with much greater surveillance by the State Governments that wholesale and retail prices continue to be reasonable and releases from stocks are made promptly to check unreasonable price increases. (Paras 6.10, 6.11 and 6.12)

Differential Freight on Movement of Salt to West Bengal (Chapter VI)

26. Only West Bengal receives edible salt in excess of 25 railway wagons per day by coastal shipping from the West Coast and Tuticorin area: while this may be the most cost effective mode of transport in national economic terms, it imposes an unreasonable burden of about Rs. 73 per tonne of salt on the consumers in Calcutta and nearly areas *vis-a-vis* consumers in other States. Therefore, the Committee recommends that this freight differential on salt for edible consumption should be compensated by corresponding payments from out of the Salt Cess Fund or other such funds like the coal Surcharge Fund, provided, however, there is the utmost vigilance on the part of the State Government to ensure that the benefit of this in the form of a reduction in the selling price is actually passed on to the consumers and not permitted to be absorbed by an increase in the effective wholesale and retail margins realised by traders. (Para 6.13)

Freight Equalisation (Chapter VI)

27. The consumption of salt forms of 0.47 per cent of the total per capita consumption expenditure. For a variety of reasons, the market for salt is far from perfect, the present margins (ex-works to F.O.R., wholesale and retail) excessive, stable fair consumer prices yet to be achieved and cost-effective transportation arrangements yet to be streamlined. In these circumstances and given the fact that there are about 4,000 salt producers and that their cost of production varies a great deal within each salt producing region and between regions, the Committee does not consider that a freight equalisation scheme for salt is feasible and likely to lead to any significant advantage to consumers at this stage. (Para 6.14)

Cost of Collection of Cess and Alternatives (Chapter VII)

28.1. The total annual cost of administration consisting of the licensing of salt works and detailed and continuous check on the release of salt is 55 per cent of the total cess collected which was Rs. 1.33 crores in 1978-79. The total annual collection is so small, the cost of administration so heavy and the controversies in this so many, that the Committee considers that the quantum of cess collected is not commensurate with the costs and total effort in its collection and therefore recommends that it should be removed altogether. If, however, the Government considers it is essential that the cost of development activities must continue to be met from revenues that must be raised from the operation of the salt industry, then much simpler methods of raising these funds are feasible. After examining several of these, the Committee considers that the simplest method will be to levy a cess of about Rs. 5 to Rs. 10 per tonne on the salt consumed by the manufacturers of caustic soda and soda ash instead of charging and collecting the cess from the several thousand widely scattered salt producers.

28.2. The removal of advantages available currently to certain classes of small producers and cooperatives through the partial or full exemption from the salt cess resulting from the above recommendations, can be compensated by the imposition of lower and favourable land revenue and assignment fees, by extending loans on softer terms and grants for labour welfare for which salt works in the non-licensed sector are not at present eligible. (Paras 7.4.2 and 7.4.3)

(Shree S.C. Aggarwal dissents from the above recommendations)

Salt Cess Act and Rules (Chapter VII)

29. The above recommendations lead to very major revisions in the Salt Cess Act and Rules. (Para 7.4.4)

Collection of Land Revenue and Protection of Central Lands (Chapter VII)

30. Land revenue on central lands used for the manufacture of salt should be collected by the State Governments and credited to the Salt Department and no separate staff of the Salt Department need be utilised for this task : the attention of the staff of the Salt Department can than be concentrated on the much more important tasks of promoting the adoption of improved technology, reduction in costs, speedy movement, etc.

Such vacant land as can be utilised for the production of salt must be so used immediately : the balance should be offered to other Central Government departments and the State Governments on reasonable terms and the land that is not required by these should then be auctioned. (Para 7.5)

Licensing (Chapter VII)

31.1. With very very rare exception, all the applications received for the manufacture of salt have been approved by the Salt Department and licenses issued. The Committee considers that delays and vexatious correspondence in licensing can be eliminated by delegating authority to the State Governments to issue licences on behalf of the Salt Department in accordance with guidelines that the Salt Department should formulate: these guidelines must include stipulations regarding the rapid utilisation of the area licensed, proper layout, flow and storage of bitterns and also that all licensed manufacturers must employ supervisors properly trained in the manufacture of salt. State Governments must constitute proper Licensing Committees which must include the Assistant Salt Commissioner. (Para 7.6)

(Shri S.C. Aggarwal, Shri K.L. Sahni and Shri S.K. Sarkar dissent from this recommendation.)

31.2. The period of licence be extended to 40 years with stipulation to ensure that the entire licensed area is worked every year strictly; and a uniform and simple procedure be adopted in all the States for transfer of licence. (Paras 7.8.1 and 7.8.2)

Development—Labour Welfare for Development (Chapter VII)

32. The total expenditure on these was negligible until 1976-77; but has increased in the last three years to reach Rs. 4.6 million in 1978-79. The Committee has received complaints of the tardy manner in which schemes are examined, processed, approved and implemented. The Committee considers that the State Governments and their enterprises (such as the State Industrial Development and Finance Corporation) are better equipped to scrutinise schemes and grant approvals quickly and, therefore, it recommends that all programmes of this type should be left wholly to the State Governments to carry out. The Salt Department should assist the State Governments in working out time phased comprehensive schemes and then monitor their implementation. Suitable funds should be made available under the Central Plan to the State Governments and their enterprises to discharge these responsibilities. (Para 7.7)

Code of Principles (Chapter VII)

33. In case, the Government does not accept the abolition of cess on salt, the code that regulates the grant of financial assistance out of cess proceeds, be amended, providing enhanced power to sanction works at various levels. (Para 7.9)

Research and Development (Chapter VIII)

34. No system has so far been developed to measure the progress in the application of improved technology or collect data in this regard. The Salt Department must take the lead in coordinating the formulation of an intensive and extensive programme of technological development in this industry, in consultation with the CS&MCRI, the Salt producing State Governments and well established consultancy design organisations. The Salt Department must accept a coordinating and overseeing role with the salt producing State Governments providing an active field extension service (initially by the loan of the staff of the Salt Department to the State Governments). The Committee has made a number of suggestions for accelerating technological progress. (Paras 8.1 to 8.6)

Specifications and Standards (Chapter IX)

35. Improvement in standards is highly desirable and the programme of steady improvement now drawn up by the Ministry of Health must be implemented. Proven technology to achieve this is available and must be disseminated vigorously by State Government salt field extension services, supported by special training courses at various levels, extensive testing by enlisting the assistance of analytical laboratories in salt works to test samples of salt produced in other salt works, etc. These efforts should be linked with the State Governments purchasing salt of progressively improving specifications as programmed by the Ministry of Health. (Paras 9.1 to 9.5)

The Role of the Public Sector (Chapter X)

36. The production of the Central public enterprise, Hindustan Salts, is equivalent to about 8 per cent of the total domestic consumption of edible salt : the potential production of State public enterprises

will be somewhat more than this when their works are completed in the near future. This large production of the Centre and State public enterprises can help maintain a degree of price stability and surveillance, assist salt deficit States in procuring salt at a fair and stable price and possibly assist in mutually beneficial long-term supply and distribution arrangements specially of iodised and fortified salts.

In close cooperation with the CS&MCRI, these enterprises can assist in training a large number of salt workers in improved techniques of salt production.

Each of the major public sector salt works should promote the recovery and collection of bitterns from all the salt works within an economical distance and establish plants to recover by-products such as bromine, potassium chloride, sodium sulphate, magnesium chloride, magnesium sulphate, etc.

The technological progress of Central and State public sector plants can be facilitated by much closer association between these and scientists, technologists, design consultants and also possibility through the institutional consultancy of the CS&MCRI. (Paras 10.1 and 10.4)

Labour and Employment (Chapter XI)

37. The problems affecting the conditions of workers are within the purview of the State Governments. The particular problem of workers in the salt industry can be dealt with more effectively by the State Governments appointing special labour welfare officers for the workers in this industry, located in the salt producing regions. Health hazards should be removed by the State Governments stipulating the facilities that every salt manufacturer has to provide as a condition of his being permitted to lease land for the manufacture of salt. The Salt Department should keep closely in touch with the progress. (Paras 11.1 and 11.2)

Packing Sizes (Chapter XI)

38. The ceiling on packing size should be reduced to 55 kgs. within three years, in conformity with the Committee on Conventions (1977) and to accord with the ceiling packing sizes for most other industrial products such as cement. (Para 11.3)

Recovery of By-Products (Chapter XII)

39. The recovery of valuable by-products such as bromine, potassium and magnesium salts should be accelerated and the Committee suggests that this be exempted from the Industrial Development and Regulation Act.

Cooperatives (Chapter XIII)

40. Although the production of cooperative salt works has increased to reach 0.90 million tonnes year it is still below the production of 1.25 million tonnes/year achieved in the unlicensed sector. The Committee emphasises the importance of greatly improving the viability of cooperative works through the extension of concessional land revenue, assignment fees, soft loans and special technological assistance so that small salt producers can take benefit by merging their works with cooperatives that are able to achieve low costs of production and by-products recovery. This should be an important objective of the Salt Department. (Paras 13.1 and 13.2)

The Revised Functions and Organisation of the Salt Department (Chapter XIV)

41.1 With the recommendations in the above paragraphs, the main functions of the Salt Department will be in production and price surveillance; streamlining storage and distribution; promotion and technological development; assistance in investment planning and monitoring the implementation of schemes; facilitating the rapid expansion of labour welfare measures and reviewing these in each salt producing regions; supporting studies and measures to accelerate exports; establishment of future quality standards and to assist in their achievement; provision of meteorological services and in promoting the formation of cooperatives.

The Annual Report of the Salt Department should contain detailed data on the progress in these areas. The Salt Department should also take the initiative in publishing a directory of design consultants in this industry. (Paras 14.1.1 to 14.1.7)

41.2 The Salt Department should consist of five main divisions for production, storage and distribution, technological development, labour welfare and economics and statistics, in the head office, directed by officers of the rank of Deputy or Assistant Salt Commissioners and regional offices in the major salt supplying States of Gujarat, Tamil Nadu, Rajasthan and possibly Andhra (where Divisional Superintendents of the Railways are located) directed by officers of the rank of Assistant Salt Commissioners to help streamline the distribution and storage of salt : in these latter regional offices, the assistance of railway transportation officers should be sought, at any rate initially to train the officers of the Salt Department in the new responsibilities of streamlining distribution. A regional office should also be maintained in the North Eastern area to assist these States in ensuring the ready availability of iodised salt. (Para 14.2)

41.3 A substantial surplus of staff is likely to arise in Group B, Group C and Group D. This surplus should be determined with the assistance of the Staff Inspection Unit. (Paras 14.2 and 14.3)

41.4 The staff declared surplus should be provided remunerative employment in the greatly enlarged responsibilities that the State Governments will now have to undertake, by preferentially licensing to it or to cooperatives that the surplus staff should be encouraged to form, new salt works and by assisting it in setting up design and consultancy organisations. (Para 14.3)

41.5 The assurances in regard to salary, allowances and other amenities, given to the staff of the Salt Department when this Department was formed in 1947, have yet to be fulfilled. The complaints received by the Committee in regard to pay scales and amenities appear legitimate and the Committee suggests that the term of reference of the study that it suggests that the Staff Inspection Unit should undertake should include this important issue. (Para 14.4)

30

REVIEW COMMITTEE ON ELECTRONICS, 1978 — REPORT[1]

Chairman Shri Mantosh Sondhi
Members Dr. B. Nag; Shri J.A. Dave; Shri M. Menezes
M. Secy. Shri N. Sivasubramanian

Appointment

On the direction of Prime Minister the Government of India in the Department of Electronics appointed a Review Committee on Electronics Vide its Order No. 19(41)(8)78-Adm.I dated December 7, 1978.

Terms of Reference

"A quick review should be undertaken of policies and organisational structures in the Department of Electronics (including the Electronics Commission), so that new directions of policy are identified as early as possible and organisational structures are fashioned to implement the new policies effectively."

Contents

Electronics: the Pace Setter; The Review Committee; Current Status of the Indian Electronics Industry; Task Ahead: Broad Strategies for Development; Annexure 4A: Estimated Production for Electronics Industry; Industrial Approvals; Annexure 5A: Illustrative list of Reservation for Small Scale Sector; Annexure 5B: Illustrative list of Telecommunication equipment which can be taken up for production in private sector; Imports and Tariffs; Annexure 6A: Illustrative list of Electronic

1. New Delhi, Department of Electronics, 1979, 207 p.

equipment whose Import is to be strictly restricted; Annexure 6B: Illustrative list of Capital Goods for electronic industry not available indigenously and to be placed under open general licence; Annexure 6C: Illustrative list of test equipment, tooling, Components, professional grade in particular and raw materials to be placed on the restricted list for imports; Fiscal and Financial Measures; Exports; Role of the Small Scale Sector in Electronics; Research, Development and Manpower; Quality Management and Standardization; Computers; Central Public Sector Undertakings; Annexure 13A: Central Public Sector Undertakings in the field of electronics; Organisational Structure; Annexure 14A: Functions, Duties, Responsibilities and Powers of Department of Electronics and Electronics Commission; Annexure 14B: Organisational Structure of Electronics Research and Development Organisation; Conclusions and Summary of Recommendations; Appendices from 2.1 to 14.6.

Recommendations

15.1 The Committee has completed, in accordance with its terms of reference, a review of the policies, procedures and institutional framework in the Department of Electronics (including the Electronics Commission). In undertaking this review, consultations in depth were held with the electronics industry in all its segments both in the private and the public sectors, Government agencies concerned with electronics directly or indirectly, R&D institutions and professional experts. As a result, the Committee has come to the conclusion that it is possible to achieve much higher and faster rates of growth in the production and use of electronics in the country than has been the case hitherto. The objective can be realised if the existing restrictive climate is replaced by one of positive promotion, consistent with the national socio-economic priorities.

15.2 Towards this direction, the Committee has recommended a package of measures in the area of industrial approvals, import and tariff policies, fiscal and financial arrangements and exports. The essence of this package is the dismantling of unnecessary controls, restrictions and regulations but with an overall coordinated and integrated approach on growth, with due regard to specific strategies of development. Multi-channel and multi-agency approvals seem to have retarded growth in the past. Streamlined procedures have, therefore, been suggested as well as approvals by a single-point nodal agency, moved by group dynamics so that the Department of Electronics can be held fully accountable for the development of the electronics industry in the country. In respect of the Free Trade Zone, it has been clearly brought out that unless we offer similar facilities, as some of our neighbouring countries do, it will continue to languish. Measures for strengthening the role of the small scale sector, especially in the production of certain types of consumer electronics and in employment intensive assembly operations, have been clearly brought out. Its complementarity to the organised sector has also been stressed.

15.3 Substantial but selective investments in production-oriented research and development programmes have been highlighted; so also the need for the development of suitable manpower. Specific measures for standardisation and quality assurance have been suggested.

15.4 To obviate stagnation in the area of computers, specific steps have been proposed for stimulating production and use of computers with due regard to the accelerated development of key sectors of the economy but fully consistent with our socio-economic requirements including the sensitive issue of employment potential. Streamlining of procedures for import of such computers which do not lend themselves to economical production in the short-term, has been suggested. An organisational re-structuring of the facilities in the public sector for the manufacture and maintenance of computers has also been proposed. The need for greater coordination at the national level for more effective utilisation of costly and powerful computer systems set up in the country has been emphasised.

15.5 A series of measures for the restructuring of the present Department of Electronics, the Electronics Commission and the organisations functioning under them have been suggested with a view to ensuring clearly demarcated functional and organisational responsibilities. With the implementation of these measures, Department of Electronics assisted by the high-powered interministerial Boards which have been recommended, would have the primacy of policy direction and implementation. The Electronics Development Commission replacing the present Electronics Commission, would essentially be a high level advisory body, free from executive responsibilities, with an enlarged membership concerning itself with studies of and advice on perspective planning for self-reliance, integrated development of the electronics industry, the inter-sectoral applications of electronics and R&D efforts. Its new role would be that of a 'think tank'. Consequently, the existing organisations supporting its activities will be merged in the Department of Electronics.

15.6 A summary of the conclusions and recommendations made by the Committee is given below.

Electronics: The Pace Setter

(1) The concept of rapid development of the electronics industry which is a forceful catalyst for the growth of our national economy fits in ideally with our national priorities and resource endowments (Para 1.7).

Industrial Approvals

Electronics Approval Board

(2) In electronics, the emphasis so far seems to have been more on regulatory rather than on developmental and promotional aspects. The Committee has reluctantly come to the conclusion that this situation in electronics seems to have stifled initiative and enterprise, even in the case of small entrepreneurs and self-employed technocrats, by subjecting them to time-consuming procedures and multi-channel scrutiny (Para 5.1)

(3) The Committee is convinced—and so are most of the industry groups and professional experts whom it met — that if the growth of the electronics industry in the country has to gain momentum the first step that would need to be taken would be to dismantle the present control structure to the extent that it does not subserve the accepted socio-economic objectives (Para 5.2).

(4) An Electronics Approval Board be set up in the Department of Electronics with Secretary, Department of Electronics as Chairman, Secretaries in the Ministry of Communications, Ministry of Commerce, Department of Industrial Development, Department of Defence production, Planning Commission and the Department of Economic Affairs or their senior authorised representatives not below the level of Additional Secretary (or Joint Secretary, where post of Additional Secretary does not exist) and the CCI&E as members. The Board should be delegated in respect of electronics, all the powers which are now being exercised by the Licensing Committee. The Foreign Investment Board, the Capital Goods Committee, the Technical Development Fund Committee, the Committee on Joint Ventures abroad and

the Import Licensing Committees within the jurisdiction of the CCI&E (Para 5.8)

Delicensing of Investments upto Rs. 10 Crores

(5) The present investment limit for delicensing be raised from Rs. 3 crores to Rs. 10 crores for the electronics industry so as to effectively delicense it, without any of the existing preconditions on limits for import of raw materials and components or locational aspects. The exception in regard to MRTP/FERA companies and reservation of certain areas for the small scale sector, as of now, may be retained, in consonance with the accepted socio-economic policy frame (Para 5.4).

Nodal Agency

(6) The existing and new units in the proposed delicensed area need, only register the details of their activities with a single nodal agency, viz., the Department of Electronics except for small scale units where such an agency may be the State Director of Industries or the District Industries Centre (Para 5.6).

Time Bound Clearance

(7) The Department of Electronics shall act as the Secretariat for the Board and accept the responsibility for time-bound package clearance of all applications within a maximum period of 45 days (Para 5.9).

Single Point Clearance

(8) (a) The applications for import of raw materials, components and tooling for electronics industry be disposed of by the Department of Electronics;

(b) Formal references to the DGTD by the Department of Electronics on all matters connected with the Electronics industry be dispensed with (Para 5.10).

Review of Non-Viable Capacities

(9) In the case of MRTP/FERA companies, all such cases where

fragmented and non-viable capacities have been sanctioned in the past should be reviewed urgently by the Department of Electronics and firm proposals submitted to the Electronics Approval Board to rectify the situation (Para 5.11).

Positive Approach to Foreign Collaboration

(10) There is clearly need for liberalising induction of foreign technology in the components field (Para 4.6).

(11) There need be only a list of banned items/processes for foreign collaboration, for clearly stated reasons, leaving the entire residual area free for foreign collaboration. Full authority be vested in the Electronics Approval Board to examine and sanction proposals for foreign collaboration, as well as equity participation, even if this involves some departures from the existing guidelines keeping the specific requirements of the electronics industry in view, but not at the cost of national interest (Para 5.15).

Production of Telecommunication Equipment also in Private Sector

(12) The private sector could supplement and augment production in the public sector of telecommunication equipment substantially; restriction on it be selectively removed and consequential changes made in the Industrial Policy Resolution (Para 5.13).

Automatic Allocation of Frequencies to Manufacturers

(13) In the case of telecommunication equipment, the Department of Electronics, in consultation with the Ministry of Communications, where necessary, should ensure that allocation of frequencies (only for manufacture and not operation) is done more or less automatically and does not tantamount to licensing, for the delicensed sector (Para 5.14).

Effective Reservation for Small Scale Sector

(14) The list of items reserved for the small scale sector be comprehensively reviewed annually (Para 5.12).

Activity Reservation for Small Scale Sector

(15) Consumer electronics, assembly of test and measuring instru-

ments and simple control and micro-computer systems are some of the areas suited to the small scale sector; in these areas therefore, the policy of the Government would need to be implemented through reservation of assembly activities for small scale sector and through ancillarisation. In addition to reserving production of some items for the small scale sector and the benefit of fiscal concessions being given only to this sector, some assembly activities should also be exclusively earmarked for this sector. Any further expansion of capacity in the area of consumer electronics in the organised sector should be subject to the stipulation that assembly operations would be confined to the small scale and ancillary units only. The organised sector should promote the small scale and ancillary units, through progressive quantitative increase in their turnover coming from such units (Para 9.5).

Mutual Dependency

(16) Effective implementation of the existing policy requires more dynamic measures and not merely static reservation of products of small scale sector or denial of opportunities for growth to the organised sector. The real growth of the small scale and tiny sectors of industry has to complement the growth of the organised sector utilising contemporary technology with mutual concern for each other's interest. The organised sector must be made to accept the responsibility for providing essential inputs to the small scale units and ancillaries in matters of technology, marketing after sales follow up and making available raw materials and components; the State Electronics Development Corporations must also be made to play a much more effective role in this direction. To enable manufacture of electronic products for various types of applications in the short run a deliberate policy of liberal imports, extension of technology, training and professional managed common facilities for the small scale sector is needed (Paras 9.6 and 9.7).

Imports and Tariffs

Rationalised Import Policy

(17) (i) Import of fully assembled and ready-to-use electronic equipment, excluding test equipment, be restricted, except in certain specified cases where the domestic requirements do not justify the set-

ting up of fabricating capacity or assembly units;

(ii) capital goods not available indigenously be placed on Open General Licence, as far as possible;

(iii) test equipment, tooling, components, professional grade in particular, and raw materials be also placed on Open General Licence except those which are being manufactured in the country in the short-term and warrant protection in the national interest; the import of the letter however being restricted;

(iv) items on restricted list be eligible for automatic licensing at 110 per cent of previous year's consumption of imported items by value, at 15 per cent for small scale sector for components and supplementary licensing, subject to the prescribed scrutiny (the Department of Electronics shall act as the nodal agency for this purpose);

(v) wherever feasible, pack values be fixed for import as percentages of the ex-factory price of the end-product, laid down from year to year, to regulate automatically the import content; and

(vi) no restriction be placed on the import of second hand plant and testing equipment except to the extent of the usual certification about the good condition, residual life and depreciated value of the equipment from a chartered engineer (Para 6.4).

No Canalisation

(18) There is no need for any canalisation of imports (Para 6.12).

No Advertisement Procedure for Capital Goods

(19) For capital equipment of the electronics industry advertisement procedure may be dispensed with (Para 6.7).

Rationalised Import Duty Structure

(20) The irrationality in customs duty structure is a deterrent to the development of the electronics industry in the country. This situation therefore needs to be rectified immediately (Para 6.9).

(21) (a) Capital goods, test equipment, tooling, raw materials and components placed on Open General Licence be wholly exempted from duty;

(b) items, not placed on OGL be assessed to duty at 100 per cent *ad valorem* except for specified items which may need higher duty protection because of their nascent development or for any other reason, depending on cost studies and in the national interest; however, the industry should be put on notice that tariff protection would be gradually reduced so that they might take steps to reduce their cost of production and build up their competitive strength in a definite time frame, of say 3/5 years, the protective duty structure being subject to periodic reviews (Para 6.10).

Set-off Against Multiple Taxation

(22) A fixed set-off worked out on an empirical basis, be given to reduce the cascading effect of multiple taxation. The existing area or quantum of central excise duties on electronics goods should not be enlarged for three years (Para 6.13).

Stable Import/Tariff Policy

(23) The import/tariff policies formulated should have a stable tenurc of at least three years (Para 6.14).

Fiscal and Financial Measures

Priority Status for Electronics and benefits thereof

(24) The electronics industry (other than the consumer sub-sector) and more especially the electronics components industry should be regarded as a priority industry and this should get reflected in the relevant acts, rules regulations and guidelines. Based on its priority status, the benefits which are available to various priority industries under the various acts, rules and regulations should be extended also to the electronics industry (excluding the consumer goods area) and especially to the electronics components industry (Para 7.3).

Higher Rate of Depreciation

(25) The rate of depreciation for electronics components industry be fixed at 20 per cent under the Income-tax Act (Para 7.5).

Partial Tax Holiday for Components Industry

(26) The partial tax holiday incentive be continued for investments

in new, electronics components industries for the next five years since the components industry holds the key to development of electronics industry but has been a late starter in India (Para 7.7).

Fruitful Interaction with Financial Institutions by Department of Electronics

(27) The Department of Electronics should interact with the financial institutions and arrange for imparting training to entrepreneurs, who need it, in project formulation and help the financial institutions by supplying them panel of independent experts for project appraisal in the sophisticated field of electronics (Para 7.9).

No Recurring Broadcast Receiver Licence (BRL) fee on Radio Sets

(28) The basis for raising revenue year after year by relating it to possession of a radio set in fast getting out of date, taking into account the technological advances, size of radio sets, their portability, extent of piracy on use of unlicensed sets, and less than 50 per cent efficiency in levy and collection of BRL fees even after 3 years of sale. The basis for raising revenue should in future be a one time levy on a graded *ad valorem* basis roughly equal to the present average life time revenue received through BRL on the sets, cheap sets of value upto Rs. 165 being exempted from even the one time levy (Para 7.11).

Exports

Export Zone (SEEPZ) facilities to be Comparable Internationally

(29) The Export Zone cannot really take off unless it offers facilities which are at least on par with those offered by other similar zones in the neighbouring countries (Para 8.11).

Full authority to Development Commissioner of Export Zone

(30) The Development Commissioner Export Processing Zone should be fully authorised to take and communicate decisions on all matters including Central customs/excise questions. The status of the Development Commissioner should be such as to enable him to effectively discharge these functions. The SEEPZ Board should be

abolished and its duties and powers handed over to the Development Commissioner SEEPZ (Para 8.13).

Concessions Essential to Revive Export Zone

(31) (a) Exemption from corporate tax and tax on dividends for SEEPZ units, existing and to be newly set up for a period of five years with an inbuilt provision to review the question of tax holiday for a further period on the merits of each case at the end of the five years.

(b) a higher rate of depreciation for Zonal units, which should at least be 30 per cent every year.

(c) abolition of the service charge levied by SEEPZ Administration.

(d) an *ad hoc* but appropriate percentage of export value to be allowed as compensation towards Central Sales-tax, State Sales-tax; Octroi, Electricity Duty, etc., be worked out by the Development Commissioner in the case of each unit and allowed under the Market Development Fund which is in fact meant to remove such disincentives of export (Para 8.14).

Single Point Approval for Export Joint Ventures

(32) Proposals for joint ventures abroad from Indian entrepreneurs in the field of electronics be henceforth received and cleared by the Electronics Approval Board; keeping in view the paramount need to have an integrated organisational approach to the growth of the electronics industry which differs from other industries in many respects (Para 8.17).

Reasonable and Simple Incentives to Promote Exports from Hinterland

(33) (a) A rate of 20 per cent cash support to electronics export would be appropriate and the rate should remain unchanged for at least three years;

(b) drawback rates be empirically fixed on the basis of a percentage to be applied to the f.o.b value of exports, if necessary, in three or four distinct groups of related equipment and components taking into account the likely incidence of customs and Central excise duties entering into products covered by each group;

(c) a simple application from the exporting units of what they require by way of duty-free imports, supported by a chartered agency's certificate, should be adequate for granting the duty exemption; in case of misuse or non-performance, panel duties may be levied. The facility should be extended to programmed but committed exports, without insistence on firm orders, subject of course, to the usual bonds/bank guarantees;

(d) replenishment rates would be necessary and need to be rationalised to facilitate import of new generations of components, designs and prototypes for product development, special toolings and drawings. Adequate flexibility should be given to the exporting units in their shopping lists taking into account the fact that there are rapid changes in the circuitry designs;

(e) liberal grants be given from the Market Development Fund not only to approved organisations and eligible merchandising Export House but also to individual units with an export performance and potential of over Rs. 10 lakhs and Rs. 1 crore per annum respectively;

(f) electronics export items other than those which require mere assembly activity with indigenously available components should also be eligible for the more liberal packing credit terms (Para 8.19).

Export Quality Assurance

(34) There is need for facilities available in the field of electronics in the country being pooled and coordinated for effective quality assurance services to the exporting units as well as to their foreign customers . Export promotion organisations in the field should assist exporting units by making available to latter at little or no cost, codified reprints of standards, including English translations, on request (Para 8.20).

Export Promotion Council

(35) For a concentrated export drive in electronics, which offers tremendous scope, there should be a distinct and separate Export Promotion Council consisting *inter alia* of representatives of the Ministry of Commerce and the Department of Electronics. The administrative jurisdiction of this Export Promotion Council should properly vest with the Department of Electronics which should have the overall and integrated responsibility for growth in electronics which needs to be stimulated also by exports (Para 8.21).

Research, Development and Manpower

R & D a must for Industries

(36) The industries in the private sector, especially those in the organised sector, be persuaded to develop in-house R&D capability which should not merely be for the purpose of obtaining fiscal reliefs but essentially for the development of indigenous technology and for adaptation and updating of the imported technology. Within the proposed framework of industrial licensing of MRTP and FERA companies and new units with an investment of more than Rs. 10 crores, and taking into account the present policy on the import of technology and foreign collaboration, measures should taken to ensure that a reasonable percentage of the turnover or profits of the industrial units is expended by them or R&D which is meaningful, relevant and commercially linked with their production. Our Research and Development efforts must be related to the requirements of our industrial production along with a high degree of cost consciousness (Para 10.5).

R & D in Materials and Components Vital

(37) A concerted effort in R & D in the area of materials and components technology should be organised by the Department of Electronics. In this effort no resource constraint, financial, material or manpower, should be allowed to come in the way (Para 10.6).

Identified R & D to be Encouraged and Promoted

(38) The Department of Electronics should continue to fund institutions like the Universities and the Institutes of Technology on well identified projects including long ranging research programmes. This would help to elevate the quality of manpower development in our academic institutions apart from other benefits which are bound to accrue as a result. The existing national research organisations in the areas of electronics should be given all the support so that the continue to grow, preferably in identified areas of specialisation so that there is no duplication of effort with consequent dilution of our scarce resources (Para 10.7).

Direction and Coordination of R & D by Department of Electronics-Setting up of ERDO

(39) The Department of Electronics should be entrusted with the responsibility for giving a sense of purposeful direction to and for the coordination of all R & D activities in the country. This should be ensured not merely through the mechanism of funding projects in various institutions but through promoting bilateral organisational linkages between industry and the R & D institutions. To achieve all this, the Committee recommends that an Electronics Research and Development Organisation (ERDO) under the Department of Electronics should be set up (Para 10.8).

Development of Manpower

(40) It is necessary that much greater attention is given to ensure that our potential engineers and technicians, fresh from the universities and institutes, measure up in quality to the high standards, with the right orientation, required by the electronics industry. This would require development of a suitable strategy and coordinated action between the Department of Electronics, Ministry of Education and the Ministry of Labour. In this we should not lose sight of the requirements of the electronics industry for highly skilled workmen, technicians, and the supervisory personnel. The Department of Electronics should also work out a scheme for the exchange of technical personnel at all levels between the industry and the educational and R & D establishments so that they are aware of each others' specific requirements thereby helping to establish linkages between the two besides providing an avenue for cross-fertilisation of ideas (Para 10.9).

Quality Management and Standardisations

Systematised Quality Assurance Institutions to Cover Whole of Industry

(41) The area of standards and quality assurance is very important and should engage the serious attention of Government and industry with a view to setting up institutionalised arrangements covering all production units in electronics. The working of the Test and Development Centres and the four regional centres should be entirely

reoriented to the requirements of the industry which should have a considerable say in their planning and management. This should be ensured by the Department of Electronics through the setting up of a suitable standing forum. The ISI and the test centres including the export inspection agencies should coordinate their efforts under the aegis of the Department of Electronics with those of the Electronics Standardisation Sub-Committee of the Ministry of Defence (LSSC) so as to ensure continuous refinement of specifications and procedures for testing, certifying and quality management. Immediate arrangements be introduced for in-house quality management by major manufacturing units. In-house inspection facilities in some of the major manufacturing units may also be recognised for the purpose of their issuing certificates of quality and conformity to specifications in respect of the products of the other units also. Surveillance by authorities and agencies nominated by the Department of Electronics, of the working of such recognised centres in the public and private sectors would also be necessary. The ultimate aim should be to link every manufacturer in the country with a recognised quality assurance centre (Para 11.3).

Incentives to Quality Consciousness

(42) To facilitate the promotion of quality consciousness, one per cent rebate on loans from financial institutions should be available to all units whose products are inspected and certified by agencies nominated or recognised by the Department of Electronics. All nationally financed test and inspection centres should make available their facilities free for an initial period of 3 to 5 years purely as a promotional activity with a view to popularise the inspection and certifying procedures among the units manufacturing electronic products (Para 11.4).

Standardisation and Specifications by Consensus

(43) The Department of Electronics should organise meets with industry annually, if not at more frequent intervals, to ensure that the national specifications get evolved over a broad spectrum commensurate with the requirements of the industry and without standardisation becoming a dogma. The Department of Electronics should provide the necessary thrust and leadership in this vital area (Para 11.6).

Computers

Need to Develop Indigenous Computer Industry

(44) Immediate measures are necessary to ensure that indigenous production of contemporary computers and peripherals makes rapid strides so that the range of computer systems produced in the country does not continue to be restricted (Para 12.5).

Measures for Rapid Development

(45) The existing organisations and others who are likely to enter the area of mini-computers and micro-processor based systems, for manufacture and sale within the country and those who have gone in for medium sized computers have the capability to satisfy a good proportion of the functional requirements of users within the country. The basic rationale of the policy measures proposed earlier, subject to certain modifications, in respect of industrial approvals including foreign collaboration, import policies, tariff structure, exports, fiscal incentives, etc., apply equally to the area of computers including mini-computers and micro-processor based systems, peripherals as well as other related items of equipment and software. These policy measures would impart the necessary dynamism for the rapid development of this sector of the electronics industry where the growth has been somewhat stunted so far and where a very large technological gap exists and needs to be bridged (Para 12.9).

Strategy for the Development

(46) Strategy for the development of the computer industry has to give first priority to the mini-computers and micro-processor based systems costing not more than Rs. 50 lakhs with maximum flexibility in the import of components. Second priority has to be for medium computers costing more than Rs. 50 lakhs. The large computer systems will naturally have to take the third priority (Para 12.10).

Rationalised Tariff Structure

(47) (i) All imported computer systems and such sub-systems, peripherals, accessories, software, etc., as are under production in the

country be subject to import duty at 100 per cent *ad valorem*; in addition, countervailing duty on par with the excise duty levied on indigenous manufacturers should also be imposed;

(ii) for the present and till the indigenous industry is in a position to market systems of value above Rs. 50 lakhs, which as per present estimate may take 4 to 5 years, import duty on systems of value above Rs. 50 lakhs inclusive of peripherals, accessories, software, etc., may continue to be levied at the present rate of 40 per cent *ad valorem*. The countervailing duty should be reduced to 8 per cent in line with the recommendations made in sub-para (iv) below. However, full rate of duty as in (i) above shall be levied on identifiable discrete units of the above imported systems which are being manufactured in India and already enjoy protective duty;

(iii) all sub-systems, peripherals and accessories which are not being produced in the country should also be subject to an import duty on 45 per cent with a countervailing duty of 8 per cent; and

(iv) excise duty on all indigenous computer systems, sub-system, peripherals, accessories, etc., should be reduced from level of 25 per cent of the general rate of 8 per cent (Para 12.11).

Merger of Efforts in Public Sector Computer Corporation of India

(48) The corporate future of the CMC lies in its forging an organic bond with a viable indigenous computer manufacturer which in this case is obviously the ECIL. This can be achieved through the merger of the computer division of ECIL with CMC into a single public sector undertaking to be called the Computer Corporation of India which should be placed under the administrative control of the Department of Electronics. Bold and imaginative corporate plans would need to be drawn up by the Computer Corporation of India so that India attains self-reliance in the whole range of computers as soon as possible (Para 12.15).

Maintenance also by Other Manufacturers

(49) Maintenance of computer systems including peripherals supplied by foreign collaborators of manufacturing units in India should also be permitted to be maintained by manufacturing cum maintenance organisations in India, in addition to the Computer Corporation of India. The choice should be left to the actual user (Para 12.16).

Sound Import Policy

(50) The basis tenets of the present policy on import of computers continue to be valid and do not call for any change (Para 12.20).

Computer Cell in Ministry of Labour for Speeding up Import Decisions

(51) For deciding on all aspects of labour interests relating to computers, the Ministry of Labour should constitute a cell in that Ministry manned by persons with knowledge of computer systems, the diversity of its applications and its impact on productivity, labour displacement, etc. The cell should work in close consultation with the Department of Electronics so that in the initial stages of the finalisation of the configuration of computer system this extremely important aspect is fully taken care of (Para 12.21).

Import Procedure too Rigid

(52) The present procedure for the import of computer systems is much too rigid and cumbersome and tends to defeat the very purpose for which computers are required (Para 12.20).

Rationalised Import Procedure

(53) Under the rationalised procedure for procurement of imported computers, for systems of value more than Rs. 50 lakhs, the user will draw up detailed specifications and systems configuration and they will be critically examined by the Department of Electronics in consultation with the user, the Cell in the Ministry of Labour, where necessary, and the Computer Corporation, the last being essential where maintenance is to be done by the Corporation. If the proposal is found to be justified, the Department of Electronics will clear the computer system for import. Thereafter, the user shall float global tenders broadly in the manner prescribed by the Department of Electronics from time to time. The user will get the selected system and the draft contract approved by the Department of Electronics which will consult where necessary, the Computer Corporation so as to ensure that the contract covers purchase of equipment, peripherals, spares, maintenance, warranty, etc. and the application for import licence will be submitted to the Electronics Approval Board as per normal procedure. Where the c.i.f.

value of the system does not exceed Rs. 50 lakhs approval for import clearance will be obtained from the Department of Electronics without the necessity of having to through the above procedure, as is being done at present for system below Rs. 5 lakhs in value (Para 12.22).

Monitoring of Imports Under Special Clearance

(54) The policy for the import of computers against an obligations for export of software and the special clearance for such imports may be continued and the use of such computers should be monitored by the Department of Electronics and the results thereof published in the annual reports of the Department (Para 12.23).

Policy on RCCs Sound

(55) The present policy for setting up Regional Computer Centres is basically a sound one and may be continued while adapting it to the changing pattern of the user demands; this, of course, has to be a continuous process (Para 12.26).

Centralised Guidance and Promotion of National Computer Effort

(56) The transfer of the National Centre for Software Development and Computing Techniques (NCSDCT) to the Department of Electronics was a step in the right direction but the follow up action for linking the NCSDCT to the Department of Electronics administratively still remains to be implemented. The NCSDCT be hived off from the Tata Institute of Fundamental Research (TIFR) and set up immediately as an autonomous registered society, administratively linked to the Department of Electronics. A computer advisory panel should be set up in the Department of Electronics directed by the Secretary, Department of Electronics and with a cross section of computer professionals, manufacturers, users, scientists and technologists engaged in research and development, represented on it to guide and promote the national computer effort (Para 12.32 and 12.33).

Review of Fast Changing Computer Area After Three Years

(57) The whole area of computer development, maintenance and related issues be subjected to a review after three years in the light of

the growth and changes that may take place during the period (Para 12.34).

Central Public Sector Undertakings

Public Sector Undertakings to be Linked to User Ministries

(58) To keep up with the frequent changes in user requirements and the associated technology and in order to ensure efficient product support, close and continuous interaction amongst the customer, the production undertaking and the user Ministry has to be maintained. This can only be effectively ensured if the undertakings are administratively linked to the user Ministries concerned (Para 13.9).

CEL to Progress Rapidly

(59) It is necessary that all possible measures are taken by the Government so that the highly laudable objective for which the Central Electronics Limited was set up are achieved as early as possible (Para 13.6).

Organisational Structure

Rationalisation of Organisational Structure

(60) The organisational structure of the Department should be suitably strengthened so as to enable the Department to discharge its onerous responsibilities fully. It would have to be substantially different from that of the Department of Atomic Energy to subserve its functions (Para 14.1 and 14.3).

Electronics R&D Organisation (ERDO)

(61) The Committee has recommended the formation of an Electronics Approval Board and an Electronics Research and Development Organisation (ERDO) under the Department of Electronics (Para 14.4).

(62) The head of ERDO should be an eminent electronics engineer or technologists of proven competence and an established reputation; he should be designated as Director General (ERDO) (Para 14.5).

(63) ERDO will have to attract scientists, engineers and technologists of proved merit. The Government should be willing to provide adequate compensation to attract Indians of exceedingly high technological competence presently working abroad. In the ultimate analysis, this approach would give dividends to the nation in the form of technological self-reliance in a highly sophisticated area which will be out of all proportion to the additional expenditure which may be incurred on some individuals. This is a matter of crucial importance in the development of electronics industry in the country (Para 14.7).

R & D Board

(64) To provide guidance and direction and in order to ensure proper coordination in respect of the R&D activities of ERDO, an R&D Board should be constituted in the Department of Electronics (Para 14.8).

Planning and Coordination Group

(65) A Planning and Coordination Group under the Department of Electronics should be set up for coordinating the growth and development of the public sector units, producing electronic items and proper utilisation of our meager resources, in areas of high sophistication and high level of investment. This applies also to the units of the Electronics Development Corporation under the State Government. It will facilitate effective coordination with other Ministries/Departments intimately concerned with the development of the Electronics Industry and also give guidance in respect of work connected with "Joint Commissions" with other countries which in some cases present good prospects for the development of the Electronics industry to the mutual advantage of both the countries (Para 14.9).

Restructuring of Electronics Commission

(66) There is no justification for the Electronics Commission to continue in its present form. Instead, it would be more useful to have a body free from executive functions charged with the responsibility of advising the Government on the development of Electronics in the country as a long term perspective covering the total spectrum. This body should accordingly be named the 'Electronics Development

Commission' (Para 14.10).

(67) Separate identity of the existing organisation under the Electronics Commission should be immediately merged in the Department of Electronics (Para 14.11).

Personnel Policy

(68) Except for appointments at relatively higher levels, such as heads of divisions, which should be on contract or tenure basis for a fixed period, all other appointments must be on regular basis save inexceptional cases. The scheme for merit promotion and grant of extra increments should also be introduced in the Department of Electronics, where the staff are engaged in activities which are predominantly of research, design and development nature, without any further delay (Para 14.13).

Effective Financial Control System

(69) Consequent on the suggested restructuring of the Electronics Commission, the normal system of financial control existing in other Departments and Ministries of the Government of India should be adopted in the Department of Electronics with an Integrated Financial Adviser at an appropriate level reporting to the Secretary, Department of Electronics and to the Secretary (Expenditure) in the Ministry of Finance as in other Ministries and Departments (Para 14.14).

Scrutiny of Government Imports

(70) The Department of Electronics should carry out import scrutiny in respect of banned items only in keeping with the practice followed by the DGTD. No further clearance with reference to the value of items above Rs. 5 lakhs is necessary, which is presently done in regard to the restricted items and even items on Open General Licence (Para 14.15).

National Radar Council (NRC)

(71) With the setting up of the Electronics Research and Development Organisation (ERDO) recommended earlier, the functions of NRC can be fully discharged by ERDO. There is no need for NRC to

continue in its present form (Para 14.17).

Defence Project Cell

(72) The activities of the Defence Project Cell in the Department of Electronics should continue in the present form as a part of the ERDO (Para 14.18).

Industrial Electronics Promotion Programme (IEPP)

(73) The 'Industrial Electronics Promotion Programme' (IEPP) for the use of control, instrumentation and industrial electronics in major industrial sectors coming under other Ministries/Departments should also in future appropriately become the responsibility of the Electronics Research and Development Organisation (Para 14.19).

31

COMMITTEE ON POWER, 1978 — REPORT[1]

Chairman	Shri V. Rajadhyaksha
Members	Dr. N.B. Prasad; Shri S.N. Roy; Shri J.C. Shah; Dr. N. Tata Rao; Shri J.M. Patnaik; Shri R.N. Bhargava; Prof. V.N. Kothari; Shri K.M. Chinappa; Shri K.V. Raghavan; Shri Muthusami Gounder
Spl. Invitee	Shri T.R. Satish Chandran
Secretary	Dr. S. Ramesh

Appointment

The Committee on Power was appointed in pursuant to a decision taken at the Conference of State Power Ministers held in January 1978 by the Government of India, in the Ministry of Energy (Department of Power), Vide its Memorandum No. 31(33)/78-US.V. dated December 27, 1978.

Terms of Reference

"The Committee will examine all aspects of the functioning of State Electricity Boards and Central Organisations engaged in electricity generation, transmission and distribution, including organisational structure, management practices, planning systems, efficiency of operations, financial performance, tariff structure and legislative framework and make recommendations for improving them."

Contents

Letter of Transmittal; Preface; Acknowledgements; Introduction; Planning for Power Development; Project Formulation and

1. Delhi, Controller of Publications, 1980, 209 p.

Implementation; Operation and Maintenance; Finance, Financial Management and Tariffs; Rural Electrification; Organisation and Management; Research and Development; Short-Term Measures to Alleviate Power Shortages; Summary of Recommendations; Appendices from 1 to 8.1 and Charts.

Recommendations

Planning for Power Development Demand Forecasting

Long-Term Forecasts

1. Plans for the development of the power industry should have a 15-20 year time-frame and the Five-Year Plans should be built into this plan so as to optimise the mix of generating sources i.e. thermal, hydel and nuclear. (Para 2.23)

2. Such plans should be based on long-term demand forecasts evolved by adopting a scenario approach which takes into account changing patterns of connected loads, the trends within different categories of consumers, the relationship between the GDP and demand for power and the progress achieved in demand management and conservation. (Para 2.24)

3. This exercise should be carried out every three years by a Committee headed by a suitably senior officer or by a Member of the Planning Commission together with representatives of the related sectors of the Central Government such as Department of Power, Coal, Industries, Agriculture and Railways. (Para 2.29)

Annual and Medium-Term Forecasts

4. Annual and Medium-term forecasts (5-10 years) which quantify the national demand, for both peak and energy, that can be met from year to year should be prepared annually by a Standing Committee consisting of the Chairman, CEA, 5 Chairman of the proposed REAs, 4 Chairmen of SEBs nominated by the Central Government and Advisers for Energy, Resources and Perspective Planning in the Planning Commission. These forecasts should replace the current system of Annual Power Surveys. (Para 2.30)

State-wise Forecasts

5. These forecasts should indicate the increased demand that it will be possible to meet in each State taking into account *inter alia* the State's on contribution to power generation, its share of Central power, historical growth rates which should take into account socio-economic objectives such as redressing regional imbalances. These allocations should receive the endorsement of the Planning Commission, the Central Cabinet and the National Development Council. (Para 2.31)

6. The plans for load growth in each State should be restricted to this additional capacity. (Para 2.32)

7. In order to optimally utilise the available load planning cells should be set up in each SEB. The growth and variability of the agricultural load will have to be given special weightage. These cells should work in close coordination with the planning groups in the REA and the CEA. (Paras 2.35 and 2.41)

Load Management and Conservation

8. For the industrial load, all States should adopt such measures as staggering off-days, high peak hour tariffs, timing of annual shut-downs for overhaul of major consuming industries so as to reduce seasonal and daily peak demand and flatten the load curve. (Para 2.45)

9. An estimated 20 per cent reduction in power usage in industry is feasible by adopting a wide range of conservation measures. Such savings should be encouraged by using a mix of fiscal incentives and penal tariffs. (Paras 2.46 and 2.47)

10. In agriculture, rostering of loads, use of properly sized and efficient pumpsets, elimination of flat rate tariffs, and installation of efficient transformers and capacitors would reduce losses, conserve power and reduce peak demands. (Paras 2.49 to 2.51)

11. A Committee should be set up to examine ways of curbing the growing energy demands of commercial offices and hotels. Appropriate peak hour pricing of domestic and commercial power and enforcement of minimum standards of efficiency of domestic and office power consuming equipment would assist demand management and help conservation. (Paras 2.43 and 2.53)

12. Power Conservation Committees should be set up in each State to draw up time bound programmes and set physical goals. (Para 2.55)

13. For each of the major industries the concerned Development Councils should set up task forces on conservation to quantify the targets that each type of industry should aim at and suggest measures for achieving them. (Para 2.55)

Capacity Planning

Role of Central Generation and Transmission

14. In order to minimise costs, additions to power generating and transmission capacity should be planned on a region-wise rather than a State-wise basis. (Para 2.78)

15. To achieve this the Centre's role in power generation will need to be enlarged so as to achieve ownership of at least 45 per cent of all generation capacity by 2000 A.D. (Para 2.79)

16. The Centre should forthwith take steps to acquire the ownership of such EHV transmission lines and sub-stations as would enable it to operate the regional grid optimally. (Para 2.80)

17. The nuclear power programme should be accelerated to attain an installed capacity of 5000 MW by 2000 A.D. (Para 2.83)

Organisational Changes

18. To implement this enhanced role proposed for the Central Government two groups of bodies, the Regional Electricity Generating Corporations and the Regional Electricity Authorities should be set up. (Paras 2.84 and 2.85)

Centre-State Financial Transfers

19. The increased investment by the Central Government in power generation will require a review of the Plan assistance to the States. This should be carried out by the Planning Commission. (Para 2.86)

Gestation Periods of Power Project

20. A two years period should be allowed for formulating thermal and nuclear projects inclusive of the time required for the issue of Government sanction. (Para 2.91)

21. The construction and commissioning period of thermal and nuclear projects could be assumed to be 5 and 7 years respectively for planning purposes and between 9 to 11 years for hydel projects (inclusive of time for preparing the detailed project report). (Para 2.92)

22. A thermal project should be assumed to be 'stabilised', i.e., available for operating at 80 per cent plant availability 12 months after it has successfully completed its guarantee tests. (Para 2.93)

23. The present practice of planning capacity to meet peak loads should continue. (Para 2.94)

24. 87.5 per cent of hydel capacity, 64 per cent of stabilised thermal capacity and 65 to 75 per cent of nuclear capacity may be taken as being available for meeting peak loads. Thermal plants in the Eastern Region can be assumed to contribute at 59 per cent of their rated capacity for peaking purposes. (Paras 2.95, 2.96 and 2.98)

25. For energy availability calculations stabilised thermal plants should be assumed to have an all-India average plant load factor of 58 per cent. The factors will vary from region to region. (Para 2.101)

26. All hydel stations should in future be designed for meeting either diurnal and or seasonal peak load and should be based on a 40 per cent plant load factor. (Para 2.102)

27. The C.E.A. should carry out a study on derating and retirement of old units, till then the current figure of 0.5 per cent of installed capacity being phased out every year can be assumed for planning purposes. (Para 2.104)

28. In place of the present deterministic approach to capacity planning, probability techniques should be used. (Para 2.105)

29. Captive generation should be encouraged in the case of total energy systems and permitted in the case of highly power sensitive units like steel or artificial fibre plants, large scale consumers like aluminium and for collieries, based on using washery rejects. (Paras 2.107 to 2.110)

Private Sector Utilities

30. The present policy of permitting growth of private sector utilities only on a selective case by case basis should not be disturbed. (Para 2.111)

Transmission and Distribution (T&D)

31. Investment in T&D will need to be stepped up to take care of

the backlog of the past and to restore the balance between generation and T&D capacities. (Para 2.116)

32. Generation capacity planning must be fully integrated with T&D planning so that both are optimised as a system (Para 2.121)

33. System studies should be carried out to optimise planning of the T&D network and the software required for this will need to be developed on a continuing basis. These studies should be undertaken for rural electrification system as well as for urban complexes. (Paras 2.122, 2.123 and 2.130)

34. Adequate provision should be made for providing reactive compensation on transmission lines to reduce power losses. (Para 2.124)

35. Monitoring and information systems on the construction and operation of transmission system should be developed for the Central and State Governments by the CEA in the same way as has been done for the thermal generating units. (Para 2.128)

36. The planning groups in the CEA, and the SEBs should equip themselves to undertake systems studies. (Para 2.131)

37. Electricity Boards should install sufficient meters to enable an energy audit to be carried out and to monitor losses. (Para 2.135)

38. Priority should be given to reduction of both transmission and distribution losses over increases in generation capacity. (Para 2.137)

39. Diversion of agreed plan funds by SEBs/State Governments to other purposes should lead to a corresponding cuts in Central plan assistance. (Para 2.139)

40. As a guideline to capacity planning the following assumptions can be made regarding trends in T&D losses.

		Percentage of Loss
By	1982/83	18
	1987/88	17
	1992/93	16
	2000/01	15

Project Formulation

General

1. In order to prepare an optimal regional plan the Regional Electricity Authorities should have a shelf of detailed project reports

(DPRs) of potential hydel, thermal and nuclear projects from which to choose. (Para 3.18)

2. Responsibility for funding and preparing DPRs for thermal and nuclear projects should be that of the owning and operating agencies but for major hydel projects the appropriate REA should provide funds. (Paras 3.19 and 3.23)

Major Hydel Projects

3. Project investment capabilities in the SEBs and organisation like WAPCOs should be strengthened and they should be provided with the latest equipment required for site investigation. (Para 3.24)

4. The output of engineering geologists will have to be increased. (Para 3.24)

5. To bring competent personnel into project investigation and motivate them, they should be given special allowances, improved welfare facilities and provided with full logistic support including helicopters and good telecommunication facilities. (Para 3.27)

6. Investment decisions on hydel and other projects should be taken after evaluating all options based on DPRs, in relation to the region's long-term plan. (Para 3.29)

7. The practice of estimating project costs at current prices should continue but the effect of inflation should be quantified when comparing actuals with estimates. (Para 3.30)

Small Hydel Projects

8. Micro Hydels should be developed for meeting the power requirements of sparsely populated areas far away from major power projects. (Para 3.31)

9. Measures for reducing the cost of small hydels should be examined. (Para 3.32)

10. Separate divisions should be set up for concentrating on small hydel projects in those SEBs which have the potential for them. (Para 3.34)

Thermal Projects

11. A project should be regarded as complete only when it has satisfactorily completed the contractual period of operation at full load

and is ready for commercial operation. (Para 3.36)

12. While a period of 5 years has been recommended as the time that should be allowed for planning purposes for completing construction and commissioning of the thermal stations, SEB's should attempt to finish the job in 4 years or less. (Para 3.37)

13. A 15-year coal production plan should be drawn up and linkages established from mining areas to power plants, building in some flexibility in the power plants to take care of unforeseen changes of linkages with specific mines. (Paras 3.39 and 3.40)

Nuclear Projects

14. A separate corporation for the manufacture and supply of heavy water should be formed. (Para 3.50)

Transformation and Distribution (T&D)

15. Improvement of the data base for formulating T&D projects should be given high priority and specialised consultancy services should be sought for this purpose. (Para 3.51)

Standardization

Thermal Stations

16. Standard lay-outs and schemes for 200/210 MW BHEL sets, sent to utility companies by BHEL, should be used for formulating new projects using this size of set. (Para 3.57)

17. Similar standardisation should be carried out in regard to KWU designs of turbo generators, AVB boilers and instrumentation system in consultation with the manufacturers. (Paras 3.57 and 3.58)

18. Feed back systems should be set up to report regularly on field experience on such standard layouts and designs so that they can be continuously updated and at the same time advantage taken of new technological developments. (Para 3.59)

Hydel Stations

19. Standard modules for ancillary and auxiliary systems should be prepared by the CEA and CWC. (Para 3.60)

20. Standard designs for low head bulb type turbines should be prepared. (Para 3.61)

21. Civil foundations, structures and generating plant for installation in seismic zones are specialised areas of standardisation to which attention should be given. (Para 3.62)

Transmission and Distribution Systems

22. Standards developed by the CEA for 400 KVA systems covering specifications and design parameters for sub-station equipment and line material should be adopted by SEBs and manufacturers. (Para 3.63)

23. Similar standards should be developed for sub-station layouts, transmission line clearances, transmission line towers, protection schemes and instrumentation and accessories especially those made by small scale industries. (Para 3.64)

24. Practices in regard to stub setting, tower erection, stringing conductors should be standardised. (Para 3.64)

Responsibility for Standardisation

25. The CEA should assume responsibility for drawing up and implementing a time bound programme in the field of standardisation and also for updating standards to keep pace with the advance of technology. (Para 3.65)

Appraisal

26. Preliminary appraisal of detailed project reports (DPRs) submitted by utilities should be carried out by the REAs. Final appraisal and sanction should continue to be done by the CEA and the Planning Commission. (Para 3.67)

Project Implementation

27. Time consuming procedures for dealing with sanctions and inputs into projects which involve external agencies in the State and the Centre should be streamlined, substituting where possible decisions across the table for correspondence and file notings. The costs of delay in decision-making should be quantified and conveyed to all internal

and external agencies concerned with implementation of the Project. (Para 3.69)

28. The DPR should specify the requirements of staff and approval of the DPR should automatically be construed as sanction for the staff. (Para 3.71)

29. Inter-State water disputes, if not resolved amongst the concerned States in 3 months, should, by law, be referred to an arbitrator to be appointed by the Central Government who should be required to submit his award in 3 months. Such an award should be made non-justiciable. (Para 3.74)

30. As an alternative the possibility of river and lake waters being declared a Central subject under a constitutional amendment may be given serious consideration. (Para 3.74)

31. Properly prepared resource based PERT charts should be made a pre-condition to the approval of DPRs and should be used as operating instruments for realistically scheduling projects and ten keeping them on target. (Para 3.76)

32. The full cost of rehabilitation of displaced persons should be treated as a part of the project cost and the responsibility for rehabilitating displaced people in suitable productive and remunerative occupations should be taken on by the project authorities who should have a fully staffed multi-disciplinary cell for this purpose. (Para 3.78)

33. Except for providing overall supervision, co-ordination and checking the quality of work done, the owners of utilities should leave the execution of the projects entirely to contractors and undertake no work departmentally. (Para 3.80)

34. The CEA and CWC should encourage contractors who work on power projects to use time saving techniques and should help them in training their staff in the theory and practice of modern project construction techniques. (Para 3.82)

35. Work on detailed designs and engineering should be done in advance of the project being sanctioned to save time. (Para 3.83)

36. Tenders should only be invited from contractors who have proven capability and equipment and even in these cases the acceptance of lowest tender should not be mandatory. (Para 3.84)

37. Shortages of construction materials should be anticipated and stocks built up in good time. Special cells for planning the ordering and follow-up of contracted supplies should be set up. (Para 3.85)

38. State Governments should ensure that there is a regular flow of funds as planned in the Annual Plans from the State Governments to

the State Electricity Boards. (Para 3.86)

39. The Railways should augment their stock of heavy duty wagons particularly in the 90 tonne to 130 tonne range. (Para 3.87)

40. A group should be set up to examine the clearance procedures required to be followed by SEBs and P&T for erecting transmission lines which run close to P&T lines and make recommendations both on expediting such clearances and on the equitable sharing of costs that are incurred in relocating P&T lines. (Para 3.88)

Equipment for the Power Industry

Hydro-electric Projects

41. Imports of large hydel turbo-generators should be permitted well in time if the gap between demand and indigenous supply cannot be bridged. An early decision should be taken on augmenting hydel plant manufacturing capacity. (Para 3.91)

42. The number and technological capabilities of manufacturers of small hydel sets should be augmented. (Para 3.93)

43. For building low head bulb type turbines foreign collaboration should be permitted and specialised units set up for manufacturing these machines. (Para 3.94)

Thermal Plants

44. Manufacturers, especially local ones, must be made to give the highest priority to spares, components, and sub-assemblies required to maximise utilisation of existing capacity even at the risk of loss of production of complete equipment. (Para 3.99)

45. The additional capacity that will be required to implement the larger power programme of the next two decades should be set up outside BHEL to encourage competition. If this cannot be done then BHEL should administratively move to the Deptt. of Power. (Paras 3.101 to 3.103)

46. The indigenous capacity for manufacturing pressure parts for boilers and boiler auxiliaries, as also for manufacturing coal and ash handling plant, coal crushers and pulverizers will have to be augmented. (Paras 3.104 and 3.105)

Transmission and Distribution Equipment

47. Critical equipment which is not produced in adequate quantities and quality, e.g., sophisticated protection systems and reactive power compensation equipment, should be freely imported. (Para 3.108)

48. The capacity for manufacturing transmission line towers will need to be augmented and this should be done largely through the small scale sector. (Para 3.109)

49. There is need for substantial improvement in the quality of equipment like distribution and power transformers, LT and HT capacitors, switches, circuit breakers and fuses. CEA, ISI and SEBs should provide technical assistance to manufacturers in ensuring that equipment is produced to meet the approved standards. (Para 3.110)

50. Additional capacity will need to be created to meet the requirements of such items as H.T. insulators and ACSR conductors. 200 KVA and 400 KVA bushings and insulators and data acquisition and control equipment will need to be imported till such time as indigenous capacity comes on stream. (Paras 3.111 to 3.114)

51. Steps should be taken by the manufacturers to ensure that equipment is supplied according to the agreed and predetermined sequence. (Para 3.115)

Quality Control

52. Bought out equipment must be carefully quality controlled by the main manufacturer. If it does not meet the specifications, imports by the main manufacturer should be permitted. (Para 3.117)

53. Hydel units should be fully assembled in the shop before despatch to the project site. (Para 3.119)

54. The quality of instrumentation and auxiliary control equipment like conductors, relays, switches, etc., procured from indigenous sources needs to be improved. (Paras 3.120 and 3.121)

55. The quality assurance systems of the main manufacturers also requires substantial upgradation as also those of the utilities. (Para 3.123)

56. The proposed Power Design & Consultancy Corporation (PDCC) should set up a quality control wing to carry out quality control of equipment on behalf of the owners. (Para 3.125)

Consultancy Services

57. A new public sector organisation, the Project Design & Consultancy Corporation, should be set up with the nucleus being provided by the staff of CEA and CWC presently engaged in this work. With this the CEA and CWC should progressively give up consultancy services beginning with thermal projects and eventually hydel projects. (Para 3.129)

58. The Water and Power Development (Consultancy) Services (India) Ltd. (WAPCOS) should become a part of the PDCC and help to equip it to provide full consultancy on hydel projects. (Para 3.131)

59. The expertise available in IITs and other academic institutions should be sought on solving complex problems relating to design of load despatch centres and 'on-line' computer systems. (Para 3.133)

60. Consultancy services should cover the entire spectrum of project formulation and implementation activities. (Para 3.137)

61. Selection of consultants should not be done simply on a 'lowest tender' basis. Minimum fees should be prescribed and choice of consultants governed by quality of advice and services offered. (Para 3.138)

62. Manufacturers of equipment should not be awarded turnkey jobs for complete power plants. (Para 3.139)

63. The owner must assume final responsibility for the performance of the contract and develop sufficient in-house capability to assess the quality of the work done by his consultants. (Para 3.140)

Operation and Maintenance (O&M)

Plant Availability and Load Factors

1. Plant availability for operating thermal units should be assumed to be 80 per cent on an average. (Para 4.6)

2. Plant load factors of 58 per cent should be considered as the norm for the system. (Para 4.7)

Interaction between Utility Companies and Equipment Manufacturers

3. A Committee should be set up composed of Member (Thermal), CEA as Chairman and senior representatives of utilities and manufacturers as Members to advise on, modifications to be made in

existing equipment and evaluating new designs of equipment to be manufactured in the country. (Para 4.28)

4. Manufacturers should prepare expeditiously comprehensive manuals for erection, operation and maintenance of their equipment for use by various levels of plant personnel. (Para 4.29)

Maintenance Measures

5. The recommendations of Reports of earlier Committees, e.g., the Kulkarni Committee and the VGB Committee should be vigorously and meticulously implemented. (Para 4.39)

6. While maintaining the improvement in the time schedules for planned maintenance the quality of the work done requires to be improved. (Para 4.40)

7. Short outages, especially at week-ends, should be planned to enable relatively minor problems like steam leaks to be attended to. (Para 4.41)

8. Detailed data about forced outages during the proceeding years should be analysed to enable an effective planned maintenance programme to be formulated by the plant authorities. (Para 4.42)

9. The CEA should take follow-up action to find out the efficacy of the preventive maintenance manual prepared by BHEL. (Para 4.43)

10. SEBs should establish independent, internal, multi-disciplinary audit groups to report independently to the Chief Executive on the quality and comprehensiveness of the planned maintenance operations. (Para 4.44)

11. Specialised maintenance task forces should be set up at all power stations and be given rigorous training in maintenance systems. (Para 4.45)

12. The CEA should arrange exchange visits between engineers, specialists and skilled workmen of different plants using similar equipment or coal. Comprehensive reports on maintenance activities and problems should be prepared and widely circulated in the CEA, and all utilities in the country down to the shop floor. (Para 4.46)

Spares

13. For equipment which is becoming obsolete, either life time spares should be ordered out or, if the numbers are large and there is adequate time, organisations such as BHEL or ILK could make these

items themselves or assist local manufacturers in producing them. (Para 4.48)

14. Local manufacturers of equipment must take full responsibility for timely availability of spares both local and imported. Manufacture of spares should receive priority over main equipment. (Para 4.49)

15. Utilities should give manufacturers the lead times specified when ordering spares. (Para 4.50)

16. A common pool of major spares should be formed for equipment of similar design and capacity and the CEA, with the help of utilities and manufacturers should take steps to organise their production. (Para 4.51)

17. Project authorities should provide at least 3 per cent of the equipment cost for the supply of start-up and essential spares in the project proposal and these should be ordered along with main equipment. (Para 4.52)

Training of Operation and Maintenance Personnel

18. A special group should be appointed by the Department of Power to study the shortcomings in the operations of the four regional Power Station Personnel Training Institutes and recommend measures for using them fully. (Para 4.57)

19. Additional training institutes to cater to the expected gap between demand and supply of engineers, technicians and operators should be started. (Para 4.58)

20. Special training courses for maintenance personnel at the officer level should be started using the resources of regional engineering colleges. Consultancy inputs should be sought from IITs for drawing up the curricula in specialised areas. (Para 4.60)

21. Operator/technician training courses should be augmented to cater to training staff for maintenance work. Training schools for this purpose should be set up by the larger SEBs for themselves or if available local ITI's can be used. In the case of smaller Boards two or three of them could get together to start up such schools. (Para 4.61)

22. Short-term courses in specific areas, e.g., power station chemistry, maintenance, planning techniques, currently being conducted by the CEA, should be held more frequently. (Para 4.62)

23. SEBs and other utility operators should train personnel for 1½ years prior to their being required for operating a plant by being taught

theoretical principles and then given practical training in the manufacturer's works and his test facilities and in such operating stations as are using his equipment. (Para 4.63)

24. Persons so trained should, when they return, be put on jobs for which they have been trained and not disturbed for at least five years. (Para 4.63)

25. Several more simulator training centres need to be established. (Para 4.64)

26. The coordination and follow up of training activity for trainees in SEBs and other utilities should be the responsibility of training officers in each plant. Trainees should be given a mix of theoretical and practical training, if possible on redundant plant. (Paras 4.65 and 4.66)

27. The CEA and REA should assume the responsibility for arranging tests for operators of power plant and issuing certificates of competency on a national basis. A similar practice should be adopted with regard to maintenance personnel. Only such certified personnel should be permitted to operate and maintain power plants. (Para 4.67)

Industrial Relations and Staffing

28. State Governments should take firm action in backing the top management of the SEBs in dealing with tactics like go-slows and curbing, indiscipline corruption and inter-union rivalries which affect the smooth and efficient operation of the plant. (Para 4.68)

29. The management should take the initiative in evolving a more participative approach to problem solving, setting up objective mechanisms for awarding rewards and penalties and creating an 'esprit de corps'. (Para 4.68)

30. Fresh recruitment should be stopped till wastage, separations or growth absorbs the surplus staff as worked out according to the norms prescribed by the Power Economy Committee (1971) up dated for the new plants. These norms should be reviewed from time to time to take into account technological changes. (Para 4.69)

31. Incentives should be given to O&M staff for exceeding preset norms of plant availability. (Para 4.69)

Partial Unavailability

32. About 1000 MW of existing capacity is unavailable in some

of the newer plans due to defects which can be rectified quickly and with marginal investments. Steps should be immediately taken to bring this capacity back on stream using the assistance of consultants and manufacturers. (Paras 4.76 and 4.77)

33. Another 1285 MW can be added to capacity by removing constraints which will take somewhat longer to remove and similar measures in this regard should be taken expeditiously. (Paras 4.79 and 4.80)

Coal

34. Coal washeries for up-grading coal should be put up if found economically viable and should be accompanied by the setting up of pit head power plants to make use of washery rejects. (Para 4.83)

35. Collieries should blend coal at the loading points, start putting up mechanical shale separating units, crush coal to the correct size and in the meantime set up facilities for manually removing shale and stones. (Para 4.85)

36. Station authorities should monitor coal despatches and they together with representatives of coal companies should jointly check receipts of coal for quality and quantity at the power stations. (Para 4.85)

37. Stations which have mechanical coal blending facilities should accumulate stocks of coal till these facilities can be utilised. Stations without blending facilities should try using bulldozers to even out fluctuations in quality between different deliveries. (Para 4.86)

38. The systems and techniques adopted by the Renusagar Thermal Power Station for dealing with the coal problem should be emulated. (Para 4.87)

39. Future power stations should be designed to burn high ash coals and made as flexible as possible. (Para 4 88)

40. To build up coal stocks greater attention should be paid to using unit trains, sea and water transport. Pipe-line transport should be tried out on an experimental basis. (Para 4.90)

Rehabilitation and Replacement of Old Plants

41. Plants which have been derated but can be restored to full capacity because of deficiencies which can be corrected should be attended to expeditiously. Multi-disciplinary groups should be put on this

task including the manufacturer's representatives. (Para 4.92)

42. Units which are uneconomical to run should be replaced. CEA should estimate the extent of such replacements over the next 5 years and allow for them in planning additions to capacity. (Paras 4.93 and 4.94)

Research and Development

43. 'Grass roots' R&D intended to deal with the day to day practical problems of thermal power plants operation should be undertaken in close collaboration with academic and research institutions like the IITs. (Para 4.96)

Hydel Plants

44. Although hydel plants have generally caused less problems than thermal units the quality control in the case of indigenous equipment especially with respect to welding, lubrication, insulation and cooling systems requires to be improved. (Para 4.99)

45. Specialised training is also required to be given to hydel plant operators. (Para 4.100)

Nuclear Plants

46. Many of the operation and maintenance procedures and practices adopted by nuclear power stations including the training of personnel, standards of house keeping are sound and can be applied to thermal stations. The Department of Atomic Energy should help to set up the necessary training inputs. (Para 4.104)

47. There should be an independent body, outside the Department of Atomic Energy, to lay down and monitor observance of minimum standards for siting, design, construction, operation, maintenance and safety of nuclear power plants on the lines of the Nuclear Regulatory Commission. (Para 4.410)

Transmission and Distribution

48. T&D losses should be reduced by metering power flows at all stages of voltage change from generation down to LT distribution, identifying sections where excessive losses are occurring and taking

corrective action. Divisional and assistant engineers should be held accountable for losses in excess of predetermined norms and vigilance squads set up to detect thefts of power and equipment. (Para 4.111)

49. The other recommendations of the Power Economy Committee 1971 for improving the T&D system also require to be expeditiously implemented. The CEA and REAs should initiate and coordinate action in this regard. (Para 4.115)

Management Information Systems (MIS) and Data Base

50. The MIS introduced for thermal generation system should be extended to the T&D and hydel generation system also. (Para 4.119)

51. Data acquisition systems should become a compulsory part of all power plant equipment so as to strengthen the data base. (Para 4.120)

Measures to Ensure Implementation of Recommendations

52. A Standing Committee of top level officers of utilities responsible for operations and maintenance of power systems should be constituted and meetings convened at regular intervals to review progress, exchange information, carry out joint studies, etc. (Para 4.121)

53. The CEA should extend the coverage of information published to include data on other parameters of plant efficiency, T&D losses, water levels in lakes, tariffs, etc. (Para 4.122)

54. The CEA, the Finance Ministry and the Planning Commission should make grant of Central assistance, clearance of projects conditional on satisfactory progress being made in implementing such of these recommendations as are accepted by Government. (Para 4.124)

Take over of Power Stations/State Electricity Boards by the Central Government

55. Only if a State Government requests that a power stations or a State Electricity Board should be run by the Centre, should the Centre accept, subject to its capability of providing the requisite level of managerial inputs. (Para 4.125)

Finance, Financial Management and Tariffs

Finance

1. Over the longer-term the utility companies should aim at generating internally about 50 per cent of the resources they need for their

expansion. (Para 5.5)

Financial Management

2. The objectives of tariff and financial policies should be clearly set out and incorporated in the Electricity Act. (Para 5.47)

3. The rate of return, to be calculated according to a recommended methodology should be 15 per cent on the assumption that the average rate of interest on loans to the SEB is 7 per cent. If the borrowing rate is increased the return should go up correspondingly. (Para 5.52)

4. Interest on works-in-progress should be debited to the revenue account and not capitalised. (Para 5.54)

5. Government should lend to SEBs at one per cent above the rate at which they themselves borrow loans from the open market maturing over periods of 10-12 years. (Para 5.55)

6. The contingent interest liabilities of Boards should be converted into interest bearing loans. (Para 5.56)

7. The present provisions for depreciation should be examined in depth by a Committee to be set up by the CEA. (Para 5.57)

8. Electricity duties charged by State Governments should not be included in the calculation of the rate of return of SEBs. (Para 5.58)

9. The question of merging the excise duty on electricity with tariffs should be referred to the next Finance Commission. (Para 5.59)

10. Electricity Boards should be statutorily exempted from income-tax. (Para 5.61)

Principles of Tariff Structure

11. No single class of consumers should be charged by the SEB a rate less than the 'cost' of providing them this power, i.e., at most the 15 per cent rate of return could be waived. (Para 5.65)

12. If the State Government feels that a particular consumer group needs special subsidies which require the SEB to sell power below cost, specific written instructions should be issued to the Board and a subsidy equivalent to the loss that the Board will suffer given to the Board and provided for as a separate item in the State Budget. (Para 5.66)

13. Groups which could qualify for such subsidies are small and marginal farmers, landless labourers and slum dwellers. (Para 5.67)

14. Subsidies for electrifying remote, sparsely populated areas should be gradually tapered off as demand picks up. Steps should be taken to see that subsidies do actually reach the intended beneficiaries. (Paras 5.67 and 5.68)

15. Peak hour tariffs should reflect the cost of incremental additions to capacity. (Para 5.69a)

16. The capacity of the consumer to pay should be taken into accounting fixing tariffs. (Para 5.69b)

17. For bulk consumers who take loads of 1 MW and above time differentiating meters should be provided. (Para 5.70)

18. Domestic and commercial consumers should be charged inverted block tariffs, i.e., rates should increase as the quantum of power taken increases. (Para 5.71)

19. Tariffs should encourage conservation by being raised to levels at which investment and effort in conservation become economically worthwhile. (Para 5.72)

20. Agriculturists and rural consumers as a class do not need subsidies and subsidies should be confined to the rural and urban poor. (Para 5.73)

21. There is no case for subsidising power intensive industries and they should be charged at least the full cost of power plus the prescribed return. (Para 5.75)

22. Inter-state competition by States to attract new industries to their States by offering concessional tariffs should cease. No subsidies should be given to industries except as a special subvention from the State Government to the Board and voted through the budget. (Para 5.77)

23. Tariff rates required to earn the specified rate of return should be based on the Boards reaching prescribed minimum norms of technical and commercial efficiency. (Para 5.78)

24. To prescribe such norms a Bureau of Electricity Costs and Prices (BECP) should be set up as statutory body. Its role should be advisory. (Para 5.79)

25. The BECP should also advise SEBs on tariff policies. (Para 5.80)

26. Flat rate tariffs should be discontinued and replaced by metered supplies. (Para 5.81)

27. The Commercial wings of the SEBs will need to be greatly strengthened. (Para 5.82)

28. The CEA should evolve detailed guidelines and proformae on

how the accounts of the SEBs and utility companies should be kept and compliance with these ensured by making suitable changes in the Electricity Act. (Para 5.83)

Inter-state Tariffs

29. All bulk power bought and sold by a State should be through the proposed Regional Electricity Authorities and there should be no bilateral exchanges of power between States. (Para 5.88)

30. Uniform, rational and equitable tariff policies for inter-State exchange of power should be evolved which will encourage inter-State power flows. (Paras 5.89 to 5.93)

Power from Centrally-owned Generation Stations

31. Allocation of power from Central Stations whether thermal, hydel or nuclear should be made on the basis of the total pool of Central power in each region and not from each station. (Para 5.95)

32. Central power should be sold at a uniform price throughout the country to SEBs. Prices should be based on a 15 per cent return on capital employed as in the case of SEBs subject to the same conditions of minimum performance norms being achieved. (Para 5.96)

Private Sector Utilities

33. Subject to their achieving the prescribed minimum norms private sector utilities should be allowed to charge tariffs on the same basis as applicable to other goods and services which are sold at administered prices, i.e., a 12-14 per cent return after tax on shareholders' funds. (Paras 5.97 and 5.98)

Rural Electrification

Planning and Project Formulation

1. Given the rising trend of petroleum prices of growth of rural electrification should be based on the assumption that there will be no addition to the number of diesel sets beyond 1990 and that by 2000 A.D. all pumpsets will work on conventionally generated power or non-conventional renewable energy resources. (Para 6.71)

2. By 1994-95 all villages in the nation should be targetted to be electrified. Simultaneously household electrification should be given much higher priority to improve the quality of life and save kerosene. The goal should be to electrify all households by 2000 AD. (Para 6.72)

3. Rural electrification schemes should be formulated as a part of a total distribution system and not in isolation and optimisation studies should be carried out to minimise investment. (Para 6.73)

4. Load growth should not be permitted to grow beyond levels which cannot be adequately serviced. (Para 6.74)

5. Rural electrification programmes should be developed on a block by block basis and besides covering agricultural pumpsets and household lighting should be dovetailed into the integrated rural development plants covering village, cottage and small scale industries. (Para 6.75)

Street Lighting

6. Street lighting dues can be paid directly to SEBs, agents or rural cooperative and deducted from the grants paid by the State Government to the concerned local bodies. (Para (6.41)

7. In planning and implementing rural electrification programmes special care must be taken to see that the smaller farmers share fully in the benefits. (Para 6.76)

8. Procedures for issuing of bank guarantees, clearances from Ground Water Boards, etc., should be simplified and mobile units set up for providing a single point clearance of all formalities required to sanction loans to small farmers. (Para 6.76)

9. Schemes such as giving a light point free to small farmers and landless labourers as is done in Karnataka should be introduced by other States. (Para 6.77)

10. Special emphasis should be given to the development of micro- and mini-hydel generation schemes. These and non-conventional energy sources should be developed in rural areas where distance and load densities make conventional RE systems uneconomic. (Para 6.78)

Data Base

11. The data base on all matters concerning RE should be greatly improved. The SEBs, and REC should set up systems which report

relevant information regularly and key information on RE should be included in the National Sample Surveys. PEO and the REC should carry out studies on the flow of benefits of RE schemes to different income groups in rural areas. (Para 6.82)

Technical Modifications

12. Special programmes should be implemented to improve the quality of supply to rural consumers by provision of capacitors, small size distribution transformers, etc. (Para 6.83)

13. The ISI should prescribe minimum standards of efficiency for pumpsets and SEBs and REC should have field level technical advisory bodies to see that farmers are properly advised on sizes and types of set. Banks and other institutions should give loans for purchasing only such pumpsets as conform to these minimum standards. (Para 6.84)

Rural Electrification Corporation and other Financial Institutions

14. The REC should arrange special courses and training programmes for improving the project formulation and implementation capabilities of the less developed States. (Para 6.85)

15. The REC should fund schemes for micro- and mini hydels and pilot demonstration schemes for development of non-conventional renewable energy resources. (Para 6.86)

16. The REC should develop schemes for encouraging household electrification. (Para 6.87)

17. The REC should not fund system improvement schemes. These should be funded by the SEBs themselves except where modifications to REC schemes have to be made on account of unforeseen factors. (Para 6.55)

18. Other financial institutions should also devote more attention to helping backward States to absorb more loan funds for rural electrification. (Para 6.88)

Organisation

19. Specialised RE groups should be set up at sub-divisional, divisional, zonal and Board levels by SEBs to ensure that RE gets concentrated attention. (Para 6.89)

20. Financial institutions in the rural areas as well as agencies set up to help the small entrepreneur such as District Industries Centres and Small Industries Service Institutes should provide the training input and seed money to get RE 'agents' started in business. (Paras 6.90 and 6.91)

Organisation and Management

Structural Changes

1. To implement the recommendation that 45 per cent of total generation should be in the Central Sector by 2000 A.D., five Regional Electricity Generating Corporations (REGCs) should be set up to construct and operate Centrally owned thermal and hydel plants. (Para 7.67)
2. To plan the development of the regional grid and operate it in an integrated way, Regional Electricity Authorities (REAs) should be set up as statutory bodies. The REAs should be administratively under the CEA. (Para 7.69)
3. The CEA should give up consultancy, work and concentrate on the policy, planning, managerial, personnel, research, commercial, financial and coordination requirements of the power industry. It should help the growth of consultants in the public and private sector, improve their technical and professional skills by organising training inputs and certify their suitability to bid for consultancy assignments. It should function as an appellate body in case of disputes. (Paras 7.70, 7.71 and 3.131)
4. The CEA should not function as the Secretariat of the Deptt. of Power. (Para 7.72)
5. A full-fledged public sector consultancy organisation should be formed — the Power Design and Consultancy Corporation (PDCC) — to take over the consultancy work currently being done by the CEA and later on by CWC and WAPCOS. (Para 7.74)
6. The PDCC should be equipped to provide the full range of consultancy services required by thermal and hydel plants and the T&D system. It should also undertake quality control of equipment on behalf of owners of the utilities. (Paras 7.74 to 7.78)
7. Steps should be taken to prevent the PDCC from monopolising all work in these fields. (Para 7.75)
8. A Nuclear Power Corporation should be set up to construct

and operate nuclear power stations. (Para 7.80)

9. The DVC should be merged with the regional REGC after paying West Bengal and Bihar compensation for their shares. (Para 7.81)

10. SEBs and not Government Departments should be responsible for constructing and operating all civil and mechanical facilities on hydel/multipurpose projects up stream of the power house and the dam except those only required for the irrigation system. (Para 7.83)

11. Those States which have departmentally run power systems should set up autonomous electricity boards. (Para 7.84)

12. The North-Eastern States and the North-Eastern Council (NEC) with the exception of Assam, should concentrate on mini- and micro-hydel projects, leaving large projects to the local REGC. (Para 7.84)

13. The Union Territories of Goa and Pondicherry should also set up their own Boards. (Para 7.85)

Internal Structuring of Organisations in the Power Industry

14. Restructuring should be aimed at a clear demarcation of responsibilities and powers of individuals so that centres of accountability can be identified, ensuring reasonable spans of control, and elevation of important staff functions like personnel, commercial, management services to Member/Director level or one level below. (Paras 7.87 to 7.90)

15. Staff and line functions should be clearly distinguished. (Para 7.91)

16. Cadres should be created for a wide range of technical and non-technical functions. (Para 7.92)

State Electricity Boards (SEB)

17. The larger SEBs should have a full-time Chairman and 6 full-time and 5 part-time members and the Electricity Act should be suitably modified to allow this. (Para 7.94)

18. The Chairman, Members and General Managers should have staff groups to assist them in selected areas where specialised inputs are required. (Paras 7.95 to 7.98)

19. The distribution function should be highly decentralised with the General Managers in charge of zones being treated as profit centres

and they in turn delegating powers to divisional and sub-divisional managers who would be held accountable for results. (Para 7.99)

20. The RE programme should be supported by specialised staff at levels from the Board down to the zones, divisions and sub-divisions. (Para 7.100)

21. Of the part-time Members on the SEBs, two should be Government representatives, one should be the Member in charge of planning and operations the concerned REA and two should be eminent professionals in areas where the Board needs advice. (Para 7.101)

22. Boards should develop sound management information systems based on advice from specialised consultants. (Para 7.102)

Regional Electricity Generating Corporations (REGC)

23. The structure of the Boards of the REGCs should be similar to the SEBs except that a Member for distribution is not needed. (Para 7.103)

24. The operations and planning Member of the REA should be an ex-officio part-time member of the Board. Two other distinguished professionals should be appointed as part-time Members. (Para 7.103)

Rural Electrification

25. Where they are seen to be working satisfactorily, rural cooperatives should be set up for the bulk purchase and sale of power and operation maintenance of the rural electrification system. (Para 7.108)

26. Where they are not successful the experiment of appointing entrepreneurs as 'agents' for a few villagers who do the same work as RE cooperatives on a smaller scale, under the supervision of the SEBs should be tried out. (Paras 7.108 and 6.90)

Regional Electricity Authorities (REA)

27. The REA should have a Chairman and 4 full-time Members, all appointed by the Central Government. (Para 7.110)

28. The REA should have the Chief Executives of all the SEBs, REGC and any other utilities in the region as its part-time Members. (Para 7.111)

29. Regular regional meetings of the various functional heads of the REGC, the REA, the SEBs and any other utility in the region should be organised by the concerned REA Member to exchange information and discuss policies and problems. (Para 7.112)

30. The REA should publish a regular bulletin, on the lines of the monthly review published by the CEA dealing in depth with various aspects of the operation and future prospects of the regional power system. (Para 7.113)

31. In case of disputes between constituent utilities of the REA on issues like power flows, tariffs power planning the final appellate authority by statute should be the CEA. Such disputes should be made non-justiciable. (Para 7.113)

Central Electricity Authority (CEA)

32. The CEA should have a Chairman and 8 full-time Members. The existing post of Member (Operations and Monitoring) should be abolished and posts for Members in charge of Planning, Personnel and Research and Development created. The 5 Chairmen of the REAs should be part-time Members of the CEA. (Paras 7.114 and 7.115)

33. To meet the new challenges that will face it the CEA will need to induct a large number of high level specialists and relatively few supporting staff. (Para 7.121)

34. Each Member should be assisted by at least two Chief Engineers. (Para 7.123)

35. There should be no fresh recruitment to permanent posts by the CEA except at the clerical/class IV level. The senior posts should be filled as a rule, either by internal promotion or by deputationists from the SEBs, REGCs and REAs except in the case of a few specialised disciplines like finance and personnel where direct recruitment should be permitted. (Para 7.126)

36. Other than the above, all fresh recruitment to the REA/CEA cadre should be done in the REAs. (Para 7.127)

37. The terms and conditions of service of the REA and CEA officers should be delinked from those of other central technical services and substantially improved. (Para 7.128)

Personnel Policies

38. Managers should be encouraged to exercise delegated

authority, streamline cumbersome procedures, and reduce paper work so as to get quick results. (Para 7.131)

39. The appraisal and promotional policies of all the public sector and Government agencies dealing with power have to be modified to bring in much greater emphasis on promotion based on merit. (Paras 7.133 and 7.157)

40. In order to encourage mobility between organisations like CEA, REAs, REGCs, and SEBs they should be staffed by officers with broadly similar experience, qualification and back-grounds. (Para 7.137)

41. The job specification drawn up for top posts in these organisations should lay stress on managerial qualities rather than on narrow specialisation. (Para 7.138)

Selection of Chairman and Members of REA and CEA

42. The guidelines and conventions regarding filling of post in central public sector companies adopted by the Public Enterprises Selection Board (PESB) should be adopted for filling up top level posts in the CEA, REAs, REGC's and SEB's. (Paras 7.139 and 7.140)

43. The Selection Boards for the posts of Chairmen and Members of the CEA and REAs should be as suggested in para 7.139. (Para 7.139)

Selection of Chairman and Members of SEBs

44. Similar procedures and conventions should be followed in filling up the posts of Chairman and Members of SEBs and the Selection Boards should be established as recommended in paras 7.141 and 7.142. (Paras 7.140 to 7.142)

45. These changes in the selection procedures for the SEBs should be incorporated into the Electricity Act. (Para 7.143)

46. The tenure of the Chairman and Members of the Board should be at least 3 and preferably 5 years. (Para 7.144)

47. If the State Government wishes to terminate the appointment of a full-time Member or Chairman of SEB before the completes his term of office, the Government should consult the appropriate Selection Committee. In case there is a difference of view the reasons for such termination should be tabled on the floor of the Legislature. (Para 7.145)

Manpower Planning

48. Recruitment and training input into the power industry should be prepared on the basis of a 10 year man-power plan updated from year to year. (Para 7.149)

Training

49. Substantial augmentation of training facilities at all levels will be required if the training inputs required are to be satisfactorily met. (Para 7.152)

50. Training managers should not be people who are considered unsuitable for appointments elsewhere but should be drawn from amongst the abler managers. They should be given a special training and allowances so as to attract good men. (Para 7.153)

51. The brighter and more promising officers should be sent to training programmes and where possible as a preparation for promotion to more senior positions. (Para 7.154)

Fixation of Work Norms

52. The extent of over-staffing of SEBs should be quantified by establishing work norms in consultation with expert bodies such as the National Productivity Council or the National Institute of Training in Industrial Engineering. (Para 7.159)

Relationship between Governments and their Utilities

54. The role of Government *vis-a-vis* the Board's of utilities should be clearly defined and should be confined to appointments of Chairmen and Board members, approval of capital expenditure over certain limits, approval of annual budgets in physical and financial terms and annual and long-term plans. (Para 7.163)

55. Government should receive periodic reports on progress in relation to budget and plans and intervene only when there are major departures. Policy directives in regard to subsidies, allocations of power, etc., should be communicated as written instructions.

56. Government nominees should not look upon themselves as spokesmen of Government when they sit as Board Members of SEBs. (Para 7.164).

Delegation of Powers

57. Power should be delegated to the extent possible retaining just sufficient checks to ensure there is no misuse. Unless there is a clear *prima facie* case of *mala fides* occasional errors of judgement should not lead to managers who exercise such powers being penalised. (Paras 7.166 and 7.167)

Materials Management

58. The materials management system of the utilities especially the SEBs requires to be completely overhauled for this purpose the services of specialised consultants should be sought. (Para 7.168)

All India Service of Power Engineers

59. The concept of an All-India Service of Power Engineers should not be accepted in its entirely. (Para 7.176)

60. There should be a common entrance exam at the Class I level for all utilities and the REA's at the State, Regional and National level. (Para 1.176)

61. A minimum of 40 per cent of the successful candidates should be taken from outside the State in the case of SEBs and outside the region in the case of REAs. (Para 7.177)

62. An All-India pool of senior managers should be formed on the basis of selection from officers at the level of Superintending Engineers and above. This pool should be the normal source of filling posts of Chief Engineers, Members Directors and Chairman of SEB's, CEA, REAs and REGC's. (Para 7.178)

63. Selection of this pool should be done by a Standing Empanelment Committee. (Para 7.179)

64. The CEA should fix guidelines for categorising posts, lay down minimum terms and conditions of pay, perquisites and other facilities and standardise recruitment rules and promotional policies. (Para 7.181)

Consumer Relations

64. The State Electricity Consultative Councils (SECCs) and the Local Advisory Committees should be serviced by independent full-

time Secretariats responsible to the Chief Secretary and the local District Collector respectively. (Para 7.187)

65. A wider range of consumer protection interests could be nominated to the Council. (Para 7.187)

66. In a situation of resource scarcity there has to be a trade-off between a higher quality of service to existing consumers and non-consumers getting access to power.

67. Rating Committees and Tribunals for setting disputes between consumers and SEB's are not recommended. (Paras 7.190 and 7.191)

68. SEBs and utilities should publish detailed information required to keep consumers fully informed about their performance, progress and future prospects. The performance for this could be produced by SECC and LACs. (Para 7.192)

69. Consumer counselling counters should be set up at divisional and sub-divisional offices and printed booklets published on the procedures for getting connections and information on tariffs, safety regulations, etc. (Para 7.193)

70. Payment of compensation by SEBs to consumers who suffer losses due to failure or poor quality of power supply is not considered to be a practical proposition. (Para 7.194)

Research and Development

State Electricity Boards

1. The absence of an 'R&D culture' in SEBs is the biggest obstacle to faster progress in the growth and utilisation of research and development inputs in the power industry and steps must be taken to bring about a basic attitudinal change. (Para 8.36)

2. A Member in charge of R&D should be appointed in the CEA and supported by senior officers in charge of major areas of R&D activity. (Paras 8.37 and 7.115)

3. Each SEB should have a full-time Chief Engineer (CE) as head of the R&D Division and he should be assisted by a carefully selected, full-time, multi-disciplinary group of scientists and technologists. Where possible this team should be composed of people already within the undertaking and their special skills and knowledge should be appropriately reflected in their status. (Para 8.38)

4. SEBs should eventually aim at spending about one per cent of

their turnover equally on building up facilities and on research staff. (Para 8.39)

5. Efforts should be first concentrated on solving problems which are responsible for the current low levels of efficiency of thermal plants and reducing high T&D losses. (Para 8.40)

6. Procedures for sanctioning funds and facilities should be simplified and authority delegated to the CE and his accounts officer to spend money within the sanctioned budget on approved projects. (Para 8.41)

7. Academic and research institutions should evolve a series of basic training and refresher courses for R&D personnel. (Para 8.42)

8. A few academic institutions should be developed as centres of excellence, each in a different scientific and technological area. (Para 8.42)

Manufacturing Units

9. An expert group should be set up to examine how the pace of in-house R&D in the large scale manufacturing sector can be speeded up. (Para 8.46)

10. The small scale sector should be assisted in improving the quality and reliability of its products. The areas of assistance could include provision of improved standard designs for products such as motors, transformers, relays and help in designing production tolls, and fixtures, products like micro switches and improvements in insulation systems. (Paras 8.47 and 8.48)

11. Testing facilities for the large, medium and especially the small scale manufacturing sector need to be augmented and improved. A three-tier testing organisation under the CPRI should be set up, the second tier comprising centrally funded regional laboratories and the third 'grass roots' tier consisting of testing laboratories in SEBs large and medium scale corporations and industrial estates which serve a group of small scale industries making products, components and equipment for the power sector. (Para 8.49)

12. There should be close interaction between these 'grass roots' laboratories and the next tier of the structure and with the local, State and regional level engineering and research institutions by inter-change of personnel within and between tiers. (Para 8.50)

Apex Body for R&D in Power

13. To evolve policies, strategies and plans for R&D in the power industry and to co-ordinate them, in apex body to be termed the National Council for R&D on power should be set up. (Para 8.51)

14. The Council should function through eight Standing Committees for each of the following subjects:

(a) Testing, certification and standardisation;
(b) Product, process and technology development;
(c) R&D training and man-power development;
(d) Generation;
(e) Power systems;
(f) Non-conventional energy sources;
(g) Conservation technologies; and
(h) Information/documentation. (Para 8.52)

15. The areas on which R&D effort and should be focussed are those in which India has a distinctive interest and/or where external knowhow is not available. (Para 8.53)

16. The Council should consist of the Secretary, Department of Power, Government of India or the Chairman, CEA, as Chairman. The Members should be the Secretaries of the Departments of Electronics, Science and Technology, the Chairman of the 8 Standing Committee, the Director General, Technical Development, other eminent people connected with different aspects of the power sector and representatives of the Ministry of Finance and Planning Commission. The Member (R&D) of the CEA should be the Council's Member-Secretary. (Para 8.62)

17. This Committee would be the high level channel of communication in R&D on power between India and other countries. (Para 8.63)

Alternative Energy Sources

Solar Energy

18. Solar energy sources (inclusive of windmills) need to be developed rapidly because of the high potential for developing them in India and the nature of the demand for power and energy especially in

the rural areas. (Para 8.64)

19. To promote rapid development of solar energy, a Solar Energy Commission on the lines of the Electronic Commission should be set up. (Para 8.67)

Magneto-hydro Dynamics (MHD)

20. Subject to the preliminary trials establishing its commercial/economic viability, the MHD programmes for direct conversion of heat into power should continue. (Para 8.68)

Nuclear Power

21. Work on improving the performance of the pressurised heavy water reactors and the development of fast breeder reactors should continue. (Para 8.77)

Fusion

22. A "State of the Art" survey should be carried out and the long- and short-term, technological and financial implications of alternative strategies for entering into fusion R&D should be worked out. (Para 8.78)

CHAIRMAN INDEX OF COMMITTEES & COMMISSIONS IN INDIA, 1947-78, Volumes 1 to 16